Ante Batović is a Cold War historian, with a keen interest in Eastern Europe and the Balkans. He has published extensively on Croatian post-war history, Yugoslav foreign policy in the Cold War and its role in the Non-Aligned Movement. He holds a master's degree in Global Politics from the London School of Economics and a PhD in History from the University of Zadar.

Benjamin Bilski is an author and editor. He is the executive director of the Pericles Foundation, which specialises in developing and publishing new research for a general audience.

'Ante Batović's book, based on extensive research in American, British, NATO, Croatian and Serbian archives, provides not just an authoritative account of an important, though relatively little-known, episode in Cold War history. It shines a spotlight more generally on how the West viewed Yugoslavia as a pivotal state in the Cold War.'

Robin Harris, bestselling author and historian

The Croatian Spring
Nationalism, Repression and Foreign Policy Under Tito

ANTE BATOVIĆ

TRANSLATED, EDITED AND EXPANDED BY
ANTE BATOVIĆ AND BENJAMIN BILSKI

WITH A FOREWORD BY
ROBIN HARRIS

I.B. TAURIS
LONDON · NEW YORK

To Ana and Martina

Published in 2017 by
I.B.Tauris & Co. Ltd
London • New York
www.ibtauris.com

International Library of Twentieth Century History 99

ISBN: 978 1 78453 927 6
eISBN: 978 1 78672 184 6
ePDF: 978 1 78673 184 5

A full CIP record for this book is available from the British Library
A full CIP record is available from the Library of Congress

Library of Congress Catalog Card Number: available

Printed and bound by CPI Group (UK) Ltd, Croydon, CR0 4YY

Contents

List of Figures

Acknowledgements

We would like to thank all the archives, libraries, universities, coffee baristas, patient wives, everyone at I.B.Tauris and Robin Harris for making this edition possible.

We are particularly grateful to the University of Zadar for supporting the development of this edition based on research that was undertaken there as part of the author's doctoral studies.

We hope that the history of the liberal movements in Croatia and Yugoslavia will be studied alongside similar movements in Cold War Eastern Europe – histories that hold lessons for our time. As the first New Talent project of the Pericles Foundation, we are pleased to present this research to a general audience and look forward to many more such projects in the future.

Foreword
Robin Harris

It is a privilege to be asked to contribute this foreword to Ante Batović's *The Croatian Spring*. To the limited extent that this honour is deserved, I must call in aid my knowledge of the language and the country, my past work on the history of Dubrovnik, my recent research for my forthcoming study of the life and times of Zagreb's Archbishop, Alojzije Stepinac (1898–1960) and, not least, my friendship with one of the few people in the West who comes well out of this study, the late Chris (Krsto) Cviić.

The Croatian Spring is an expanded, adapted and translated version of the doctoral thesis defended by Dr Batović at the University of Zadar in 2010. As such, it is evidence both of the quality of work being undertaken by the younger generation of Croatian historians and of the need for more of this work – and other classic works in Croatian – to be translated into English. In this case, the author's own linguistic skills – honed over the last few years while living and working in Britain – avoided the need for an outside translator. That is an advantage, because much translation from Croatian into English is extremely poor. Batović's efforts were seconded by Benjamin Bilski, whose self-imposed mission of bringing such work to the attention of the English-speaking world, through the Pericles Foundation, must also be warmly commended.

The story of the movement which became known – albeit only in retrospect, after its suppression by the regime – as the 'Croatian Spring' is not well known in the West. This is understandable, though regrettable. Unlike the 'Prague Spring' of 1968, it was not suppressed by Russian tanks, and though it resulted in purges, imprisonment and a fair amount of brutality, it was over quite quickly. Tito summoned the liberally minded Croatian Communist Party leadership to his residence in Karađorđevo, on the eve of a meeting of the Presidium of the League of Communists of Yugoslavia on 31 November 1971, to signal that he had lost confidence in them. The first sign that a major purge was afoot was a speech by Vladimir Bakarić, the old guard Croatian communist leader and a serial opportunist, on 7 December, disowning Mrs Savka Dabčević-Kučar, the most popular and charismatic Croatian Spring leader. The 'resignations' then began in a rolling programme, reaching out from the Central Party in Zagreb and supplemented by accompanying purges of other institutions. Yet, compared with Czechoslovakia in 1968 – let alone the cruel repression in Hungary in 1956 – it was relatively tame stuff.

As Chris Cviić, writing for *The Economist* one of those pieces that caused anger in Belgrade and risked apoplexy in the British Foreign Office, noted:

> It did not prove necessary even to use the tanks and troops that had surrounded Zagreb ... The arrest of intellectuals and other 'undesirable elements' identified with the sacked leaders went just as smoothly. Not one, out of more than a hundred, apparently slipped through the net ... It was, as Lloyd George once said about another country, a rape, but only a little one; and everything was over before you could say 'Long live the self-managing, socialist, federative republic of Jugoslavia'.

Cviić's piece was headlined, 'An Old Man in a Panic'. The British Ambassador in Belgrade, a warm admirer of the Marshal, thought that, to judge from Tito's self-confident demeanour, 'Old Man at a picnic' would have been more appropriate. But, whatever the 'Old Man's' innermost thoughts – which now, as at most other time, remain shrouded behind the numerous masks he adopted – this was no picnic for Croatia.

Ante Batović is inclined to think that, had the liberal reformist Croatian leaders remained in power, and had their less numerous equivalents prevailed in the other Yugoslav Republics, the bloody conflicts of the early 1990s would have been avoided. He considers that the break-up of Yugoslavia was inevitable, once the Cold War ended. But he believes that it might have been managed peacefully. The parallel of Gorbachev's agreeing to the fall of the Berlin Wall could be used to support that hypothesis. On the other hand, the history of nineteenth-century Serbia and of the first (Serb-dominated) Yugoslavia might suggest that the drive for a Greater Serbia, never far below the surface of political culture in Belgrade, could never have permitted peaceful disintegration. About these possibilities, though, different views can obviously be held.

Since its expulsion from Soviet-controlled Cominform in 1948, Yugoslavia had enjoyed informal but effective Western security guarantees and economic and other assistance. Tito's regime remained repressive. Especially in Croatia, its prisons were full of political suspects and, notably, priests. The West was prepared to overlook that, at least once Washington decided that the break with Stalin was real and lasting. (Britain regarded Tito as its own protégé and its diplomats almost always strove to depict him in dispatches in a favourable light.) Tito was even permitted to enjoy special international status as the leader of the 'Non-Aligned Movement' and to pursue an unwelcome pro-Arab policy in the Middle East, because of Yugoslavia's deemed strategic importance in the Eastern Mediterranean and as an independent (i.e., not Warsaw Pact) European Communist state.

Tito played up the Soviet threat once again in order to persuade the Americans that they must stand by him in the run up to the crisis of the late sixties and early seventies. The likelihood, by now, that any pro-Soviet alternative would emerge, at least unless there was chaos in the event of his death, was clearly minimal. A full scale Soviet invasion, even after the shock administered by the suppression of the Prague Spring, was also highly improbable. Judging from messages delivered by Brezhnev, what the Soviet Union feared was any further out-of-control liberalism in a Socialist country. Ideological contagion, rather than geopolitics, was apparently what was worrying the Kremlin. But one has to add 'apparently'. The Soviet archives, which would presumably reveal Moscow's real worries and intentions regarding Yugoslavia for the whole period, are currently inaccessible.

These external factors provide the framework for what occurred. But internal factors were always the driving force. Ante Batović describes and seeks to assess the relationship between the different causes of discontent. These were economic, social and political – but, in the case of Croatia, and much to the irritation and incomprehension of Western observers, they were, above all, cultural and national.

The most important date in the transformation of Yugoslavia from a hard-line Communist regime to a system in which the Party still monopolised power but allowed a substantial amount of freedom to those it did not consider a threat is not 1948 – the break with Stalin – but 1966 – the fall of the powerful Security Chief, Aleksandar Ranković. Ranković's alleged sins were many, including bugging Tito. But, above all, he represented centralism (against the individual Republics), was viewed as an obstacle to economic reform, effectively controlled the Secret Police and was the regime's top Serb, and so viewed, rightly or wrongly, as a covert Serb nationalist.

The post-Ranković era was marked by a lurch towards liberalism in a number of forms. These were frequently incoherent, occasionally contradictory, and all eventually doomed to fail. Batović describes skilfully and in detail what occurred. Economic reforms disappointed because moves towards greater initiative (more 'self-management') took place without the required disciplines imposed by competition and the threat of bankruptcy. Republics squabbled about which should benefit from foreign cash. Bringing the Party closer to the people meant diluting its Socialism and increasing the force of nationalism. The latter was particularly the case in Croatia, which not just from 1945 but from 1918 had resented what Croats saw as political, financial, cultural and religious discrimination from Belgrade. The reform movement is thus a fascinating tale of diversions, route changes, and speed alterations, ending in inter-connected multiple-collisions.

Liberalism – even when practised within the approved Party framework – involved an encounter with reality. Economic realities were hard enough to face. But the fact that many, perhaps most, of the Croatian population had no sympathy for Yugoslavia and preferred their own national symbols, myths, linguistic distinctiveness and leaders involved challenges that Communism was unable to withstand without the use of repression.

It is necessary, though not always easy, to distinguish between those elements of the Croatian Spring programme which represented the views of the Croatian Party Leadership – Dabčević-Kučar, Miko Tripalo and others – and those which were forced upon them by non-Communist opinion. While the Party Leaders emphasised economic reforms, the question of foreign currency retention, and the rights of the Republics at Federal level, the non-Communist (or nominally Communist) intellectuals, students and *Matica Hrvatska* (the venerable Croatian cultural institute) were much more interested in language issues and the link with Croatian national identity. Western diplomats, by and large, had limited time for the first set of demands and reserved special scorn for the second set, though those in Zagreb showed a markedly better grasp than those in Belgrade.

American diplomats reported the mass gathering of 200,000 in Zagreb's Ban Jelačić Square addressed by Savka Dabčević-Kučar on 7 May 1971. The diplomats were puzzled by the wide-spread weeping when the Croatian national anthem was played. They noted that Dabčević-Kučar's speech was interrupted by applause on 40 occasions – but that these outbursts were reserved for jibes against 'statists', 'Serbian great state hegemonists' and the like. The American consul-general attended a performance of the Croatian national opera, Nikola Šubić Zrinski, on 2 October 1971. At the end, the crowd erupted to sing Croatia's national anthem, 'Almost all in the theatre seemed carried away by the moment except for a few in boxes who may well have been connected with organs of public administration. There was no radiance in their faces, and their lips were still'.

Chris Cviić's commentary in *The Economist* was almost unique in expressing what Western Governments were still, in their keenness to shore up Tito's position and Yugoslav unity, unwilling to accept. Cviić noted that nationalism in Eastern Europe could not be compared to that in Western Europe, because it represented the only way to express freedom for peoples who had no access to free elections. He conceded that in the cases of Albania and Romania, nationalism (in the service of local Communists) had not brought liberalism

> But liberalism and nationalism did march in step on two important occasions in the recent past. One was Czechoslovakia's liberalisation between 1966 and 1968. The other was Jugoslavia's between 1966 and 1971. Neither could have taken place if the reformers had not been joined by 'impure' nationalists.

The West's errors in the case of the Croatian Spring were part of a long litany of misunderstanding, which extended well into the 1990s. While it is probably true, as Batović observes, that British and American diplomats at the time of the Croatian Spring did not have 'an intentional bias' in favour of Serbia and the Serbs – their limited knowledge of national differences would, anyway, have precluded this – they did consistently downplay the complaints of the Croats. Given the fact that bereft of Croat support, or at least acquiescence, neither the first nor the second Yugoslavia could attain stability without a high – and ultimately self-defeating – degree of coercion, this Western prejudice made for flawed assessments and, ultimately, for bad policy. That leaves aside the further question of whether Western powers should, on moral grounds, have pressed Tito (or, indeed, the Karađorđević dynasty earlier) to treat national and religious minorities better.

Ante Batović's book, based on extensive research in American, British, NATO, Croatian and Serbian archives, provides not just an authoritative account of an important, though relatively little-known, episode in Cold War history. It shines a spotlight more generally on how the West viewed Yugoslavia as a pivotal state in the Cold War. It raises a number of important questions – not least about the real intentions of the Soviet Union – that should prompt further research. Finally, it should encourage more attempts to edit and translate high-quality studies – like *The Croatian Spring*.

Introduction

There are moments in the lives of every nation and state that play a pivotal role in their historic development. The Croatian Spring, a national liberalisation movement that developed between 1966 and 1971, played such a role in the life of the Croatian nation and Yugoslav state.

Even after 45 years, this decisive period in the history of socialist Yugoslavia still provokes a great deal of controversy among the citizens, historians, politicians and nationalities who once shared the state of the South Slavs. The reason probably lies in the abrupt and ruthless end to efforts to modernise and democratise the Yugoslav communist system. The purge of the liberal leadership in Croatia and other Yugoslav nations, from December 1971 onwards, caused ideological traumas and irreparable divisions.

This book is an attempt to shed more light on the events of the late 1960s and early 1970s in Croatia and Yugoslavia. The approach is rather unconventional. Unlike most previous studies of the period, the main focus is not exclusively on Croatia and its internal struggles, but on the wider effects of the Croatian developments on the Yugoslav federal structure, its domestic politics and its foreign policy orientation.

Along with archival sources and contemporary accounts, the story was primarily written with the help of outsiders – foreign diplomats and journalists who observed the transformation of Croatian and Yugoslav society in this short but tumultuous period. Their reports and articles reveal both prejudices and biases, but also pragmatism and realism that is often blurred by the emotional and ideological ties of the participants in these events.

This study will try to reveal, explain and intertwine relations and ideas that defined the period, from global, regional and local perspectives. It will also combine international views on domestic developments by considering diplomatic reports and their impact on the foreign policies of other states in order to present a comprehensive view that includes the effect of global events on the complexities of Croatian and Yugoslav politics and society.

The international context is the Cold War, which defined and directed the postwar development of socialist Yugoslavia from its beginnings to the very end. Starting with the split with Stalin in 1948, Yugoslavia charted a third way with the introduction of self-management as its guiding economic philosophy, positioned between socialism and capitalism, and non-alignment as its main geopolitical policy. The collapse of the Yugoslav state was a direct consequence of the disintegration of the Communist bloc and the end of the Cold War.

This book revolves around the ideas of nation and nationalism, on the one hand, and democracy and liberalism on the other. This presented the main challenge for multinational Yugoslavia and a constant dilemma for Tito's communist regime, ever since it decided to introduce a new brand of 'communism with a human face'.

The study tries to compare the Croatian developments with similar movements in other Eastern European communist countries, such as Hungary in 1956, Czechoslovakia in 1968, and the protests of intellectuals and students in Poland until 1968. The interaction between Yugoslavia and the rest of Eastern Europe was dynamic. The events in Hungary in 1956 and Czechoslovakia in 1968 not only had a deep impact on Yugoslav foreign and domestic politics, but, equally importantly, Yugoslavia's 'soft socialism' and independence from the Soviet Union made it an influential role-model for Eastern European societies.

In the overall Yugoslav framework special emphasis is given to local developments in Croatia, because the Croatian communist leadership was

2

the prime mover and main ideologue of the efforts to modernise Yugoslavia in the late 1960s. The events in Croatia in the year of crisis of 1971 would also be the main catalyst for Tito's decision to put an end to the Croatian Spring. The primary reason was the regime's fear that an uncontrolled outburst of nationalism combined with liberalism might undermine the power of the Communist Party and break Yugoslavia apart.

In the short term Tito was probably right. The repression that followed did suppress national aspirations and preserve the power of the Party and the integrity of Yugoslavia. But in the long run it only aggravated long-standing national antagonisms, primarily between the Serbs and the Croats. The permanent removal of a new generation of leaders, not only in Croatia but also in Serbia, Slovenia and Macedonia, meant that the field was opened for others incapable of resolving the crises of the 1980s, setting the country on the course to war.

Because of its multinational structure, and long-standing divisions that had haunted the country since its establishment in 1918, Yugoslavia would probably not have survived the end of the Cold War and the collapse of the communist bloc, regardless of how the political crisis of 1971 was resolved.

This leads us to the key message of this book: leadership does matter. With the purge of the progressive and liberal political elite in all the Yugoslav republics, Tito might have eliminated the very force that could have given Yugoslavia a chance to negotiate a peaceful dissolution which might have prevented the bloody drama that unfolded 20 years later.

Instead, after 1971 Yugoslavia continued with further decentralisation, and even controlled liberalisation, but without the necessary democratic input that could have allowed a forum for an open discussion and potential resolution of national and inter-republican issues. The deposed leaders in Croatia, Serbia, Macedonia and Slovenia were trying to promote just that – the introduction of democratic elements into the Yugoslav single-party system in spite of the harsh realities of the environment in which they had to operate. For this reason they deserve a special place not only in the history of their respective nations but also in the wider context of the struggle against communist totalitarianism in Europe.

The book is divided into 11 chapters that cover different stages in the development of the national and liberal movement. The first two chapters describe the global circumstances of the Cold War and the development of socialist Yugoslavia from its establishment in 1945 until 1965, when a significant shift towards stronger economic liberalisation and decentralisation acted as a catalyst for similar political processes.

The third chapter gives a deeper insight into the 1965 economic reform and the removal of Aleksandar Ranković, the powerful secretary of the Yugoslav Communist Party and Tito's right-hand man, who controlled the Yugoslav security apparatus.

The fourth chapter tackles long-standing and contentious language issues that erupted in 1967 when a group of Croatian intellectuals published the 'Declaration on the Position of Croatian language' which directly challenged the existence of a joint Serbo-Croatian language and demanded the introduction of a Croatian language as an official language in Croatia.

The fifth chapter explains the process of decentralisation and democratisation in both the Yugoslav League of Communists and the Federal state, giving more powers to the republics and allowing greater media freedom.

Chapter 6 describes the positive and negative impact of decentralisation and democratisation on Yugoslav foreign policy and its non-aligned orientation, with the examples of the Middle East 1967 war, the Czechoslovakian crisis in 1968, and Chinese engagement in the Balkans in the wider context of the Sino-Soviet split.

Chapter 7 presents the developments in Croatia that followed after the tenth meeting of the Croatian League of Communists, in which the national question was reaffirmed with the claim that every nation in Yugoslavia had the right to openly express its national identity, instead of promoting uniform 'Yugoslavism'. The chapter also describes the visit by President Richard Nixon to Yugoslavia in 1970 and US policy towards Yugoslavia.

Chapter 8 is the focal point of the book, with a detailed account of the events of 1971 in Croatia that eventually led to the culmination of the political crisis in Yugoslavia and Tito's decision to purge the progressive Croatian leadership.

Chapter 9 gives an overview of two state visits that marked the period: that of the secretary general of the Soviet Communist Party, Leonid Brezhnev, to Belgrade in September 1971, and Tito's visit to Washington in November 1971. Both visits and their outcomes represent an example how

Cold War politics, and Yugoslavia's balancing act between East and West, played an important role in the unfortunate unravelling of the 1971 crisis.

Chapter 10 revolves around the December 1971 purge after the Karađorđevo meeting, and its consequences for the future of the Yugoslav state; the fate of the deposed political and student leaders; and the reactions of foreign governments and the international community.

Finally, Chapter 11 deals with the aftermath of the crisis, attempts by the Yugoslav leadership to contain the crisis and political trials, and Tito's decision to expand the purge to other republics, and specifically to Serbia. The chapter also gives an account of Foreign Office attempts to influence British press reporting of the events in Croatia and Yugoslavia, and the different views of British and American diplomats in Zagreb and Belgrade regarding the events in Croatia, and the reactions of NATO and the Soviet Union.

The Croatian Spring and other liberal movements in Yugoslavia in the 1960s and 1970s – and their suppression – represent a crucial episode in understanding the bloodshed in former Yugoslavia that followed two decades later. It also shared many common characteristics with other movements for individual and national liberty in Eastern Europe during the period of communist repression. This movement deserves greater recognition in the historiography of the region, and I hope this study will restore the Croatian Spring to its properly deserved place in European postwar history.

1

The Cold War World

The Impact of *Détente*

Global international relations in the immediate period after World War II were marked by a gradual escalation of tensions between the former Allies, led by the United States and the Soviet Union. From 1947 onwards, the conflict was primarily ideological, but in some parts of the world, such as Korea, it led to open war. The first phases of the Cold War lasted until Stalin's death in 1953. In the short interim period of the thaw from 1953 to 1956, when the Soviet Union was under the collective leadership of the Politburo, it took the initiative in improving relations with the West. This period ended when an internal fight for supremacy within the Soviet leadership was resolved and Nikita Khrushchev emerged as the party leader in 1956.[1] The period of his leadership was marked by a stream of foreign policy crises: the intervention in Hungary and the Suez crisis in 1956, the confrontations in Berlin, and the Cuban missile crisis in 1962. Such foreign policy risks, in a period of military and economic inferiority, further weakened the Soviet Union and compromised its international reputation. This was one of the key reasons for Khrushchev's fall in October 1964. His successor, Leonid Brezhnev, would conduct a more prudent foreign policy, while expanding Soviet military capabilities to establish parity with the West. After Khrushchev's fall, the Soviet Union would find itself for the second time under the leadership of the Politburo. With the USSR still humiliated by the Cuban crisis, Soviet policy towards the West took a more conservative course under Brezhnev's leadership.[2]

In order to compensate for its global military weakness, the Soviets built a remarkable arsenal of strategic weapons in the period from 1965 to 1968 under the supervision of Brezhnev's close associate, the Central Committee Secretary for Military Industry, Dmitri Ustinov. He ordered the development of intercontinental missiles, nuclear submarines and strategic bombers. This helped to establish a strategic equilibrium with the United States by 1969, but at the cost of 18 per cent of the Soviet defence budget.[3]

The danger of nuclear conflict and the high production cost of nuclear weapons were two of the key factors that led to *détente* and a period of decreased tensions between the superpowers. This period lasted from the early 1970s to the final breakdown of *détente* with the Soviet invasion of Afghanistan in 1979. The first signs of *détente* could already be seen in the late 1960s, as a consequence of internal processes on both sides and their international activities. In the Soviet Union the economy was heavily burdened by huge military expenditure, as well as by the US's superiority in technology, industrial power and international trade. In addition, the Soviet Union was involved in a long-standing ideological conflict with the People's Republic of China that started immediately after Stalin's death and culminated in an armed conflict on the Sino-Soviet border in 1969. The United States, on the other hand, was gradually losing its economic pre-eminence because of the rise of Western Europe and Japan. Simultaneously, it was involved in an expensive and unpopular war in Vietnam.

President Richard Nixon, elected in 1968, and his national security adviser Henry Kissinger recognised an opportunity in these international circumstances to improve the international position of the US. After 20 years of open hostility towards Mao's China, Washington started a more conciliatory policy towards the communist regime in Beijing, while China was weakened by internal instability and international isolation caused by the Cultural Revolution. The American initiative resulted in the visits to Beijing of Kissinger in 1971 and Nixon in February 1972. Both Beijing and Washington had a mutual interest in limiting Soviet influence. By establishing relations with the People's Republic, Washington achieved two goals. It weakened Moscow's position and at the same time put diplomatic pressure on the Soviet Union over the negotiations with North Vietnam to end the war in south-east Asia.[4]

Sino–American negotiations helped to end the American military engagement in Vietnam, but they also changed the balance between the Cold War blocs and significantly influenced the global *détente* process. The Sino–American rapprochement led the Soviets to take a more conciliatory position towards the West.[5] Already in 1972 a first agreement on limiting the production of nuclear weapons was signed in Moscow (SALT I), and by 1974 several similar agreements were signed that drastically reduced the danger of nuclear destruction and led to improved relations between the United States and the Soviet Union.[6]

Global *détente* permitted the European *détente* that had already started in the mid-1960s and continued in the 1980s after global *détente* no longer existed. Unlike global *détente*, which focused on relations between the US and the USSR and on nuclear weapons, the European *détente* included a wider area of cultural and economic cooperation between East and West, along with cooperation on resolving European border disputes. The process of *détente* in Europe had several unique attributes. European leaders on both sides of the Iron Curtain wanted to conduct a more independent policy from the Cold War superpowers. The best examples were De Gaulle's France and Ceaușescu's Romania. In addition, the Europeans were fully aware that a potential war between the blocs would first destroy Europe. In 1964 De Gaulle established diplomatic relations with communist China and signed cooperation agreements with the Soviet Union. In this way, he wanted to reduce European dependence on the United States. Naturally, he wanted to strengthen France's influence and become leader of an independent European foreign policy. This initiative, however, was short-lived. France did not have the political strength to achieve major changes in Europe.[7]

An initiative that would have far greater influence in establishing European *détente* came from Bonn. The future West German Chancellor Willy Brandt, while mayor of West Berlin, was deeply aware of the negative impact of the division of Berlin that symbolised the division of Europe.[8] The formation of the West German coalition government in 1966 in which Brandt became foreign minister marked a change in West German policy towards Eastern Europe and opened the door to *Ostpolitik*. Bonn started to establish diplomatic relations with Eastern European states, reversing the Hallstein doctrine of non-recognition of communist states that recognised East Germany (the German Democratic Republic, or GDR).[9] Not by accident, Romania was the first Eastern European state with which Bonn established diplomatic relations in 1967. For years, Romania had tried to conduct a more independent foreign policy from Moscow. The further improvement of relations with other Eastern European states was blocked by the East German leader Walter Ulbricht, who accused Bonn of trying to dissolve the monolithic unity of the Communist bloc.[10] In addition, Bonn's unwillingness to recognise East Germany as an independent state, and its unresolved eastern borders with Poland and Czechoslovakia, prevented the establishment of better relations with both the GDR and the Soviet Union. The only visible progress between West Germany (the Federal Republic of Germany, or FRG) and the East was the establishment of relations with Yugoslavia in 1968.[11]

Along with the conciliatory attitude coming from Bonn, the turning point that changed the course of Soviet policy towards better relations between the blocs in Europe was, paradoxically, the Warsaw Pact intervention in Czechoslovakia in 1968. The paradox was that the crackdown on the Prague Spring opened a deep chasm within the international communist movement, while at the same time enabling the beginning of *détente* in Europe.[12] While Brezhnev feared that the intervention in Czechoslovakia could lead to open war in Europe, it strengthened his position in the Soviet leadership, giving him the credibility to start negotiations with Western leaders. The intervention proved to all satellite states in Eastern Europe what they could expect if they tried to follow the Czechoslovakian path. In 1972 Brezhnev declared: 'Without Czechoslovakia there would be no Brandt in Germany, nor Nixon in Moscow, and there would be no *détente*.'[13]

This time, the initiative for constructive solutions to Europe's problems came from Moscow. Brezhnev could not count on support from the Nixon administration, and instead turned to Bonn. In their new approach, the Soviets did not insist on Western recognition of the Oder–Neisse border with Poland as a precondition for opening talks. The border issue was simply added to dialogue. The only precondition was international recognition of the GDR. The West responded with an initiative to improve the situation in Berlin, which Moscow did not oppose. Simultaneously, the Polish government proposed to resolve the border dispute in a bilateral agreement. The final move occurred with the election of a new West German government in September 1969, with Willy Brandt as its Chancellor. Brandt won the election with promises to pursue *Ostpolitik* and strengthen the bond between the Germanys. The FRG signed the Nuclear Non-Proliferation Treaty (NPT) in November 1969, and in August 1970 Brandt and the Soviet Prime Minister Alexei Kosygin signed the Moscow Treaty, which recognised Europe's existing borders.[14] Brandt performed a massive U-turn and supported the recognition of the GDR with the motto 'One nation, two states', which did not imply a recognition of the permanent division of Germany. The negotiations were difficult, because Ulbricht obstructed progress. But after his removal in 1971, events progressed more rapidly.[15] By 1972 the FRG had signed several 'eastern treaties' that regulated relations with its eastern neighbours. The Moscow Treaty settled relations with the Soviet Union and in the Warsaw Treaty of 1970 West Germany accepted the Oder–Neisse border with reservations.[16] In addition, Brandt's symbolic act of showing remorse in the Warsaw ghetto in 1970 marked the end of open disputes between West Germany and Poland. The apogee of *Ostpolitik* was the settlement of the division of Berlin in September 1971, and the treaty with the GDR in December 1972, which coincided with the rise of Soviet–American *détente*.[17]

Soviet Interests in Yugoslavia

The key dilemma for Yugoslav foreign policy in the complex postwar international order was how to combine Yugoslavia's attachment to the international communist movement with the policy of non-alignment and the system of economic 'self-management' that introduced elements of the free market. With this in mind, the relationship to the Soviet Union was of special importance. Similarly to the West, the Soviet Union had a strategic and ideological interest in strengthening its influence in Yugoslavia. Surrounded by the Soviet East European satellites, Hungary, Bulgaria and Romania, and in a strategically important position, the non-aligned Yugoslavia was particularly sensitive to the messages coming from Moscow that could be interpreted as interfering with its domestic policy. The Yugoslavs were also alarmed by any signs of increased Soviet influence in the Balkans and the Mediterranean. The key Yugoslav asset was its access to the Adriatic Sea and the Mediterranean. Western politicians and military officials often emphasised that the protection of Yugoslav independence from Moscow's influence was a key strategic requirement for keeping the Soviets away from the Mediterranean.

The Soviet attempts to reach the Mediterranean were simply a continuation of a long-standing Russian policy to secure access to warm seas. The USSR had an option to use its Baltic and Far East bases and ports, but with a better climate the Black Sea and the Mediterranean offered more favourable strategic and economic benefits. In addition, this was the fastest way to the Indian Ocean, the Middle East and the Atlantic.[18]

The Black Sea, however, was limited by Turkish control over the Bosporus and the Dardanelles Straits, as well as by the Montreal Convention of 1936, which prevented unlimited passage to shipping without Turkish consent. In the interwar period such a policy suited the newly created Soviet state, which did not have a significant naval capability in the Black Sea. Turkish control also prevented other fleets from entering the Black Sea, and this protected the Soviet Union. After World War II and in the new circumstances of the Cold War, however, the Soviets increased their attempts to expand control to the Mediterranean.[19] The Turkish crisis of 1945 revealed that the West would not simply allow Soviet expansion. Stalin's attempt to gain control over the straits failed when the United States intervened by sending what would become the 6th Fleet to the eastern Mediterranean, which thereafter remained under the firm naval and military control of the West.[20]

The Suez crisis of 1956, however, changed the geostrategic relationship between the great powers in the Mediterranean. Great Britain and France lost a great deal of their influence in the region, and the United States filled the vacuum left behind after their retreat. After 1953, Moscow started to change Stalin's uncompromising policy towards the Third World that resulted in rejecting potential allies.[21] The new Soviet leadership had a far more flexible attitude towards anti-colonial movements and newly formed Third World states. They emphasised the 'Soviet readiness to cooperate in the national development of non-socialist countries'.[22] The Soviets found new allies in decolonised countries. These were not necessarily interested in Soviet communist ideology, but welcomed Soviet material and political support in their fight against neo-colonialism. At the same time, many

Third World countries saw in the Soviet socialist model a means to modernise their economies. They were also forced to implement this model because they were unable to adapt fast enough to market-driven capitalist economies, which involved an unpleasant relationship with their former colonial masters.[23] Egypt and Syria were the champions of such models in the Middle East and North Africa. Egypt was of particular interest to Moscow for its strategic position and the role it had as the leader of Arab resistance to western neo-colonialism. Before 1961, however, Egypt did not interest the Soviets in strategic terms, because the USSR's key stronghold in the Mediterranean was the Albanian port of Valona. Only after Tirana's split with Moscow in 1961 over the Soviet conflict with China did Moscow start to intensify the build-up of its naval capabilities in Egypt and Syria. By 1964, the Soviets were establishing the 5th *Eskadra* (fleet) to balance the American 6th Fleet. The height of Soviet military and political expansion coincided with the Arab–Israel Six-Day War in June 1967. Until the war, Nasser was not at ease with Soviet attempts to strengthen their military influence in Egypt. The Arab defeat, however, completely changed the perspective. It damaged Nasser's reputation in both Egypt and the Arab world, while Israeli military supremacy along with the occupation of Sinai became a serious threat to Egypt's security. In order to preserve his position in power and prevent further Israeli actions, Nasser was forced to ask the Soviets for extensive military and economic support. In the period after 1967, Soviet military and economic assistance, along with a military presence, brought Egypt to a state of complete dependence on Moscow. It also allowed the Soviets to strengthen their position in the Mediterranean.[24] The Soviet position would be endangered in 1972 when Nasser's successor, Anwar Sadat, requested the withdrawal of the Soviet military from Egypt, although that did not prevent the Soviet Union from assisting Egypt militarily in the Yom Kippur war of October 1973.[25] Eventually in 1976 the Soviets were completely thrown out of Egypt when Sadat decided to establish close cooperation with Washington.[26]

Soviet political and military support to the Nasser and Sadat regimes during the 1967 and 1973 wars required uninterrupted airborne and naval supply lines between the Soviet territory and Egypt. In this context, the geographic position of Yugoslavia increased its strategic value, because it provided the shortest airborne and naval corridor to Egypt. In 1967,

Yugoslavia's President Josip Broz Tito approved the use of Yugoslav airspace for Soviet aircraft transporting military assistance to Egypt and Syria, and of the Yugoslav port of Rijeka. A similar situation occurred during the 1973 war.[27]

Increased Soviet engagement in the Middle East and Mediterranean also brought changes to Soviet policy towards the Balkans. The Balkans ceased to be a periphery in comparison to the rest of Eastern Europe and the so-called 'Iron Triangle' of East Germany, Czechoslovakia and Poland. In these new circumstances the Balkans provided a potential new access to the Mediterranean.[28]

But Yugoslavia was determined to limit Soviet attempts to use the facilities of the Adriatic ports. Several times the Soviets sought to gain Yugoslav permission for unlimited use of its naval capabilities for repair and supply of the Mediterranean 5th *Eskadra*. Yugoslav legislation of 1965 and 1974 was quite restrictive and precise in defining the terms under which foreign navies could obtain access to Yugoslav territory. The laws permitted the presence of a maximum of three foreign ships and two auxiliary ships in Yugoslav territorial waters at the same time. The 1974 law also limited the tonnage of foreign military vessels being repaired in Yugoslav shipyards. Foreign warships could stay in shipyards for a maximum period of six months, only Yugoslav workers could repair them, and the repairmen had to have permission from the Yugoslav government. A maximum of one-third of a ship's crew was allowed to disembark at any time, and foreign states were not allowed to store fuel on Yugoslav territory.[29]

Unlike its ties to the West, Yugoslavia's relations with the Soviets were influenced equally by ideological and military-strategic considerations. Ever since 1948, relations were burdened by ideological differences, which continued after the re-establishment of state and party connections. The Soviet leadership blamed Tito's regime for liberalisation and reduction of state and party control over society, which could potentially endanger communist domination and cause instability in multinational Yugoslavia. Of equal concern to the Soviets was the destabilising potential of the Yugoslav brand of liberal self-managing socialism to the orthodox communist regimes of Eastern Europe.

In the first years of political and economic liberalisation in the 1960s, Soviet critiques were primarily aimed at the decentralisation of the Yugoslav self-management system and the treatment of national questions. From the late 1960s the Soviets also started to express concern about the establishment of a national defence system, the influence of Western trends and the mass departure of Yugoslav workers to the West. From 1968 onwards, comparisons between Tito's regime and Dubček's Czechoslovakia were of particular concern. Both the Western and Yugoslav press promoted the idea that Moscow wanted to reactivate the 'Cominformists' – the Yugoslav followers of Stalin who fled to the Soviet Union in 1948.[30]

Moscow certainly did not want to exert direct pressure on the Yugoslav regime, out of fear that this could strengthen the pro-reform movement which wanted stronger ties with the West. In addition, the Soviets did not want to destabilise the country in a way that might endanger the communist regime or the integrity of the Yugoslav state. This would also imply a direct conflict with the West, which was not in the Soviet interest after the damage caused by the intervention in Czechoslovakia, while the *détente* process was gaining momentum. In the period when Tito's departure was imminent because of his age, the Soviets kept an eye on the situation and prepared the ground to strengthen their influence in the power struggles after Tito's death. In the absence of access to Soviet archives, however, the nature and development of Soviet intentions towards Yugoslavia can still only be inferred, rather than definitively established.

The View from the West

Although Yugoslavia was a non-aligned country, it enjoyed the benefits of a Western country in many regards. It was a member of the IMF, the World Bank, GATT and the IFC, and it had a special status in the OSCE. As a consequence of economic reforms, ties with the West were beginning to strengthen.[31]

Western states, and the United States in particular, had clear political interests in assisting Yugoslavia economically. The British Consul General in Zagreb, Geoffrey Baker, exemplified Western attitudes in his report to the British Ambassador in Belgrade, Dugald Stewart:

> Individually and collectively, the NATO powers dispose of a number of potential effective means for exerting a positive

influence on the course of developments in Yugoslavia. They range from economic assistance and political support to vague hints that NATO would not countenance an extension of Soviet power to the shores of the Adriatic.[32]

A similar situation occurred with military relations. The key problem for the Yugoslav armed forces was their dependence on Soviet weapons. This had nothing to do with ideology or attachment to communist ideals, but with the fact that Soviet equipment was more accessible to Yugoslavia. The Yugoslav Chief of Staff, Viktor Bubanj, confirmed this to the American Ambassador, William Leonhart, in March 1970. Bubanj complained that the key obstacles to access to Western military equipment were its price, the firm preconditions for use, and the absence of a bartering mechanism that existed between socialist states and allowed easy access to Soviet weapons. Despite this, Yugoslavia tried to diversify its sources for military equipment, especially after the suppression of the Prague Spring in 1968, establishing military relations with Sweden, Italy, Switzerland, France and the United Kingdom.[33]

Economic Relations and the West

The beginning of economic reforms and the opening of the Yugoslav economy after 1965 led to closer economic ties with the West. Simultaneously, the number of Yugoslav workers in Western European countries increased. The period of 1966 to 1973 was marked by closer ties to the West, followed by a reversal after 1973.

According to statistical reports, Yugoslav exports to Western countries increased from 48 per cent of total exports in 1966 to 56 per cent in 1973, followed by a period of stagnation throughout the rest of the 1970s. Simultaneously, exports to Eastern bloc countries reached their lowest point in 1969, at only 31 per cent. From 1973 onwards exports to Eastern European countries started to rise again. The import data gives us a slightly different picture. Imports from the West reached their peak in 1970 with 69 per cent of total imports and by 1980 had gradually fallen to 59 per cent. Such early stagnation of imports from Western countries is a reflection of the deficit in the balance of payments that burdened the

Yugoslav economy. In parallel, imports from the Eastern bloc had fallen to 21 per cent by 1970, and then gradually increased throughout the 1970s. Although we can assume that the end of political liberalisation in Yugoslavia in 1971 and 1972 influenced the trends in its foreign trade, a stronger orientation towards the east after 1970 can be partially explained by the recession in Western economies after 1971 and the oil shock after 1973. From 1974 onwards, the number of Yugoslav foreign workers in the West started to decrease.

Statistical data also show that the strong Yugoslav engagement with Third World countries was not followed by strong economic results. Trade with Third World countries fell in the period from 1955 to 1961 from 21 to 13 per cent, and by 1972 to 7 per cent. This was completely opposite to the intense political relations envisaged by the Yugoslav policy of non-alignment.[34] This fact can also be linked to the intensification of economic relations with Europe after 1965 and Yugoslav requirements for modern technology and finished products that the Third World countries could not offer. Trade with the non-aligned world was reduced to raw material imports and exports of Yugoslav industrial products that were more afford-able than Western goods and of better quality than Eastern bloc products.[35]

Trade with OECD countries started to increase from 1960 onwards. Fifty per cent of Yugoslavia's exports went to OECD countries, while more than 60 per cent of its imports came from those countries. Trade relations were particularly strong with EEC countries, which accounted for 40 per cent of total imports, led by Italy and Germany. An extremely important part of Yugoslavia's economy was tourism, which brought large quanti-ties of foreign currency into the country. More than 80 per cent of tourists came from Western European countries, which strengthened economic ties and also deepened Western influence.

Relations with West Germany were of special importance. The FRG was traditionally an important trade partner; German tourists were an impor-tant source of foreign currency; and, from the mid-1960s onwards, ever more Yugoslav citizens went to work in the Federal Republic. After 1966 there were increasing attempts to re-establish diplomatic ties, which was a direct consequence of Brandt's *Ostpolitik* and the rejection of the Hallstein doctrine.[36] Trade relations with West Germany allowed Yugoslavia easy access to modern technology and loans, and also opened the multi-million

West German market to Yugoslav products. The positive consequences of the re-establishment of diplomatic ties in 1968 were an increase in trade, access to loans, better status of Yugoslav workers, and enhanced cooperation with the West German government in suppressing criticism of the Tito regime that came from Yugoslav immigrants in Germany.[37]

The period of the 1960s and early 1970s was also marked by increased economic migration. This was a direct consequence of the 1965 reforms that led to increased unemployment, which would last until 1969. The devaluation of the dinar was an additional factor that made Western countries attract Yugoslav workers. These migration trends went in parallel with political and economic liberalisation. Until 1962 it was neither popular, nor desirable, to work abroad. Until then, emigration mainly occurred for political reasons, although the regime tolerated these outflows of the workforce as early as the 1950s. The first organised data on emigration showed that there were only 3,000 workers from Yugoslavia in Western Europe in 1954, of whom 2,000 were in West Germany. By 1961, the number had increased to 28,000, of whom 17,800 were in West Germany. But by 1973 around 830,000 Yugoslavs were working in Western European countries, which marked the peak of emigration. Together with the beginning of economic liberalisation in 1963, even the communists had come to approve of this sort of emigration. It was the easiest way to solve the problem of unemployment, especially in rural areas where most of these workers came from. In addition, the remittances that they sent home became an important source of hard currency for the regime. By the end of the 1960s the policy of open borders became an official part of the political programme, equally acceptable as 'self-management' and 'market socialism'.[38]

It is interesting to track the nationality of emigrants. In the first phase of emigration until 1963, most emigrants came from the Socialist Republic of Croatia, with more than 50 per cent of the total number. This share gradually decreased after 1963 while the percentage of emigrants from Yugoslavia's other constituent republics increased. The percentage of Croats, however, still remained proportionally high in comparison to the other nationalities. For example, according to the 1971 census, 39 per cent of emigrants were Croats, while 28.5 per cent were Serbs. The Serbian numbers were proportionally fewer because the Serbian population was nearly double that of the Croats. Additional data that supports the fact that the Croats led this economic migration was the number of emigrants from Bosnia and Herzegovina, of whom 42.4 per cent were Croats, while the total number of Croats in the population of Bosnia and Herzegovina was only 20.6 per cent.[39]

A similar situation occurred with tourism, a branch of the economy that was just as important for Yugoslavia's hard currency reserves as the remittances from workers abroad. This would become a significant political problem and the source of inter-republic conflicts in the period of liberalisation. In 1950 the number of tourists visiting Yugoslavia was 41,000; by 1961 this number had risen to 1,755,000; and in 1973, the number peaked at 6,149,000 tourists. In the period between 1963 and 1973, Yugoslav tourism went through its highest growth rate, stabilising after 1973. The country's most open period, the 1960s, was reflected in the number of foreigners entering: between 1960 and 1965 the number of visitors increased from 1,157,000 to 8,316,000 per year. In 1966, it increased to 16,820,000; and in 1970, to 29,393,000 visitors. The numbers decreased drastically in 1971 to 21,752,000, which can be explained by the beginning of a long-standing economic crisis in the West that started in 1971.[40] These trends can also be confirmed by the higher numbers of Yugoslav citizens crossing the borders: in 1960, 200,000 visited a foreign country; in 1964, 440,000; in 1965, the numbers increased to 1,284,000; and they continued to increase until 1970, when 14,474,000 travelled abroad.[41]

An important part of economic liberalisation was the Law on Foreign Investments that was passed in 1967. Yugoslavia was the first communist country that attempted to attract foreign investment in this way. The aim was to draw in Western capital and technology, and at the same time, to guarantee security for investments in Yugoslavia. For these reasons, parts of this law were also incorporated in the constitution of Yugoslavia. Despite these efforts, the interest of Western companies was relatively insignificant. The law did not give them any guarantees that their investments would pay off. It limited the transfer of capital and ownership to 49 per cent. The transfer of profits was limited by a relatively small retention quota, and the law also required that 26 per cent of profits had to be reinvested in the company. In addition, there was an issue over invested capital after the expiry of a five-year contract, where the investment of technology and intellectual property was not treated as a part of the investment. Western companies complained that the law was very selective because it sought a gradual increase in Western capital without providing adequate returns. The Swiss publication *Business International* concluded: 'The Yugoslavs prefer investments such as Fiat, that invests in technology, modernises Yugoslav industry and increases exports.'

An additional problem was income tax, which for joint investments amounted to 35 per cent, while for domestic companies the rate was 4 per cent. Yugoslav legislators had difficulty in reconciling the need for foreign investment within the self-management system that automatically treated assets as public ownership. As it was, the law did not produce the results that the Yugoslav regime expected. From 1968 to 1970 only 20 joint-venture contracts had been negotiated with foreign companies, of which 18 were with Western companies and two with Eastern bloc companies. The biggest joint venture was the cooperation between Zastava from Kragujevac and the Italian car giant Fiat, amounting to $114 millon, of which Fiat invested only $21 million.[42]

A bigger problem for the Yugoslav regime was the ideological influence that accompanied Western investment, which introduced liberal ideas and trends into the country. This influence was strengthened by Yugoslav emigration to Western countries. A Radio Free Europe reporter, Slobodan Stanković, summarised the regime's dilemma:

> In Yugoslavia it is not foreign capital as such which is feared but rather the ideological influence, which is – as it now seems – impossible to stop. This is also true in relation to Yugoslavia's manpower export, since more than one million Yugoslav citizens live and work in Western 'capitalist' countries, and thus fall under the influence of a 'non-socialist' way of life.[43]

The British ambassador Terence Garvey described Western influence on Yugoslav society in his last report before leaving Belgrade. In a charmingly written report from April 1971, he gave an overview of developments in Yugoslavia over the past ten years. He emphasised the changes and transformation that the country had gone through:

> In 1958 Yugoslavia used to be a static rural society. It is now in a condition of constant motion. The new town-dweller retains, for the most part, a root in the countryside to which he returns

when he can but his children are increasingly exposed to the culture of the telly, the football match and the pop record. He wears quite good ready-made suits. His daughters follow the vagaries of Western fashion, mini, maxi and midi, and he and his wife are bewildered by their long-haired, blue-jeaned sons. He reads tabloid evening newspapers and the stodgy morning Press is feeling the draught. Western films and the output of the Western avant-garde dramatists fill the theatres of Belgrade and Zagreb. *Hair* has been playing to full houses for 18 months. I am told that *Oh Calcutta!* is coming. Most of the attributes of the permissive society have infiltrated here against the weakening resistance of the Party. I was first alerted to this development through one of the Belgrade weeklies before coming here in 1968; I came upon an illustrated section entitled '*Seksi Humor*'. But things have moved far and fast since then. Today no holds are barred.[44]

2

Yugoslavia, 1945–65

The Early Postwar Years

From its formation, communist Yugoslavia was in many regards different from other Eastern European countries. This was primarily a consequence of developments during the war, when a strong anti-fascist movement formed under the patronage of the Communist Party of Yugoslavia. From 1945 onwards, the party took complete political and military control of the entire territory of the Kingdom of Yugoslavia, as well as parts of Istria and Dalmatia, which at the time still formally belonged to the Kingdom of Italy.

Unlike other Eastern European countries, the Yugoslav Communist Party did not require significant support from Soviet troops who, in the second half of 1944, had reached the country's eastern borders. At the same time the British liberated Greece. In such circumstances it was necessary to strengthen the military and political position of the Yugoslav communists, especially with regards to the Western Allies and the Royal Yugoslav government in exile in London. In order to achieve this, with Tito's approval, Moscow launched an offensive to liberate eastern parts of Yugoslavia, including Belgrade. The Soviets required, and asked for, permission to do this from the Yugoslav communist war government (AVNOJ)[1] and the headquarters of the Yugoslav army, to pursue military operations in

Yugoslav territory. In accordance with this agreement, the Soviets promised to withdraw from Yugoslavia and cede control to the Yugoslav partisans after the conclusion of military operations. This move had great political significance, because it represented recognition of the legitimacy of AVNOJ, while preventing a potential British invasion of Istria.

In this context, it is worth examining the controversial Moscow percentages agreement between Stalin and Churchill in October 1944. In this deal, they established zones of interest, such as Romania (90 per cent Russia and 10 per cent 'the others'), Greece (90 per cent Great Britain 'in accord with USA', 10 per cent Russia), whereas Yugoslavia was split 50–50.[2] The deal actually suited Moscow's interest because it affirmed Soviet claims in the Balkans. On the other hand, it did not have any effect on the partisan movement, nor did it limit Soviet help for Yugoslav communists who already had *de facto* control over most of the country. This is the reason that Tito could easily ignore the agreement after the war, and strengthen his authority independently without any significant participation of pre-war royalist politicians.[3]

Unlike Poland, Czechoslovakia, Hungary, Romania and Bulgaria, where the process of establishing communist regimes had lasted three years after the war had ended, in Yugoslavia the Communist Party had already established full control during the war. It formalised its authority after the elections organised under Allied pressure in accordance with the Tito–Šubašić agreement made with the royalist government in exile. Cooperation between the Yugoslav communists and the pre-war royalist government was a precondition for the international recognition of the new state. The Belgrade Agreement between Tito and Prime Minister Šubašić from November 1944 envisaged, in accordance with AVNOJ's decision, that the king should not return to Yugoslavia, but transfer his authority to a three-member Royal Regency. King Peter II appointed Srđan Budisavljević, Ante Mandić and Dušan Sernec – a Serb, a Croat and a Slovene. The agreement envisaged the formation of a joint government composed of members of the People's Committee of the Liberation of Yugoslavia and members of the royalist Yugoslav government. Consequently, on 7 March 1945 the Temporary People's Government of the Democratic Federative Yugoslavia was formed. Simultaneously, both the wartime royalist government and the People's Committee were dissolved.[4]

Josip Broz Tito became the prime minister and defence minister in the new temporary government. The royalist members were Milan Grol, who became deputy prime minister, Ivan Šubašić, foreign minister, and Juraj Šutej, a Minister Without Portfolio.[5] However, the multi-party elections for the constitutional assembly turned into a democratic farce: the Popular Front, controlled by the Communist Party, won 90 per cent of 7.4 million votes. This also differentiates Yugoslavia from other Eastern European countries, where postwar elections were held in a more democratic environment. In Czechoslovakia and Hungary, communist parties did not win outright majorities. Albania followed Yugoslavia's example by abolishing the monarchy, in January 1946, while in Bulgaria and Romania this would occur later.[6] While other communist regimes were more dependent on Moscow, the Yugoslav communists were eager to implement Soviet practice and Stalinist methods to organise their public authority.[7]

The immediate postwar period was marked by the strengthening of the communist regime based on the Soviet practice of a centralised, state-managed economy and industrialisation. Until World War II, Yugoslavia was a predominantly underdeveloped country with a weak industry and 76 per cent of the population living in rural areas.[8] The first task the new government undertook was to pursue a rapid industrialisation based on heavy industry and large industrial facilities that require huge investments and long-term planning. The existing industries, banks, warehouses and small shops were all nationalised by 1948 in accordance with the First and Second Law on Nationalisation, while only small agricultural holdings, small craft workshops, individual homes and apartment buildings remained in private hands.[9] The first Five Year Plan started in 1947 under the leadership of Boris Kidrič, who replaced Andrija Hebrang as the head of the Economic Council and the Ministry of Industry.[10] The plan envisaged a five-fold increase in industrial production and a 1.5-fold increase in agricultural production.

Under the 1946 constitution, unofficially referred to as 'Stalin's constitution' for its similarities to the 1936 Soviet constitution, the new state was organised as a federation of six republics. In addition, two new autonomous regions were created within Serbia: Kosovo and Vojvodina.[11] The creation of the autonomous regions, especially Vojvodina, was the first example of an ethnic conflict in socialist Yugoslavia. Vojvodina's autonomy was a compromise between Serbian demands based on the majority Serb population regions of Bačka, Banat and Srijem, and Croatian historic and ethnic claims to Srijem.[12]

In the international arena, Yugoslavia had become the Soviet Union's staunchest ally while relations with Western countries were burdened by unresolved territorial disputes, along with ideological differences. The animosity of Yugoslavia's communist leaders towards the West and the United States was already obvious. Western diplomats were already united in their opinion that Yugoslavia was the most faithful and militant satellite of the Soviet Union.[13]

The fact that the Soviets did not contribute significantly to the liberation of Yugoslav territory from German occupation, nor did they help to establish communist control over Yugoslavia, gave Tito much greater freedom of action, both internally and externally. Yugoslavia was the only country in Europe, besides the Soviet Union and Albania, where the communist regime established its authority without external pressure.[14] The Soviets did not like Yugoslavia's independent actions on several fronts that could bring them into direct conflict with the West. The principal areas of dispute were Trieste, the Austrian–Yugoslav border, Yugoslav help to the Greek communists, the so-called Balkan Federation, and Yugoslavia's policy towards Albania. Additional areas of bilateral dispute were the establishment of joint Soviet–Yugoslav enterprises in river and aerial traffic, the creation of a joint bank, and the status of Soviet experts working in Yugoslavia.[15] Another source of contention in the relations between the two states was the Soviet Union's attempt to infiltrate the Yugoslav police and party structure with its agents.[16]

The question of Trieste, and relations with Italy and Austria, became an issue from the moment the Yugoslav army entered Trieste and parts of Carinthia, and came into conflict with British and American units over the control of the area in April 1945. Although the Yugoslav units eventually withdrew from Trieste and Carinthia, the issue of the Venezia Giulia region and Istria was only partly settled at the Paris Peace Conference of 1946. The 1947 peace treaty between Yugoslavia and Italy gave Yugoslavia the territory that Italy had gained during World War I, whereas Trieste remained under Allied control until it was ceded to Italy in 1954.[17]

The idea of the Balkan Federation, in which communist Yugoslavia would have a leading role, was born during the war. In the spring of 1943, a member of the Yugoslav communist leadership, Svetozar Vukmanović Tempo, suggested the establishment of a Balkan headquarters under the command of the Yugoslav Communist Party to coordinate the military actions of Albanian, Bulgarian and Greek partisans. Although the initial plan failed, because of opposition by Bulgarian and Greek communists and Soviet reluctance, the idea to unite the Balkan countries under a communist regime was revived in the middle of the Greek civil war of 1944–9, in which the Greek communists fought the royalists, who were supported by the British and later also by the Americans. In 1946 Yugoslavia became a key supporter of the Greek communists.[18]

Yugoslavia organised camps to train the Greek communist rebels and supplied them with weapons and other equipment.[19] This was in direct opposition to the 'percentages agreement' and Stalin's decision to allow Britain to maintain its influence in Greece. Another problem for the Soviets was the increasingly close relationship between Bulgaria and Yugoslavia, especially after meetings between the Yugoslav and Bulgarian leaders, Tito and Dimitrov, in Bled and Evksinograd, in which they agreed to the creation of a Yugoslav–Bulgarian Federation. Stalin lost his patience after Tito's attempts to integrate Albania into Yugoslavia. Albania had been under strong Yugoslav influence since the end of the war, and until 1948 the Soviet Union had no authority there. The breaking point was Tito's decision to send two Yugoslav divisions to prevent a potential attack from Greece. At the same time, Yugoslavia, Bulgaria and Albania prepared plans for economic and military integration.[20]

The break with Stalin's Soviet Union was a surprise for both the public in Yugoslavia and for the West. Overnight Yugoslavia was transformed from the most faithful Soviet ally into a bitter critic of Stalinism and the Soviet model of socialism. Immediately after the war, Yugoslav and Soviet views were very similar. Only after 1947 did the Yugoslav interpretation of communist legitimacy start to be questioned by Moscow. The main reason was that in other communist countries the Soviet Union and the Red Army were portrayed as the greatest liberators of those countries and the ones who brought communist regimes to power. In Yugoslavia the communist party had created its own legitimacy by fighting its way to power without

25

significant Soviet participation. The Yugoslav model was a direct challenge to the Soviet concept of a monolithic communist bloc and to Stalin's Cold War policy that gained momentum in 1947.[21] In this context, the true cause of conflict was the struggle for Moscow's prestige in the communist world, where Stalin was portrayed as the undisputed authority.

The *Informbiro* Resolution and the Conflict with Stalin

The Soviet–Yugoslav conflict was preceded by a period of close coop-eration between the two communist parties and the creation of the Information Bureau of the Communist Parties (Cominform or *Informbiro*, its Yugoslav name), founded in Szklarska Poręba in Poland in 1947. The creation of Cominform was Stalin's response to the American initiation of the Marshall Plan, which was meant to strengthen Western European economies and democracies. At the same time, the Marshall Plan sought to counter communist influence in Western European political systems.[22] Cominform was meant to be Stalin's lever to subordinate the European communist parties to Moscow. Although Tito was initially the most vocif-erous promoter of Cominform, he was not yet aware that it would become Stalin's most powerful weapon in his ideological fight against Yugoslavia.[23]

The open conflict began in February 1948 when Stalin called for a meeting in Moscow with the Yugoslav and Bulgarian party officials, Edvard Kardelj, Vladimir Bakarić, Milovan Đilas, Koča Popović, Svetozar Vukmanović Tempo and Georgi Dimitrov, whom he accused of not con-sulting with Moscow on their respective foreign policies.[24] Stalin blamed Dimitrov for announcing the creation of a new federation in Eastern Europe, while Tito was criticised for his decision to send the Yugoslav army into Albania. At the same meeting, Stalin unexpectedly requested the uni-fication of Bulgaria and Yugoslavia as the Bulgarian–Yugoslav Federation, which would subsequently be joined by Albania. The surprise was even greater because in 1945 Stalin had rejected the idea.[25] His motives are still unclear, but it was probably a negotiation tactic to pre-empt Dimitrov's ideas on the creation of an Eastern European federation and Tito's attempts to unite Albania with Yugoslavia. Stalin's move heightened Yugoslav sus-picions that in this attempt at unification he was seeking to strengthen

Soviet influence in Yugoslavia. After all, Bulgaria was under complete Soviet control. This was why the Yugoslav leadership rejected the proposal and continued to strengthen Yugoslav influence in Albania, along with assisting the Greek communists.[26] In early March 1948, the Politburo of the Yugoslav Communist Party (KPJ) concluded that the Soviet leadership did not respect Yugoslav political ambitions and that it sought to enforce its will through political and economic pressure. Shortly after, Soviet experts were withdrawn from Yugoslavia, and in March 1948, the Central Committee of the Soviet Communist Party accused the Yugoslav leadership of pursuing anti-Soviet policies.[27] The Soviets halted negotiations on the Soviet–Yugoslav trade agreement, which presented a great challenge to the recently initiated Five Year Plan. The Soviet Communist Party forwarded its accusations and conclusions to all Cominform members. Manoeuvring behind the scenes lasted until Moscow's open strike against the Yugoslav leadership in June 1948.

The first victims were two high-ranking party officials Andrija Hebrang and Sreten Žujović. Žujović, who secretly cooperated with the Soviets, opposed Tito's anti-Soviet attitude, while Hebrang was already in disgrace with Tito, and characterised as a Soviet man. Both were imprisoned for fear that the Soviets would try to kidnap them and move them to Moscow.[28] These accusations against important officials exacerbated the conflict with Moscow. In his so-called second letter to the Central Committee of the Communist Party of Yugoslavia, Stalin denigrated the Yugoslav communists' contribution to the fight against the Germans, while claiming that the Yugoslav communist regime was created by the Red Army and the Soviet Union.

The final break came when the Yugoslavs declined to attend the Cominform summit in Bucharest from 19 to 23 June 1948, where the conflict with the KPJ was scheduled to be discussed. At the summit, the *Resolution on the State of the Yugoslav Communist Party* was adopted. It contained a series of accusations against the Yugoslav communist, and represented an open Stalinist attack on the Yugoslav communist leadership. The KPJ was expelled from the Cominform, which came as a complete surprise to the Yugoslav public, and was also the first time the conflict between the two communist states had come out into the open. All economic ties between Yugoslavia and the Eastern bloc were cut off too.

The publication of the Cominform resolution and the Yugoslav reply in the newspaper *Borba* on 28 June 1948 initiated a series of mutual recriminations. More dangerous for the fate of Yugoslavia, however, were the economic and military measures that the Soviets and the other Eastern European countries started to pursue in order to suppress the Yugoslav heresy and to dethrone Tito's regime. The conflict between Cominform and the Yugoslav communist leadership also led to purges in other Eastern European countries.[29] By 1951, many high party officials in the communist movements of Albania, Bulgaria, Hungary, Czechoslovakia, Greece, Poland and Romania were accused of giving support to Tito, and removed from their positions or executed.[30]

The later Yugoslav historiography would try to portray the initial Yugoslav appeasement of Stalin as a well-thought out tactic on the path to independence, in order not to give the Soviets any evidence in support of their accusations of heresy. But there is enough evidence to suggest that in this initial phase of the conflict the tone of the resolution had come as a surprise, and the Yugoslav leadership genuinely hoped to find a conciliatory solution. They did not want to give the Soviets a justification for a military intervention, which was a credible threat.[31] For this reason, the first reaction of the Yugoslav communist leadership was to emphasise its allegiance to the Soviet Union and to Stalin, while rechanneling the conflict from the party to the state level.

The Cominform resolution was understood in Yugoslavia as an attack on the Yugoslav state, and not as an ideological conflict between the two parties as the Soviets had formulated it.[32] The Yugoslavs downgraded relations with the West in order to defend themselves against the Soviet accusation of abandoning Marxism-Leninism. This actually worked in the Soviets' favour, because it coincided with the Western proposal to cede Trieste to Italy, in the middle of parliamentary elections in Italy. Yugoslavia continued to pursue the Soviet model of development, which was most obvious at the Third Plenum of the Yugoslav Communist Party Central Committee (CK KPJ) in January 1949, when the decision was made to collectivise agriculture on a mass scale. As a consequence, the number of *kolkhozi*, collective farms shot up from 14 in 1945, and 1,218 in 1948, to 6,238 in 1949, reaching its peak with 6,913 in 1950.[33] The move led to strong resistance among the peasant population and a 41 per cent drop in wheat production.

Total agricultural production fell to 73 per cent of pre-war levels.[34] Such an agricultural policy was particularly controversial because 50 per cent of party members originated from rural areas. There was a particular danger that the regime would lose its core supporters. Another question, however, was whether ideology was the only reason for collectivisation, or whether the regime was looking for a quick fix to overcome economic problems caused by the war and the Soviet blockade.[35]

The strongest pressure from the Eastern bloc could be felt in the spring of 1949, when the show trials against alleged Titoists began in Eastern European countries. By the summer of 1949, there was a real danger of military intervention in Yugoslavia by the communist countries. This coincided with the first successful detonation of the Soviet atomic bomb in September 1949, which increased tensions. A second Cominform resolution, colourfully titled *The Communist Party of Yugoslavia Owned by Murderers and Spies*, openly called for toppling 'Tito's regime of terror'. This was carried symbolically on Yugoslav National Day (or 'Republic Day') on 29 November, 1949. The resolution was the final signal to Yugoslavia's leaders that there was no possibility of reconciliation with Stalin's Soviet Union.[36]

Bonding with the West

The establishment of cooperation with the West after the initial conflict with Cominform was slow and burdened by suspicion on both sides. This animosity was primarily caused by unnecessarily negative attitudes that the Yugoslav communists took after the victory over Nazi Germany. The position of the newly founded communist state towards recent war allies became clear at the London conference of foreign ministers in 1945 and the Paris Peace Conference of 1946. Western states clashed with Tito's regime over Trieste and the future Yugoslav–Italian border. These relations were worsened by an incident when the Yugoslavs shot down an American plane and forced another to land in August 1946. These events almost led to open conflict with the United States.[37] Tito was still determined to attach Yugoslavia to the Soviet Union and rejected the Marshall Plan in 1947.[38]

Western diplomats did not pay much attention to the tensions between Tito and Stalin before the first Cominform resolution of June 1948. In 1947,

British and American diplomats started to report on a potential Yugoslav–Soviet conflict, but neither Washington nor London acted on this information.[39] This made the surprise and shock even greater among Western officials and publics when the first resolution was published. Apart from the highest leadership, most Yugoslav officials were also surprised by this course of events.

American support for Yugoslav independence from the Soviet Union did not come overnight. This was understandable considering the unpleasant experiences that the United States had had with the Yugoslav regime, starting with worsening bilateral relations, the Trieste issue, and support for the Greek communists.[40] Despite ideological obstacles, however, the Truman Administration quickly recognised the opportunities of Yugoslav independence from the Soviet Union. For the State Department, the Yugoslav heresy was a good way to break the monolith of the communist bloc, while the Armed Forces, the US Congress and the American public were equally interested in the geostrategic potential these developments offered.[41]

With Yugoslavia in the Soviet bloc, the Soviets had access to the Italian border and the eastern Adriatic coast. In the new circumstances, however, the potential for Soviet pressure on Italy and Greece was significantly reduced, while isolating Albania from the rest of the communist bloc. Despite the ideological background, the West would support Yugoslav attempts to portray the conflict with Moscow as an attack on a sovereign state. Such a policy called into question the doctrine that subsumed national sovereignty to the unity of the communist movement, potentially reducing Soviet influence in other Eastern bloc countries.[42]

Western intelligence services did not consider the threat of a Soviet military intervention realistic. But in the summer of 1949, when tensions were heightened, Western diplomats began to fear that the Soviets might indeed attack Yugoslavia. Western officials starting sending clear messages to the Soviets that an attack on a sovereign state would not be tolerated.[43] This was a signal to Stalin that Yugoslavia would not be left at his mercy.[44]

In October 1949, the West supported Yugoslavia's candidacy for Non-Permanent Membership in the UN Security Council. This was the first event that elevated the conflict to an international level. The unofficial agreement between the great powers was that the seat should belong to an Eastern bloc country, which should have been Czechoslovakia. Western countries ignored the Cominform proposal and supported Yugoslavia's successful candidacy, dealing a blow to Soviet attempts to isolate Yugoslavia. The move also decreased the potential for a Soviet attack on Yugoslavia, while the West used the Soviet–Yugoslav conflict in its own propaganda against communism.[45]

Another two events directly influenced Yugoslav attitudes towards more active cooperation with the West. On the global level, in June 1950, North Korea attacked the South, with Soviet support, intensifying fears that a similar scenario could unfold in Yugoslavia with the Soviets organising an armed attack via their satellites. On the local level, a drought hit Yugoslavia in the summer of 1950, bringing the country to the edge of famine and worsening an already catastrophic economic situation caused by the Soviet blockade.[46]

The American policy of aiding Yugoslavia was unofficially characterised as 'keeping Tito afloat', which involved providing enough aid to preserve Yugoslav independence. The critical period was immediately after the economic ties with the Eastern bloc countries were cut, which represented 50 per cent of Yugoslav foreign trade. The first sign of American help for the Yugoslav regime was to allow the use of gold reserves inherited from the Kingdom of Yugoslavia and frozen since the German invasion in 1941. Access to British and American oil was granted in June 1948, which was in direct contradiction of the American policy that forbade exports of commodities and products of military importance to the Soviet Union and its satellites.

In September 1948 the American embassy in Belgrade suggested that Yugoslavia should be excluded from this policy, and in December the British signed a one-year trade pact with Yugoslavia.[47] The first American credit line to Yugoslavia of $20 million was approved in September 1949, and more significant help started to flow in the second half of 1950 after Yugoslavia formally requested economic aid.[48] The turning point came again on 'Republic Day' on 29 November 1950, when the US Congress, at President Truman's proposal, approved a bill on urgent aid to Yugoslavia that officially regulated American aid.

Yugoslavia also received aid from American allies, especially the UK, France and West Germany, and loans from the World Bank. It was estimated that during the period of closest relations with the West between 1950 and 1955 Yugoslavia received around $1.2 billion in food, machinery and military equipment from the US alone. Most aid came in the form of donations of products; loans and direct purchases were only a small part of the package.[49]

The Truman Administration used Yugoslavia as a Trojan horse against the unity of Soviet and Eastern bloc influence on Western European communist parties. This would continue during Eisenhower's presidency. According to Secretary of State John Foster Dulles, 'Titoism' had become a tool of liberation from the Soviet bloc. The British, on the other hand, were more reluctant to support Tito's branch of national communism, because they feared that the model could endanger their interests in Africa and Asia.[50]

The consequences of political, economic and military cooperation with the West would define the future course of Yugoslav domestic and foreign policy. It is hard to know what would have happened had the break between Tito and Stalin not occurred in 1948. This could have happened at some other time, considering their earlier mutual disagreements and distrust. But it is likely that Yugoslavia would have become a closer Soviet ally and accepted the Soviet and economic model of development. It would have been reduced to just another Soviet satellite.

Relations with the West significantly improved and there are several examples of Yugoslavia softening its previous attitudes. The stick-and-carrot approach that the West discreetly pursued in order to gain concessions from Yugoslavia in exchange for financial support was most obvious in the case of Greece. Yugoslavia ceased helping the Greek communists, who supported the anti-Yugoslav resolutions of the Cominform.[51]

The tensions surrounding the border with Austria eased, and the status of Trieste would be finally resolved with the London Memorandum of 1954, which also regulated and normalised relations with Italy. The Treaty on Friendship and Cooperation between Yugoslavia, Greece and Turkey of February 1953 and the creation of the Balkan Pact in August in 1954 represented the high point of cooperation between Yugoslavia and the West. The Balkan Pact was supposed to be part of a chain devised by the United States to encircle the Soviet and Chinese spheres of influence. These plans, however, would not succeed after Yugoslavia normalised relations with the Soviet Union following Stalin's death.[52] At the United Nations, cooperation with the West became common practice: on several occasions Yugoslavia voted in favour of Western resolutions and against Soviet proposals.[53] Finally, the events of 1948 made way for a new phase in Yugoslav foreign policy that manifested itself through a non-aligned policy and the establishment of closer relations with Third World countries. It also established a policy of a path to socialism that was independent from the Soviet Union and the Eastern bloc.

The Belgrade Declaration on the Independent Path to Socialism

The internal consequences of cooperation with the West could be seen in the abandonment of communist rigidity and Stalinist methods. The process of collectivisation was halted, the liberalisation of everyday life began and the bureaucratic apparatus was decentralised.[54]

Stalin's death on 5 March 1953 was a turning point for relations between the USSR and Yugoslavia. Ending the personal animosity between the two dictators enabled a process of reconciliation to begin, although official Soviet policy would not change immediately. Ideological attacks continued throughout 1953. Only after Khrushchev took control of the Soviet Communist Party did relations start to improve, resulting in the Belgrade Declaration of 1955. In the summer of 1953, the Soviets suggested the exchange of ambassadors; and in 1954, the Soviets and some of its satellites re-established economic ties with Yugoslavia.

In this period, the Soviet leadership was in a state of flux. After Stalin's death, his closest associates distributed positions of responsibility among themselves. Georgy Malenkov formally succeeded to Stalin's position as head of state when he became Chairman of the Council of Ministers. Lavrentiy Beria remained in his position as the Minister of the Interior and chief of the secret police (NKVD). Vyacheslav Molotov continued as Minister of Foreign Affairs. Nikita Khrushchev took control of the party apparatus. The first victim of the internal conflict was Beria, who was arrested in July 1953 and formally accused of trying to establish relations with Tito and the head of the Yugoslav secret police, Aleksandar Ranković. Beria had promoted better relations with Tito, while Molotov considered Tito to be a traitor to the communist movement.

Before he was arrested, Beria prepared a letter for Aleksandar Ranković, in which he proposed the restoration of closer relations between the two countries. In the end, Molotov prevailed with the arms-length formula that applied to the West: the 'equal relations that exist with other bourgeois states aligned with the North Atlantic aggressive bloc'.[55] Eventually, the reestablishment of links to Yugoslavia was justified with the words: 'When we have diplomatic relations with Tito's masters (the Americans), why wouldn't we have them with Tito?'[56]

The Sino-Soviet agreement of October 1954 actually preceded the Soviet rapprochement with Yugoslavia. It had many elements that Yugoslavia had formulated in response to Soviet attacks since 1948, including equality between socialist states. It was also reflected in the Soviets waiving their share in Sino-Soviet joint enterprises. In all other Eastern bloc countries these enterprises were organised in such a way to use the economic potential of the satellite countries in the Soviet Union's favour. The quiet acceptance of the Yugoslav position in the negotiations with Mao Tse-Tung enabled a renewed opening with Tito. The Soviets wanted to preserve the unity of the communist bloc after Stalin's death, and in the middle of the infighting that was raging inside the Kremlin peace with Yugoslavia's communist leadership was portrayed as a victory in the propaganda war with the West. Liberal reforms in Yugoslavia slowed down after the expulsion from the Central Committee of Milovan Đilas in January 1954. A close associate of Tito, Đilas promoted democratic socialism and reform in a series of articles between October 1953 and January 1954 in *Borba*, the official newspaper of the Yugoslav Communist Party. His expulsion from the Central Committee demonstrated that Yugoslavia was not yet ready to abandon communism, which also helped the process of reconciliation with the Soviets.[57]

When a Soviet delegation made its historic visit to Belgrade in May 1955, Khrushchev was already the most powerful man in the Kremlin. The visit was one of his international initiatives meant to strengthen the Soviet Union's international standing, as well as his own position vis-à-vis Molotov. Along with strengthening the Sino-Soviet bloc, Khrushchev was in a hurry to sign the Austrian Peace Treaty in May 1955. And, by the end of the year, he had made a deal with the West German Chancellor Konrad Adenauer to establish diplomatic ties between the Soviet Union and the Federal Republic.[58]

Tito and Nikolai Bulganin, the Premier of the Soviet Union, signed the Belgrade Declaration, emphasising that this was an agreement between two sovereign states and not between two communist parties. This was a huge victory for the Yugoslav communist leadership over the Soviet Union. The Soviets unilaterally accepted responsibility for the conflict, but more important was their acceptance that 'different forms of socialist development are an exclusive matter of the nations of individual states'.[59] This formulation of non-interference in the political, economic and ideological affairs of another state would have far-reaching consequences for future Yugoslav–Soviet relations, as well as on Soviet policy towards Eastern Europe. It provided a foundation to resist Soviet influence in other Eastern European countries. This led to a delicate balancing act between the USSR's need for security on its western borders, while loosening its ideological grip over Eastern European countries. At the same time, this policy also cast doubt on Moscow's supremacy in the socialist world, which was particularly obvious in the case of Sino-Soviet relations. Such contradictions in Soviet policy would have tragic consequences in Hungary in 1956, in Czechoslovakia in 1968, and on the resistance in Poland and Romania, as well as affecting the conflict with the Chinese and Albanian communists, and weakening the Soviet position in the ideological fight with the West.

Yugoslav–Soviet relations would never reach the level of armed conflict or the political and economic blockades of 1948–53. But tensions did arise on many occasions, primarily because the Soviets feared that Yugoslavia's promotion of its independent path to socialism could endanger its influence in Eastern Europe. The honeymoon lasted from the signing of the Belgrade Declaration in May 1955 until the Hungarian revolution in the autumn of 1956. This period was marked by bilateral contacts and mutual visits by Yugoslav and Soviet leaders. The most important event was the 20th Congress of the Soviet Communist Party in February 1956, in which Khrushchev famously denounced Stalin, a speech that was only made public when despatched to Belgrade and Washington on 18 March. The reason Belgrade received this information so early was that the speech also included recognition of Yugoslavia's unique form of socialism. The denunciation of Stalinist terror, combined with this recognition, raised high hopes in other countries. Another important event was Tito's visit to

Moscow in June 1956 and the signing of the Moscow Declaration, which continued the process started in Belgrade, as an agreement between two communist parties.[60] It even seemed that Khrushchev was starting to acknowledge Tito's opinions and influence in Eastern Europe, which were particularly obvious during the Hungarian events later that year. The two Soviet military interventions in Hungary on 23 and 31 October, however, put an end to this period of goodwill. Tito's support for the Hungarian leaderships, and his attack on the Soviet decision to intervene militarily, were not welcomed in the Kremlin, and led to a renewed economic blockade by the Eastern bloc.[61]

But the fight over Hungary did not last long, and better relations resumed after Tito and Khrushchev met in Bucharest in August 1957. The Yugoslavs recognised the German Democratic Republic and intensified anti-Western propaganda. At the same time, the Soviet bloc unfroze loans that had been assigned to Yugoslavia before the intervention in Hungary.[62]

A new crisis occurred in November 1957, when the Soviets proposed a resolution on communist unity that emphasised the USSR's leading role in the communist movement, minimising the importance of 'national' communism. The Yugoslav leadership understood this move to be directed against their country's independence, and they declined to sign the document at the celebration of the 40th anniversary of the October Revolution in Moscow.[63] This period of Yugoslav–Soviet tension would last until 1962. It was marked by Sino-Soviet tensions and characterised by vicious attacks on Tito. At the VII Congress of the Bulgarian Communist Party in Sofia on 3 June 1958, Khrushchev's speech regressed into a rant against Yugoslav 'revisionism', and repeated the vocabulary of the 1948 resolution, accusing Tito of being a Trojan horse within the communist camp. This occurred against the background of the Sino-Soviet struggle for supremacy in the communist world. The Chinese Communist Party was particularly harsh towards any attempt at reconciliation with the West and liberal trends within communist movements. This is the reason why the Chinese led the attacks on Yugoslav 'revisionism', which also implied an attack on Khrushchev's policy of destalinisation. The Yugoslav and Soviet parties would eventually reconcile in 1962 when an open conflict between the Soviet Union and China had become inevitable, and the positive trends continued with Leonid Brezhnev's rise to power in 1964.[64]

Balancing East and West

From the beginning of the 1960s, the worsening state of Sino-Soviet relations affected Soviet policy towards Yugoslavia. After the Soviet and Chinese Communist Parties broke ties at the 22nd Congress of the Soviet Communist Party in October 1961, the propaganda war against Yugoslavia that started in 1958 would ease. Already in 1960 Yugoslav and Soviet politicians were re-establishing contact. Tito and Khrushchev met in New York at the UN General Assembly, and in the following year the Yugoslav foreign minister Koča Popović visited the Soviet Union, while his Soviet counterpart Andrei Gromyko visited Yugoslavia in 1962. This rapprochement would continue with mutual visits by Tito, Khrushchev and Brezhnev until 1968. Warmer relations were helped by Yugoslav support for the Soviets against China at the 22nd Congress. The 1960s were also marked by Yugoslavia reaching out to Third World countries, which led to the founding conference of the Non-Aligned Movement in Belgrade in 1961, as well as by attempts to preserve good relations with the West. The balancing game between the East and West, to the background of the era of decolonisation, enabled this opening to newly independent states.

As a consequence, relations with other Eastern European countries also improved and the Yugoslavs established some sort of *détente* with the Soviets. Good relations continued after Khrushchev's removal in 1964. By the time the Yugoslav economic reforms and liberal changes started in 1965 and 1966, Soviet–Yugoslav relations had reached new heights. Economic cooperation was established by Yugoslav participation in Comecon (the Council for Mutual Economic Assistance) from 1964, and the two countries shared similar views on international issues, such as the Vietnam War and policy towards China.[65]

In the period of warmer relations between the Soviets and Yugoslavs after the Belgrade declaration of 1955, Western aid to Yugoslavia decreased, as did military ties. But Tito managed to allay Western fears that this rapprochement would lead Yugoslavia into the Soviet bloc. He made clear that he would not worsen his relations with the West on account of improved relations with the East.[66] The visit of American Secretary of State John Foster Dulles to Tito's residence on the island of Brijuni, during his European tour in November 1955, confirmed the continuity of stable ties with the West.[67]

By 1954 the structure of economic ties with the West had changed. The UK and France gradually phased out aid to Yugoslavia, while the US decided to offer loans and food surpluses. In addition, Yugoslavia started to take advantage of new sources of financing, primarily West German loans and stronger trade with Italy after the settlement of the Trieste question in 1954.[68] Continuing good relations were particularly important for the economy: the ups and downs of economic trends did not always follow the fluctuations of political relations. In the 1950s, both political and economic relations with the US depended primarily on the state of Yugoslavia's relations with the Soviet Union. Although successive American administrations continued to support the Yugoslav economy with exports of food surpluses, technology and loan assistance on beneficial terms, the obstacle was the US Congress. On several occasions the House of Representatives sought to prevent American presidents from strengthening Yugoslav independence through economic assistance.

This was emphasised in the period of good relations with the Eastern bloc in 1955–6, and again when Yugoslav–Soviet relations improved after a dip following the intervention in Hungary. In this period, the trial of Milovan Đilas began, and Yugoslavia recognised East Germany.[69] This was the reason US Ambassador Riddleberger was withdrawn, the US limited the flow of economic aid and completely cut off arms deliveries and West Germany imposed the Hallstein doctrine on Yugoslavia.[70] Similarly, the US Congress softened its attitude to Yugoslavia in times of strained relations with Moscow, such as during the Hungarian intervention and the so-called second conflict with Moscow and Beijing from 1958 to 1960.

By 1959 American aid based on contracts and agreements from the early 1950s had largely ceased. The two countries established economic relations that were not dependent on the political will of Congress. Relations with the US were strained once again, however, when Belgrade established better relations with both the East and the Third World. This called into question economic ties with the West, which the Yugoslavs badly needed to implement the next Five Year Plan. At the end of the 1950s, a group of Western countries led by the US secured a $275 million loan for this plan, while the Soviet Union promised $800 million. This situation caused a conflict between the Kennedy Administration and the US Senate, which sought to terminate US aid to Yugoslavia.

Consequently, several new Bills were introduced that limited presidential authority over American foreign assistance and abolished Yugoslavia's Most Favoured Nation status.[71] Despite these occasional problems with the US, Yugoslavia managed to maintain good economic and political relations with other Western countries, and in 1966 became a member of GATT (General Agreement on Tariffs and Trade).[72]

Non-Alignment Policy

The second pillar of the Yugoslav system, along with 'self-management', was the Non-Aligned Movement. The policy of non-alignment was directly linked to the 1948 split with Stalin, and operated similarly to self-management. It developed gradually and adjusted to changing circumstances.

Yugoslav officials had established their first postwar contacts with Asia and Africa, via communist and socialist organisations in Western Europe, and through their occasional contacts with Asian communists. These included the conference of Asian communists in Calcutta in 1948. Until 1949, Yugoslav policy towards Asia had been pro-Soviet, and the Yugoslav media were very critical of Western attempts to preserve their colonial empires.[73]

The Korean War and the fear of Soviet attack forced the Yugoslav leadership to change its foreign policy. Yugoslavia supported the American initiative to defend South Korea, but opposed the decision to cross the 38th parallel after the successful landing at Inchon in September 1950. It did this because it believed that it could be interpreted as interference in a country's internal affairs, which would set a dangerous precedent in light of a potential Soviet invasion of Yugoslavia. Yugoslavia's reaction was an early sign of the non-aligned policy that would take shape by the mid-1950s.[74]

Yugoslavia's cooperation with Third World countries at the UN over the Korean War was the first example of multilateral cooperation between its diplomacy and the newly independent states of Asia and Africa.[75] This was an isolated case, however, since Yugoslavia had not formulated a clear policy or strategy towards the Third World.[76] Still, close ties with India and Egypt, co-founders of the Non-Aligned Movement, began to take shape when all three countries were Non-Permanent Members of the Security

Council in 1950–1, where they coordinated their position on the Korean crisis. This cooperation would continue and include countries (such as Indonesia and Burma) with similar views on the divisions between the blocs, colonialism and poverty. By 1952 Yugoslavia had strengthened formal diplomatic ties with India, Burma, the Arab states, Indonesia and Ethiopia. In 1954 and 1955 Tito visited India and Burma, followed by visits to Ethiopia and Egypt – immediately before the Suez Crisis.[77]

During those years Yugoslavia was isolated by the Soviet Union and its satellites, and cooperation with the West was difficult, because of harsh economic reality and the possibility of eastern invasion. In such circumstances, it was impossible to pursue extensive foreign policy activities. On the other hand, in order to break its diplomatic isolation and avoid overdependence on the West, Yugoslavia needed allies who could not threaten her economic and political independence.

After Stalin's death the balancing act continued between the normalisation of relations with the Soviets and the continuation of close relations with the West. So cooperation with the non-aligned countries was a natural solution and a justification of this high-wire dance between East and West. In this context, Yugoslavia froze its Balkan Pact activities, and the Soviet break with the principles of the Belgrade and Moscow Declarations in the following years convinced the Yugoslav leadership that closer alignment with the Eastern bloc would threaten its independence. In reaching out to Third World countries, Tito reduced pressures that came from within the party leadership which sought closer links to the East, as well as from pro-Western factions that favoured further liberalisation and decentralisation. Another reason was the potential for the Yugoslav economy to enter new markets. Underdeveloped Third World economies that could not afford sophisticated Western technology were eager to forge better economic ties with Yugoslavia.[78]

By organising the first conference of non-aligned countries in Belgrade in September 1961, Yugoslavia became a leader of the newly established movement. The conference attracted 25 countries, institutionalising ideas and attitudes that those countries shared and promoted in the 1950s. The person most responsible for the organisation of the conference was Tito himself. The event elevated him as a statesman of wider importance, considering the size and clout of his country.[79]

Titoism and Workers' Self-Management

In the immediate postwar period from 1945 to 1949, political author-ity and economic management were centralised according to the Soviet model. But as an important consequence of the fight with Stalin, a process of decentralisation started in 1949. This included the implementation of 'Titoism' and the unique 'Yugoslav path to socialism'. These key elements of new Yugoslav policy were the development of 'workers' self-management' as domestic policy and non-alignment as foreign policy. Both ideas, which most characterised Yugoslav socialism, were developed in the early 1950s as responses to Soviet critiques and attacks on Soviet Stalinist practices. In May 1949 a Law on People's Committees was passed, with the aim of decentralising the economy and state apparatus by transferring authority to regional and local administrations.

In this new economic system all the means of production would remain the property of the state, but the state would not manage the production. Instead, it would be overseen by the workers and managements of individ-ual companies. To this end, the parliament (or Federal People's Assembly) adopted a basic law on the management of state companies, agricultural companies and higher economic enterprises by 'workers' collectives' on 27 June 1950. This was the beginning of the implementation of the idea of 'workers' self-management' that had been a part of Marxist and anarchist thought since the nineteenth century.[80] The system of the Soviet planned economy was gradually abolished: now the state was only *directing* the economy by creating the basic conditions for economic growth. State bureaucracy was reduced, many federal economic ministries were abol-ished, along with the Federal Planning Commission, and the management of a large number of industries was transferred to the republics.

By April 1959, the entire economy was under the authority and juris-diction of the regional governments of the republics. Because of strong resistance from small farmers, Soviet-style collectivisation was abandoned and the market-driven pricing of agricultural products was permitted. In March 1953, the state permitted workers' agricultural cooperatives to be abolished. As a consequence, in Vojvodina alone, the most agriculturally developed part of Yugoslavia, two-thirds of farmers left the cooperatives within nine months.[81] The state was no longer issuing production plans,

41

but rather investment plans. The state's new role was to direct the economy rather than administer it. This process faced difficulties because the Eastern bloc's blockade and sanctions brought economic growth to a halt, while the droughts of 1950 and 1952 badly affected agriculture. Until 1953, the economy was in a worse state than it had been in 1948. Economic growth only accelerated from 1953 onwards with Western support. In 1953 economic growth was estimated to be as high as 18 per cent, and the number of employed that had fallen by 210,000 from 1951 to 1952, increased by 102,000 in 1953.[82]

The reform of the state and party apparatus was also under way. The new constitutional Law on the Basics of Social and Political Management of the FNRJ of January 1953 replaced the 1946 constitution and stayed in force until 1963. This changed the administration of federal and republics' assemblies, and the republics lost some of their formal rights: they were no longer defined as 'sovereign republics' with rights of secession. The basic law also introduced the new role of the president of the Federal Republic, which Tito assumed. The Council of Ministers became the Federal Executive Council.[83] This process was preceded by reform of the Yugoslav Communist Party (KPJ) at its 6th Congress in November 1952. The most important change was the formal division between party and government. The Congress changed the party's name to the League of Communists of Yugoslavia (LCY): its new role was ideological and political work and not the administration of the state. The party organisations within state institutions were abolished and LCY members could only act individually and not as members of a Communist Party branch. The role of the largest political organisation, the 'People's Front', with seven million members, was also changed at its own congress in February 1953. The newly named 'Socialist Union of the Working People of Yugoslavia' gained greater authority and formal independence from the party.[84] The next few decades of socialist Yugoslavia would be marked by the contradictions between the efforts to reduce the role of the party in everyday life, while preserving its leading role in political and social life.

The liberal trend that was formally confirmed at the 6th KPJ Congress was slowed by the Milovan Đilas affair. Đilas had been a member of Tito's inner circle, along with Edvard Kardelj, another key party ideologue engaged in the anti-Stalinist fight. After the 6th Congress, Đilas started to promote the reduction of the party's role in society. In articles published in *Borba* and *Nova Misao* in 1953–4, he criticised the privileged position of the communist structures and promoted greater democratisation, which his party comrades viewed as a form of self-abolishment of communist authority in Yugoslavia. The party leadership and Tito himself felt threatened by the positive reactions to Đilas' articles.[85] In January 1954 the Central Committee removed him from his position as president of the Federal People's Assembly and he resigned from the party three months later.[86]

Liberalisation of Economic Life

The Đilas affair slowed the process of liberalisation for the next decade until the mid-1960s when liberal forces would predominate again. The halt in political liberalisation did not put an end to decentralisation of state administration, the further development of 'workers' self-management', and strong economic development. In this way decentralisation was a substitute for democratisation. In the period from 1954–61, average annual economic growth was 12 per cent, while the increase in personal expenditure was 10 per cent per year. By 1971, around 5.5 million people had left the countryside and moved to towns and cities, while agricultural production increased by 60 per cent compared to the pre-war period.[87] The administrative system was further decentralised by transferring authorities from federal and republic institutions to local administrative counties, municipalities and communes.[88]

A recession that started in 1962, however, led to a new discussion about the future of the country. Yugoslavia found itself caught between its efforts to adjust to market mechanisms and its attempt to exercise state control over the economy. Most economic measures announced from 1952 onwards, that were supposed to increase economic autonomy and decrease state interference, were never implemented. Around 80 per cent of companies' income remained in state hands. It became necessary to bridge the gap between the theory and practice of the Yugoslav self-management system.

The state tried to solve the problem by introducing economic reforms in 1961 that allowed enterprises to control their net incomes, while the state maintained control over the overall economy by controlling price indexes and foreign exchange rates.[89] The income system also had its negative side that was manifested in an uncontrolled increase in salaries, independent of productivity or performance. High inflation and other economic problems opened old wounds between the Yugoslav nations. These led to political conflicts as they competed for a share of centralised federal funds aimed at correcting the imbalance between developed and underdeveloped parts of Yugoslavia.

The 1961 economic reform was partially stopped due to negative experiences with the system of free income distribution, as well as political resistance to further decentralisation and economic liberalisation. The discussions about economic reform turned into a serious political fight at the meeting of the LCY Executive Committee in March 1962. For the first time, two different visions of the political and economic future of Yugoslavia clashed openly. On one side, the politicians of the developed economies Slovenia and Croatia were in favour of further development of the market economy and political decentralisation; on the other side, a number of Serbian communists were in favour of greater political and economic centralisation.[90]

The discussion on economic reform resumed in July 1962 at the 4th Plenum of the LCY but remained confined to a small circle of politicians and economic experts until 1964. But by early 1964, the severity of the country's economic problems and an outbreak of strikes forced the leadership to open the discussion to the public. Preparations for drafting a new constitution were completed by the spring of 1963, along with the drafting of templates for new constitutions for the republics and municipal statutes. Although the 1963 constitution was supposed to be a temporary solution in the further development of the self-management system, it set up the legislative framework for further liberalisation of the economy and the autonomy of business. In early 1964, the contributions to public investment funds were abolished and their funds were transferred to banks, which became the key providers of loans for the first time in communist Yugoslavia. Nonetheless, the policy of artificial price fixing of indices and exchange rates remained in place, creating inflation and other problems for the normal functioning of the economy.[91]

The Federal Assembly was organised as a representative body with five chambers, of which four were tasked with economic and social responsibilities, while the federal council represented the republics. It also incorporated the Chamber of Nationalities, with representatives of the republics and autonomous regions. Members of all chambers were elected proportionally according to population size, while only the Chamber of Nationalities had equal numbers of representatives from each republic, and half the number of representatives from autonomous regions.[92] All representatives were elected by the assemblies of the republics, autonomous provinces and local municipalities. A similar model was introduced for the republics and autonomous provinces.

In 1964 the republics once again gained the right of self-determination and secession that had been abolished in 1953. The new constitutions also formalised the powers of the Federal Executive Council, which had an equal number of representatives from each republic. The republics gained broader legislative powers, as well as access to arbitration at the Yugoslav Constitutional Court in cases of a clash between federal and republic laws.[93] Such an expanded system of representation, while not as democratic as in Western Europe, was still a novelty for the Yugoslav public and politicians, because it abolished the practice of dictating decisions without political or electoral deliberations. These changes brought new life to the Yugoslav parliamentary system. In order to establish a balance and satisfy the party's conservatives, the new constitution introduced the roles of vice president of the Federal Republic and prime minister of the Federal Government. Aleksandar Ranković became the new vice president, and was now formally Tito's deputy and potential successor. Petar Stambolić became the prime minister, also known as the president of the Executive Council.[94]

Postwar social changes in Yugoslav society were the main reason for such radical changes in the legislatures. By the early 1960s Yugoslavia had reached the level of a medium-developed and relatively industrialised country. The social composition of society and leadership structures had also changed. The prewar communists and veterans, who led the country in the first 15 years after the war, were being replaced by new politicians who had grown up in different social and political circumstances. In addition, the gradual liberalisation of social and economic life, along with greater republican and local autonomy, forced parliamentarians to actively fight for their constituencies and gain as many concessions from the federal government as possible.

The resistance by party conservatives formed the greatest obstacle to further reforms. They sought to prevent or delay the process of democratisation out of fear that decentralisation would diminish party control, and therefore reform had to start within the party. But this resistance would ultimately be overcome at the LCY 8th Congress in December 1964. At this congress the party reached a formal political consensus to continue with more liberal economic reforms. But support for reform was not wholehearted, and the congress was the beginning of an open conflict between reform supporters and their hardline communist opponents.

National Awakenings

Postwar Yugoslavia sought to resolve the national question by focusing on the development of socialism, with nationality subordinated to socialist society. In practice, the government hoped that economic development and improved living conditions would lessen national tensions.[95] The practice of gradual liberalisation of economic and political life, however, only worsened the conflicts between nationalities.

With memories still fresh of the bad experiences of the Kingdom of Yugoslavia, which had been dominated by the Serbs, the communist regime devoted great attention to the problem of nationalism. Communist Yugoslavia formally resolved the national question by establishing the federal state and by granting formal autonomy to the republics. It also introduced the formal equality of all nations living in multinational Yugoslavia. Great attention was devoted to proportionate representation of all nationalities in the party, state and military structures. Every outbreak of national sentiment that was not directed or controlled by the authorities was severely punished. Although the regime never insisted on creating a Yugoslav *nation*, it supported the process of integration within society as a whole. This was particularly emphasised in the creation of 'Yugoslavism' and 'Titoism' by the party's key ideologue, Edvard Kardelj, in the 1950s.

Yugoslavism was supposed to be a compromise between the idea of national communism and ethnic nationalism. In this sense, Yugoslav nationalism was meant to become a new form of supra-national relations based on the development of a socialist society, above ethnic and cultural communities. At the same time, it would not undermine the right of the

Yugoslav nations to retain and develop their own national identities. But national sentiments could only be pursued within the limits of official party attitudes. This contradictory policy was pursued in culture, education, science and the media.[96]

In the immediate postwar period before 1952, the republics' party and state leaderships had very limited influence on the creation of federal policy. During the reform period of 1950–65, the federal state transferred a large share of its administrative and economic responsibilities to the republics, local municipalities and business and industrial enterprises. By protecting their economic interests, the republics became the most stringent advocates of their respective national interests. Economic disputes led to so-called 'dinar nationalism' between the party leaderships of the more developed north-western republics of Slovenia and Croatia and the lesser-developed south-eastern republics. With the country's overall liberalisation, these animosities started to affect all levels of society and were expressed by an awakening of nationalist awareness.

The problem of an economic gap between the wealthier north-west of the country and the poorer south-eastern regions was particularly demonstrated by the issue of aid to underdeveloped areas, especially Bosnia-Herzegovina, Kosovo, Montenegro and Macedonia. Throughout the 1960s the federal state invested heavily in the industrialisation of these areas through a centralised fund specifically devoted to developing them. The results were poor, however, because funds were wasted on 'political factories' that could not function without state subsidies and lacked a skilled workforce. Although, this practice was not limited only to underdeveloped republics, it caused dissatisfaction in the better-developed republics that contributed a larger share of their GDP. They did not wish to finance failing economic experiments outside their borders.

The underdeveloped republics argued that they actually contributed to the technologically advanced economies of the developed republics by providing cheap commodities. The biggest problem was the south-eastern republics' economic productivity in comparison to the western part of the country. In practice, this meant that one dinar invested in Slovenia was three times more productive than a dinar invested in Serbia. One dinar invested in Croatia was twice as productive as a dinar invested in Macedonia.[97] By the beginning of the 1960s, the gap between the developed

47

and underdeveloped parts of the country was bigger than after the war. In 1947 individual income in Macedonia was 31 per cent below the national average, while by 1963 the gap had increased to 36 per cent. The average national income in the most developed republic, Slovenia, in 1947 was 62 per cent higher than the national average; in 1963 this had increased to 95 per cent.[98]

Another negative aspect of the economic reforms was 'economic particularism'. This took the form of autarkic economies at the regional and republic level, while the overall economic integration of the country was neglected. The main reason for this was the non-existence of market mechanisms in the Yugoslav economy, which was still run by political rather than economic logic. As in other communist state-run economies, in the absence of clear ownership, meaningful market competition and the profit motive, there was no incentive for economic efficiency. This led to absurd duplication of industries and infrastructure. The efforts of the federal government to integrate similar industrial enterprises across the country were rendered futile by the passive resistance of the individual republics, which preferred to develop industries within their own borders.[99]

The speed and manner in which economic reforms were pursued led to the first national conflicts within the party organisation. As early as 1958, regional discontent had erupted in a miners' strike in Trbovlje, Slovenia.[100] The conflict about the future of Yugoslav development culminated in the initiation of new economic reforms in 1965, and the removal of Aleksandar Ranković in 1966. As Tito's number two, he was a powerful party secretary and the chief of the Yugoslav secret police. His support for the centralised state carried weight in both the party and government. Equally important was his Serbian nationality, which gave him a reputation as a protector of Serbian interests. By promoting centralisation, he would be accused of promoting Serbian hegemony that the regime perceived as the key national problem of prewar Yugoslavia. As head of the secret police Ranković surrounded himself with other Serbs and built a network of confidants within the party organisation and federal institutions with the purpose of controlling social and political life in Yugoslavia. All this gave him a reputation of being a Serb nationalist.

This was most certainly exaggerated, because Ranković was primarily a convinced communist who believed in a strongly centralised state system.

He feared that economic reforms and decentralisation would lead to a weakening of the party's political power and the break-up of the country. He merely used his Serbian nationality, and the fact that Serbs were the largest nation in Yugoslavia, in the service of creating a communist political and social order.[101]

From 1966 onwards liberalisation was followed by a weakening of state and party control over society. The initial economic differences would next take on a strongly nationalist character, throwing Yugoslavia into deep economic and political turmoil. The irony is that Ranković's fears turned out to come true.

3

Economic Reforms and the Fall of Aleksandar Ranković

'Currently we are swimming in a sea of glee.'[1]

The Economic Reforms of 1965

The attempts to partially stabilise the Yugoslav economy with the 1961 reforms turned out to be unsuccessful. The economy continued to be unstable. Prices rose, followed by chronic illiquidity, and the balance of payments deficit continued to increase. During the 1950s economic growth depended to a large extent on Western aid. By the beginning of the 1960s Western aid had been reduced, while payments on previous loan were due. Heavy industry and infrastructure that were built with Western support had not started to contribute to economic growth. Manufacturing industry required imported commodities that were purchased at artificially low prices, supported by low tariffs and an overvalued dinar. Such a policy caused an enormous balance of payments deficit and problems with repaying foreign loans. On the other hand, the price of commodities was so low that domestic producers did not have an incentive to increase their production, forcing manufacturers into the spiral of importing the commodities they needed.[2]

At the second plenum of the Central Committee of the League of Communists of Yugoslavia (LCY) on 17 June 1965, a package of laws was adopted and approved by the Federal Assembly that consisted of several measures relating to economic problems. This was an attempt to revitalise the Yugoslav economy and correct the mistakes that followed the economic development of the early 1950s, when experimentation with 'workers' self-management' began.[3]

The policy of price control needed changing. The state was controlling and directing the economy by fixing the prices of manufactured products, energy, commodities and semi-manufactured products at unrealistically low levels. The key lever of this policy was a complex system of subsidies, which could no longer function when industry became relatively well developed.

The balance of payments deficit was another major problem. Exports covered only two-thirds of imports, while in trade with the West exports covered only three-fifths of imports. With the reduction of Western aid, this deficit started to cause significant problems to the economy. The country had tried to solve it once already in 1952 by opening up the economy and integrating into world markets. By the mid-1950s, economic growth was based on heavy industry and the economy started to adapt to foreign trade.

With different exchange rates for different sectors, the state sought to direct production and trade flows. It stimulated the export of agricultural products with low exchange rates, while discouraging exports of heavy industrial products with high exchange rates. Similarly, imports of machinery and commodities were supported by low exchange rates, while imports of manufactured and luxury goods were discouraged by high exchange rates.[4] Such policies encouraged monopolistic behaviour, with domestic producers preferring to sell their manufactured goods domestically instead of increasing their quality and value for export to Western markets.[5]

In order to increase exports, in 1962 the state started to stimulate exports of certain products with subsidies to close the gap between high production costs and low export prices. In this way, businesses had no incentive to increase their efficiency, or the quality and value of their products. On the other hand, the state was also subsidising imports by artificially lowering world market prices.

By 1964, these wasteful export and import subsidies had reached a value of 400 billion dinars (approximately $500 million at the time),[6] which was around 20 per cent of the total value of Yugoslav exports. In fact, subsidised enterprises were not making money by exporting their products abroad, the state did not benefit from receiving foreign currencies, and domestic consumers were buying goods at higher prices compared to other countries. In trade with communist countries, the balance of payments issue was solved by the so-called 'clearing mechanism', the barter of goods for goods. But with the West, only hard currency trade was allowed. This made it necessary to establish a balance between imports and exports to stabilise the dinar by allowing the currency to float at market exchange rates.

Reforms would include the further devaluation of the dinar. In 1945–9 the price of the dinar was fixed at 50 dinars per dollar, but by 1952 it had risen to 300 Din/USD, in 1961 to 750 Din/USD and, by 1965, it was further devalued to 1,250 Din/USD.[7] Other reforms included lower protectionist tariffs and a decrease in export subsidies, in order to support exports and the overall efficiency of the economy. This was primarily related to the manufacturing goods industry, which would gain the option to acquire commodities more cheaply from world markets and export finished products more easily. The measure was intended to force domestic industry to produce goods more efficiently.

On average the prices of new products and services were increased by 24 per cent. By 1965 the state controlled prices by lowering the price of commodities in comparison to the price of finished goods. The combination of these factors, along with an increase in wages, high levels of investment and industrial development, resulted in increased consumer spending and high inflation. The administrative increase in prices was needed to reflect the real value of products in world markets. Sixty-seven per cent of industrial products increased in price in order to establish parity with global prices; 12 per cent of products were increased to reflect the true cost of production; and 21 per cent of products were not price-controlled. The prices of agricultural products increased on average by 33 per cent, industrial products rose 14 per cent, of which commodities and semi-manufactured goods rose by 23 per cent, and finished products by 8 per cent. It was expected that the price of coal would increase by 36 per cent and electricity by 34 per cent. The increases in commodity prices were the highest, at three times the price of finished products, which only revealed how unrealistically they had been undervalued.[8] In the next few years, there would be attempts to abandon the price-control system completely, but in light of Yugoslav market failures the state never relinquished price controls.[9]

Another goal of the 1965 reform was further decentralisation of business management: enterprises would keep a larger share of their income, which they could distribute to meet their own needs, in accordance with the theory of self-management. In the period 1961–4, the state retained 54 per cent of all business income, while only 46 per cent remained for salaries and reinvestment. From 1964 onwards, the state started gradually to decrease taxes on income and profit, and with the 1965 reform this system of distribution was completely abolished. With the new income redistribution, businesses could keep 71 per cent of their income, while local tax rates were reduced from 49 to 29 per cent.[10] The goal was to stimulate the reinvestment of profits, but in practice businesses largely rewarded themselves with higher salaries.

Controls on incomes and salaries were abolished, and a new system was introduced in which businesses distributed income in accordance to their performance. This led, however, to a big imbalance in salaries between companies in similar industries, as well as to pressure to increase salaries in unprofitable enterprises. Since businesses were forced to increase their salary budgets, they reduced the proportion of capital for reinvestment. They covered this gap with bank loans. As banks hoped that the reduction in taxes would increase the levels of reinvestment rather than salaries, they limited loans, which in turn led to a crisis of illiquidity and sudden drops in production.[11]

In March 1965 the Federal Assembly adopted the *Law on Banks*, with the purpose of changing the role of banks in the financial system of the country and supporting the development of a market economy. The banks ceased to be the mere distributers of state funds, but instead became independent enterprises, responsible to their clients rather than to the state. Since the 1961 reforms, the banks could issue short-term and long-term loans from the state funds they managed. Most banks, however, functioned on the local or republic level, while there were only three federal banks, headquartered in Belgrade, that distributed federal investment funds. These were the Yugoslav Investment Bank, the Yugoslav Agricultural Bank and the Yugoslav Bank for Foreign Trade. When the investment funds were abolished in 1964, these three banks lost their original purpose and in practice became commercial Serbian banks. They held on to the remaining capital after the investment funds were abolished. The fact that by 1964 these funds included contributions from all the republics would soon become a political problem that would further worsen economic relations between the republics.[12]

Equally important was the decision to establish the Federal Fund for Accelerated Development of Underdeveloped Republics and Kosovo in February 1965, popularly known as the 'fund for the underdeveloped'. The fund was supposed to replace unpopular social investment funds that created tensions between republics by non-transparent and inefficient distribution. Such a decision represented a compromise between the interests of individual republics and the state's attempts to develop poorer regions more efficiently. All federal units were supposed to contribute 1.85 per cent of their GDP to the fund. The collected funds were distributed among the underdeveloped republics of Bosnia-Herzegovina, Montenegro and Macedonia, and the autonomous region of Kosovo.[13]

None of these measures succeeded in stabilising the Yugoslav economy, primarily because of political resistance. It soon became apparent that the Yugoslav economy was not ready for such drastic reforms. Their consistent implementation called into question the basic tenets of the theory of 'self-management' and destabilised sensitive economic and national relations between the Yugoslav republics and nations.

The negative side of the reforms revealed itself in the weakening of macroeconomic policy as a consequence of decentralisation and a widening gap between the regions and nations. The devaluation of the dinar, along with increases in prices and salaries, led to inflation; the banks' limitations on loans led to a drop in investments, production and economic growth, as well as to rising unemployment. In the period 1964–7 the number of unemployed rose by 69,000, while the number of workers moving abroad increased from 138,000 in 1964 to 401,000 in 1968.[14]

The reforms not only widened the gap between the economically developed north-west and the underdeveloped south-eastern republics, but also intensified a clash between the supporters of two different concepts of economic and political development. Until the early 1960s political alliances were primarily forged by shared economic interests, especially between Slovenia and Croatia versus the rest of the country. Serbia, with a strong economic base in the north and an underdeveloped south, was in favour of promoting aid to underdeveloped republics and concentrating industry in Serbia in accordance with the 'Danube concept' of development. Accordingly, the key industrial zone would be developed along the Danube basin, around Belgrade, Pančevo and Smederevo. This was in strong opposition to the 'Adriatic concept' of development, which promoted a maritime orientation of the country.[15]

By gaining larger political and economic autonomy in the beginning of the 1960s, the republics started to differentiate along economic as well as ethnic lines. Supporters of liberalisation and decentralisation, and those who backed a strong centralised state, existed in all the republics. But because of their role in the creation of the Yugoslav state in 1918, the position of Belgrade as the capital and the centre of the federal administration, and the fact that they were the largest nation, the Serbs were traditionally more in favour of centralisation. Such attitudes, along with an ever-present fear of 'Greater Serbia's' pre-war attempts at domination, made other republics, such as Macedonia and the autonomous regions Vojvodina and Kosovo, reluctant to forge economic and political alliances with Serbia. Only Montenegro, which was traditionally close to Belgrade, established formal cultural and economic ties with Serbia.[16]

One of the more visible consequences of the economic reforms was the liberalisation of society and social life. Growing open criticism of the political and economic system manifested itself in all aspects of everyday life. The cabarets of Belgrade and Zagreb subtly mocked Yugoslav political controversies.[17] The American consul-general in Zagreb, Helene Batjer, made a note in her reports to the State Department on the media reactions to plays performed at the first Yugoslav cabaret *Jazavac* ('The Badger'). Batjer noted that the Zagreb newspapers limited themselves to commenting on the artistic side of these satirical plays, which combined the works of the Serbian playwright Branislav Nušić (1864–1938) and the French dramatist Jean Anouilh (1910–87). But they neglected to mention that these performances were adapted to criticise Yugoslav society and politics. In December 1964, she attended one of the shows and noted that ideological holy cows were largely spared but criticism of practical problems faced by Yugoslav communists were so harsh that many wondered how far this could go.

The show started with a critique of government ministers, who were portrayed as persons without faces, whose professional qualifications were determined by the size of their ears and bottoms. The narrator told the audience after the performance that he received many anonymous threats and warnings and that nobody was listening long enough to discover that Branislav Nušić had written the play 60 years earlier.

The second act was a satire on irrational public investments. The narrator played the president of a south-Serbian municipality who exclaimed that his city wasn't getting enough federal money until he suggested a project of keeping a whale alive in his town. The whale struggled to adjust to his new environment, but with the help of federal funds, a canal was dug to the sea, so the whale could have access to fresh seawater. Eventually the whale was happy and Belgrade recognised the value of this investment, deciding to establish a federal institute for research into the behaviour of deep-sea animals on land.

In the third act, an entrepreneur from Zagreb complained that the city was not what it used to be, because all the money went to finance failed investments in the rest of the country. He himself could hardly afford a new country house, a car or a garage, and he personally knew many people who suffered similarly from high taxes.[18]

Alongside economic affairs, foreign diplomats continued to pay close attention to the nationalist question. The critique of nationalism at the Third Plenum of the CK LYC encouraged the American consul-general in Zagreb to write an extensive report on Croatian and Slovene nationalism.

> For the leadership to state that nationalism is supported only by 'class enemies' and a few misguided Communists is false, unless the regime considers over 80 per cent of the population of Croatia and Slovenia to be 'class enemies' and if this is true, it is to admit that neither its earlier brutal police nor its later carrot-and-stick tactics have had any effects on these populations. Using such an old revolutionary cliché for the nationalist problem can only mean that the top leadership is out of touch with its people and modern life, or it is at a loss as to how to handle the problem and thus has fallen back on outmoded verbiage. (Most former class enemies are either out of the country, dead or quietly living in the country afraid to utter a word about nationalism.)[19]

Batjer estimated that 50 per cent of Croatian and Slovene party members had nationalist tendencies. Both communists and non-communists were manifesting their nationalism openly, to the extent that foreigners often ended up defending the federation. Nationalism was mainly expressed with language differentiating between 'us' and 'them', where 'us' referred to Croats and Slovenes, while 'them' referred to federal and high party officials, assuming that they were mostly Serbs.

Batjer believed that nationalism was primarily a protest against years of material deprivation, political repression, failed investments in under-developed areas, poor living conditions in small and dilapidated buildings, unfulfilled promises and, perhaps most importantly, against Belgrade's domination and dictates. Nationalism prevailed mainly among young people who were indifferent to the partisan generation of their parents, and sought a more important role in the social and political life of the country. They also believed that they had the right to express their opinions openly and to prosper, regardless of whether they were party members.

The business community wasn't immune to nationalism either. It used the liberal face of the economic reforms in order to address the problems of foreign trade, foreign currencies, foreign investments and loans. Slovenia and Croatia sought to attract foreign investments and loans, in order to overcome the problems of obtaining federal funds. Croatian and Slovenian entrepreneurs, together with their politicians, formed an alliance in Belgrade to achieve these goals. Social and cultural life in Croatia and Slovenia was oriented to the West, the American diplomats frequently observed. Historically, their populations had a sense of belonging to Western Europe and wanted to stay there. They felt that the culture east of the river Vrbas was oriental and backward. Batjer emphasised that the two republics' cultural and sporting cooperation with Italy and Austria was stronger than with the rest of Yugoslavia.

Batjer also explained the role of the Catholic Church. She noted correctly that the church was traditionally a symbol of nationalism in western Yugoslavia, and one of the key indicators of increased nationalism was the growing interest in Catholic religious life. She added, however, that Cardinal Franjo Šeper, who succeeded Cardinal Alojzije Stepinac as Archbishop of Zagreb in 1960, was careful not to allow a more active role for the church at a time when all church activities were under close surveillance by the state. The American diplomats were aware of the role of the church in the preservation of Croatian national identity, and of the difficulties the church faced after 1945. This was particularly obvious before 1966, the year the Vatican and Yugoslavia established diplomatic ties, when the regime would not tolerate any cooperation with the church authorities.[20] But for the American diplomats this was also evidence of a warming of the political climate in Yugoslavia.

The American consul-general concluded that the trend towards increased nationalism would depend on the ability of the regime to stabilise the economy and to allow greater participation of the public in the political and social life of the country.[21]

The Expulsion of Aleksandar Ranković

By the end of 1965 it was obvious that the reforms were a failure. In face of the country's growing economic problems, the party leadership sought to place the blame on the opponents of decentralisation. Tito started to denounce Serbian and Montenegrin political circles for their boycotts of economic change.[22] The conflict with Aleksandar Ranković also had a personal element. He was the most popular and most influential Serbian politician. As Tito's deputy, he was perceived to be his potential successor. This conflict had been brewing slowly since 1962, when Ranković opposed the party officials Edvard Kardelj and Vladimir Bakarić's attempts to gain Tito's support for greater autonomy and power for the republics, which he termed 'federalising the federation'. This was the prelude to the events of 1966 that culminated in the removal of Ranković.[23]

The opposing sides were at loggerheads over the failures of the reforms, which resulted in high prices, unemployment and inflation. The party leadership sought to mitigate these problems from late 1965 and at the Third Plenum of the CC LCY in February 1966, when in the course of the meeting it became apparent that the pro-reform forces were gaining the upper hand. Despite his preference for centralisation, Ranković supported the official party line and condemned Serbian nationalism.

The conflict peaked in July 1966, when at the Fourth Plenum of the CC LCY, also known as the 'Brijuni plenum', Ranković was denounced for his political views and his mismanagement of the Yugoslav secret police

(Udba), which he had founded and led since the war.[24] The formal reason for this drastic move was Udba's alleged bugging of the Yugoslav leadership, including Tito himself, from as early as 1945. The truth surrounding the wiretapping affair remains unknown to this day. Considering the powers that he had amassed, it was certainly within Ranković's capabilities to eavesdrop on anyone in the country, but it is unlikely that he could have concealed such a wide and systematic programme for more than 20 years.[25]

Vojin Lukić, one of Udba's top officials at the time, wrote in his memoirs that the federal Udba had information as early as June 1966 that Vladimir Bakarić had already disclosed the decision to remove Ranković to an ambassador stationed in Belgrade, but this claim cannot be verified.[26] Additional pressure on Ranković came from the problem that many viewed him as the 'Soviets' man'.[27] Tito was aware that Udba carryed out surveillance of all aspects of public and social life. Particularly dangerous was its infiltration of the federal institutions, where it could influence political decision making.

The surveillance scandal erupted when microphones were found in Tito's Belgrade residence in June 1966. The Executive Committee of the CC LCY immediately set up a technical commission, headed by the Macedonian Krste Crvenkovski, with the power to investigate. Along with Crvenkovski, the commission included representatives from all the republics: Đuro Pucar, Blažo Jovanović, Dobrivoje Radosavljević, Miko Tripalo and Franc Popit. At the same meeting Ranković offered his resignation, which was duly accepted.[28]

The Fourth Plenum of the CC LCY was held on Brijuni island on 1 July 1966, with only one item on the agenda: to reveal the circumstances surrounding the wiretapping affair and the responsibility of Udba's leadership. Based on the findings of Crvenkovski's commission, the plenum accused Ranković and his associate Svetislav Stefanović, the head of the federal Udba, of monopolising the secret service in pursuit of their personal political interests. Ranković, while the founder and most influential figure in the Udba, had handed formal control to his close associate Stefanović in 1953. The plenum not only removed top Udba officials, but also aimed to reform the security service completely. The key accusations included the abuse of power and illegal wiretapping in order to discredit or blackmail individuals, as well as infiltration of federal institutions and services, in particular

the Federal Secretariat of Foreign Affairs, businesses and municipal institutions. They were also charged with establishing a smuggling network and
illegal international trade.[29]

The commission's report described a vast state-within-a-state apparatus:

> The State Security Service maintained a closed structure, with a
> particularly strong influence on domestic security institutions.
> It remained a firmly centralised organisation and its vertical
> integration included only one or two officials. As an organ-
> ism, it became completely isolated from any public scrutiny or
> control. It maintained a strong and massive apparatus in every
> republic and in federal institutions. Any attempt to change this
> failed. The idea that this service should influence all aspects of
> social life was continually reinforced.

A particularly strong accusation was Udba's active distortion of public
opinion polls in order to influence political decisions related to economic
and political changes in the country. The commission recommended a
thorough reorganisation of the security services and the expulsion of
Svetislav Stefanović from the LCY and all public offices. The commission
also recommended that the Plenum should accept Ranković's resignation
from all party duties.[30] And on 14 July 1966, the Federal Assembly accepted
Ranković's resignation as vice president of Yugoslavia. He was replaced by
another Serb, Koča Popović. This was a tactical move to temper any negative nationalist reactions from Serbia.

The downfall of Aleksandar Ranković was the greatest surprise for the
international community since Tito's break with Stalin of 1948. The British
ambassador to Belgrade, Duncan Wilson, reported quickly on these
events, with the help of Bill Deakin, an operative of the British Special
Operations Executive during World War II, and the first Western Allies'
representative to join Tito's partisans in 1943. Deakin kept good contacts
with his wartime Yugoslav comrades 'who were still nesting comfortably
about two-thirds of the way up the official three', and therefore presented
an invaluable source of information for British diplomats.[31] It was Deakin
who first discovered and reported to Wilson the news about the wiring of
Tito's house through Avdo Humo, who was in charge of the enquiry into
Udba activities.[32]

Wilson noted that over the years Udba had tried to become a party-within-the-party and sought to prevent the development of 'self-management' trends, which it viewed as a weakening of party control. At the same time, he made it clear that the reform of the security services was not a sign of party's wish to diminish its role in society, but to break a strong and irresponsible group within its ranks, as well as projecting a liberal image to the public. By removing Ranković, Tito also got rid of his most powerful potential adversary. Wilson emphasised

> Any effects on foreign policy will of course be indirect. Probably Tito will incidentally enjoy using the purge of the UDBA as proof of his 'liberalism' to Western and uncommitted nations. He may well hope to be setting another brilliant example to Eastern Europe at a time when the Romanians have been stealing the limelight. He is however unlikely to want at this moment to create difficulties for the Russians, whose European policy he seems to have been supporting faithfully. Given Rankovic's and the UDBA's record rounding up Stalinists after 1948, the Russians may be quite happy in the short run to see him removed. In the long run they and other Eastern European Communists may reasonably doubt once again whether the Yugoslav leaders have chosen the right way of strengthening the Party's position.[33]

The British assessment was that the CC LCY might seriously affect further development of communism in Yugoslavia, and potentially elsewhere. According to Wilson, Tito had been planning to remove Ranković since the Third Plenum of February 1966 when he spoke about the resistance of high police circles to economic reforms. The official explanation was that Udba would not be able to adapt to the process of democratisation and self-management, and that it had become an adversary to the party as such. For this reason, it needed to be put under the control of the party and representative bodies. Wilson noted that, in the past two years, he did not have the impression Yugoslavia was a police state. Diplomatic representations were not under strong surveillance by Udba, contacts with foreigners were allowed, and the average citizen didn't notice the activities of the secret service. In the case of Ranković it was ultimately a question of the relationship between Udba and the party, rather than the relationship between Udba and the people. Udba was accused of manipulating party members by encouraging them to give their opinions on certain issues, and then reporting them for these statements. Wilson also noted that Udba had been spying on high state and party officials, including Tito himself. Ranković was accused of spreading rumours about the question of Tito's successor and of comparing this with the situation in the early Soviet Union after the death of Lenin. Tito denounced Ranković at the Veterans Association meeting for supporting Serbian nationalism and boycotting economic reforms.

Wilson believed that Ranković viewed self-management and decentralisation as forces that threatened the power of the party, which could strengthen the forces of nationalism when Tito died. Wilson added that Ranković had been preparing for this moment and tried to use Udba and the Serbian party to establish a stronger centralised government. Public reactions were divided as many Serbs viewed Ranković's fall as part of broader anti-Serbian action. On the other hand, the role of the party was compromised by Udba's methods. Wilson continued,

> I should emphasise once again that the Central Committee decisions are not intended to go very far, in any Western liberal sense. President Tito has specified in his speech to the Veteran's Union that the Communist Party has no intention of fading away, and that there is no room for Djilas' ideas (a rare public mention of that dreaded name), or for Western liberalism.[34]

The British diplomat believed that the problem of Udba arose as a by-product of economic reforms and administrative decentralisation. The dilemma between party and state security control on the one hand, and decentralisation on the other, was common to all Eastern European countries. An additional problem was posed by the potential of conflict between the republics. The poorer republics were afraid that economic decentralisation and self-management would impoverish them even further. Moreover, the party feared that the process of liberalisation and Ranković's removal could encourage freedom of speech, especially by magazines and newspapers that were already targeted by the regime for their 'subversion'. If the regime felt compelled to repress them, this could severely damage the liberal image that Tito wished to project internationally.[35]

The CIA's report on Ranković's removal from August 1966 included a thorough analysis of Yugoslavia's postwar development and the potential scenarios following the Brijuni meeting. The American sources of information and analysis were similar to the British. They also observed that Ranković's involvement in boycotting the economic reforms led to a conflict with the liberal wing of the party and with Tito himself. The CIA dismissed the possibility that Ranković was actively planning to remove Tito, but more likely wished to succeed Tito after his death. The Americans did not challenge the official Yugoslav version of events that emphasised the eavesdropping scandal. The CIA assessment was that Ranković assumed that his position would be endangered by the 1967 elections, when most of his associates were likely to lose their seats and positions – and he would lose the Vice Presidency. This was a part of a newly proclaimed policy that forbade holding party and state positions simultaneously. Many members of the party and the public did not wish to see him as Tito's successor, given his past as head of state security in the early years of the regime. And many Croats and Slovenes disliked his Serbian background and his strong political base in the largest republic.

Tito denounced Ranković for his misconduct, and reminded the public about Ranković's repressive role in the postwar years. In this way he managed to portray himself as the protector of a more liberal and democratic Yugoslavia, which naturally strengthen his position in this conflict.

According to the CIA, Ranković had a special role in placing his people in the foreign ministry. In 1964, he presided over an investigation that led to the removal of the head of the foreign ministry's own intelligence service, which was promptly followed by the appointment of a confidante of Ranković and Stefanović. According to the CIA's trusted source, Ranković used this internal intelligence network to take complete control of the foreign ministry. He also managed to put pressure on Yugoslav foreign trade companies to employ his people. These foreign trade companies were owned by the state, but had a monopoly on all imports, which gave them great financial power and control over hard currency flows. He did not succeed, however, in establishing control over the armed forces. The key person who prevented this was the State Secretary for People's Defence, Ivan Gošnjak. In 1964 Gošnjak removed his deputy Otmar Kreačić; who, despite being a Croat, was loyal to Ranković. The CIA report also indicates that Ranković was planning to put Kreačić at the head of the defence ministry after Tito's death. But there is no clear evidence for this last claim.[36]

Nationalist antagonisms made the removal of Ranković particularly sensitive, and for this reason it became a priority to neutralise negative reactions from Serbia. The commission that was supposed to deal with the Ranković case was composed of representatives from all the republics, while the Slovenes and Croats at the plenum were careful not to openly criticise Ranković. This was left to the Serbian officials Jovan Veselinov and Dobrivoje Radosavljević. They were also careful about the nationalities of the officials who would replace Ranković and his close associates. Three Serbs took his jobs: Mijalko Todorović replaced him as Party Secretary, while Milentije Popović took his place on the Executive Committee of the CC LCY, and Koča Popović became vice president.[37]

With Ranković removed from the vice presidency, Tito reopened the question of his succession. The American assessment was that none of the existing officials could replace Ranković and assume Tito's authority should he die or retire.

> Edward Kardelj, a Slovenian and author of many of the liberal reforms in Yugoslavia since 1952, is now senior party secretary and ranks next to Tito in point of service. He lacks, however, the political power base and charisma necessary to assume authority. Veljko Vlahović is popular in the party and has made his mark as an ideologue, but as a Montenegrin he also lacks an extensive power base. Todorović, although a Serb with roots in the largest of the Yugoslav republics, is too new to the office to be considered as a replacement for Tito.'[38]

The general conclusion of the American intelligence assessment was that the stability of Yugoslavia was safe with Tito firmly in control, and that Ranković's removal was evidence that Tito was willing to do whatever was necessary to ensure the stability of the regime after his death.

> Tito apparently hopes to gain such wide acceptance for his policies, both among regime officials and with the general population, that any new leaders would find it difficult if not impossible to retreat from the country's present liberal course. He must realize, of course, that there is an inherent contradiction between a party dictatorship – which the hierarchy will try

to maintain at all cost – and the present policy of increasingly reducing the party's role to that of a persuading and guiding, rather than directing, force in the country. Given a few more years he may resolve this dilemma. Given only a short time, an eruption of violence is possible.[39]

The American consulate in Zagreb reported on 12 July 1966 that the police and the army appeared to have increased their public presence in Croatia, compared to other republics. The police increased their visibility during the weekend of 1–4 July in Zagreb, and similarly in Ljubljana and Rijeka (Fiume). On 1 July the army was put on a state of preparedness and the consulate discovered that that the Zagreb and Ljubljana television stations had been placed under police surveillance. One high Croatian official confirmed that this was a precautionary measure in order to prevent potential action by nationalist elements.[40]

The consulate also noted that around fifty employees of the Zagreb television station were arrested upon arrival at work on 2 July, and taken away by the police. By 19 July, when the consulate filed its report, they hadn't yet returned to work. The reason for this was the fear of potential diversions, and the hijacking of the media sparking a rebellion in Croatia.[41] On 1 July an armed guard surrounded two American professors when they mistakenly found themselves close to a television transmitter on Sljeme Mountain, near Zagreb.[42] While these incidents highlighted the regime's fears, everyone the Americans spoke to in Croatia and Slovenia agreed that the country could expect a better future. The Americans quoted the Austrian consul-general in Zagreb, who described the public euphoria as, 'currently we are swimming in a sea of glee.' The American embassy in Belgrade commented on the Yugoslav events with the following words:

> Downfall of Rankovic and related events seem, over long term, to be in line with US interests. Long-time aims of US policy have been to support liberalization of Yugoslav society and to maintain Yugoslav independence from any centralized communist control, principally from Moscow. Rankovic was party leader with authoritarian bent who envisaged role of party as one of controlling and commanding Yugoslav society. He thus was guide and symbol for party functionaries who were unable to adjust to changing internal order and therefore felt themselves

most threatened by liberalizing tendencies associated with economic and social reform. Of the top leaders Rankovic was also
most palatable to Soviets, if indeed he was not a pro-Soviet.[43]

The Croatian media were quick to criticise reports in the Western media
that linked the fall of Ranković to Yugoslavia leaning to the West and the
capitalist system. The new American consul-general in Zagreb, Robert
Owen, who succeeded Helen Batjer, did not fail to notice that the Croatian
media only criticised the economic aspects of Yugoslavia moving closer
to the West, while it was silent about the ideological shift towards greater
individual liberty. Another critique from the Zagreb media was aimed at
the Western perception that Yugoslavia was a step closer to a multi-party
system. Owen was particularly amused by the comparisons that Zvonimir
Kristl made between the Yugoslav and American political systems in the
Zagreb daily *Vjesnik*. Kristl observed that 'there is no ideological difference
between the American Republican and Democratic parties – it is just that
there are two candidates for every political position, whereas the development of another party in Yugoslavia would be for the purpose of destroying
socialism.'

Owen tried to put himself in the position of Kristl's readers, and asked:
'Why can't we have another party within the socialist ideology if having a
second party is as safe ideologically as you say it is in America?'[44]

With this in mind, the American embassy in Belgrade recommended
to the American journalists accredited in Yugoslavia that they refrained
from commenting on the events surrounding the fall of Ranković. They
did not want to overplay this as a Western victory which might jeopardise
Yugoslavia's liberal path. Despite the conclusion that Yugoslavia would
remain a one-party state, the embassy recommended that the United
States should continue to give material support for economic reforms.
If the reformists succeed in introducing more humane and democratic
elements into the political and social structures, this could have positive
consequences, not only for Yugoslavia, but also for attentive neighbouring
communist countries.[45]

The Yugoslav embassy in Washington was also interested in the
American government's position on the removal of Ranković. The Yugoslav
press attaché, Cvijeto Job, was particularly unhappy with the reports of

the *New York Times* Belgrade correspondent David Binder, who justified Ranković's behaviour in one article, arguing that Tito brought it upon himself with his indecisiveness.[46]

Equally important for the future of socialist Yugoslavia were the decisions taken at the Fourth Plenum on the reorganisation of the LCY, which would last until 1967. The results would be further liberalisation of social life and the inevitable weakening of party control over society.

4

The Language Question

'They can understand each other perfectly well.'[1]

'If you really wanted to get tempers going in the Balkans, the defi-nition of what constitutes a language is sure to cause problems.'[2]

Towards a Joint Language

The first serious crisis following the Brijuni Plenum of 1966, which at the time was understood as the most serious public incident in Croatian–Serbian relations, concerned the question of language.[3] The language had an important role in the policy of creating a unified Yugoslav nation, with one joint and prevailing language. Naturally, the Serbian and Croatian languages had a major role in this process. This was not a new phenom-enon. In 1850 the Vienna Literary Agreement represented the beginning of efforts to codify and unify the Croatian and Serbian languages.[4] With the establishment of the first Yugoslav state in 1918, the Serbian language was enforced in state administration, education and public life.[5] In order to rectify this situation, at the second meeting of AVNOJ[6] in January 1944, it was decided to publish all decisions and proclamations in the 'Serbian, Croatian, Slovenian and Macedonian languages'.[7] In the constitution of the new Federal Republic of Yugoslavia of 1946, the languages weren't mentioned specifically, but Article 65 declares that all official documents should be published in all languages of the people's republics. The official gazette of the federal republic was published in Serbian, Croatian, Slovenian and Macedonian.[8] The 1963 constitution declared that all federal laws must be published in the languages of all Yugoslav nations: Serbo-Croatian, Croatian-Serbian, Slovenian and Macedonian.[9]

Although it was federal in theory, the early Yugoslav state was, in practice, a Stalinist centralised state. Only after the divorce with Stalin's Soviet Union would there be some relaxation of party dogmatism. Language policy related to the Serbian and Croatian languages, however, did not follow the trends of 'democratisation, de-bureaucratisation, de-étatisation' (reducing the role of the state) that started in the early 1950s with the rise of the doctrine of 'self-management'.[10] On the contrary, in practice these two languages played a part in the broader campaign to establish a 'national Yugoslavism'. This was felt particularly in culture and the arts in the period between the mid-1950s and the Eighth Congress of the LYC of 1964.[11] With the creation of the joint language of Croats, Serbs, Montenegrins and Bosnian Muslims, the regime sought to neutralise potentially contentious issues that affected sensitive national differences. This was particularly obvious with the official language of the Croatian Serbs and in the multinational areas such as Bosnia and Herzegovina.

The Novi Sad agreement of 1954 was the final outcome of efforts to create a unified language standard (*lingua communis*), as a consensus between 25 Serbian, Croatian and Montenegrin linguists. They signed an agreement that the new language was one language with two pronunciations or dialects, the western *ijekavian* and the eastern *ekavian*, and two alphabets, Latin and Cyrillic. Accordingly, *ijekavian* pronunciation with Latin script became 'Croatian-Serbian', whereas *ekavian* with Cyrillic or Latin became 'Serbo-Croatian'. The agreement also included the decision that the 'Serbian' and 'Croatian' languages could not be mentioned in isolation, but only as the Croatian-Serbian or Serbo-Croat portmanteaus. Finally, the agreement also led to the development of a joint dictionary and handbook of grammar and orthography, along with a codification of

69

common terminology 'for all spheres of economic, scholarly, and cultural life'. The Croatian historian Miroslav Brandt recollects that in 1954, there were rumours in Zagreb cultural circles that the federal authorities had forced Croatian linguists and authors to agree with Serbian linguists on a joint grammar, alphabet *and* pronunciation. The Croatian linguist Ljudevit Jonke, one of the signatories of the agreement, believed that the creation of a joint language was initially supposed to be a compromise between Croats adopting the *ekavian* dialect and the Serbs abandoning the Cyrillic alphabet. According to Jonke, with the Novi Sad agreement, the Croatians managed to avoid this scenario.[12]

In 1960 the Serbian and Croatian cultural societies, *Matica Srpska* and *Matica Hrvatska*, published their separate versions of a joint grammar. The Zagreb edition was entitled *The Grammar of the Croatian-Serbian Literary Language*, and was printed in the *ijekavian* dialect and the Latin alphabet. The Belgrade edition was printed in the *ekavian* dialect and in Cyrillic, with the title *The Grammar of the Serbo-Croatian Literary Language*.[13] The new handbooks regulated the use of joint grammar, two alphabets, two pronunciations (or dialects), and the eastern and western forms of transliterating foreign words. Individuals were permitted to choose which variant of the language they preferred, but not to mix them in official use.

The language disagreements were heightened in the more liberal political atmosphere following the fall of Aleksandar Ranković. In November 1966, Slovenian and Macedonian cultural institutions demanded that their constitutional language rights should be honoured. On 3 February 1967, Slovenian cultural and scientific institutions sent an open letter to the Ljubljana television station demanding the exclusive use of the Slovenian language on television. The demand was based on a part of the Slovenian constitution which regulated the use of the Slovenian language on television. In reality, more than half of TV programmes in Slovenia were transmitted in Serbo-Croatian. The reactions that followed were not negative, because of the special position that the Slovenian and Macedonian languages had in Yugoslavia's overall language policy. The demands of the Slovenian intellectuals were partially adopted, which inspired the Croatian intellectual community to formulate a similar proclamation.

70

The Declaration on the Title and Position of the Croatian Language

Although there had been disputes between Serbian and Croatian linguists on how to implement the Novi Sad agreement since its signing, the impetus to issue the declaration was the publication of a joint dictionary in 1967. On this occasion, Ljudevit Jonke warned that the dictionary had unitarist tendencies, with the attempt to combine the eastern and western variants of certain words without noting explicitly to which language particular words belong.[14] On the demand by the Croatian linguists to distinguish between the Croatian and the Serbian forms of particular words in the dictionary, the Serbian linguist Pavle Ivić replied that from a linguistic point of view it was one language, completely understandable to the inhabitants of most Yugoslav republics. There was therefore no need to specify what was perceived as common knowledge. In terms of the legislative aspects of this problem, Ivić questioned what the position of the Croatian Serbs and the three nations in Bosnia and Herzegovina would be, if this demand were accepted.[15]

Matica Hrvatska had already prepared more than 75 per cent of the material for the joint dictionary, but due to public pressures and the inability to find common ground with the Serbian representatives, it formally abandoned the project in November 1970. The rest of the dictionary would be published by *Matica Srpska* alone, in Novi Sad.[16]

The language dispute intensified further with the publication of yet another joint-language dictionary by Miloš Moskovljelić in 1966. His dictionary favoured only the Serbian language variant. In his dictionary, Croatian words and expressions were degraded to the level of local dialect, and the Serbian language was elevated to be the standard literary language. The Yugoslav authorities seized it and burned the whole print, while the author and Belgrade publishers *Nolit* and *Tehnička Knjiga* ('Technical Books') were punished.[17] A joint project on the history of the Communist Party of Yugoslavia turned out to be equally contentious, as nobody from Croatia participated and it was published in all the country's languages except Croatian. The key critic of this publication was Franjo Tuđman and his associates in the Institute of the History of the Worker's Movement in Croatia.[18]

For this reason, the management board of *Matica Hrvatska* decided to form a commission in March 1967, with the goal of formulating Croatian attitudes on the problem of language and publishing them in the form of a declaration. Miroslav Brandt, together with Radoslav Katičić and other members of the board, led this initiative.[19] The 1967 *Declaration on the Position and Title of the Croatian Literary Language* was published on 17 March in *Matica Hrvatska's* magazine *Telegram*.[20] In his memoirs, one participant Stjepan Babić remembers how the declaration was implemented by Miroslav Brandt, Dalibor Brozović, Radoslav Katičić, Slavko Pavešić, Slavko Mihalić, Tomislav Ladan and probably also by Vladimir Blašković or Jakša Ravlić.[21]

The declaration spoke openly and boldly about the difficulties of everyday use of the Croatian language, which was being discriminated against in public institutions in comparison to the Serbian variant of the joint language. This was primarily obvious in state institutions, the media and the army. The declaration was supposed to be a public amendment to the 1963 constitution. As such, it suggested that 'the constitution established a clear and an unambiguous equal status for all four official literary languages: Slovenian, Croatian, Serbian and Macedonian.' The declaration proposed changes to Article 131 of the 1963 constitution, which called for all 'federal laws and other official decisions of federal bodies to be published in authentic texts in all four literary languages of the Yugoslav nations, Serbian, Croatian, Slovenian and Macedonian.' Such an amendment would remove the vagueness of the existing definition on the use of Serbo-Croat or Croatian-Serbian, which did not clearly define the uniqueness or differences between the two languages. The most contentious suggestion in the declaration was that public servants, teachers and officials, regardless of their national or territorial background, should use the language of the region where they worked. This was in direct contradiction to the constitution, which clearly defined that all official languages were equal and could be used without discrimination throughout Yugoslavia.[22] The document was signed by 130 Croatian intellectuals, on behalf of 18 public and scientific institutions. Eighteen of the signatories were members of the LCY, among them the most famous living Croatian writer, Miroslav Krleža, who was also a member of the Central Committee of the LCY and a close friend of Tito.[23]

Political denunciations and vilification of the declaration started even before it was published in *Telegram*. The public learnt about the declaration when the Croatian daily *Večernji List* published an announcement on 13 March on the plenum of the Society of Writers of Croatia, where the problems of language would be discussed. On 15 March, the plenum unanimously approved the declaration, as did the management board of the Croatian Society of Translators and the Department for Modern Literature of the Yugoslav Academy of Arts and Sciences. The first public reactions were neutral, and at times positive. But after the declaration was published in *Telegram* on 17 March, however, the first attacks occurred. On 19 March Croatia's most popular daily, the party-controlled *Vjesnik*, denounced the declaration and in the following days more denunciations followed by party bodies, along with protests organised in the Zagreb factories *Rade Končar, Prvomajska, Janko Gredelj* and *ELKA*.[24]

On 20 March *Vjesnik* started publishing a series of articles by the Croatian communist high official Miloš Žanko, attacking the spirit of the declaration.[25] In support of the denunciations, he quoted a letter at the meeting of the Management Board of Socialist Alliance of the Working People of Croatia, sent to him by a Croat who worked in the Federal Executive Council (FEC). Criticising Žanko for his attacks on the declaration, the anonymous author wrote that they (the Croatian officials in FEC) most strongly feel 'the greater-Serbian Communist hysteria directed against the Croatian people.'[26] Žanko used the letter to attack the nationalist outburst that followed the declaration, never straying from party doctrine.

The American consul-ceneral to Zagreb, Robert Owen, who described Žanko as the 'state party bulldog', noted in his report to the State Department that the Croats who agreed with the spirit of the declaration, if not with every word, represented the majority: 'Whether or not a Croat on the Federal Executive Council ever really sent such a letter to Žanko, that letter typifies the way many Croatians feel.'[27]

On 22 March, Owen wrote an extensive report on the reactions that followed the publication of the declaration. For him the greatest surprise was that leading party and republic officials did not see it coming. This was confirmed by the head of the Croatian Communist Party, Vladimir Bakarić, at the meeting of the presidium of their central committee in April 1967.[28]

Miko Tripalo, another high Croatian communist official, remembers that his party colleague Ivan Šibl discovered that the Society of Croatian Writers was preparing a public discussion that might harm 'the atmosphere and the balance of power in the midst of the discussions on national relations'. Subsequently, the Executive Committee of the Central Committee of the Croatian Communist Party appointed Duje Katić, Ivan Šibl and Pero Pirker to investigate and to put an end to the publication. This effort did not succeed, because the editor-in-chief of *Telegram* Mirko Bošnjak complained that stopping the edition would be too costly at that stage.[29] Miroslav Brandt recalled that the Central Committee only found out about the declaration on 16 March, when the Croatian daily newspapers were preparing to publish it. A member of the Central Committee, Duje Katić, threatened the president of *Matica Hrvatska,* Jakša Ravlić, with the abolition of the organisation if the declaration was published. Ravlić managed to postpone the publication in daily newspapers but not in *Telegram*.[30]

Owen noted accurately that the Croatian intellectuals could not remain silent after the Slovenian request of February 1967, but also that the Slovenians were also in a much stronger position to issue these demands. According to Owen, the timing and manner in which the declaration was published only showed that the party was too optimistic when it assumed that with further liberalisation it would gain people's trust. He thought that an open public preparation of the document could have had a much more positive outcome. On the other hand, publication without the party's approval showed that the atmosphere since the Brijuni meeting of July 1966 had changed, and that the fear of the party was diminishing. As a result, the party was losing the influence it once had and was surprised by the lack of support it was receiving. The denunciations of the declaration in the dailies *Vjesnik* and *Borba* were even stronger, which caused an even bigger backlash.[31]

The Serbian Society of Writers responded to the Croatian declaration with their own document, entitled '*Something to think about*', in which they demanded that Serbs living in all the republics have the right to use their language and that only the Cyrillic alphabet was to be used in Serbia.[32] Demands to punish the signatories of both documents soon followed. Both documents were denounced as examples of nationalist outbursts, but their publication and the reactions to them revealed that long-standing nationalist tensions in Yugoslavia had not been overcome. Similarly to the Đilas and Mihajlov cases, Bakarić resorted to the familiar tactic of conspiracy theory, by explaining the declarations away as foreign plots. The director of the School for Socio-Political Sciences, Branko Pribičević, went so far as to imply to the American diplomat that the CIA and other foreign intelligence services were responsible for the declaration.[33]

The US embassy in Belgrade emphasised Bakarić's negative reaction to Franjo Tuđman's role in this affair.[34] The Slovenian source, who knew Tuđman, characterised him as an 'extreme Croatian nationalist' who was protecting two of his employees. They had ties to the Yugoslav dissident Mihajlo Mihajlov, whose activities Tuđman considered useful to Croatian aspirations. The American assessment of the Croatian-Serbian language conflict was that it could turn into a serious political crisis. And without an agreement between the Croats and the Serbs, Yugoslavia could not function as a unitary state.

Contrary to initial information, Owen implied in his 12 April report that the Croatian political leadership knew about the declaration and even supported its publication. According to him, their goal was to create an artificial crisis to weaken communist hardliners, in order to strengthen the position of the liberal wing of the party.[35] Serbian sources told the Americans that the fate of Miroslav Krleža, as the most prominent participant, would be an important test for the Croatian party and its determination to act against the 'chauvinism' of the declaration. Apparently Tito tried to convince Krleža to resign from the Central Committee. Because of Serbian cooperation in removing Aleksandar Ranković, the Serbs expected the same from Croatians against their own nationalist outburst.[36] Krleža resigned at the Seventh Plenum of the League of Communists of Croatia (LCC) on 19 April 1967. At the same plenum, Bakarić tried to justify Krleža's actions by saying that he was the only member of the Central Committee of the LCC who had signed the declaration, and he had done so believing it was going to be an amendment to the constitution. Miko Tripalo noted that, a few days after the declaration was published, he was invited to Belgrade to speak with Tito and Krleža. Tito demanded that Krleža withdraw his signature, but Krleža himself suggested that he would resign instead from the Central Committee without public embarrassment. Tripalo eventually persuaded Tito to accept this resignation.[37] Rumours were circulating in

Zagreb that Krleža had fled to France or Austria, but he continued writing and simply kept out of political life.[38]

The Americans expected that the negative reaction to the declaration would slow down the process of liberalisation. This process was particularly important for the State Secretariat for Foreign Affairs, where 'as a direct result of language dispute, a planned overhaul of foreign office to eliminate conservatives has now been postponed'.

> Such a postponement has implications both for nationality question and for Yugoslav foreign policy. Conservatives in FONOFF (Foreign Office) tend to be Serbs, and their replacements in many cases would have been Croats and Slovenes, national groups (now under-represented in FONOFF) which are more liberal and western-oriented.[39]

They further assessed that the whole thing would probably harm the party's reputation. The fact that almost one hundred communists signed the Croatian and Serbian documents implied to the public that either the party was directly involved or there was a complete lack of party discipline. The very efforts made to suppress the accusations that the party was weak and indecisive only confirmed their veracity.

There was a danger that the Croatian affair would strengthen the party hardliners, but even Tito's public support for a firmer policy failed to reverse the liberal trend. Even after the escalation of the language war, the Central Committee of the Yugoslav party continued to warn about the dangers of 'bureaucratic centralism'. In order to alleviate pressure from critics, the party had to be *seen* disciplining the cultural and ideological elites. The American ambassador in Belgrade, Charles Burke Elbrick, believed that the linguistic dispute would not affect the processes within Yugoslav society. More importantly for American interests, he believed that, despite the temporary slowdown, the overall process of liberalisation would continue.

> Certainly Croat (and Slovene) nationalist appetites should be gratified by a liberalizaton which results in increased control by republics of their own economic resources, in larger republican voice in federal policy (including foreign policy), and in general decentralization of power within both the state and the party.[40]

He substantiated this by quoting the position of the CC LCY, that further liberalisation was probably the best solution for nationalist disputes.[41] The American diplomats in Zagreb noted an event that occurred on 15 April 1967, when during the weekend several hundred pamphlets were dropped from a high rooftop into the city centre.

> Citizens! Do not allow the CK to manipulate you via radio, television and the press. The communists and thoughtful citizens are in favour of the Declarations. Only Dictators don't allow them to express their opinions.

Passers-by managed to collect several copies before the police arrived and confiscated the rest. Several people were arrested and taken in for interrogation. There was no mention of this incident in the press, and the Consulate could not get any confirmation from the authorities. Consul-General Owen commented:

> Whoever prepared the text of the leaflet seemed to be well informed about the mood of the Croatian people concerning the Croat-Serb language controversy and their feeling of disdain for the Party leadership for generating an excessive reaction to the Declaration.[42]

A direct consequence for the signatories of the declaration was their expulsion from the League of Communists, forced resignations from their jobs and other sanctions. Throughout 1967, the American Consulate continued to report cases of resignations by people who were involved in drafting and publishing the declaration. A report on 19 April was devoted to the forced dismissal of the entire management of *Matica Hrvatska*, the Croatian Philological Society and the members of the Parliamentary Council on Science Ivo Frangeš, Ljudevit Jonke and Rudolf Filipović. Franjo Tuđman resigned from his post in the Institute of the History of the Workers Movement of Croatia, even though the institute had not participated in the declaration.[43] He was also thrown out of the League of Communists for his nationalist attitudes and his refusal to criticise his own work. Owen was not surprised by Tuđman's expulsion from the LC, considering the public criticism he had received from Vladimir Bakarić, who headed the Croatian LC.[44]

In May the Consulate learnt from a reliable source that Miroslav Krleža and Večeslav Holjevac, the former mayor of Zagreb, had moved out of the public eye until the affair surrounding the declaration had subsided.[45] In June *Vjesnik* published a series of articles with excerpts from Krleža's early novels as part of the 50th anniversary of the October Revolution. This was a sign that his literary reputation would spare him from the consequences of his participation in the declaration affair. One source revealed to the consulate that Krleža continued to use his office in the Yugoslav Lexicographic Institute, and that he had lost much of his previous enthusiasm, due to recent events. For this reason, he had accepted an invitation to visit West Germany. Owen added that Krleža had the reputation of being a germanophile and that people liked to call him 'Fritz'. In one of the anecdotes that circulated after the declaration was published, Krleža's wife asked him whether he supported the declaration. He replied, *Aber natürlich!*[46]

In a conversation with one of the editors of the Yugoslav Lexicographic Institute, Owen learnt that Krleža had no plans to leave the country, that he was active and in good spirits. The editor also mentioned that other signatories might be lucky that Krleža had participated in drafting the declaration, because it was awkward for the regime to punish such an important and popular figure. For this reason, other participants were punished only mildly.

The *Telegram* announced that on 29 September Radio Zagreb would broadcast Krleža's drama *Golgota*; and in October the daily *Večernji List* reported the publication of the 25th volume of his collected works, which included his novels *The Flags*.[47] This was a clear sign that Krleža had escaped serious consequences following the affair.

The fact was that, in spite of strong public reaction, all the participants in the declaration received relatively mild punishments. Despite his resignation from the Institute of the History of the Workers Movement of Croatia, Franjo Tuđman remained a member of the Croatian parliament, while Vjećeslav Holjevac retained his office as the president of *Matica Iseljenika*, the association that dealt with Croatians abroad. Krleža resigned from his post in the CC LCC, but even before the affair he hadn't been very popular there.[48]

Despite the fuss, the declaration had a certain impact on broader Yugoslav language policy. In December 1967, the Federal Executive Council decided that all federal documents would henceforth be published in the languages of all the republic's nations. Some documents had only been published in Serbo-Croatian and the Latin alphabet before, which was inconsistent with the Yugoslav constitution.[49]

The party managed to put an end to the language affair in December 1967, when the Executive Council of the Central Committee affirmed the Novi Sad agreement with its two variants of one language. Any further attempt to separate the languages was declared to be 'ideologically reactionary' and 'scientifically conservative'. It was emphasised, however, that efforts should be made to introduce greater use of the Croatian variant in Croatia and in federal institutions. Consul-General Owen commented that this was an impossible attempt to de-nationalise the languages. His Croatian sources were sceptical about the party's attempts to suppress growing Croatian national sentiments that considered language to be at the very core of Croatian identity.[50]

In March 1968, the consulate reported another language incident. At the celebration of the 150th anniversary of the birth of the Croatian poet Petar Preradović, one of the speakers declared that a language could not be imposed from above, but had to develop naturally as part of broader national development. The comment received a standing ovation, which alarmed the party, who interpreted the statement as a criticism of the party's reaction to the declaration. This was all the more serious because the celebration was co-organised by the Yugoslav Academy of Arts and Sciences, the Croatian Society of Writers, and *Matica Hrvatska* – the same organisations who had initiated the declaration. The consulate was quick to notice this and concluded that the supporters of the 'two-language theory' were not defeated but still had the ability to embarrass the Croatian communist regime. This only complicated the efforts by the Croatian party to secure a better position for Croatian at the federal level.[51]

A sharp reaction by the regime did not put an end to the language disputes. In June 1968, the Socialist Workers Alliance of the People of Yugoslavia organised a discussion in Belgrade on the language question. The participants were joined by three Croatian linguists from the Faculty of Philosophy of the University of Zagreb, Milan Moguš, Krunoslav Pranjić and Zdravko Malić. They developed the thesis that there was linguistic, legal and political justification for two variants of one language. From a linguistic point of view, they could be treated as one national language; but from the political, legal and constitutional perspectives, they had to be treated as two languages. With this in mind, they proposed the formulation of a law that would establish four separate official languages: Slovenian, Macedonian, Serbo-Croatian and Croatian-Serbian.[52]

Although politically more correct, this proposal was in line with the declaration which sought to introduce two separate languages, rather than two variants of one language as in the Novi Sad agreement. The compromise was that they used the terminology of the Novi Sad agreement, with 'Serbo-Croatian' and 'Croatian-Serbian', rather than the 'Serbian' and 'Croatian' that the declaration called for. The language disputes between Serbian and Croatian linguists would continue throughout 1969–70, until in April 1971 Croatian cultural institutions completely abandoned the Novi Sad agreement.

Western media described the declaration in the context of the ever-present national problems of Yugoslavia. The *New York Times* reported on the declaration for the first time on 22 March 1967. Richard Eder started his article, 'Serbo-Croatian Dispute Becomes Political Issue in Yugoslavia', with the words:

> When a Serb says no he says 'ne', and it sounds like 'nEH'. When a Croatian says no, he says 'nije' and it sounds like 'nYEH'.

Eder spoke to a Slovenian writer who told him that the difference between Croatian and Serbian could be compared with the differences between the British and American ways of using the English language. But the writer also emphasised that behind the linguistics lay deeper inter-republic and national problems.[53] Several days later, Eder spoke to a prominent communist journalist, a member of the liberal wing of the party. The journalist rhetorically asked Eder:

> 'Do you know how much it cost to put this country together, and how little it would take to wreck it?' He continued: 'It is even better that a few persons be killed than that thousands die in the kind of war that would occur here if there were ever an effort to split Yugoslavia according to national lines'.

Eder explained the strong reactions to the Serbian and Croatian language documents as an attempt by party liberals to prevent the reintroduction of party dictatorship. But despite all the efforts to decentralise and liberalise the country, Eder believed that even the most liberal politicians in Yugoslavia were not certain whether abolishing dictatorial methods would lead to the resurgence of nationalist hatred and violence.[54] The *Vjesnik on Wednesday* countered that the *New York Times* was over-dramatising the situation.[55]

The *Times* of London commented on the declaration:

> Never in the history of modern Yugoslavia have relations between the Serbs and the Croats been so charged with emotion and never since the creation of President Tito's federal republic of equal nations has there been so much indignation and political alarm, so many hurriedly convened conferences of party executives in Zagreb and Belgrade as during past week.

The *Times* wondered whether Croatian linguists were indeed worried about Serbian language dominance, or whether they simply sought to create new obstacles between Serbs and Croats. The article questioned whether the joint language would really take away from the Croats their constitutionally guaranteed rights to their own language, or whether the signatories of the declaration started a discussion on a 'non-existent language question to force an old national issue', because the differences between Serbian and Croatian could be compared to the differences in the English-speaking world. The *Times* added: 'By separating the two languages are they not aiming at separate states?'[56]

In another article, The *Times* took a more conciliatory position and reported that the political storm over the language question had subsided. But the question remained whether the Serbs and the Croats should have one joint or two separate languages:

> When the present remorse and self-criticism are over, Croat and Serb linguists will have to sit down in an atmosphere free of politics and national suspicions to discuss whether to keep their linguistic union or whether each nation is to have its own language, regardless of the fact that the two are almost identical.

The Times reported that Tito acknowledged that the declaration, and the reactions to it, had taken him by surprise. Tito mentioned two signatories of the declaration, Vlatko Pavletić, the president of the Croatian Society of Writers and an established member of the Communist Party, as well as Miroslav Krleža, who was perceived to be the mastermind behind the declaration.[57]

The Economist observed that the declaration was exclusively political, rather than cultural or linguistic. Most Serbs and Croats accepted the Novi Sad agreement and the fact that the language was the same, with different alphabets and some differences in pronunciation and vocabulary.

> They can understand each other perfectly well and all important books and newspapers are printed in both alphabets.

The Economist pointed out another problem that arose from the language affair. It was the new avant-garde role of the party, with the comment:

> What makes this kind of crisis particularly tricky for president Tito and his colleagues is that, if they are to be true to their principles, they can no longer make use of the party to impose discipline and stifle opposition. The party's role is to guide, not to dictate.[58]

In another editorial, *The Economist* linked the Croatian-Serbian language dispute to Yugoslavia's international position, including its relations with the Eastern bloc and the Soviet Union. Ahead of the meeting of the heads of Eastern bloc countries at Karlovy Vary, Czechoslovakia, in April 1967, *The Economist* acknowledged that one of the informal themes of the meeting would be Yugoslavia's liberal path and a decreased role of the League of Communists in social and political life.

> Whenever a member of the Russian delegation finds himself privately confabulating with two or three east European colleagues, Jugoslavia will crop up. The Russians are worried about what they see as Jugoslavia's rake's progress from economic liberalisation to political liberalisation to eventual political suicide.

The Economist continued that the Soviets did not fear these developments, as part of Yugoslav internal affairs, but were more afraid of Yugoslavia's liberal influence on Eastern Europe. For this reason, Soviet papers fiercely criticised Yugoslav reforms, arguing that liberalism would not solve the country's problems. The Soviet media argued for stronger repression, especially of the media. For the Soviets, the incidents of the declaration, the Mihalov case, and the case of the philosophical magazine *Praxis* (which had been critical of 'self-management' and Tito's regime), were dealt with too softly and should not have received the level of attention that they did. *The Economist* emphasised that despite constant criticisms coming from the East, as well as the dangers of separatism, Yugoslav leaders were continuing to pursue reforms with determination.[59]

Western media commentaries were largely negative about the declaration, as it was perceived that the Croatian and Serbian languages were essentially the same. But foreign commentators were aware that this was a political, and not a linguistic, question. Unlike the British consulate in Zagreb, the US consulate followed the affair closely. The consulate reports reveal sympathy and understanding for the Croatian society and nation, more so than the embassy in Belgrade, but the consulate was critical about the manner in which the declaration was mishandled. Generally, the American observers supported the Croatian efforts to call their own language whatever they wanted, but they were not willing to sacrifice good relations with Tito's regime. They were also pragmatic about the fact that changes in Yugoslavia could only be achieved by institutional reforms and not by individual actions.

The British and American media reported similarly on the declaration. In most cases the Anglo-Saxon journalists simplified the linguistic aspects of the issue by comparing it to variations of the English language. The political element of the language dispute was explained as the latent conflict between the Croats and Serbs, which was aggravated by liberalisation and decentralisation, along with the fight between party liberals and communist hardliners. Western media and diplomats correctly understood the declaration in the wider context of liberalisation, which could have grave consequences for the stability of Tito's regime. Such a scenario would suit neither the West nor the Soviet Union. Therefore the West was ready to tolerate the authoritarian nature of the Yugoslav regime while unobtrusively supporting the liberal trends that would not endanger the international position of a non-aligned Yugoslavia.

5

Liberal Reforms

After the Brijuni Plenum

The most important decision of the Fourth Brijuni Plenum of the LCY Central Committee (CC LCY) of July 1966, along with the removal of Aleksandar Ranković, was the organisational reform of the League of Communists of Yugoslavia.[1] The commission mandated to carry this out, led by Mijalko Todorović, presented its conclusions at the Fifth Plenum of the CC LCY the following October. The Presidium of the LCY was established with 35 members, 11 of whom formed its Executive Bureau. The reforms abolished the position of LCY Secretary General, who was replaced by the president of the LCY, Tito. The Executive Committee became the main executive body, while the Presidium was focused on political decisions and oversaw their implementation. Five new commissions were formed for international relations, the international workers movement, socio-political relations and socio-economic relations, as well as one for 'social, ideological and political questions of education, science and culture', along with a commission on nationalities and inter-republic relations. The commissions were meant to serve as the instruments of communication between the Central Committee and party members.

The system of the appointment of party members to positions of responsibility was changed to a more decentralised one. Until the Brijuni Plenum, Ranković, in his capacity as Organisational Secretary of the CC LCY, held the key role in this process.[2] In line with this new direction of economic reform and decentralisation, the commission devoted more attention to proportional participation of all the republics and nationalities in central party bodies.[3] The principle of parity was introduced and the local branches of the League of Communists in every republic and autonomous province were represented equally in the Executive Bureau and Presidium.[4] Equally important was the decision to allow the republic party leaderships to appoint officials to federal party bodies, which before the Fourth Plenum had been the monopoly of Ranković. The positive side of this policy was greater influence of the republics on the federation. At the same time, the republics' representatives started to protect the interests of their republics more vigorously, because their political futures depended on it. The negative aspect of the process manifested itself in the competition between the republics that led to confrontations and conflict within the party leadership.[5] Party officials could not hold state duties, and professional party staff could not hold political duties. These changes reduced direct party control over federal and republic assemblies, which increasingly reflected the wishes of the people rather than the party leaderships.[6]

Along with party reform, a direct outcome of the Brijuni Plenum was constitutional reform, starting with amendments to the 1963 constitution.[7] The representatives of Bosnia and Herzegovina initiated the changes in the Chamber of Nationalities of the Federal Assembly because they were dissatisfied with the distribution from the under-development fund.[8] This was a sensitive issue, because it was the first time that one of the republics had used its constitutional right to protect its interest in the Chamber of Nationalities. Considering that Bosnia and Herzegovina was the most multi-national republic, there was little chance that they would be accused of nationalism. The investigation that was conducted at their request revealed that the fund had acted in accordance with existing law, but the Bosnian-Herzegovinian initiative was the first sign of a new liberal climate. At the same time, the discussion led to the introduction of constitutional amendments in line with the decision to allow the republics greater decision making powers.

According to the 1963 constitution, the Chamber of Nationalities was a part of the Federal Chamber, with ten representatives from each republic and five representatives from each autonomous province. It worked independently from the Federal Chamber when the agenda called for a discussion on amendments to the constitution, questions of equality between nationalities, or constitutional rights of the republics. These deliberations were initiated either by a majority of representatives, or at the request of the president of the Federal Assembly.[9] Until 1976, however, the Chamber of Nationalities had only a symbolic role. Edvard Kardelj explained this as the party leadership's wish to deal with sensitive nationality issues through direct negotiations with the republics' parties, in order to avoid a public discussion in the Federal Assembly.

With the new amendments to the constitution, the Chamber of Nationalities became independent from the Federal Chamber and it gained the ability to deliberate independently on laws related to the economic interests of the republics. The number of deputies needed to gather the Chamber of Nationalities was lowered from ten to five, which automatically increased the influence of autonomous regions, who had five deputies each.[10] In April 1967 the Federal Assembly adopted the first six amendments relating to increased powers for the republics, which included abolishing the office of Vice Presidency of the Federal Republic that had been created in 1963 for Aleksandar Ranković.[11] Amendment I increased the authority of the Chamber of Nationalities, while Amendment III significantly curtailed the federal government's use of federal funds for economic investment.[12] The fourth amendment allowed the republics' assemblies to independently appoint their republic's public prosecutor, who had hitherto been appointed by the federal public prosecutor. The fifth amendment abolished the vice presidency, and his authorities were transferred to the president of the Federal Assembly.[13]

Additional amendments introduced in December 1968 further increased the autonomy and the influence of the republics. These included granting the assemblies of the republics and autonomous regions the authority to appoint their own representatives to the Chamber of Nationalities. The republics could appoint 20 representatives, and each autonomous region appointed ten – doubling the size of this chamber.[14] Although the Chamber of Nationalities gained additional powers with the 1967 amendments, it still was not completely equal to other chambers in the Federal Assembly. For this reason, Amendments VII to XIX of December 1968 abolished the Federal Chamber, elevating the Chamber of Nationalities to an equal position with other chambers of the Federal Assembly.[15] In theory, this implied the introduction of the principles of confederalism, although in practice it was not likely that the republics' delegations in the Chamber of Nationalities would abuse their voting rights. Every decision had to be approved by a majority of deputies, so at least in theory there was no possibility of institutionalising a republic's independent course.[16]

Another sign of the increased influence of the republics was the changes to the way in which representatives were elected, on all levels from local to federal. Unlike the 1963 and 1965 elections, there were more candidates than seats, and the party did not interfere directly with the selection of candidates. It did, however, require the approval of the Socialist Alliance of the Working People of Yugoslavia – a movement that was not formally part of the League of Communists but was, in practice, under its control. One responsibility of the Socialist Alliance was to organise elections. This was particularly important for the Chamber of Nationalities. In this sense, the 1967 and 1969 elections for the Federal Assembly probably represented the most democratic process in the history of socialist Yugoslavia. This process, however, also had its negative side. In a *New York Times* interview in July 1967, the Croatian party official Miko Tripalo did not conceal his disappointment with the candidates who were elected.[17] Due to negative experiences with some individuals elected in 1967, despite the party's unofficial disapproval, the Socialist Alliance sought to limit the number of candidates, which in turn invited negative reactions from the press and public.[18]

After the 1967 elections, the Federal Assembly became the forum for lively debates that were unimaginable only years before. Contrary to the political leaders' expectations, this practice created informal factions inside the assembly, based around ethnicities and republics. The factions started to treat the assembly as the stage on which to fight for their republic's interests, instead of addressing the problems of the federation as a whole. This led to increased conflicts between the republics' representatives and their respective interests. The constitutional changes, therefore, did not ease national and inter-republic problems, nor did they contribute to the integration of Yugoslavia. On the contrary, liberalism prompted stronger nationalist animosities. This forced the party leadership to preserve its role as arbiter, which would use its authority and political influence if the republics could not reach a compromise. This would undermine the integrity of state institutions, as well as the whole idea of a decreasing role of the party in everyday policy making.

During the preparations for the Ninth Congress of the LCY planned for March 1969, it was becoming obvious that the strengthening of the republics would have unintended consequences. Since the republics had become the real centres of power, the most prominent politicians did not want to lose their local offices, and so they selected less influential public figures for the federal bodies.[19] There was a danger that this practice would weaken the LCY leadership. Consequently, the party would lose the ability to be an efficient arbiter in resolving disputes in the country's increasingly spirited political life.

Immediately before the congress, Tito consulted with the party leaders of the republics, and decided to strengthen the federal party leadership by gathering the most influential representatives from each republic. Tito warned them that the republics were exerting too much influence on the federal party leadership. For this reason, the most influential representatives were told to join the Executive Bureau of the Presidium (of the party).[20] This manoeuvre by Tito had an additional motive: he wanted to prevent any politician from gaining too much authority that could endanger his own position, or even be regarded as his potential successor. After Ranković, Tito was well aware of the threat of a powerful number two. For the rest of his life, no one would ever be allowed to come as close.

This time, the likeliest potential contender was Mijalko Todorović, who had been Secretary of the Executive Committee since the Fourth Plenum at Brijuni; he was also the key operative and organiser of the Ninth Congress. His position was that the LCY should be reorganised in such a way that the Central Committee should be abolished, with only the Presidium and its Executive Committee remaining. He also wanted to decrease the political role of the LCY and detach the political party from state structures more clearly.[21] Todorović also wished to include more younger people in the party structure, which was a direct reference to the older generation of 'dinosaurs' who had dominated political life since the war, and who never stopped using the wartime partisan heritage as the main source of their legitimacy.[22]

Todorović's programme was adopted by the majority of the party's organs, but at the last stage, Tito overruled them by deciding to form the executive committee with two representatives from each republic and autonomous province.[23] The Croatian historian Dušan Bilandžić interpreted this as an attempt by Serbian liberals, who took over after the fall of Ranković, to 'Sukarnoise' Tito. Indonesia's President Sukarno's power bases were chipped away, after which he was easily overthrown by the army. In Tito's case, the plan was to take away the key levers of his power: the party, the army and the secret police. According to Bilandžić, the plan of the Serbian leadership was to establish Serbian dominance over Yugoslavia with the help of Belgrade as the financial capital, foreign trade enterprises and the diplomatic service.[24] It is impossible to verify such a counterfactual interpretation, but it is nonetheless interesting to consider what Tito feared and wished to prevent.

Croatia, Bosnia and Herzegovina and Macedonia appointed their respective party presidents and secretaries to the Executive Bureau, while Serbia and Montenegro appointed lower-ranking politicians. Slovenia appointed Edvard Kardelj, and the still relatively unknown Stane Dolanc;[25] Croatia appointed Vladimir Bakarić and Miko Tripalo; Serbia appointed Mijalko Todorović and Miroslav Pečujlić; Bosnia and Herzegovina appointed Nijaz Dizdarević and Cvijetin Mijatović; Montenegro appointed Veljko Vlahović and Budislav Šoškić; Macedonia appointed Krste Crvenkovski and Kiro Gligorov; and the autonomous regions sent one representative each: Stevan Doronjski for Vojvodina and Fadil Hodža for Kosovo. Tito became the head of the Executive Committee.

At the first meeting of the Executive Committee, Tito proposed that the chairman should rotate alphabetically every month, an inclusiveness that eroded the efficiency of the body because there was no continuity. Tito managed to preserve his powers as ultimate arbiter and, as the Serbian politician and historian Latinka Perović concluded, by 'incorporating not only Todorović, but all other leading party members in one amorphous organ, he exempted himself from it'.[26] The fear was that the formation of a strong federal body would slow the process of decentralisation, but this didn't happen, because the republics still decided whom to send as representatives to

Belgrade. They were still under the strong influence of their electoral base, which made negotiations at the federal level more difficult.

The Ninth Congress of March 1969 concluded the process of the federalisation of the party, which had started at the Sixth Congress of 1952.[27] For the first time in the postwar history of the Communist Party of Yugoslavia, political forces moved from the periphery to the centre, rather than from the centre outwards. The best example was the election of LCY officials, that started with local and republic organisations and ended with federal party bodies. Just as significant was the equal representation of all the republics and autonomous provinces in the Executive Bureau.[28] Despite Tito's initial idea of strengthening the federation by forming a strong federal party body, and in the process streamlining decision-making processes, in practice the move ended up strengthening the party leaderships of the republics.

The US State Department observed that the Ninth Congress had a strong anti-Soviet atmosphere and decisively promoted a liberal and independent path.

> New elections resulted in an unprecedented rejuvenation of the party hierarchy and the retirement of Tito's partisan 'old guard'. Tito's defense of Yugoslavia's policies and his readiness to fight for this country's independence evoked sympathies both in the West and apparently also in Eastern Europe.[29]

The process of decentralisation of the party had one unintended consequence: it reduced the ideological influence of the party over social and political life. In June 1971, a Montenegrin member of the Executive Bureau, Veljko Vlahović, described this situation. He concluded that the republics were not mere decentralised subsidiaries but were viewed as equal with the state structures of the federal republic. His view was that the decentralisation process of the party should not be the same as the decentralisation of the state, because the state should not assume the party's ideological avant-garde role.[30]

Ranković's considerable influence worked in favour of a highly centralised political system. Ranković believed in a centralised party and a centralised state, where power resides at the top of the pyramid and is limited to a small elite group. Ranković's ideas of centralism naturally were designed to operate in his own favour, and in favour of his own, largely Serbian group. This why many who did not oppose centralism as such, did oppose Ranković's version of it. It was too exclusive, advancing the interests of one group and one nationality at the expense of the others. The downfall of Ranković resulted in discrediting of this Serbian idea of centralism and damaged the idea of centralism as such. And it liberated centrifugal forces that had long been bottled up.[31]

American Observations

American diplomats in Zagreb and Belgrade reacted to the reforms, and especially to the problems of nationalism that preceded and would be exacerbated by them. In a lengthy report to the State Department in February 1967, the American ambassador in Belgrade, Charles Burke Elbrick, emphasised the national problem as the key for the survival of the Yugoslav state. The Serbs favoured a centralised federation for economic and political reasons, and because, as the largest nation, they were traditionally accustomed to dominating the multinational Yugoslav state. The Serbs and Montenegrins believed they could gain more economic benefits in a more centralised system. Slovenia and Croatia, on the other hand, feared Serbian domination and economic exploitation from the centre. Bosnia and Herzegovina, although multinational, preferred the concept of stronger centralisation due to its underdevelopment. Although lagging in development, Macedonia preferred greater autonomy because of negative experiences with Serbian nationalism in the past. Elbrick also observed that the fall of Ranković did not entirely suppress centralist forces. It evoked negative reactions with many Serbs, who viewed it as a direct strike of the other republics on Serbia. One Serbian university professor told the American diplomats that even Serbs who felt 'Yugoslav' until then had started to view themselves as only *Serbs*. Elbrick added that the system of 'self-management' and the LYC liberalisation were two additional forces that might endanger the Yugoslav federation.

A Slovenian political scientist who spoke to the Americans believed that Yugoslavia would turn into a confederation after Tito's death, with only the army and the foreign secretariat remaining of the federal state. He also believed that no one could stop this process, and that he, as a Slovene, supported it. Of this prediction Elbrick commented: 'Such an extreme situation is not unthinkable, but on the other hand, there are significant factors that keep Yugoslavia together.' He was primarily referring to Tito, who was believed to be the *only* supranational Yugoslav leader. Both the centralists and the liberals regarded him as irreplaceable, fearing that without his ability to balance these camps either side might lose crucial influence.

The younger generation that grew up after World War II were not as divided along national lines. And so it became normal for young Serbian liberals to support Croatian and Slovenian leaders like Bakarić and Kardelj, with whom they shared progressive ideas, against Serbian centralist hardliners.

Finally, Elbrick concluded that despite liberalisation, the party still represented the key force of Yugoslav unity:

> The LCY is an organization whose legitimacy rests on its ability to exclude or control potential rival. In communist states that ability has traditionally depended on a rigidly centralized party organization and a rigidly centralized state. These facts of survival are obviously well know to Yugoslavia's political leaders, and while they may be talking about introducing more democracy into 'democratic centralism,' they have not forgotten the value of centralism. (…) The party is now faced with a dilemma to which it has not yet found a solution. It must decide how long it is prepared to tolerate a trend towards decentralization which imperils its own control over political power. (…) Little in the experience of communist parties and states will be of help to the Yugoslav party in its search for a new balance, because its dilemma is a uniquely Yugoslav one.[32]

The American report also paid close attention to a speech that Miko Tripalo had given at the People's University of Zagreb in December 1966. Serbian communists reacted negatively to his speech, in which he argued that the economic reforms were more successful in Croatia than in other republics. The Americans believed that this was directly aimed at Serbia, but it was framed as an attack on the federal administration in Belgrade that Croatians believed was under heavy Serbian influence. One statement in the speech attracted particular attention: 'The federation must be structured according to the consent between the republics, and not according to the predominance of the largest nations.'

The Serbian LCY demanded that Tito intervene and force Tripalo to retract his remarks. Tito declined, and also received support from Vladimir Bakarić and Mika Špiljak, the president of the Croatian government. The American observers believed that the Croatian communists had finally consolidated their position after the fall of Ranković and were determined to pursue their pro-reform course despite resistance from other republics.[33]

In Zagreb, the American consulate reported in September 1967 on disturbances in Croatia and Slovenia. Nationalism was still ever-present, but there was a change in the way in which the federal model was criticised. The attacks on the federal centre were not as direct as before, but they were rather aimed at achieving greater economic and cultural freedoms, with a final goal of replacing the federal with a confederal state model. The American diplomats noted several examples of this from their contacts from different professions and social milieus:[34]

> For the first time the party is being openly criticized from liberal as well as conservative positions over the slow pace of liberalization since Brioni. The coalition between liberal politicians and the intellectual community, which held together firmly in its opposition to the common enemy, Rankovic, is showing fissures now that Rankovic has been toppled and the liberal politicians have assumed a more influential role in the regime. This was in a way inevitable, since the very victory of the liberal politicians over Rankovic created a favourable political climate for the criticism which is now being turned against those politicians. (...) Since the downfall of Aleksandar Rankovic on July 1, 1966, the Yugoslav political scene has been characterized by a tendency for power to flow away from the center. Underlying this tendency are three basic centrifugal forces which have received impetus from the convulsions surrounding the Rankovic affair. These are: the pressures of some nationalities (principally the Croats and the Slovenes) for more autonomy; the decentralizing thrust of the economic reform and the self-management system; and the growing liberalization of the League of Communists of Yugoslavia.[34]

After the Ninth Congress of 1969

One of the most important decisions made by the Presidium of the Central Committee of the LCY was to adopt the Croatian proposal to introduce a parity principle. The Executive Bureau adopted a model that would affect 'all organs of the Federation which decision significantly affects the equality of nations and nationalities, republics and autonomous provinces'. With this measure, they tried to resolve the problem of Serbian overrepresentation on federal bodies. As the centre of the federation was Belgrade, it was natural for the majority of civil servants to be Serbs. The Serbian representatives, on the other hand, believed that political appointments should be made proportionally according to quotas of *both* the republics and nationalities. In this Serbian model, the majority of civil servant positions would still be filled by the local Serbian population. Miko Tripalo was appointed as the head of the commission that was supposed to resolved this issue. He tried to find a compromise between the Serbian proposal and the proposal favoured by the other republics. The commission concluded that the republics and autonomous regions could appoint political officials in accordance with the parity system, while the professionals and civil servants would be chosen with more consideration towards proportional representation. The commission also concluded that a blind pursuit of the proportionate system would negatively affect the representation of the smaller republics and autonomous regions. The commission also preferred representation according to the republican, and not the national or ethnic model. Croatia supported this republican concept, fearing that the national model would draw in Serbs from other republics; while Bosnia and Herzegovina supported the national model, because they were multi-national already.

The quota system functioned well at the highest levels, but at lower levels and in some sectors such as the army and police, republics and nationalities were not proportionally represented.[35] The republican model was strictly applied to the highest state offices, while the national approach was favoured for lower-level positions in the federal system. Ministerial positions in the federal government were appointed strictly on the basis of republican parity. But the duties of the deputy minister, the undersecretary and the deputy undersecretary were appointed on the basis of *both* the republican and national approaches. For example, if the Croatian

republic could appoint 100 jobs, and 10 per cent of the Croatian population were Serbs, then 10 per cent of the Croatian appointments would be
Croatian-Serbs.

In accordance with this dual quota system (below the ministers),
officials represented at the federal level were (ethnically) 39.4 per cent
Serbs, 19.1 per cent Croats, 10 per cent Slovenes, and Macedonians and
Montenegrins 7.8 per cent each. The lower echelons of government, however, remained predominantly Serbian. In the general administration, Serbs
made up 66.6 per cent and Croats 8.9 per cent of civil servants. A similar
situation occurred in the Federal Assembly, where the republican model
was introduced for the highest offices, while other posts were distributed
in accordance with the nationality model.[36] Although the quota system was
the best solution given the circumstances, and as such it strengthened the
Yugoslav multinational and federalist structure, this agonising over percentages, quotas and sub-quotas would ultimately leave actual qualifications for the job as an afterthought.

The professionalism and efficiency of the Yugoslav civil service was
always strained because of token placements in lieu of qualifications. The
newly appointed Yugoslav prime minister Mitja Ribičič warned against this
development in April 1969. He spoke against the practice by the republics'
leaderships of appointing people whom they knew were not up to the task.
Regardless of this, they insisted on this system in order to fill their allotted
quotas.[37] Although the system was carefully thought out, it led to conflicts
and disagreements over its everyday implementation. In October 1969,
Vjesnik on Wednesday reported that the Federal Assembly Commission
for Appointments had rejected the Croatian proposal to appoint Nikola
Šimetin, who was a director of the Commercial Investment Bank of Split,
for the position of State Secretary of Foreign Trade. The Commission
instead proposed a candidate from Bosnia-Herzegovina, Muhamed
Hadžić. The Chamber of Nationalities eventually accepted this proposal.
Vjesnik on Wednesday viewed it as an obvious example of unfairly overrul-
ing the Croatian proposal, considering that Croatia had the largest share
of Yugoslav foreign trade. It then became obvious that the federal government did not always consult the republics over their candidates. In addition, some individuals had worked in federal institutions since 1945 and
did not have active contacts with their republican bases any more. In the

first two decades after the war, the federation had created its own professional civil machinery without the participation of the republics. *Vjesnik on Wednesday* added:

> Formally the representation of the republics in the federal institutions paints a very pretty picture of acceptable harmony. But it is impossible to determine what this really means, and what is the true national structure, considering all the ingredients of the cadre appointment policy.[38]

The Spring Leadership

In line with the new organisational scheme of the LCY, the Croatian party elected its new leadership at the Sixth Congress of the LCC in December 1968. Miko Tripalo was elected as the Secretary General of the Executive Committee of the LCC, which marked the beginning of the creation of the new party leadership who would lead the Croatian party through the tumultuous years that followed.[39] The following people were elected to the Executive Committee of the Central Committee of the LCC: Miko Tripalo, Dušan Dragosavac, Dušan Bilandžić, Jure Bilić, Ema Derossi-Bjelajac, Marko Koprtla, Ante Josipović, Milka Planinc and Jelica Radojčić.[40] The Sixth Congress also removed most of the old guard, lowering the average age of CC LCC to 45.[41]

In the same period, the parties of the other republics elected new leaders who were younger, better educated and less ideologically burdened. They built their political careers after the war and had completely different goals, methods and leadership skills. In Serbia the new party leaders were Marko Nikezić and Latinka Perović; in Vojvodina Mirko Tepavac; in Macedonia Krste Crvenkovski and Slavko Miloslaveski; and in Slovenia Stane Kavčić.[42]

American diplomats observed that there was a consensus in Zagreb that the new government headed by Savka Dabčević-Kučar, known as the 'tiger lady of economic and social reforms' was a much better choice than her predecessors.[43] The American consul-general in Zagreb, Robert Owen, reported in May 1967 on the consular visit that he and his colleagues paid to the new prime minister. He described her as a dynamic, intelligent and self-confident woman who coped well with her role. She left an impression of a strong and confident supporter of economic reforms, a flexible and pragmatic leader who looked to the future without any dogmatic convictions. Owen added that she had a strong personality, which left no doubts to her subordinates who was in charge. Although she spoke in Croatian through a translator, it was obvious that she understood English well and she replied to questions before the translator had finished. She even corrected the translator several times. Owen concluded with the observation that she was 'attractive and well groomed.'[44]

Savka Dabčević-Kučar served as Croatian prime minister until the Ninth Congress of the LCY of March 1969, when she became president of the Croatian party, the LCC; the previous president, Vladimir Bakarić, left with Miko Tripalo for Belgrade to serve on the newly founded Executive Bureau. Pero Pirker replaced Tripalo as new Secretary General of the Croatian party. The former mayor of Rjeka, Dragutin Haramija, became the new Croatian prime minister, and Srećko Bijelić became the new head of the Zagreb party.[45]

Zagreb sources told the American diplomats that there was a positive consensus in Croatia surrounding the departure of the most influential politicians to Belgrade. They believed that this would make the pursuit of economic reforms more efficient, while removing party conservatives. The choice of Dabčević-Kučar was expected, due to her reputation and energetic pursuit of economic reforms and Croatian interests in the federation. According to the American consul-general, she had an intelligent and appealing image on television, typical of the new generation of communist leaders.[46]

The Slovenian Road Affair

The Slovenian road affair followed shortly after the 1969 elections, revealing that Yugoslavia was still a long way from full integration. In July 1969 a crisis surrounding the distribution of World Bank funds for Yugoslav road and construction projects erupted in Slovenia. In 1968 each republic was obliged to provide estimates to the Federal Executive Council that would be forwarded to the World Bank. The crisis arose when the Slovenian proposals were not approved by the federal government, and not forwarded to the World Bank. This created an unprecedented political crisis and public outcry in Slovenia. The Slovenian government supported this wave of public discontent and demanded that the federal government change its decision. The Slovenian Socialist Alliance and the Slovenian Economic Council reprimanded the federal government, while the Slovenian Central Committee also reacted, but more mildly, requesting the federal government to reassess its decision.

Even the Slovenian representatives on the Federal Executive Council, Marko Bulc and Mitja Ribičič, then the federal prime minister, were both forced to react and maintain an unbiased position. Ribičič, however, supported the government's decision and forcefully explained that the decision was reached in line with the procedures and rules adopted by federal bodies and supported by all the republics. The Slovenian proposal failed to incorporate two basic elements: it did not include the republic's funds and it was not prepared in line with the World Bank's rules.

The affair soon turned into a wider national problem, prompting reactions from all republics. Croatia supported the Slovenian position while Macedonia and Serbia reacted negatively. This already revealed how decentralisation and economic reforms were perceived in different parts of the country. This was actually already an established position, with less developed republics more interested in more centralised governance. In particular, the centralised distribution of funds always favoured the lesser-developed economies.[47]

In the end, Tito and the party leadership had to cut the knot. The Executive Bureau of the LCY met in Brijuni with the party representatives of all the republics, as well as with federal and republic officials, to discuss the road affair. The Bureau supported the government's decision because the Slovenian proposal was too expensive and badly prepared. These were the only reasons why World Bank funding was postponed but not fully aborted. Passions in Slovenia subsided only when a full transcript of the Brijuni meeting was published, with a detailed explanation of how the World Bank tender process really worked. The Slovenian government accepted the explanation and withdrew its accusations against the federal government. The final explanation was that the crisis was caused by lack of information and distrust between different institutions.

The Executive Bureau meeting also tackled the problem of inter-republic relations, along with reprimanding the Slovenian leadership for inflaming the public outcry. The discussion revealed that the road affair was a consequence of unresolved economic problems, including the issue of irrational federal investments and distribution. Of particular importance for Croatia was the problem of banks and the concentration of joint capital and international loans at Belgrade banks and enterprises. Bosnia and Herzegovina wanted the establishment of a separate fund for the development of underdeveloped republics and Kosovo, in which this underdeveloped republic would have a significant role.

The road affair increased economic and political tensions in Yugoslavia, signalling unresolved problems under the surface. The affair also revealed that the federal centre had not entirely succeeded in balancing greater autonomy of the republics with conflicting economic interests. From 1966 onwards, political pressure would become an important negotiating tool between the republics and the centre.[48]

The Liberalisation of the Media

The period after 1966 saw a renaissance of cultural and scientific institutions, and relative freedom of speech in magazines and newspapers. The Croatian cultural institution *Matica Hrvatska* ('Croatian Matrix') was the best example in Croatia, along with the Yugoslav Academy and the Society of Writers. In this period, *Matica* alone ran nine magazines and published five digests. These three institutions published a number of magazines and newspapers, including *Kritika, Kolo, Forum, Republika, Telegram, Hrvatski književni list* ('Croatian literary magazine'), along with others that tackled different topics from all aspects of life.[49] Most of them quickly developed in the eyes of the regime a reputation of promoting nationalism. This was particularly related to *Matica Hrvatska*, and magazines such as *Kritika* and *Hrvatski književni list*. On the other hand, the regime accused *Matica Srpksa*, the Serbian Philosophical Society and *Prosvjeta*, the Cultural Society of Serbs in Croatia, of being key promoters of Serbian nationalism. Unlike in previous cases, however, the party tolerated these tendencies.

In March 1969, *Matica Hrvatska's* weekly *Telegram* resurrected the language discussion in line with the 1967 *Deklaracija*. This time, however, although there were some public complaints, there was no official action. A similar situation occurred several months later when *Kritika* again challenged the concept of the Serbo-Croatian language. The emphasis was on

negating Yugoslavism and its enforcement in all aspects of life, and especially in language. A direct cause for this was the publication of the first
two volumes of the Dictionary of the Croatian-Serbian Literary Language
that the Croatian linguists immediately objected to for its attempt to combine the Croatian and Serbian linguistic forms into one artificial political
construct. Cultural circles were on the frontline of affirming and shaping
national identity, while the party structures were more cautious.[50] Despite
tolerating these trends, the Croatian political leadership remained firm in
distinguishing between legitimate protection of the national interest and
nationalism. This led to situations where Croatian communist leaders like
Bakarić were particularly critical of *Matica Hrvatska* and the Croatian
Society of Writers for their nationalist attitudes. But despite these criticisms, the fact remained that this degree of liberalisation would not have
been possible without high-level party support.

The main promoters of media liberalisation in Croatia were the publishing house *Vjesnik,* and the station *Radiotelevizija Zagreb,* along with
the daily *Slobodna Dalmacija* ('Free Dalmatia'), *Novi list* ('New magazine'),
Glas Istre ('Voice of Istria') and *Glas Slavonije* ('Voice of Slavonia').[51] *Vjesnik*
was at the time the largest publishing house in Yugoslavia. Its newspapers
Vjesnik, Vjesnik u srijedu ('Vjesnik on Wednesday') and the evening daily
Večernji list systematically promoted Croatian economic and national
interests. This had been particularly obvious since 1963 when Božidar
Novak took over as director. In a highly professional manner *Vjesnik*
devoted a lot of space to foreign policy. Under the direction of the former
editor-in-chief, Franjo Barbieri, *Vjesnik* had been sending reporters and
establishing offices around the world since 1950.

Vjesnik on Wednesday (*VUS*) was particularly interesting. It was
launched in 1952 and it got its name because Wednesday was traditionally
a day off for *Vjesnik's* journalists. It devoted a great deal of space to covering the Western world and news from Western sources. It also adopted
Western journalistic practice without strong emphasis on party policy,
which was usually the case with other newspapers.[52] The golden age of
Vjesnik on Wednesday started when two experienced journalists took over,
Neda Krmpotić from 1964, and Krešimir Džeba from 1966. In this period
the newspaper had a circulation of 400,000, of which 300,000 were paid-for.
Vjesnik on Wednesday was so influential that Edvard Kardelj declared that

it was the key weapon for creating opposition to the party. The political department of the Yugoslav People's Army portrayed *VUS*'s reporting and writing as an attempt to destroy Yugoslavia.[53] For its criticism of the federal administration and reporting on the negative sides of Yugoslav communism, the Belgrade magazine *Jež* ('Hedgehog') called *VUS* the *Vustaša* – a play on words referring to the *Ustaša*, the Croatian fascist movement of World War II. Immediately after the 1966 Brijuni Plenum, *VUS* started to report on issues related to the removal of Aleksandar Ranković, primarily on irregularities in the functioning of the security services, the Ministry of the Interior, the secret police and the judiciary. *VUS* reported on these matters throughout the second half of 1966. After that, the paper started to challenge the legitimacy of the Yugoslav system, highlighting whenever parliamentarians in the Federal Assembly criticised and rejected legislation proposed by the government.[54] 'Bureaucratism' and 'centralism' became two enemies of Yugoslav socialism overnight after the fall of Ranković, which helped to open a discussion on many unresolved issues. In 1967, *VUS* started to write about the democratisation of foreign policy, the status of Yugoslav workers abroad, and problems with the economic reforms. At the end of 1967, the Croatian economist Vladimir Veselica began criticising the monopoly of the so-called state banks, and the non-transparent spending of the federal funds. The *VUS* journalist Salih Zvizdić began to investigate the immense fortune accumulated by 're-export enterprises', the largest of which was the Belgrade-based Genex. In 1969, *VUS* turned its focus to the national question, which had been present before but was now discussed more openly rather than under the cloak of an economic discussion.

A similar situation occurred with television. In the period of the swift development and urbanisation of Yugoslav society, television became increasingly important. Radio-Television Zagreb was the first broadcaster in Yugoslavia to introduce regular and continuous programming, in 1958, and immediately became part of a joint Yugoslav TV system.[55] Immediately after the removal of Ranković in 1966, the republican radio and television stations gained more autonomy, putting an end to the pursuit of a joint Yugoslav media space. At the end of 1966, the Committee on Programming of Yugoslav Radio and Television decided that every TV studio should be free to create its own programming and news. Under the leadership of Ivan Šibl and Ivo Bojanić, Radio-Television Zagreb attempted to achieve greater autonomy from the federal centre, even before the fall of Ranković. In 1962, Šibl cancelled the transmission of the Belgrade news on Radio Zagreb; and in 1964 TV Zagreb started to include its own independent news programmes in its schedule. On 1 October 1968, it started to broadcast its independent news in full. The Belgrade studio, however, thanks to its proximity to the centre of power, retained its privileged position as both the Serbian and the federal broadcaster.

Political pressure on the media started to grow after the Ninth Congress of the LCY, where Tito called for 'holding the front against liberalism and against those who support the return of the multi-party system'. The liberalisation of the media created problems for Tito in his relations with the Soviets. In May 1969, the Soviet ambassador to Yugoslavia, Ivan Benediktov, handed Tito a note from the Central Committee of the Soviet Communist Party and the Soviet government, demanding that the Yugoslav authorities discipline the press in return for normalisation of state and party relations between the two countries. The note emphasised that,

> The precondition for normalising relations between the Soviet Union and Yugoslavia are improvements in informing on the internal and foreign policy of our countries, both in the press and through other channels.

The Soviet ambassador emphasised that some Yugoslav publications tended to have a 'non-objective and opinionated character' towards the Soviet Union and the Soviet Communist Party. The ambassador also reminded Tito of his statement that 'the freedom of the press cannot be unlimited' and that it 'cannot be allowed to rage'. The Soviet demands were rejected with the following 'disclaimer':

> The writings of our press, and its position within our society, is an internal matter of our political life based on self-management, which is built on the open expression of opinion; the creation of policy by democratic means, including foreign policy. [...] The articles and other materials published in Yugoslav media do not require approval by the state, party or other institutions: the writings in our press, literature or other means of informing the public, whether related to internal or foreign policy, are not, and cannot be, an exact reflection of our official policy.[56]

Despite the formal rejection of the Soviet demands, the media were instructed not to criticise the Soviet system and policy in a way that might endanger the normalisation of state relations. *Vjesnik* was particularly singled by the Soviets, and Brezhnev himself warned that *Vjesnik* was a hotbed of 'anti-sovietism and anti-communism'.[57]

6

Democratising Foreign Policy

Decentralisation of the federation, along with liberalisation and greater autonomy of the republics after 1966, also affected Yugoslav foreign policy. Until then the foreign policy was the exclusive domain of Tito, the Party and the foreign ministry. Active foreign policy was one of the pillars of Yugoslav socialism and reflected Tito's personal prestige, enhancing his political legitimacy. The media criticised this exclusivity and began to write about foreign policy by openly promoting the interests of the republics, who wished to participate more actively in shaping foreign policy.

Croatia in particular wished to pursue better relations with its neighbours, Italy, Hungary and Austria, because of historic links and the position of the Croatian minority in Austria. There was a strong initiative to enhance relations with the Croatian diaspora, especially in the Americas, and to improve the conditions of Croatian workers in Western Europe. For this reason, in November 1967 the Executive Committee of the Croatian parliament established a Council for International Relations, with a mandate to cover all aspects of Croatia's special interests in foreign affairs. In February 1968 the Republic Chamber of the Croatian parliament in turn established its own foreign policy sub-committee and international cultural ties. In May 1969, the Croatian parliament added the Foreign Policy Commission. All these committees and sub-committees were in parallel to similar structures created by the Croatian party and other institutions. The Central Committee of the LCC had its own international relations committee along with the Commission on International Problems and Social Cooperation, operating under the umbrella of the Socialist Alliance of Working People of Croatia. In Zagreb the Institute for International Law was also active, along with the African Institute and the Croatian United Nations Society.[1]

In addition, the economic institute and the Croatian chamber of commerce kept close track of Croatian businesses abroad, notably large construction and manufacturing companies, including Rade Končar, Ingra, Ina and Croatian shipyards. Republican institutions cooperated with federal organs, especially with the government and the foreign ministry, on matters important to Croatian interests. During 1967–8, the representatives of the Executive Council of the Croatian parliament participated in negotiations with Italy on maritime delimitation, and the agreement regulating Italian fishing in Yugoslav waters. The Croatian representative participated in the work of a joint commission for individual traffic crossing the border with Italy, in the joint Yugoslav–Hungarian Commission, and in the Commission for Minorities.[2]

One of the first criticisms in the Croatian media of Yugoslav foreign policy after the Brijuni Plenum of 1966 was an article in the *VUS* newspaper about the Predrag Ajtić case. Ajtić was a Kosovar Serb who was removed as ambassador to Bulgaria by Ranković in 1963 because he opposed Ranković's methods in the foreign ministry. He was rehabilitated after the Brijuni Plenum and *VUS* reported on his case with Western-style sensationalism. In November 1966, the Ajtić case openly revealed how Ranković established control over appointments in the foreign ministry through the security services.[3]

From December 1966 *VUS* published a series of eight articles entitled 'Who should create Yugoslav foreign policy?', in which Yugoslav officials discussed different aspects of foreign policy.[4] Of particular interest was an interview with Mladen Iveković, the president of the Commission for International Problems and Social Cooperation from January 1967, in which he expressed his opinion on how to open up and democratise foreign policy. This was particularly important in the relations between the federation and the republics in handling foreign policy problems.

Indirectly challenging Tito, he emphasised that 'the republics and their respective social and political organisations need to include in their everyday duties the supervision and correction of federal foreign policy.' According to Iveković, Croatia was particularly interested in issues related to its workers in the West and the wider diaspora. Along with this, there were issues surrounding the appointments of Yugoslav diplomats and Yugoslav policy towards underdeveloped countries. The article on Iveković continued:

> When approaching the issue of our diplomatic and consular service, and their officials, which became acute after the Fourth Plenum [of CC LCY in 1966], the Socialist Republic of Croatia will have to engage more as one of the factors that will give aid to the federal institutions in their search for optimal appointment solutions. In doing this, the republics need to exercise their influence through municipal, republican and federal parliamentary systems.[5]

Underneath this meta-language, Iveković expressed a serious demand for greater authority in directing Yugoslav foreign policy, as well as increased Croatian representation among Yugoslav diplomats.

In the same series of articles, Josip Šentija, a member of the Executive Committee of the Main Committee of the Socialist Alliance of the Working People of Croatia, argued that foreign policy should not only be created at the centre:

> Yugoslavia should not focus on creating a powerful authoritarian palace in *Knez Miloš* street [the seat of the foreign ministry in Belgrade], but behave similarly to other world powers where states with their civil servants and their administration reflect their internal and foreign stability.

Šentija pointed out that the republics' assemblies never discussed foreign affairs, although they had a right to do so according to the constitution. According to him, it was necessary to introduce this practice.[6]

Joža Zemljak, a member of the main committee of the Socialist Alliance of the Working People of Slovenia, expressed the same view, that foreign policy should be more accessible to the public. As a long-standing official of the foreign ministry, he observed:

Anybody who worked in the foreign ministry could feel how strong the forces were that wanted to keep foreign policy in a very narrow circle. This created an atmosphere with the view that Yugoslav ethnic diversity is an obstacle that requires special safety measures; that the members of national minorities are unwelcome, and so on, and so on.[7]

Zvonimir Komarica, the director of the Institute for Migrations and Nationalities, pointed out the problems with 270,000 workers abroad. He referred to the lack of Yugoslav diplomatic and consular representation in Western European countries, and in particular to activists:

> Some groups of our citizens from some parts of Croatia and Hercegovina call them 'ambassadors'. This was a direct reference to the fact that these 'ambassadors' solve their problems with their employers and the authorities more easily and quickly than the official Yugoslav diplomatic and consular representatives.

His idea was to allow municipalities and towns where these people come from to help with addressing their practical problems abroad, while the federation would only be in charge of international agreements and social security conventions. A good example of this practice was TV Zagreb's programme '*To our citizens in the world*', targeted at Croatians working abroad.[8]

The question of Yugoslavia's foreign policy goals sparked an intense debate in the media. This was a reflection of the different concepts of state development that existed within the state and party leadership at the federal level. Along with the traditional issue of finding a balance between East and West, the practical dilemma was whether to orient the economy and society more towards the developed West, or to follow the official line of favouring relations with Third World countries and the Non-Aligned Movement. A good example was a debate between the Belgrade daily *Politika* and the Zagreb weekly *Vjesnik on Wednesday* on the purpose and meaning of Yugoslavia's non-alignment policy. The foreign policy commentator of *Politika*, Juraj Gustinčić, published an article in October 1967 which was an obvious criticism of the country's non-aligned policy and Tito's pro-Arab stance during the Six-Day War of June 1967. In an article entitled 'No Illusions', Gustinčić criticised Yugoslavia's diplomatic activities. He pointed out that this activity had been reduced to asking 'the big ones to do something, to guarantee something, to establish a balance to prevent war.' He added that it was an illusion to expect that small countries could do something without big ones. In the case of Yugoslavia, this was reflected in the inability to engage economically on a large-scale in Third World countries. He concluded that 'we have to first put the house in order where we live, and that is Europe.'[9]

Vjesnik on Wednesday replied in an article by Josip Vrhovec that Gustinčić was positing a false dichotomy between Europe and non-alignment, between the rich West and the poor countries of the Third World. According to Vrhovec, the concept of non-alignment does not suggest peace at any price. The policy of non-alignment was the most difficult, but also the most realistic choice for Yugoslav foreign policy.[10]

A public opinion poll published in June 1970 revealed that the Croatian public was quite realistic about the global role of Yugoslav foreign policy. Despite the official position that the Cold War bloc division was counter-productive, 58 per cent of those polled agreed that world conflicts could be solved only by agreement between the great powers, while a smaller number believed that problems could be solved by force, and 47 per cent supported the 'United Nations solution'. Eighty-four per cent did not consider Yugoslav foreign policy to be carried out badly, and believed it should not be changed.

Equally interesting was that, despite the small percentage (7.8 per cent), the number of people who supported the United States and the West as potential allies was double that of supporters of the Soviet Union and other socialist countries. There was a significant difference between polls taken in June 1968 and October 1969 – before and after the Soviet invasion of Czechoslovakia of August 1968. In June 1968, both the USSR and the US had 12 per cent support, while in October 1969, support for the USSR dropped to 6.3 per cent and support for America rose to 12.6 per cent. In June 1968 and January 1969, no one considered Yugoslav foreign policy to be 'completely wrong' and it should be completely changed. In October 1969 and June 1970, small percentages did agree with this statement, which is a sign that some people were not only dissatisfied with Yugoslav foreign policy but felt sufficiently free to say so.[11]

Figure 6.1 Public opinion polls on Yugoslav foreign policy.

How do you view your country's foreign policy?	June 1968	January 1969	October 1969	June 1970
Overall positive and should not be changed	75%	85.4%	73.7%	84.5%
In general positive, but should rely more on US and the West	12%	5.9%	12.6%	7.8%
In general positive, but should rely more on Soviet Union and East	12%	4.6%	6.3%	3.7%
Entirely negative and should be changed completely	–	–	3.5%	1.2%
No answer	1%	4.1%	3.9%	2.7%
Total	100	100	100	100

Two Meetings, Two Concepts

Two meetings held in 1969 and 1970 clearly reveal two opposing concepts in the pursuit of foreign policy goals and the work of the diplomatic service, reflecting two competing views, of the central government versus the republics – both legitimate but irreconcilable. Presidium of the LCY discussed the practical problems of the Foreign Service; and in February 1970, the Commission for International Policy and Relations in the International Labour Movement (of the Croatian party) discussed a study on the democratisation of foreign policy written by Dr Davorin Rudolf.[12] This latter report reveals some of the regional grievances to the federal government, which especially includes criticism of the Federal Assembly, the foreign ministry, and indirect criticism of Tito himself.

The study convincingly revealed that Yugoslav foreign policy was still very much a closed area decided by a small number of individuals, without the participation of those who were empowered by the constitution to conduct foreign policy. This was primarily a criticism aimed at the Federal Assembly for their dereliction of duty. According to the 1963 constitution, the Federal Assembly was defined as the body with rights and obligations responsible for defining and overseeing foreign policy. The author could not, however, find 'a single document to demonstrate that the Federal Assembly had done this'.

The study concluded that the executive bodies of the party and state monopolised foreign policy and therefore it was impossible for the Federal Assembly to carry out oversight as defined by the constitution. The conclusion was supported by very precise data, documentary evidence and public statements by officials. In the period from 1963 to 1967, the Federal Assembly discussed 2,136 items on its agenda, of which only 60 were related to foreign policy. A similar situation continued even after constitutional amendments were adopted in 1967 and 1968, and also after the 1967 and 1969 elections. Throughout 1968–9, foreign policy was discussed six times and during the four most important annual discussions about foreign policy, only 16 parliamentarians participated, discussing foreign policy 28 times in total.

The minutes from the meetings of federal bodies revealed that there was obvious discontent with this situation. Marko Barišić, a member of the foreign policy committee of the Socio-Political Chamber of the Federal Assembly, declared:

> I can only conclude that the members of this committee had extreme difficulties in their attempts to discuss foreign policy in the Federal Chamber. All parliamentarians of the past four years can confirm this. We argued that if the Federal Chamber can continuously discuss agriculture, pension funds, and economic reforms, which were always the focus … why can't we speak of foreign policy? We fought hard to be able to discuss this in the Federal Chamber.

Vera Aceva, another committee member, confirmed this:

> The Federal Chamber wasn't bothered much with foreign policy. The committee tried to discuss certain issues, but most parliamentarians were not even informed about many topics, not to mention that they were never active participants in creating foreign policy. I also have to say that the committee assembled twenty days after the Czech events, and in such a situation the Federal Assembly should have been brought together immediately.

Veljko Mićunović, a Yugoslav diplomat and a member of the Committee for Foreign Affairs and International Relations of the Federal Chamber, depicted this amateurism with the following words:

> There was no discussion in the Federal Assembly in 1967 and 1968, primarily because – whether we wanted this or not – the

situation is the same as when we started our mandate in 1967. It is because 'these things' are still firmly in hands of the government and other federal organs, and the assembly and its institutions are kept out of the loop, and are forced to follow events with a delay. There was no debate because the Federal Assembly is still not considered relevant in shaping foreign policy decisions. It seems that its opinion does not matter. Although the laws and the constitution have been changed, the practice has not changed. And these matters are only discussed in the assembly *post festum;* and even then, only partially and with difficulty.

The parliamentarian Josip Đerđa stated in 1968 in one of his speeches at the Committee for Foreign Affairs and International Relations, that:

The constitutions of other countries do not grant as much responsibility over foreign policy to their assemblies as ours does; but on the other hand, not one assembly in the world makes use of these responsibilities as little as we do.[13]

The study revealed that the Executive Council of the Croatian Parliament (Sabor) proposed 23 candidates for 23 vacant posts in the federal foreign ministry, in the period from early 1968 to October 1969. Of these, only eight were appointed, of which only four were appointed to the posts they were put forward for by the republic. The other four were dispatched to other offices and countries. Special attention was given to the lack of Croatian diplomats in neighbouring Italy, Hungary and Austria. For example, at the beginning of 1969 there were no officials from Croatia in the Yugoslav embassies in Rome, Budapest and Vienna. The report listed a number of additional grievances: repeated requests to send Croatian diplomats to countries with a Croatian diaspora were ignored: not enough Croatian diplomats were sent to countries with large numbers of Croatian workers; nor to countries like Libya where Croatians enterprises were active; nor to Chile, where there was a large Croatian community; nor to Pittsburgh, where the Croatian Fraternal Union of America repeatedly asked for the Yugoslav consul-general to come from Croatia. In Austria and Germany there were very few diplomats from Croatia, although the largest Croatian economic diaspora lived there. In West Germany, Croatia only had a consul-general in Stuttgart. In this sense, the report concluded:

> Although we understand the need of the foreign secretariat and the federal government to influence the new appointments to diplomatic positions, it is impossible to escape the fact that the cooperation surrounding the appointments between the foreign secretariat and the executive council of Sabor is irregular and uncoordinated, and that the foreign secretariat easily, and without a sense of responsibility, neglects the positions and interests of the Socialist Republic of Croatia.

The party commission's discussion in February 1970 on the Davorin report brought to light that the problems related to foreign policy were much wider and encompassed a complex range of issues, including: the economic monopolies of foreign trade companies; the appointments policy in the foreign affairs system; the relations between the republics and the federation; and the issue of national and republican representation in federal institutions. According to data presented by the Croatian official Budimir Lončar,[14] the foreign secretariat had 1,667 workers, of whom 14.8 per cent came from Bosnia-Herzegovina, 8 per cent from Montenegro, 27.2 per cent from Croatia, 3.6 per cent from Macedonia, 4.8 per cent from Slovenia, and 41.1 per cent from Serbia. Nationality distribution, however, was more unbalanced. Montenegrins, Macedonians and Slovenes were roughly equally represented according to the populations of their respective republics, but Croats were underrepresented at 14.4 per cent, and Serbs overrepresented at 63.1 per cent. In addition, 4.2 per cent declared themselves as 'Yugoslavs' and 11.9 per cent 'others'.[15]

American diplomats in Belgrade noticed this imbalance. In an April 1970 report, they acknowledged that the Serbs and Montenegrins were indeed overrepresented in comparison to their share of the total Yugoslav population, while the balance according to the republican system was relatively fair. According to their data, the Yugoslav diplomatic service had an ethnic composition of 53 per cent Serbs, 12 per cent Montenegrins, 18 per cent Croatians, and 6 per cent Slovenians. The republican composition was 38.6 per cent from Serbia and 25.6 per cent from Croatia.

Mladen Iveković, a long-standing diplomat and ambassador to Italy and West Germany, mentioned that Croatia had a significant number of officials, especially ambassadors, and that 50 per cent of high-ranking diplomatic officials came from Croatia. According to him, however, these people were not put forward by the Croatian government but appointed on the basis of their former affiliation to the security services. He added that attachment to the security services in the Ranković era was the key criterion for gaining official authority in the foreign ministry. The Croatian leadership not only complained about the composition but also about the quality of the Croatian quota. At the meeting of the LCY Executive Bureau in March 1971, Savka Dabčević-Kučar declared that the Croatian leadership distrusted the Croatian officials in the foreign secretariat and she asked for a review of everybody from Croatia who worked there. She particularly referred to officials who did not support the changes of the 1966 Fourth Plenum. She specifically singled out Zvonko Grahek, Ljubo Drndić and Šime Jelić, whom she considered to be remnants of the Ranković era.[16]

There was an additional problem of the monopolies of foreign trade enterprises which abused their financial power and links to security services. Similarly to the foreign ministry, the security services placed their people in these monopolies but used additional leverage from above and below to influence foreign policy. Based on his experience as ambassador to Indonesia, Budimir Lončar explained how the Belgrade foreign trade companies exploited their monopolistic position, reaping rewards with other people's money while forcing others to pay compensation when their investments failed. The federal administration granted exclusive rights for trade with south-east Asia to the Belgrade-based company Inex. In practice, Inex used this position to increase its profits by monopolising the distribution of short-term loans from Yugoslav companies in south-east Asia to their local partners. When these local business partners or countries failed to repay the loans Inex withdrew from its obligations and forced the Yugoslav companies (such as OKI and Pliva) to settle the debts. A similar situation occurred when the government, with approval from the Federal Assembly, decided to import raw materials from developing countries, in line with Yugoslavia's non-alignment policy. The initiative eventually failed because the Belgrade-based Genex decided to buy raw materials more expensively from the London and Singapore markets, where it could make bigger profits.[17]

Before the Rudolf report was published, the Executive Bureau of the Presidency of the LCY met on 1 July 1969 to discuss the problems of appointments in the Yugoslav Foreign Service. There was a practical problem in the everyday functioning of the service, which required professional civil servants as well as a centralised system of decision making. The state secretary for foreign affairs, Mirko Tepavac, confirmed that the parity formula was the key criterion for political appointments in both the secretariat and diplomatic missions. But Tepavac warned that strict adherence to the parity formula might lead to a collapse of the foreign diplomatic service. This was particularly obvious when the republics demanded to propose representatives for particular offices. He made it clear that this distribution should not be an exclusive right of the republics. He also complained that he was receiving too many applications for the most prestigious offices and embassies, leaving the secretariat unable to fulfil other essential tasks for several years.

Another major problem was the issue of professional competence. According to Tepavac, Yugoslavia was the world champion in appointing people to diplomatic missions without any political preparation or experience in Foreign Service. For example 26 per cent of American heads of diplomatic missions were political appointees; while in Yugoslavia out of 69 ambassadors only 28 (40 per cent) had prior experience in Foreign Service, while 60 per cent had no such experience. The statistics revealed that this imbalance between political and professional appointees only applied at the ambassadorial level, while the first secretaries and consul-generals were largely professional. This professionalism was possibly due to the lack of interest for these jobs from politicians.

Figure 6.2 An overview of diplomatic staff appointments in 1969.

Diplomatic posts	Political appointees	Professional foreign service
Ambassadors	41 (60%)	28 (40%)
First Secretaries	2 (40%)	3 (60%)
Consuls-General	8 (24%)	25 (76%)
Total	51 (48%)	56 (52%)

Tepavac observed that the Croatian quota was predominant in the foreign secretariat structure. This was especially relevant to high offices and the heads of diplomatic service. For this reason the secretariat actually tried to reduce the number of appointments from Croatia. To make matters worse, the blind implementation of the republican quota led to situations where individuals were eager to re-establish their ties with their republics, which also included changing nationality several times for career purposes. The consequence was greater attachment to the republics than to the institution for which they worked. The appointments problem compromised the overall effectiveness of Yugoslav representation abroad. For this reason Tepavac was opposed to the exclusiveness of quota systems, except in cases where the right nationality was needed abroad. An additional problem related to both the republic and ethnic quota systems was the unequal treatment of civil servants, who were appointed automatically on the basis of republican recommendation while professional individuals not on these lists were sidelined.[18]

Vjesnik on Wednesday reported in January 1970 that the first tender for traineeships in the foreign secretariat failed because of the small number of applicants. Out of 100 candidates, 50 were rejected for failing to meet requirements like a university degree and knowledge of foreign languages. An additional problem was the ethnic composition of those who did pass the first minimum criteria. For example, no one from Slovenia made it to the second round, while there were five successful candidates from Montenegro, six from Bosnia-Herzegovina, four from Macedonia, ten from Croatia and 23 from Serbia. Most candidates already lived in Belgrade. In addition, low salaries and the lack of career prospects complicated attempts to attract competent and talented individuals.[19]

Figure 6.3 Foreign Service appointments by Republic origin 1 June 1969.

Republic origin	Total	Serbia	Croatia	Slovenia	Bosnia-H	Macedonia	Montenegro
Ambassadors	71	17	20	7	11	8	8
First Secretaries	6	1	4	0	0	0	1
Consuls-General	23	5	6	6	1	3	2
Total	100	23	30	13	12	11	11

The ethnicity or nationality of appointees was often more important than their quality. At the 1969 meeting, Tepavac provided an example of the behaviour of Yugoslav diplomats at the Conference of European Security (the Helsinki process), where the secretariat had to prepare all the materials because they could not trust that Yugoslav interests would be presented properly by the appointed diplomats. It was often the case that the secretariat would send materials in a foreign language to the foreign missions, and it would immediately become apparent that the Yugoslav diplomats were unfamiliar with the language of the country to which they were assigned – even if they had claimed to be so in the application process. To discover the true position of the Yugoslav government, foreign ambassadors in Yugoslavia would simply communicate directly with the secretariat.

Edvard Kardelj complained that the republics were dominating the appointment process, even if the candidates proposed by the republics had to be approved by the federal government before they were forwarded to the foreign secretariat. It became a common practice that ambassadors answered to the executive councils of their republican governments rather than to the foreign secretariat. In theory, the ambassadors were responsible for their embassies, but in practice some departments within the embassy were so independent that they didn't even bother to inform the ambassador of their activities.[20]

The republicanism issue in the Foreign Service attracted a lot of attention from Western diplomats because it affected their everyday communication with Yugoslav officials. Their reports confirmed that the parity principle functioned well at the level of ambassadors and consuls-general, and that every diplomatic mission had to reflect multi-ethnic Yugoslavia. This was the reason why all diplomatic staff had to receive the approval and support of their republics and autonomous provinces. In practice, however, this made everyday work more difficult. Dugald Stewart, the British ambassador to Belgrade in 1971–7, highlighted the case of a Yugoslav embassy in one of the Western capitals where the ambassador and first secretary had an argument. Subsequently, the first secretary requested that the incident should be officially reported to his republican government. Another example involved the government of a Western country that was making preparations for a ministerial visit to Yugoslavia.

It became apparent that the Yugoslav ambassador to this country was channelling the arrangements to his republican government instead of to the foreign secretariat.[21]

The US Ambassador William Leonhart reported in November 1969 that the greatest problem for the Yugoslav diplomatic service was the republican quota system. According to him, a large number of high diplomats were recruited from the secret services immediately after the war. Until the fall of Ranković, the diplomatic service was not attractive for young people. In addition to low salaries, Leonhart mentions nepotism as one of the reasons why intelligent students had no wish to apply for jobs in diplomacy. Additional problems emerged with the sudden increase in the numbers of Yugoslav workers abroad requiring more consular staff, as well as the need to coordinate foreign policy activities in light of the greater influence of the republics in foreign affairs.[22]

American reports in October 1971 confirmed that pressures from the republics created practical problems for the foreign secretariat. A large number of experienced diplomats with origins in Montenegro and the Croatian region of Dalmatia were causing new problems.[23] Immediately after the war, Udba officials and partisan commissars were the main candidates for the diplomatic service, came primarily from these two regions and would not relinquish their privileges.[24] Montenegro and Croatia, therefore, had only a limited number of slots available. For example, this led to a dispute over the appointment of Mišo Pavičević as ambassador to Rome. He was a Montenegrin who was blocked by Slovenia and Croatia, who wanted their own ambassadors in neighbouring countries.[25]

The constitutional amendments of June 1971 further complicated this situation. According to the 35th amendment, each republic was given the right to establish their own institutions abroad, that is, from the Yugoslav republics to provinces, cities and German *Länder*. The republics used this right to create their own miniature foreign ministries, who promptly started establishing their own contacts and, in some cases, overreaching themselves.

Immediately after the amendments were adopted, Serbia established its own commission for foreign affairs. A Serbian government source admitted to a British diplomat that this commission, in practice, would be the Serbian foreign ministry.[26] Similar developments took place in other republics. Slovenia and Croatia established relations with provinces in neighbouring countries even before the amendments were adopted.

The American consul-general in Zagreb, Orme Wilson, reported in July 1971 that Croatian international activities significantly increased after this amendment was adopted. The Croatian prime minister, Dragutin Haramija, led delegations to Austria in June 1970, to Hungary in March 1971, and to the Italian regions of Friuli-Venezia-Giulia in June 1971. Jakša Bučević, a member of the delegation to Hungary, told Wilson that it was treated by the Hungarians as an official state delegation.[27] During his visit to Italy, Prime Minister Haramija stated that Croatia would develop its economic and cultural international relations, but this did not imply the pursuit of an independent republican foreign policy. In June 1971, a delegation from the Zagreb Chamber of Commerce visited Madrid and negotiated economic cooperation with the German city of Mainz. At the same time, the Croatian parliamentary delegation negotiated economic cooperation with the German *Land* Baden-Würtenberg.[28]

American diplomats were particularly interested in the republics' contacts with the Eastern bloc. A delegation of the Soviet Communist Party visited Slovenia and Croatia in January 1971, making a stop at the Rijeka shipyard *Viktor Lenac*, and also meeting Croatian officials Pero Pirker and Srećko Bijelić. In February the Soviet Minister for Foreign Trade, Nikolai Patolichev, met Croatian prime minister Haramija in Zagreb.[29] Although Croatian officials were eager to emphasise the economic and culture aspects of this cooperation, Wilson believed that Croatia would soon come into conflict with Belgrade if these activities started to affect overall Yugoslav economic policy.[30]

International Developments in 1966–9

Although Yugoslavia managed to stay out of the Cold War blocs, it could not avoid the impact of the bloc divisions. This was particularly obvious in the late 1960s when *détente* was born. In Yugoslavia's case this coincided with the period of liberal reform and the adoption of Western cultural and economic trends. Immediately after the removal of Ranković, Western diplomats started to notice changes and an opening to the West in Yugoslavia's foreign policy and economy. Good examples of these trends can be found in the Yugoslav reactions to global developments in the Cold War.

These include the Israel–Arab Six-Day War of June 1967, and the Warsaw Pact intervention in Czechoslovakia in August 1968. The reactions of the public and political leadership to these events are good indicators of changes that the country was going through. In addition, a good example of the Yugoslav position in the geopolitical game was the short-lived Chinese initiative in the Balkans caused by worsened Sino-Soviet relations after Czechoslovakia.

The Middle East Crisis of 1967

The crisis in the Middle East in 1967 significantly shook the foundations of Yugoslav foreign policy: non-alignment and peaceful coexistence. Tito's initial reaction to the Israeli pre-emptive strike and rapid Arab defeat in the Six-Day War was to condemn Israel and its Western allies, especially the United States. Yugoslav newspapers were full of articles denouncing Israeli aggression. *Vjesnik's* commentator Joško Palavršić, and its correspondents in New York and London, Josip Vrhovec and Milovan Baletić, sharply criticised the pro-Israeli policy of Washington and London, while Paris correspondent Milan Beslać praised De Gaulle's neutrality.[31] At Tito's initiative, Yugoslavia's carefully balanced foreign policy made a sharp turn towards the East and the Arabs. Tito's decision to participate in the meeting of the leaders of socialist countries in Moscow in June 1967, organised in response to the Israel's pre-emptive strike, was unprecedented.[32] Western diplomats were very interested in Tito's decision to sign the Moscow declaration condemning Israel. According to British diplomats, there were two reasons for this decision:

> The first would run as follows: The aging Tito has for some years been suffering from *nostalgie de Moscou*, a yearning for a united World Communist movement in which he could be fully at home without sacrificing his independence […] The disappearance from the political scene of all of his major original 'non-aligned' cronies except Nasser and pushed him further in the same direction.[33]

The second reason for his support to the Soviet position in the Middle East crisis was his attempt to save the Non-Aligned Movement. Tito saw the Arab defeat as the defeat of non-alignment:

> Without non-alignment, and pending further *détente* in Europe, Yugoslavia has no home except Eastern Europe; and there she cannot feel comfortable.

His visit to Moscow was therefore an attempt to save the Non-Aligned Movement from complete disintegration, and to save Nasser, rather than an attempt to move closer to the East. In that sense, the Yugoslav position on the UN declaration by the Non-Aligned Movement on the Middle East situation was opposed to the Soviet position.[34]

The decision to support the Soviets was even more surprising because several months before, in March 1967, Yugoslavia had refused to participate in a similar meeting in Karlovy Vary, Czechoslovakia.[35] *Vjesnik's* Moscow correspondent Mirko Bilić objected to Western commentators who thought that Tito's participation implied an eastward turn.[36] Well-informed observers noticed that not everybody in the Yugoslav political leadership was happy with the degree of support for the Soviet position. Clear differences emerged between the foreign secretariat, headed by Mark Nikezić, and Tito's cabinet.[37] The foreign ministry was unhappy with Tito's anti-American rhetoric. At a transition meeting between the old and new Yugoslav ambassadors to Washington, Veljko Mićunović and Bogdan Crnobrnja, Nikezić complained that Tito's anti-American statements were exaggerated and counterproductive. At the time, Tito was promoting conspiracy theories, accusing the United States of being behind the Greek military coup of April 1967 and anti-Yugoslav statements by Italian politicians. Nikezić also rejected Tito's 'theory' that Yugoslavia was the main obstacle to the United States's attempt to 'conquer' the Mediterranean.[38] The Yugoslav diplomats agreed that this anti-American attitude was unhelpful for attempts to deal effectively with the Middle East crisis, but rather harmed opportunities to stabilise the Yugoslav economy that depended on American support.

The Yugoslav politician Koča Popović openly expressed his reservations about Tito's Moscow trip, while other members of the Executive Bureau, Mijalko Todorović, Lazar Koliševski and Nijaz Dizdarević, gave him tacit support.[39] In an interview with the *New York Times*, Miko Tripalo admitted that there was strong resistance to Tito's Middle Eastern policy and cooperation with the Soviets, especially among intellectuals and the bureaucracy. He also admitted that, despite the official position, there was some support for Israel among the Yugoslav public.[40] The information service of the Central Committee of the LCC noted in its report that while there was much support for the government position on Middle Eastern events, some people opposed it. These included questions and observations, such as: 'Why did Tito support the Arabs when they persecute communists?'; 'Tito's statement in support of the Arabs came too early. It would be better if Yugoslavia had waited longer'; 'Why are we interfering in this conflict? Let them mind their own business.' There was also some open sympathy for Israel.[41]

British and American diplomats in Belgrade were quick to react to this new trend. According to them, the new liberal trends were particularly visible in the criticism of Tito's pro-Arab line, which many viewed as a slide eastward.[42] The diplomats considered Tito's strong support for the Arab cause to be counterproductive, because it unnecessarily worsened relations with Israel and destroyed the potential for mediation between the parties to the conflict. The situation was further worsened by the indecisiveness and disagreements among the leading non-aligned countries. For the first time, the public showed signs of discontent with official foreign policy. All decisions about the Yugoslav position had been taken in Tito's office, without the participation of the foreign ministry or the party, who were both ignored until the crisis was over.

The diplomats further observed that the public had become more critical of foreign policy because the country was more open to visitors and travel abroad. It also had greater access to information from newspapers, radio and television. These changes and the Middle Eastern crisis forced Yugoslav policymakers and diplomats to develop a more pragmatic foreign policy towards Europe and non-aligned countries.[43]

The new generation of moderate and more pragmatic politicians in the foreign secretariat were professional diplomats who promoted political and economic cooperation with the West. These included the Minister of Foreign Affairs Marko Nikezić and his associates. On the other hand, the older generation of conservative politicians with Partisan roots, such as

Josip Đerđa and even Tito himself, were critical of moving away from the policies of non-alignment and the introduction of Western liberal trends.[44]

The key discussion was between supporters of Europeanisation, who believed that non-alignment was an economic burden without results, and the supporters of non-alignment as the principal foundation for Yugoslav foreign policy. British diplomats referred to this as the 'battle between the pragmatists and romantics'. Tito was obviously a staunch supporter of non-alignment, while a 'return to Europe, but not Eastern Europe' was supported by Marko Nikezić, who was Serbian, as well by as younger leaders from Slovenia and Croatia. The conflict was principally generational, not national. The younger leaders did not have pre-wartime experiences in mind, but rather the 1948 break with Stalin. For this reason, the return to the socialist camp would not have party support. Because of his own pro-Soviet nostalgia Tito was very sensitive to Soviet criticisms, but he would never subsume Yugoslav independence to a new kind of Comintern.[45]

Czechoslovakia in 1968

Yugoslavia reacted with approval when the pro-reform Aleksander Dubček replaced the discredited Antonin Novotny as the head of the Czechoslovakian communist party. Brezhnev tacitly approved of this change when he refused to support Novotny during his Prague visit in December 1967. In early January 1968, Dubček took over as chairman of the party, while Novotny remained head of state as president of the Republic. Although the initial Soviet reaction was favourable, subsequent events would change their minds.

The short episode of Dubček's political liberalisation, from January to August 1968, had a strong impact on developments in Yugoslavia and on Yugoslav–Soviet relations. The slogan 'socialism with a human face' was well received in Yugoslavia, because it was partially inspired by Yugoslavia's 'self-management' socialism. In addition, the events in Czechoslovakia confirmed to the Yugoslav leadership that the self-management model and the 'unique path to socialism' were starting to gain more support across Eastern Europe.

It is therefore not surprising that, along with China and Romania, Yugoslavia reacted particularly negatively to the Soviet invasion. The occupation endangered the future of *détente* and Soviet relations with confused Western European communist parties.

The Czechoslovakian public boycotted the new leadership that was forcibly installed by the Soviets. On the first day of the intervention, the Czechoslovak party leadership condemned the action as a breach of international law, and the Czech foreign ministry formally protested to all the countries who had participated in the intervention. The Czech foreign minister Jiri Hajek condemned the action and at the Security Council demanded the withdrawal of the occupying forces. The initial crisis subsided only when under intense Soviet pressure Dubček managed to convince the state and party leadership to accept the Moscow Protocol, signed immediately after the intervention. In practice, this document forced Czechoslovakia to reverse the liberal process and return to the fold, and also imposed the permanent stationing of Soviet troops.[46]

The military occupation of Czechoslovakia dealt a heavy blow to Soviet–Yugoslav relations. Yugoslavia and Czechoslovakia maintained a close relationship during Dubček's reign because there were many similarities between both countries' systems and aspirations. Both countries were multinational constructs with nationalist sensitivities. Czechoslovakia, however, was in a different international position. Unlike independent Yugoslavia, Czechoslovakia was a part of the Eastern 'lager' and under strong Soviet influence. Tito warned the Soviets on several occasions that the military intervention was not a good solution for their Czechoslovak problem. Along with Yugoslavia, Caeușescu's Romania also tried to chart an independent foreign policy by seizing the initiative in the Czechoslovakian crisis. Such an alliance, between Yugoslavia, Czechoslovakia and Romania, echoed the 'Little Entente' that the three countries pursued between 1920 and 1938 against a renewed Habsburg Empire and Germany.[47] This little anti-Soviet entente, however, was too superficial and unrealistic to be effective. Their only common denominator was the communist system and a temporary shared goal of limiting Soviet influence – but for different reasons.

Yugoslavia wished to promote its non-aligned position and 'unique form of socialism', and had the greatest freedom of action. Romania was constrained by its membership of Eastern European associations and the Warsaw Pact. As such, it was impossible for the Romanians to promote an independent foreign and military policy, and the Romanian regime was just as rigid as any other Eastern European communist government. Romania supported Czechoslovakia to limit its dependence on Moscow, but not its liberal reforms.[48]

The Yugoslav leadership was taken by surprise by the Warsaw Pact intervention on 21 August 1968. There were no clear signs that something like this would occur and very few observers expected such a harsh Soviet reaction. The Czechoslovak leadership had been careful not to antagonise the Soviets or to repeat the mistakes of Hungary in 1956. The rise of *détente* was thought to be a signal that the Soviets would not risk their international reputation.

The Yugoslav leadership immediately condemned the intervention, fearing that it might spread to other 'disloyal' socialist states. Tito and Ceauşescu met on 24 August in Vârşet on the Yugoslav–Romanian border. They exchanged information about their talks with Dubček and agreed to resist potential Soviet aggression.[49]

What was the Western response to the events in Czechoslovakia, and a possible attack on Romania and Yugoslavia? The United States and their Western allies considered the Romanian problem a part of the internal affairs of the socialist bloc. Romania was part of the Warsaw Pact and therefore NATO could not intervene militarily.[50] Yugoslavia, on the other hand, was in a different geostrategic position and independent from the Warsaw Pact, so it could expect more active Western support in case of an attack.

Over at the UN Security Council, Soviet Ambassador Jacob Malik defended the invasion as 'fraternal assistance' against 'anti-social forces'.[51] The West had no desire to intervene in Czechoslovakia, nor to gain it as an ally, and despite open criticism it tacitly accepted the Soviet Union's excuses. A British Foreign Office report clearly indicated, however, that this would not be the case with Yugoslavia:

> An attack on Yugoslavia would show that there had been a radical change in Soviet policy from a conservationist policy (involving military force if necessary) designed to keep the Warsaw Pact intact, to an expansionist policy, prepared to use military force in order to put down a country (admittedly a communist country) whose attitude the Russians found embarrassing. If

that change in Soviet thinking had come about, it could contain the most serious implications for their attitude to yet other countries, e.g. in Asia Minor or the Middle East. The consequence of an invasion of Yugoslavia for the balance of power in Europe and the security of N.A.T.O. are obvious. Greece, and Turkey, would become highly vulnerable. The whole of the Eastern Mediterranean would be directly threatened. Soviet forces would face Italy across the length of the Adriatic. The Soviet occupation of Albania, which in the state of mind which they would have developed would seem inevitable, could well lead to Chinese reactions. It is most unlikely that the Chinese would give the Russians serious trouble on their borders, but they might be tempted to adopt a more forward and aggressive policy towards North Vietnam.[52]

There were problems related to a potential Western intervention in favour of Yugoslav independent, however. The United States was in the middle of an election campaign and the outgoing Johnson Administration did not want to make any long-term commitments, in addition to the general moral objection to supporting a communist state. The British also quoted the State Department position:

> The U.S. owes no moral debts to Yugoslavia and would not be justified in acting to support a regime which, while comparatively liberal compared with its other Communist counterparts, is none the less undemocratic. Support for the Yugoslav resistance to the Soviets in both a pre- and post-invasion situation would only therefore be justified on the basis of U.S. and Western politico-military self-interest.[53]

It was not realistic to expect NATO to offer direct military support to Yugoslavia. Such a move would require approval from the US Congress and Senate, which would be too difficult to obtain. Instead, NATO would have the opportunity to conduct other precautionary measures in the Mediterranean. The US had other options to aid Yugoslavia bilaterally, both militarily and economically. In this case, aid would be limited to small arms suited for guerrilla warfare. Heavy armaments would be much more difficult to deliver, and would be ill-suited to Yugoslavia's armed forces, which were predominantly equipped with Soviet heavy materiel. The UK and France would probably participate in this, while West Germany, due to its sensitive geostrategic position, would be neutral. The US explicitly ruled out deploying ground forces, and limited itself to offering military aid only if Yugoslav formally requested it.

On 23 August, two days after the Warsaw Pact intervention, the Yugoslav party leadership met at Brijuni to discuss the Czechoslovakian crisis. Yugoslavia did not have a properly developed military strategy to respond to a potential attack from the east. The majority of military assets were stationed along the western borders. This situation caused a conflict within the political and military leadership about strategic priorities. General Ivan Gošnjak, who had been minister of defence from 1953 to 1967,[54] was blamed for failing to develop and implement a doctrine of eastern defence.

He also did not support the concept of the so-called 'Total People's Defence', the idea that every individual should be ready to fight at all times. It was a somewhat modernised version of the wartime Partisan ideal. In their memoirs, both Tripalo and Dabčević-Kučar blamed Gošnjak for his complete failure to organise Yugoslavia's defence in light of the Czechoslovakian crisis. They also mentioned the argument between Gošnjak and Koča Popović about the possibility of a Soviet attack.[55]

The situation in Czechoslovakia shook the foundations of Yugoslav military strategy, which was organised exclusively to resist an attack from the West. Despite its defence planning, it was clear that Yugoslavia had no chance of resisting a direct confrontation with Warsaw Pact forces. This led the implementation of the 'Total People's Defence', which implied preparations for long-term guerrilla and urban warfare rather than direct confrontation. A bill to set up the strategy was passed and by early 1969 and it embraced everybody from schoolchildren to the formal military structure, creating a reserve force of almost all able-bodied men and women aged 16 to 65. They were obliged to undergo combat training and perform other duties in order to create a deployable force of between 1 and 3 million.

In order to avoid another economic meltdown, similar to 1948, Yugoslavia improved economic ties to the West by signing economic agreements with the EEC, and obtaining loans from the World Bank and the US Export–Import Bank. It soon became obvious, however, that the Soviet military threat was overestimated. And while relations with the Soviets started to improve, the long-term consequence was that the Yugoslav political elite was drifting away from the wellspring of socialism towards the West.

The Yugoslav public closely followed the events in Czechoslovakia. A unified public opposition was soon created against a potential intervention and any forceful imposition of an unacceptable regime. It was one of the rare moments when the Yugoslav communist regime had unequivocal support from the whole country. One indicator was a sudden increase in the membership of the League of Communists, immediately after the invasion. The structure of new members revealed a significant increase in the number of young people, which had been decreasing prior to the events in Czechoslovakia. In the first six months of 1968, 20,953 new members were accepted into the party, while in the second half of the year, this number increased to 145,487, of whom 30 per cent were young adults.[56]

China and the Balkans

The unintended consequence of the invasion of Czechoslovakia was the establishment of relations between Yugoslavia and the People's Republic of China. Active Chinese engagement in the Balkans and south-eastern Europe began in the early 1960s. It was closely related to the worsening relations with Moscow. A direct result was a break between Moscow and the regime of Enver Hoxha in Tirana, and Albania's alignment with China. The Albanians hoped that, with Chinese support, they could avoid the expansionist influence of both Moscow and Belgrade, while continuing to pursue their own unique path to Stalinism. On the other hand, although aid to Albania was a burden on the Chinese economy, it served China as an ideological weapon against Moscow.[57]

Increased cooperation between Beijing and the communist regime of Romania was also a function of worsening Sino-Soviet relations, as well as of Romania's attempt to reduce Moscow's influence. Cooperation with China intensified after Nikolai Çeauşescu became the head of the Romanian communist party in 1965, and he started to promote a more independent foreign policy.[58] After heavy floods in Romania in 1970, substantial aid arrived from China. Senior Romanian officials visited Beijing several times, and China announced $244 million in infrastructure aid.

The possibility of Chinese experts coming to Romania and Albania, along with planned investment projects, must have alarmed Soviet officials.[59]

The state of Sino-Yugoslav relations was always related to the state of Sino-Soviet relations. China, however, did not always follow the Soviet position towards Yugoslavia. At the time, China was a harsher critic of Yugoslav socialism than Moscow. In 1956, the Chinese communist party gave support to independent communist regimes in Eastern Europe – including Władisław Gomułka's return to power in Poland. China's position on the Hungarian intervention was similar to Yugoslavia: they criticised the first Soviet intervention, but supported the second intervention that crushed the Hungarian liberal revolution. On the other hand, Beijing disapproved of Belgrade's constant criticisms of the Soviet and other communist parties. This situation changed drastically in 1957 with the deterioration of Soviet–Yugoslav relations caused by Moscow's attempts to strengthen its position within the communist bloc. Although Khrushchev did not want to repeat the 1948 episode, relations between Yugoslavia and the Soviets chilled in the period 1957–61. The radicalisation of Chinese policy that resulted in the Great Leap Forward of 1958–61 was a big factor in Sino-Soviet relations, and the attitude of both powers towards Yugoslavia. China criticised Khrushchev's policy of improving relations with the West and his tolerance of the liberal Yugoslav heresy. In order to attempt to repair its broken relations with China, Moscow put a brake on its opening to the West and Yugoslavia. In September 1958 China withdrew its ambassador to Yugoslavia, suspending bilateral relations for eleven years.

The further worsening of Sino-Soviet relations in the early 1960s led the Soviets to realise that additional compromises would have no effect on their influence on China. As a consequence, Soviet–Yugoslav relations started to improve. In this new situation, Yugoslavia became an informal Soviet ally in its attempts to isolate the Chinese party within the international communist movement. Moscow started to defend the Yugoslav regime against attacks from Beijing, while Beijing sought to balance this by becoming the principal patron of Albania. This in turn worsened both Sino-Soviet relations and Albanian relations with Yugoslavia. In addition, with Yugoslavia's help, the Kremlin attempted to strengthen its influence over Third World revolutionary movements. In the period 1963–8, good relations were manifested by Yugoslavia's membership of Comecon in 1964; close military and economic cooperation; and joint support for Arab regimes in 1967.

The key factor for the restoration of relations between Belgrade and Beijing was the Soviet intervention in Czechoslovakia. Both China and Yugoslavia were harshly critical of the Soviet invasion. Although Chinese attacks on Yugoslavia continued until late 1969, trade ties were re-established early that year. Trade cooperation increased from $1.5 million in 1969 to $14 million in 1970. Simultaneously, the two countries exchanged ambassadors and restored diplomatic relations. Yugoslavia maintained its neutral position towards the Sino-Soviet border conflict of 1969, but also supported the China's membership of the United Nations and reduced anti-Chinese rhetoric in the Non-Aligned Movement. The long-standing rift between the two countries formally ended when the Yugoslav State Secretary for Foreign Affairs Mirko Tepavac visited Beijing in June 1971.[60]

Both sides had their reasons for establishing a new strategic cooperation. In Yugoslavia's case it was the fear of Soviet expansion after Czechoslovakia, while China was seeking to improve its international standing, which had been weakened during the Cultural Revolution that started in 1996. Both sides had a mutual interest in reducing Soviet global and regional influence. Although Beijing tried to use the negative reactions after Czechoslovakia to prise Eastern European regimes away from Moscow, Chinese influence was greatly limited by distance. Prime Minister Zhou en Lai declared: 'Fire cannot be put out from a distant well.'

The restoration of relations with China also influenced Yugoslavia's relations with Albania. Despite political differences, Yugoslavia wanted to have better relations with Albania because of its Albanian minority in Kosovo. After Czechoslovakia, relations between Belgrade and Bucharest also warmed, which included Yugoslav support for Romania's attempts to formulate a semi-independent foreign policy. All of these developments alarmed Moscow, which feared the creation of an anti-Soviet coalition in the Balkans under Chinese patronage. The Yugoslav regime, however, was careful not to antagonise the Soviets and refrained from openly supporting Chinese initiatives in the Balkans.

The short-lived Chinese initiative in the Balkans subsided after 1971, when China became an important international power, with the establishment of ties between Beijing and Washington. The new alignment with the United States changed China's position towards Moscow, and reduced the need to forge alliances in Eastern Europe.[61]

7

Nixon in Yugoslavia

'Long live Croatia, long live Yugoslavia.'
— President Richard Nixon

The 10th Meeting of the CC LCC

The biggest international event of 1970, for both Yugoslavia and Croatia, was the visit by President Nixon to Belgrade and Zagreb. This came on the heels of two major domestic events that characterised the development of the national-liberal movement in Croatia – the 10th meeting of the Central Committee of the LCC, and Tito's September announcement of further federal reforms at a meeting with Zagreb party officials.

The immediate catalyst of the political clash at the 10th meeting was the awakening of media freedoms with the support of the Croatian party. The true reasons, however, were much deeper. The conflict between the party liberals and the hardliners was caused by a series of public attacks on the Croatian literary journal *Hrvatski književni list* (*HKL*) by Miloš Žanko, the vice president of the Federal Assembly and a member of the Croatian Central Committee.[1] Žanko had a reputation of being a hardline party functionary, and he was reviled by many in Croatia after he led an attack on the 1967 language declaration. He characterised *HKL* as the vanguard of

Croatian nationalism and 'petty bourgeoisism'. *Vjesnik* declined to print Žanko's articles for its 'pogrom character', so Belgrade's *Borba* printed them instead.²

The debate between Žanko and *HKL* attracted Tito's attention. In conversation with Tito on 21 February 1969, Žanko denounced other newspapers as nationalist, including *Telegram, Hrvatsko Kolo (The Croatian Circle), Kritiku, Vjesnik u srijedu (Vjesnik on Wednesday)* and *Naše Teme (Our Themes)*.³ He became Tito's main informer in the fight against greater media freedom in Croatia, and established a direct line of written communication with the President. *HKL* was banned shortly after, and Žanko turned his attention to the *Matica Hrvatska* and the journal *Hrvatsko Kolo*, which Tito compared to the Ustaša movement's publications in exile.

Probably encouraged by Žanko's intervention, Tito asked to review the Croatian party analysis of *HKL* himself, and wrote in the margins: 'Why has this harmful journal not yet been forbidden?' He added: 'Such analyses reveal ideological and political blindness. Even according to the constitution, such journal–pamphlets must be silently shut down immediately.'⁴

Another series of articles by Žanko from November 1969 were even more critical of the Croatian media. This time the main targets were *Vjesnik* and *Radio-television Zagreb*, as well as *Hrvatski književni list, Kritika, Hrvatsko Kolo, Dubrovnik, Dometi* ('Range'), *Jezik* ('Language'), *Telegram, Glas Koncila* (the Church newspaper *Voice of the Concilium*), *Mali Koncil (Little Concilium), Marulić* and *Vjesnik on Wednesday*. Žanko also named several individuals whom he accused of fomenting nationalism: Petar Šegedin, Vlado Gotovac, Branimir Donat, Trpimir Macan, Grgo Gamulin, Vlatko Pavletić, Tomislav Ladan, Bruno Bušić, Marko and Vladimir Veselica, Šime Đodan, Hrvoje Šošić, Krešimir Džeba, Neda Krmpotić, Igor Mandić and Father Živko Kustić. These men and woman were public figures, economists, writers, journalists and a priest.⁵

The last straw was Žanko's direct criticism of the Croatian political leadership, including Bakarić. He accused them of nationalist and anti-socialist behaviour. Bakarić and other Croatian leaders reacted immediately along with *Vjesnik, Vjesnik on Wednesday, Telegram* and *Glas Koncila*. At the meeting of the republic's leadership on 13 December 1969, the Secretary of the Central Committee, Pero Pirker, informed the other members that Tito denied any involvement in Žanko's actions.⁶ The president of the Central

Committee, Savka Dabčević-Kučar, criticised Žanko for his manner, but at the same time she also stressed the Croatian party's efforts to suppress nationalism in the republic. The meeting revealed changes in the mood and political climate, because most members of the Central Committee wished to discuss these problems openly and publicly, and not simply use repression as Žanko was trying to do. The transcript of the meeting clearly reveals that the Croatian leadership believed that Žanko was in touch with certain circles within the administration who wanted to discredit Croatian leaders. For this reason the 10th meeting of the LCC was organised and used to denounce Žanko.[7]

According to the memoirs of Miko Tripalo and Savka Dabčević-Kučar, Tito initiated the decision to remove Žanko on the occasion of the meeting. He apparently found out that Žanko was in touch with some Serbian high party officials, in particular Mijalko Todorović and Milentije Popović, president of the Federal Assembly. They wanted to compromise the Croatian leadership with Žanko's help, and in this way compromise Tito, who enjoyed strong support in Croatia. Savka Dabčević-Kučar found out about this 'plot' at a meeting with Tito in Sisak in November 1969. She noted that on this occasion Tito told her that there was a 'conspiracy' going on in Serbia against the Croatian leadership. According to Tito, the initiator of this plan was Popović, along with Žanko and the president of the Chamber of Nationalities of the Federal Assembly, Mika Špiljak. Savka Dabčević-Kučar made it clear that she wasn't certain that Tito was telling the truth or what his motives were. But it is possible that Tito wanted to compromise a potential rival in Popović, boosting his standing as ultimate arbiter while playing both sides of the liberal and hardline-communist divide. According to Savka's testimony, Žanko's removal was initiated by Tito, which was eased by the fact that Žanko was already a thorn in many sides since his opposition to the 1967 language declaration.[8]

Božidar Novak, the director of the *Vjesnik* publishing house and a member of the Central Committee of the LCC, believed that Žanko acted with Tito's direct approval. Novak also believed that Žanko enjoyed Tito's support until he started to insinuate that the Croatian leadership was responsible for rising nationalist tensions in Croatia.[9] The fact that Tito harshly attacked Žanko for his behaviour and criticisms at a meeting in Zagreb on 19 December 1969 only confirmed for Novak his reading that

Žanko had enjoyed Tito's support until very recently. Novak also believed that Tito denounced Žanko so that the Croatian leadership would handle the nationalist problem themselves.[10]

Tito's support helped the Croatian party to get rid of Žanko, but he had not expected that the 10th meeting of the LCC would move strongly towards greater liberalism and nationalism.[11] Immediately after the LCC meeting, in January 1970, the Executive Bureau of the LCY convened in Belgrade. At this meeting, Tito recalled Žanko's complaints about the weak response to the rise of nationalism in Croatia, but Žanko had gone too far when he published his articles in *Borba*; but at another meeting Tito emphasised that he never supported the liberal position of the Croatian leadership.[12]

The Croatian historian Dušan Bilandžić believed that Tito ordered the Croatian leadership to convene the 10th meeting to remove Žanko in order to balance Belgrade's hegemony. Tito needed this in light of his own problematic relationship with the Serbian political leadership after the removal of Ranković. In Tito's great game of holding the country together, as well as preserving his own status, he required careful balancing between opposing political camps, nations and the Cold War blocs.

The Serbian leadership, Milentije Popović, Koča Popović, Mijalko Todorović, Marko Nikezić and others, were more inclined towards the West, while Tito, despite ideological differences, had a greater affinity for the Soviet Union. In order to neutralise reactions in Serbia after the removal of Ranković, several Serbian politicians were brought into the highest echelons of state and party leadership. Mijalko Todorović became the Secretary of the Executive Committee of the Central Committee of the LCY; Koča Popović took Ranković's seat as vice president of Federal Republic; and Milentije Popović replaced Edvard Kardelj as the president of the Federal Assembly. It became obvious at the 9th Congress of the LCY in 1969 that Todorović was attempting to limit Tito's influence by creating a less centralised party. This was the reason why Tito changed his mind at the 9th Congress, deciding to form a new Executive Bureau with all the top party brass, where he could keep them under control. In this way he neutralised Todorović, who could have become the head of the party if the proposed changes had been carried out. On the other hand, Croatian politicians also opposed the Serbian proposals while they sought Tito's support for their pursuit of political and economic reforms.[13]

The 10th meeting of the LCC dismissed nationalism as the greatest threat to the development of socialist Yugoslavia, and instead elevated that 'unitarism' that promoted 'Yugoslavism' by denying national feelings as the 'greatest problem'. Savka Dabčević-Kučar believed the reasons for the rise in nationalism lay in unsolved economic problems and other disagreements between Yugoslavia's leaders. She was convinced that the extensive authority that the federation possessed over the economy was a part of this 'unitarism'. The 10th meeting clearly expressed a negative view of nationalism, with a special emphasis on *Matice Hrvatska* and the Society of Writers of Croatia. But with its liberal tone, the meeting did lend legitimacy to those forces that would lead to a national revival in the future.[14]

The 10th meeting was not welcomed by all in the Yugoslav political leadership. Immediately afterwards, the Presidium of the Central Committee of the LCY met at Brijuni to discuss their conclusions. The main objection was that the meeting was exclusively oriented to denouncing Žanko. The president of the Federal Government, Mitja Ribičič, complained that Žanko had been removed by Stalinist methods. The last sentence of the formal report of that meeting, added at Tito's suggestion, attacked Žanko and his circle of support. This was an indirect attack on Belgrade's federal structures and perceived Serbian dominance. Despite Tito's stature, such a conclusion by the LCY was received badly by some members of the Presidium. It soon became apparent that there was resistance to Žanko's removal, especially in the Belgrade press. The Croatian leadership had the impression that the support given to Žanko in his position as vice president of the Federal Assembly was a direct attack on them.

The conflict surrounding Žanko's removal peaked at an LCY Executive Bureau meeting in March 1970. Edvard Kardelj and Cvijetin Mijatović, the representative of Bosnia-Herzegovina, criticised Croatia for antagonising other republics and the federation by exaggerating the fear of unitarism. The Macedonian representative, Krste Crvenkovski, in turn attacked the Serbian leadership for not reacting to Žanko's articles in *Borba*, which he described as the 'Serbian newspaper full of insinuations against other republics'. Marko Nikezić retorted that *Borba* was a federal newspaper, and if there were any disagreements about this then *Borba* could be moved out of Belgrade.[15] As a good parent, Tito put an end to the discussion by supporting the Croatian position, which he later publicly reiterated in Opatija, Croatia, and again at the opening of Rijeka airport on the island of Krk. He stated that the 10th LCC meeting had been constructive and that he was not opposed to its conclusions. Tito's intervention temporarily calmed passions and tensions in the party leadership, and gave a boost to Croatian aspirations.[16]

The 10th LCC meeting was received badly in Serbia by politicians, media and the public alike, especially the suggestion that Žanko was in a conspiracy with federal elements and Serbian politicians. Particularly offensive to the Serbs was the idea that unitarism was a bigger danger than nationalism and separatism. Zdravko Vuković, the director of Radio-Television Belgrade, wrote in his memoirs that there was a big revolt against Žanko's defamation and many asked, 'What *did* the Croats want?'[17]

The increased tensions surrounding nationalism and persistent requests to pursue economic reforms with a special emphasis on the banking system and the distribution of foreign currency placed the Croatian leadership in an awkward position against the leaderships of the other republics. Its traditional partners in more developed regions like Slovenia started to treat Croatian developments with suspicion. On the other hand, the lesser developed Macedonia, while agreeing with Croatia's fight against unitarism, also became suspicious because economic reforms endangered Macedonia's share of federal funds.[18]

The 10th meeting of the LCC was also a turning point for the development of the Croatian liberal and national movement. The liberal trends that had started to develop in 1966 now became stronger with a powerful nationalist character. Although the 10th meeting is remembered mainly for the removal of Miloš Žanko from the Federal Assembly, it had a strong impact on developments in the whole of Yugoslavia. According to Dušan Bilandžić, the meeting 'shaped a political platform on the position of Croatia within Yugoslavia and the future reform of the federation.'[19] Direct television broadcasts of the meeting were also a novelty, allowing the public to see political deliberations at the party level for the first time.

The Economist emphasised that the meeting was important for the removal of Žanko and the reaction from other republics. According to the magazine, the main reasons for Žanko's ousting were his articles in *Borba* and the attempt to discredit and remove Croatia's political leadership, who had a reputation of calling for political and economic reforms, especially since the Slovenian leadership was compromised by the World Bank road loan scandal. Žanko's removal had the support of the Croatian political leadership. The fact that he wasn't popular among the Serbian minority in Croatia also helped. The majority of Croatians saw Žanko as a victim of the political fight between liberals and hard-liners, and Croatia's potential defeat as the defeat of liberalism itself.[20] American diplomats clearly noticed this deliberate ambiguity in Tito's behaviour:

> Tito's habit has been to use his power sparingly. He has avoided showdowns where possible. He admitted at the Brioni Plenum that he had been aware of the Ranković problem since 1962 but had not move against Ranković then, fearing the effect on the unity of the party and the leadership. His genius lies in his flexibility, in his astonishing receptivity to new ideas regardless of their ideological orthodoxy or of his own predilections. There is little evidence to indicate that his personal orientation is particularly liberal, yet he has allowed himself to be pulled in a liberal direction by the arguments of his advisors. But in accepting new ideas Tito never quite seems to abandon old ones. This is why his speeches often give the impression that he has one foot on the accelerator and the other on the brake. While this makes for a certain indecisiveness in public, it also enables Tito to appear to be on everybody's side at the same time. This quality of sympathizing with all points of view is a key element in his extraordinary popularity and in the indisputable political fact that both liberals and conservatives consider him indispensible.[21]

British and American diplomats followed Žanko's case with great interest.[22] The British ambassador to Belgrade, Terrence Garvey, described the situation in Yugoslavia in his 1970 annual report:

> 1970 brought Yugoslavia to a critical point on her long road back from Stalinism. Over 20 years she had evolved by stages towards multi-national regionalism but her institution had lagged behind social change.

He wasn't convinced that Žanko was trying to carry out a coup against the Croatian leadership, but that it was a case of personal animosity between him and Savka Dabčević-Kučar. The British consul-general in Zagreb, Joseph Dobbs, sent an extensive report to the Belgrade embassy about the 10th LCC meeting:

> The discussion was the strongest imaginable reassertion of the political and economic rights of Croatia within a united federal Yugoslavia and a rejection of any tendencies which might lead Yugoslavia back to an authoritarian central state. Several speakers, especially among the younger leaders, made it clear that they were also dissatisfied with Zagreb's present position economically in relation to Belgrade [...] In short, they were reasserting the determination of the people of Croatia to be allowed to runt their own affairs in their own way and to have a due share in the wealth which the workers in Croatia created and their due part in deciding how that wealth was to be divided.[23]

The prevailing opinion in Zagreb was that Žanko's removal could not have been done without Tito's approval. The Serbs in the Croatian party were as critical of Žanko's behaviour as the Croats, and helped with his removal. Dobbs described the atmosphere of the 10th meeting as:

> Speakers in the debate, while being frankly anti-Belgrade, were careful to avoid appearing as anti-Serb. But in the comments I have heard privately in Zagreb, the undertone is strongly anti-Belgrade, anti-Serb and anti-Russian.[24]

Everyone in Zagreb was astonished by the publicity and openness of the discussion. It was filling the newspapers and interrupting regular TV programming. Dobbs was told that the people of Croatia stood unanimously behind their party leaders:

> There is no doubt that the reaction of the man-in-the-street here to the plenum has been extremely favourable. [...] The man-in-the-street here likes to see his authorities standing up to Belgrade in such a decisive manner but people here are also enormously impressed by the openness of the debate and the pain, straightforward, unideological – 'manly', as one local resident put it to me – way in which the Party leaders put views that all Croats share.

He reported that the bond between the party leadership and the public was stronger than ever before, and he compared this with the popularity of Ceauşescu in Romania after he resisted Soviet economic domination. He also observed that, unlike in Croatia, the Žanko affair had passed almost unnoticed in Slovenia. The American consul-general in Zagreb, Robert Owen, was also surprised by the openness and spontaneity of the meeting. He believed that the Croatian party under new liberal leadership had made great progress in introducing democratic methods in the discussions on party matters.[25]

The British ambassador, Terence Garvey, reported that the key word at the 10th meeting was 'unitarism'. Garvey observed that in the Yugoslav context 'unitarism' had more than one meaning. The meeting appeared to reveal three of them: Greater Serbian chauvinism and nationalism, linked to the pre-war period; Greater Croatian neo-*Ustaši* chauvinism; and 'bureaucratic centralism', the attempt by the federation to reduce the autonomy of the republics. Without apparent contradiction, all three meanings were personified in Žanko.[26]

Žanko's removal was the signal from Zagreb to Belgrade that Croatia would resist centralist tendencies. Ambassador Garvey linked Žanko's case to more general economic and political trends in Croatia and Yugoslavia. This was against the background of Croatia's dissatisfaction with the five-year economic plan that the Croatian leadership considered to be too centralist. In addition, economic reforms brought unsolved problems to the surface, such as the distribution of funds and the inefficiency of investments made with Croatian money in less developed parts of the country; the issue of the banks and state investment funds; the distribution of hard currency; and the retention quota (the foreign currency retained by the republics). At a meeting of the Zagreb party faction *Aktiv* on 13 December 1969, Vladimir Bakarić blamed the centralist tendency of the Belgrade bureaucracy for poor economic results. He named officials in the federal administration and the Serbian capital who were 'manipulating' the federal machinery in Belgrade. At the same meeting, it was also decided that the rumours about the rise of nationalism in Croatia had to be stopped. Žanko's articles were the most recent example of such rumour-mongering, supported by 'unitarists'. According to Garvey, the key goal of the 10th meeting was to assure the Croatian public that the LCC would continue to pursue the reformist path and to secure its public position as the protector of Croatian national interests.

Žanko's articles served the Croatian leadership well. By attacking Žanko, they managed to promote themselves as the true representatives of reform, self-management, and Yugoslav socialist patriotism. But Garvey also pointed out the dangers of these positions:

> Their room for political manoeuvre is pretty circumscribed: on one side there is pressure from Belgrade to run the Yugoslav economy rationally; on the other there is a the risk, not immediate but inherent, that, if this pressure gets too strong, Croat nationalist sentiment will get off the lead, with unpredictable consequences.[27]

Žanko's negative writings on the situation in Croatia were soon linked to the revival of *Informbiro* (the Yugoslav name of Cominform) actions in Yugoslavia. The newspapers *Politika* and *Vjesnik on Wednesday*, as well as the weekly magazine *Nin* (acronym for 'weekly information newspaper'), regularly provided examples of such neo-*Informbiro* activities.[28] The American diplomats singled out an interview with Pero Pirker in March 1970, in which he spoke about the importance of the 10th meeting. For the Americans the interview was important, because it provided insight into the situation in Croatia by a high party official. But Consul-General Owen was not convinced by Pirker's claims about the threats of unitarism, or the linkage between radical leftist students with Soviet-oriented hardliners. In this vein, he observed:

> We continue to believe that the primary purpose of the LCC leadership in initiating its 'anti-unitarist' campaign is to strengthen the Croatian Party's case for the Reform and against those who oppose it, and that this struggle should be seen primarily within a domestic Yugoslav political context. Pirker's pitch may thus have been intended for listeners in Belgrade, perhaps specifically to catch the attention of the President, who has just returned from a lengthy trip abroad.[29]

An unexpected technical problem arose when Žanko refused to resign from his position in the Chamber of Nationalities in the Federal Assembly; there was no law that could authorise his removal. The delegates of this

Chamber were nominated by the republics and autonomous regions.[30] The Croatian parliament hurriedly passed a new law on recall on 17 March 1970, and Žanko was duly removed from office on 7 April with a large majority.[31] He was formally relieved of his duties in the Federal Assembly in April 1971, and replaced by Josip Đerđa.[32] British diplomats commented on these developments, 'Our verdict is that Žanko's views were not so much unwise as untimely. In this country, even more than in our own, timing can be more important than substance.'[33]

And US Consul-General Robert Owen concluded on the Žanko case:

> As Dr. Zanko packs his bags in Belgrade – or at least clears his desk in the Federal Assembly – it is perhaps not too early to give a judgement on the strategy of leading Croatian communists during the 'Zanko affair.' We would tend to rate their political performance during the first quarter of 1970 at a near 'A plus.' By seizing the initiative and turning Dr. Zanko's accusations against Croatian chauvinism into a counteroffensive against real or alleged 'Unitarist' elements, such Croatian leaders as Savka Dabcevic-Kucar, Pirker, Bakaric, and Tripalo managed do defend legitimate pride in Croatian identity while enhancing the Croatian party as a champion of economic reform. Now that Zanko has lost his parliamentary mandate and suspected unitarist element has been chastised, the party leadership in Croatia appears to have emerged from manoeuvring of the last three months with a renewed sense of strength matched by a pragmatic intent to avoid new controversy for the immediate future.[34]

The spirit of the 10th meeting was felt in all aspects of social life. The death of the former mayor of Zagreb, Većeslav Holjevac, in August 1970 was an indication of the informal rehabilitation of the signatories of the 1967 language declaration. Zagreb called for a day of mourning and all important Croatian officials attended the funeral, including Bakarić, Dabčević-Kučar, Haramija, Blažević and Špiljak. Orme Wilson, the new American consul-general in Zagreb, succeeding Robert Owen, described the ceremony:

> Too much significance should not be placed on the rehabilitation of figures like Holjevac, Krleza and Tudjman. However, it

is nevertheless an interesting sign of Croatian times that while Holjevac is laid to rest with full honors his former tormentor, Milos Zanko, is tasting the dregs of disgrace.[35]

Nixon in Yugoslavia

President Richard Nixon visited Yugoslavia from 30 September to 2 October 1970. The visit formed part of his European tour, which included Italy, the Vatican, the 6th Fleet in Naples, Spain, the United Kingdom and Ireland.[36] His visit was a reflection of increased US initiatives towards Eastern Europe, in particular towards countries that conducted foreign policy more or less independently from the Soviet Union. Nixon had already visited Romania in August 1969, which was the first visit of an American president to a communist Eastern European state, apart from the Soviet Union.[37] The visit to Yugoslavia served as an acknowledgement of US support for Yugoslav independence and integrity. In addition, visits to the 6th Fleet and other Mediterranean countries were a clear sign of active and permanent American engagement in the Mediterranean. This was directly related to the situation in the Middle East, and growing Soviet influence in the eastern Mediterranean.[38]

The transcripts of the conversations between President Nixon's National Security Adviser, Henry Kissinger, and American and foreign officials reveal that uncertainty surrounded the President's visit to Europe and Yugoslavia. This was due to potentially wider political implications of the Middle Eastern crisis, as well as less important diplomatic disagreements.

During the preparations for Nixon's European tour, a conflict erupted in Jordan in September 1970, between the Jordanian Government and the Palestine Liberation Organisation (PLO). The immediate cause was the Palestinian hijacking of three European commercial planes, with a large number of hostages, which were forced to land in the Jordanian desert. Jordan's King Hussein declared martial law and established a military government on 15 September 1970 and launched attacks on PLO guerrillas the next day. Iraq threatened to intervene on behalf of the Palestinians, and Syria had already started a military incursion into Jordanian territory. The United States considered a military intervention to save the Hashemite Kingdom, but that would almost certainly provoke the Soviets to get involved. The Mediterranean fleets of the US and the Soviet Union moved closer to the Lebanese and Syrian coasts, and Israel was also ready to intervene if Syria openly attacked Jordan. A wider crisis was ultimately averted, when the Palestinian rebellion was crushed and King Hussein concluded a truce with PLO leader Yasser Arafat in Cairo on 27 September.[39]

Although Yugoslav diplomats could not have known the details of the frantic atmosphere in the White House as the Jordanian crisis unfolded and escalated, the crisis came close to forcing the cancellation of the visit and thereby worsening Yugoslav–American relations. The preparations were complicated by Nixon's statement at a news conference in Chicago on 17 September, when he spoke favourably about military aid to Israel and the potential of an American–Israeli joint intervention in Jordan. He also said he planned to strengthen the 6th Fleet in the Mediterranean. Considering the Yugoslav position on the Middle East crisis, and the status of the great powers in the Mediterranean, such a statement could have had serious consequences. Kissinger told US Secretary of Defense Melvin Laird that Nixon had made the statement without his or anyone's advice, and that it could endanger the visit to Yugoslavia.[40]

In a conversation with Secretary of State William Rogers, Kissinger again expressed his surprise and dissatisfaction with Nixon's statement: 'This could mean the end of the visit to Yugoslavia. I don't think he [Tito] can afford to have us now.'[41] On 19 September, the Yugoslav foreign ministry suggested that the Prime Minister, Mitja Ribičič, release a statement on the situation in Jordan. The goal was, as the foreign ministry formulated it, to 'confirm the Yugoslav position regarding the significant worsening of the crisis and the growing danger that the American demonstration of force turns into a military intervention'. The foreign ministry also believed that such a statement was necessary in light of 'the visit of President Nixon, in order to declare our positions, and to avoid potential disagreements and distortions of our positions'. The foreign ministry also sent messages to the Yugoslav embassies and missions in all the Arab countries, the Soviet Union, United States, China, France, and the United Kingdom, as well as to Romania and Poland, to explain the Yugoslav position on the Jordanian crisis.[42]

The statement confirmed the well-known Yugoslav position on the situation in the Middle East: support for Arabs in general (without specifying which) against Israel, while calling for a ceasefire between the Jordanian government and PLO. Equally important was the warning that any interference, or military intervention, would worsen the situation. This was also a message and a warning to the United States. The Yugoslav ambassador to Washington, Bogdan Crnobrnja, did not mention the Middle Eastern crisis in a conversation with Kissinger relating to the preparations for the visit. The American side must have been aware of the potential of Tito's reaction. At the height of the Jordanian crisis, on 21 September, Kissinger told Nixon that they should cancel the visit before someone else did. There were also problems with visiting the US 6th Fleet, on high alert at the time. Kissinger was inclined to postpone the entire European tour because he was concerned about a fragmented American leadership if the crisis escalated into a regional conflict. Nixon, however, decided to continue with the preparations.

Also problematic were some aspects surrounding the visit's protocols. The Yugoslavs did not dispatch the official invitation to the American president until 14 September. Nixon and Kissinger believed that Tito was assessing the potential consequences of Nixon's visit to Italy and the 6th Fleet. Tito's pro-Arab policy was also an issue, as well as the Yugoslav fear that their population might show more public affection for the American president than for the Yugoslav regime.[43] On 12 September Kissinger told Bob Haldeman, Nixon's Chief of Staff, that they would have to cancel the visit to Yugoslavia unless they soon received a formal invitation.[44] Finally on 14 September, the Yugoslav side formally extended the invitation, and preparations could proceed.

Another contentious issue was Nixon's itinerary: the White House wished to link the visits to Italy and Yugoslavia in order to reduce potential criticisms over Nixon's planned visit to Franco's fascist regime in Spain. Yugoslav diplomats wished their country to be linked neither to the Madrid regime nor to the 6th Fleet headquarter in Naples. Kissinger therefore asked the Yugoslav ambassador to suggest what would cause the least offence to Yugoslavia.[45] On 15 September, Ambassador Crnobrnja requested that the Americans announce their visit to Yugoslavia separately from the visits to the 6th Fleet and Spain. The Ambassador made it clear that he had very strict instructions from Belgrade on this.[46] Another problem for American protocol was how to organise the visit to the Avala

World War II memorial, which the Yugoslavs had proposed. Nixon was not keen but Kissinger insisted on including it to show respect for Yugoslavia's wartime past, and because of the danger that the Yugoslavs might cancel the whole visit over this symbolic gesture. Over Yugoslavia, Kissinger showed a remarkable talent for diplomacy: 'It is much worse if we force the Yugoslavs to cancel the ceremony than for us to accept it. Better for us to lose this argument than to win. If we win we lose.' Kissinger skilfully resolved the issue by pointing out to the Yugoslavs that there would be a similar ceremony in Spain.[47]

The White House and the State Department were considering several options over the visit to Belgrade. Zagreb was the most attractive option for a second stop, because it was the second-largest city and the capital of Croatia, and its airport could accommodate Air Force One, the presidential Boeing 707. Other options included visiting Brijuni, Tito's birthplace Kumrovec, the Macedonian capital Skopje, the newly built dam on the Danube at Đerdap, and the Federal Assembly. Along with a meeting with Tito, the Americans would also meet Prime Minister Ribičič, the president of the Federal Assembly Koča Popović, local officials in Zagreb and Skopje, and Patriarch German of the Serbian Orthodox Church, who at the time presided over the World Council of Churches. The final decision was made to visit Belgrade and Zagreb, because 'these two have the best audience', as well as Kumrovec.[48]

Henry Kissinger drafted a memorandum with instructions for the President, in which he pointed out the key issues in every country on the European tour. According to Kissinger, Yugoslavia was playing the most complex game of all the Mediterranean countries included in Nixon's itinerary. Kissinger highlighted the fact that Yugoslavia emphasised its non-alignment, but at the same time wished to retain its position and role in the communist movement. Although Yugoslavia often had foreign policy goals that conflicted with those of the United States, it was aware that its security and occasional skirmishes with the Soviets depended on America's role in preserving the Cold War balance and its presence in the Mediterranean.

Kissinger prepared an extensive memorandum on potential topics that might arise in the conversations with Tito and other Yugoslav officials. It is useful to quote this memo at length, entitled *Goals, Plans, Games, Themes,* because it accurately depicts Kissinger's views on Yugoslavia's international position and the US's role in preserving Yugoslav non-alignment:

> Before your arrival in Belgrade, most of the emphasis in public and governmental assessments of your trip will have revolved around the visit to the Fleet and its implications for our Middle Eastern, Mediterranean and even worldwide policy. Tito, although in effect having enjoyed substantial protection and assistance from us since he broke with the Soviets in 1948–49, nevertheless has been very clear in attempting to preserve a form of diplomatic neutrality as between East and West. He has publicly dissociated himself from our Vietnam policy and has been critical of our Middle Eastern actions and policies. The Yugoslavs, by insisting on delaying by a day the announcement of your visit, attempted to detach themselves from your visit to the Fleet (even though Tito knows its value to his own security).
>
> Tito personally, and the path he has sought to map for his country, is in many ways full of paradoxes and ambiguities. Thus, he remains firmly a Communist and (despite all his troubles with Moscow has never quite rid himself of the magnetism it still vaguely exerts on Communists of all stripes); yet he is also a fierce nationalist and, though very conscious of Soviet physical proximity, rejects Soviet hegemony in his region. He has, indeed, occasionally nurtured dreams of playing a regional leadership role himself, always raising Soviet objections. Tito has tried to preserve his Communist credentials, yet he has quite consciously relied on Western aid of all kinds. He knows very well that his defiance of Moscow has largely rested on our holding up our end of the basic power balance; yet he has preached non-alignment. He has adapted economic, political, administrative and cultural patterns and practices from the West.
>
> In dominating Yugoslav life and policies for 25 years he has frequently sought to give his country a role quite out of proportion with its size, location and potential. In some respects, he succeeded: he successfully broke with Moscow; he managed to make himself something of a model for other Communists (though less so than he hoped and Moscow feared); for a while his non-aligned world and its conference appeared to acquire some coherence and force, but now, apart from the tarnished Nasser, he remains the lone pillar (the likes of Nehru, Sukarno,

Nkrumah, etc., having disappeared) and the movement itself lacks momentum, purpose and force. (He has just returned from the Lusaka conference on the non-aligned, which caused hardly a ripple.)[49]

Historically, one of the greatest question marks that hangs over any assessment of Tito's accomplishments is what happens after he is gone. At 78, the time is not far off and he has taken measures to provide for an orderly succession by collectivizing the Party leadership and, most recently, announcing a similar approach to the Government. (This effort at collectivization, and playing down his own role, may not be solely related to the succession but to some vague sense on Tito's part that the era of the single, all-powerful leader may have run its course generally. Moreover, it would not be inconsistent with his ego for him to suppose that no single individual could replace him, anyway.)

Beyond this, there remains the question whether the diverse, vigorous and proud nationalities that make up the Federation will hold together once Tito's magnetism and unifying role are gone. Tito's efforts to create stable governing institutions are undoubtedly in part designed to cope with this problem of cohesion. One aspect of it is the question of whether the Soviets would seek to inject themselves into a succession struggle. (Apart from occasional jitters about possible Soviet military action, as at the time of Czechoslovakia, Tito remains very alert to any Soviet efforts to build up connections among Yugoslav political groups.)

While you will get a warm and friendly popular reception, it is unlikely to expect the dramatic and moving character of last year's demonstration in Bucharest. The occasion will be less emotion-packed for a people that has long since enjoyed extensive contact with the outside world; nor as dramatic an act of emancipation from Soviet overlordship. Tito, himself, will receive you with dignity and quiet satisfaction that the President of the United States has come to see him. Assured of his towering eminence, he will not, as Ceausescu did last year, regard and use your presence at his side as a means of consolidating his political position at home.

Tito likes along conversations and he likes to talk a great deal himself. At his age and with his background he will not be reluctant to give advice or express criticism (even when, with his sense of power realities, he comprehends that if his advice led to a decline in American power and manoeuvrability, the security of his own country could suffer).

Along with this extensive analysis of Yugoslavia's realities and Tito's personality, Kissinger added a few additional goals for Nixon's visit. The purpose was to establish personal contact with Tito, to emphasise American interest in Yugoslavia's progress, and to promote Yugoslavia's unique political system and international position. This was particularly related to Yugoslavia's non-acceptance of the Brezhnev Doctrine, which had been used to justify the invasion in Czechoslovakia, and to the promotion of liberalisation in Eastern Europe and the Soviet Union.[50] The Yugoslav reaction later showed that Nixon and Kissinger succeeded in their objectives. This was confirmed in a conversation between Kissinger and the former Secretary of Defense, then president of the World Bank, Robert McNamara. Kissinger told McNamara that the visit to Yugoslavia made the whole tour worthwhile and would have positive long-term consequences.[51]

Tito had the skill to insert himself into international affairs as a trusted arbiter, elevating Yugoslavia's importance. During Nixon's visit to Belgrade, the formal dialogue in the morning of 1 October 1970 between Nixon's team included Kissinger, Rogers and Leonhart, and Tito's entourage that included Ribičič, Tepavac and Ambassador Crnobrnja. The items on the agenda included a wide range of international affairs, including bilateral relations, the Middle East, 'Black Africa', Algeria and Vietnam. Tito had connected well to Middle Eastern leaders and movements, and conveyed their messages to Nixon and Kissinger, who in turn asked Tito to use his influence for achieving ceasefires. Tito was asked about the opinions of African states of American aid, and responded that 'aid without interference will end well.' Regarding Vietnam, Tito proposed a third way between the stalemate on the diplomatic front and the uncertain progress on the military front, suggesting a provisional joint government between North and South Vietnam to choose their own government, adding that just like Algeria, he was convinced the Vietnam question cannot be settled by military victory by either side.[52]

The American embassy report noted the positive impressions in Yugoslavia left by Nixon's visit. Ambassador Leonhart wrote that the visit had a huge impact on Yugoslav media and the public. Particularly impressive were Nixon's direct speeches to the crowds in Belgrade, and even more so in Zagreb. Many citizens told the American diplomats they were surprised by the President's direct approach. In private conversations with Yugoslav officials, the American diplomats discovered that Nixon's visit was well received in top-level meetings of the Yugoslav leadership. Tito and the State Secretary for Foreign Affairs, Mirko Tepavac, spoke for an hour and a half about Nixon's visit to the Presidency of the Central Committee of the LCY. Similarly, Prime Minister Ribičič reported on Nixon's visit to the Executive Council. In a private conversation with Leonhart, Ribičič mentioned that this was one of the most important visits ever to Yugoslavia by a foreign statesman. He added that Tito liked people who 'don't speak through a curtain', which is why he liked Churchill, and viewed Nixon in a similar light. Many heads of diplomatic missions in Belgrade told Leonhart that they had never seen so much enthusiasm among the people of Belgrade. The Zagreb consulate confirmed a similar mood in Croatia. Leonhart's report concluded that the stability of this part of Europe, as well as the establishment of good processes of communication between East and West, remained important for the United States. The President's visit only strengthened these policy goals.[53]

The Croatian and Serbian diasporas reacted differently to Nixon's visit. A part of the Croatian diaspora believed that by visiting Yugoslavia Nixon had given undeserved support for Tito's communist regime, but the president of the exiled Croatian Peasants' Party, Dr Juraj Krnjević, reacted positively to Nixon's visit and his Zagreb statement, 'Long live Croatia!' In these cases, the State Department tried to justify supporting a communist regime. On the other hand, when the Serbian politicians in exile Milan Gavrilović and Branislav Stanišić complained about Nixon's visit from a 'Greater Serbia' perspective, the State Department did not react.[54]

In bilateral talks during the visit, the Yugoslav and American officials mostly discussed foreign policy topics and Yugoslav–American relations. The American embassy recommended to the White House that it should avoid treating Yugoslavia as a part of the communist bloc, a country behind the Iron Curtain, or even as an Eastern European country. The embassy also recommended not commenting on relations between the nationalities and the republics, and added that negotiations on material support should be concrete and precise, 'because the Yugoslavs quickly interpret general discussions as promises'.

It is interesting to include here the conversation between Kissinger and foreign minister Tepavac during the flight from Zagreb back to Belgrade. The topic was Vietnam. Kissinger complained that the North Vietnamese were treating them like children taking an exam, in which they were required to learn and respond to questions without the possibility of a discussion. This remark was related to the Paris talks that would eventually lead to the end of American engagement in Vietnam. Kissinger hinted that the Yugoslavs might influence the North Vietnamese negotiators to be more flexible. Tepavac agreed. He confirmed that Yugoslavia had contacts with North Vietnam, including in Paris. He was ready to talk with them, and try to convince them 'not to treat the US like a child and to be more realistic with their demands'. Kissinger also mentioned that it would be useful if the Yugoslav side could study future American proposals, which Yugoslav diplomats could discuss with the North Vietnamese in any way they found appropriate.

For Tepavac, however, a conversation about the Brezhnev Doctrine was more important. He was concerned about the vague statement given by the American Secretary of State, William Rogers, that the United States believed that the Soviet Union would be more careful in applying the Brezhnev Doctrine to Yugoslavia. Tepavac wanted to clarify whether this meant that the US was having second thoughts about helping Yugoslavia in case of a Soviet attack, and whether the US had communicated directly with the Soviets over this. Kissinger replied that, regardless of how Rogers's statement was formulated, the Soviets must know that they couldn't do anything against Yugoslavia without grave consequences.[55]

Tepavac next asked Kissinger whether he could ask him 'an airplane question', that is, an exclusively personal question. He asked whether an attack on Yugoslavia would result in World War III. Kissinger replied that such a possibility could not be ignored. Tepavac then asked whether there would be a reaction to an attack, to which Kissinger replied that this depended on many factors and primarily on whether the Yugoslavs would fight to defend themselves. Tepavac replied that the majority of the population would defend Yugoslavia. It should be noted that the potential attacker was never named in the conversation. The conversation revealed that the

Yugoslav leadership genuinely feared a Soviet attack. At that moment, the plane landed in Belgrade, and the conversation ended.[56]

Although Nixon's visit had a sensational response, the most controversial moment was his final toast in the Banski Dvori, the seat of the Croatian government, where he ended his speech with, 'Long live Croatia, long live Yugoslavia!' These words have been interpreted differently by historians and the public over the past 45 years. To this day, many still view these words as American support for Croatian independence. But there is too much evidence to the contrary. The statement was simply a courtesy meant to give support for the integrity of the Yugoslav federal state, which could be compared to the American federal structure. The fact was that the US wanted to see a more liberal and less centralised Yugoslavia as part of their goal to reduce Soviet influence in Eastern Europe.[57] In addition, successive American administrations hoped that a more liberal and decentralised Yugoslavia would more easily overcome its economic and ethnic problems. In this sense, Nixon's statement can be viewed as support for greater political and economic autonomy, but only within the bounds of a federal Yugoslavia.

The only mention in American diplomatic documents of Nixon's toast was a report on the conversation between Adolph Dubs, the head of the Soviet Department at the State Department, and Radovan Vukadinović, professor in political science at the University of Zagreb. At the time, Professor Vukadinović was a visiting researcher at Columbia University's Research Institute on Communist Affairs. Vukadinović described the situation in Yugoslavia as 'a strange and dangerous time for the country.' He hoped that the US would continue to support Yugoslav unity, to which Dubs replied that Nixon's visit and Tito's visit to the US, planned for 1971, was evidence that the American administration supported Yugoslav national integrity and unity. Vukadinović added that some in Croatia interpreted Nixon's speech as American support for Croatia's efforts to move closer to the West, as a counterbalance to East-leaning Serbia. Dubs objected that this interpretation of Nixon's speech was incorrect, and reiterated that the US government supported Yugoslav unity.[58]

The Yugoslav diplomatic community did not receive Nixon's statement well. Ambassador to Washington Bogdan Crnobrnja noted in his July 1971 report on Yugoslav–American relations that Nixon's visit to Zagreb was not accidental but needed to be understood in the context of the internal crisis that Yugoslavia had been going through. According to Crnobrnja, by visiting Zagreb Nixon had shown increased interest in the Western part of Yugoslavia in the context of strategic positioning in the event of a split between the country's east and west. He continued, 'The period since Nixon's visit has convinced the Americans that they were right to visit Zagreb.'[59]

The differences in interpretation continued. In December 1976, the top Croatian official Jure Bilić mentioned that Nixon had emphasised the historical contribution of the Croatian nation, while neglecting sufficiently to emphasise the concept of Yugoslavia and the Yugoslav nations. Bilić stated, 'When I saw Nixon's gaffe, I had the impression that he had already started the process of breaking up Yugoslavia.' He added a conspiratorial flourish – that foreign intelligence services were involved in the Croatian crisis of December 1971. The State Department reacted to his statement by complaining to the new Yugoslav Ambassador, Dimče Belovski, and demanding an explanation of the accusation that President Nixon supported Croatian separatist tendencies. The State Department spokesman made the following statement:

> We asked the Yugoslavs for an official explanation because these charges from a senior Yugoslav official involved an attack on the policy of a former president and might be construed as having implications today.[60]

8

1971: Yugoslavia in Crisis

'The poachers must be got to take over the job of gamekeepers.'
– Ambassador Terence Garvey[1]

The year 1971 witnessed an accumulation of crises in different areas that would ultimately lead Tito to purge the liberal leadership in Croatia and across Yugoslavia from December onwards. The national crises persisted despite well-intended constitutional amendments and economic decentralisation, which ultimately failed to balance national and economic aspirations with the requirements of the federal state. The year of crisis witnessed further decentralisation, even if liberalisation was hampered by the perceived rise of nationalism and the party's resolve to stay firmly in control. Student protests, émigré nationalists, renewed language disputes and pressures from the delicate Cold War balance were all factors in Tito's decision finally to take action after his repeated warnings to the Croatian liberals.

Constitutional Changes

On 21 September 1970, at the meeting of the Zagreb party, Tito announced major changes in the functioning of the state administration.[2] The existing system transferred many powers from the federation to the republics, giving the republics *de facto* control over the Federal Assembly, which oversaw the work of the federal government. In practice, the republics often used their newly acquired powers to block the government's economic decisions. 'Republican particularism' began to suffocate the work of the federal administration, of which the 1969 Slovene road affair was a good example. In addition, the decision making process was paralysed by strict implementation of the dual quota system, which left behind considerations for either a federal national interest and the competence of civil servants. It became harder to forge common ground between republics on the everyday functioning of the state. This was particularly obvious in the Coordination Commission of the Federal Executive Council and the Chamber of Nationalities of the Federal Assembly. In order to alleviate this situation, Tito once again took the initiative. In August 1970, he proposed the creation of a collective state presidency. He had two major reasons for this move: similarly to the Executive Bureau of the party, the new state presidency was supposed to gather the most influential politicians from around the country. Secondly, the presidency would assume the political role for major decisions, leaving the Executive Bureau with the responsibility to carry them out.[3]

The existence of the state presidency would make the decision making processes of the party presidency easier, and return to the party the role of the 'creator' and not the 'executor' of political decisions. In addition, the collective presidency was intended as a solution to the problem of Tito's succession, to prevent a potential fight for his position. The goal was to create a body that would not exclusively represent the interests of the republics but the country as a whole. The key of a successful reorganisation was the relationship between the future presidency and the republics, and the transfer of some powers back to the presidency. Tito emphasised that the presidency would not be composed of the highest representatives from the republics but rather the most able people from all the republics. They were supposed to represent an independent body which would solve national problems and not merely be beholden to their local interests. Tito's announcement was once again met with unease in Belgrade, because he did not make it at the meeting of the LCY presidium, which was held in Zagreb at the same time, but at a semi-formal gathering with the Croatian party leadership. This move was interpreted in Belgrade as downgrading the party presidium and demonstrating Tito's favouritism towards Croatia.[4]

The Presidium of the LCY formed a working group in 1970 that was supposed to create a platform for the transformation of existing state administration. On 25 September, Edvard Kardelj presented a draft with constitutional amendments to the Executive Bureau with an emphasis on the creation of a new presidency of the Socialist Federal Republic of Yugoslavia.[5]

The British ambassador to Belgrade (1968–71), Terence Garvey, defined this policy in his October 1970 report:

> The reorganisation is designed to kill two birds with one stone: the problem of the succession and the problem of the cohesion of Yugoslavia. But the succession problem is only a particular case, exemplifying (albeit in critical form) the problem of cohesion which is the main issue.[6]

The problem of Tito's succession was only the tip of the iceberg, but it attracted the most interest in the West. The solution was in the creation of the new presidency composed of representatives of all the republics and regions, as well as representatives from party structures, the socialist alliance, the unions, youth organisations, and the army. Tito would retain his role as president of the Presidency for life, while after his death, the post would be rotated annually around the representatives of the republics.

A bigger problem was the long-term sustainability of the Yugoslav federation. The process of decentralisation that started in the 1950s had irreversibly changed the attitudes of the republics towards the federal state. All the republics were autonomous units with their own state structures that had gained increasing powers throughout the 1960s. The 1967 and 1968 constitutional changes strengthened the role of the Federal Assembly, and the constitution allowed the Federal Assembly to make decisions only with the consent of all the republics. The greatest loser was the Federal Executive Council, which could not function efficiently without the approval of a Federal Assembly that was now effectively controlled by republican factions.[7]

According to Ambassador Garvey, only the Federal Executive Council was paying attention to the common national interest. The republics that represented the interests of their enterprises did the complete opposite:

> In consequence the economy is not developing as is should, and the cohesion of the Federation is placed under increasing strain because the existing institutions enable and encourage the republics (particularly the Croats, but also the Slovenes) to go it alone. This situation is fraught with long term danger, particularly when, as many fear, the Russians may put the screws on Yugoslavia once Tito is out of the way.[8]

Ambassador Garvey's main argument in support of preserving the efficiency of the Yugoslav federation was to continue with the independent development of the Yugoslav model of socialism. Even more important for him was the establishment and efficiency of a single market for 20 million consumers of Yugoslav products, which was supposed to be in everyone's interest. For this system to function, however, the federation required the authority to regulate and coordinate the interests of all the republics. Previous experience showed that the past federal governments could not pursue this goal effectively. Garvey compared the Federal Executive Council to a gamekeeper without a gun trying to control well-armed poachers. In that sense, in order for the federation to function, the poachers had to take the role of gamekeepers, that is, the republics had to assume responsibility for rational management of the federation.

The reorganisation included further reductions in federal powers, which were now limited to foreign policy, defence and the common market, while everything else was meant to be transferred to the republic. The national quota system would be used to further decentralise federal bodies, to complete the process that had started in 1965. Garvey observed, 'This process is designed to remove the abiding neurosis in some of the republics (Croatia first and foremost) that someone ('they') at the centre is trying to push them around.'

The newly created state presidency, in practice, took over several powers from the Federal Assembly. The purpose of the presidency was also to handle the economic and political issues, rather than the Federal Executive Council that lacked the ability to do so. The question Western diplomats were asking was why would the republican representatives in the presidency behave any differently than before? After all, they had represented, would continue to represent, and exclusively represent the interests of their republics. Edvard Kardelj believed that once they assumed responsibilities for the federation, they would act differently. Naturally this process included a strong role of the party that was supposed to provide a moral compass. Garvey was sceptical: 'I should guess, myself, that this last is, in the long-term, a losing battle but I would not discount the chances of Kardelj's main argument proving valid.'[9]

On 9 December 1970, Tito addressed the Federal Assembly and proposed to initiate the process of drafting and adopting amendments to the constitution, based on Kardelj's proposals. In the period between December 1970 and June 1971, 22 constitutional amendments were adopted that significantly restructured political and economic arrangements in accordance with Kardelj's vision. The most important change was the introduction of the collective state presidency, which reconfigured relations with other federal bodies as well as relations between the federation and the republics. The amendments also left foreign policy, monetary policy and national defence policy with the federation.

The state presidency, with Tito as president for life, now had a direct line to the Federal Assembly without mediation by the Federal Executive Council. This meant that the state presidency could propose federal laws and constitutional amendments directly. The republics would gain greater responsibilities towards the common interest: major federal decisions now required unanimous approval by the republics, including fiscal and monetary policy, foreign trade, customs, price controls, funding of underdeveloped areas, and the funding of federal bodies. Several amendments called for the creation and functioning of a common market, and prohibited republican legislation in conflict with these provisions.

The republics were defined as 'states' based on the 'sovereignty of nations', which at the time did not add much. But with the onset of the wars of the 1990s, these provisions were a powerful legal instrument used by Slovenia and Croatia to declare independence from federal Yugoslavia. Lastly, the constitutional amendments enshrined the concept of 'Total People's Defence', with concomitant mass military exercises for all able-bodied men and women ready to repel any Soviet or Western invasion.

With the new amendments alone, however, the process of reorganisation was not complete. Immediately after the 22 amendments were approved, Edvard Kardelj's coordination commission proposed more draft amendments about the work of the Federal Assembly and the system of self-management, the commune system at the municipal level, and the judiciary. These would all be enshrined in the 1974 constitution.[10]

The 1971 constitutional changes were the fourth attempt by the Yugoslav leadership since 1963 to solve the permanent political and economic crisis of the multinational state. The only constant factor in all these efforts was increasing decentralisation and the strengthening of the republics. The main consequences included increasing difficulties in the management of the federal state bodies. The process of decentralisation went so far that Western diplomats started to wonder whether it could go any further without Yugoslavia becoming a confederacy. By August 1971, the newly appointed British Ambassador Dugald Stewart was more pessimistic than his predecessor on the future of Yugoslavia:

> Yugoslavia is now so undisciplined that the present Constitutional changes led to raucous public bargaining by Republican leaders and in consequence to a severe political crisis.[11]

The West and the Croatian National Question in 1971

Western diplomats were continually preoccupied with the tensions between the Yugoslav nations and republics. British and American diplomats were very aware of nationalist difficulties, and treated them as a great threat to the integrity of the Yugoslav state which were interrelated with economic tensions. In February 1971, the British consul-general in Zagreb, Joseph Dobbs, wrote an elaborate report on nationalism in Croatia. He wanted to establish the extent to which it was a threat to the Yugoslav state:

> It is natural, before coming to Yugoslavia, to imagine a country inhabited by Yugoslavs. Living here you find out that the people around you think of themselves as Serbs, Croats, Slovenes etc. They belong to Yugoslavia rather as a Belgian or a Dutchman belongs to Benelux. The primary loyalty is to their historic nationality. This, at any rate, is the impression one gets here in the north.

[...] Only a few years ago there was a distinct gulf, in the attitude towards nationalism, between the man in the street in Croatia and the Party authorities. I am told that immediately after the war it was unwise even to call yourself a Croat: in those days all had to be Yugoslavs. It is now quite different. [...] Everyone tells you, especially people in the cultural world, that things are far freer now than even a short time ago. Matica hrvatska – the publishing house and society for the advancement of Croatian culture – is thriving as never before; and the views of the Croatian intelligentsia on the need to preserve the distinctiveness of the Croatian language, which were taboo in 1967, are tacitly accepted by the Croatian political leadership today.[12]

Dobbs observed that not only the older generations, who remembered pre-war Croatia, were the ones promoting national feelings, but the younger generation were doing so as well. A good example was the election of Zvonimir Čičak as the student Vice Chancellor of Zagreb University. He won the support of the majority of students and university professors, primarily for his non-communist and Catholic reputation, and because he stood against the party candidate. There was no doubt that the average Croatian student favoured Croatian nationalism more than Marxism or self-management.[13] The key change in the attitude towards nationalism happened after the 10th meeting of the CC LCC that had a strong pro-Croatian and anti-Belgrade character, especially on the economy. Since then the Croatian party had proved to be an uncompromising protector of the Croatian national interest, although it was careful to distance itself from more extreme manifestations of Croatian nationalism. Even Miko Tripalo, who was one of the most influential Yugoslav politicians, was behaving like an exclusively Croatian politician, especially with regard to economic nationalism.

The Croatian fight for securing her economic interests was the central theme in all political speeches by Croatian leaders and the priority in all of *Vjesnik*'s publications. The main argument was that Croatia was not receiving a fair share of investment capital and foreign currency, although Croatia contributed 40 per cent of Yugoslav foreign currency income. The Croatians also complained that as a net exporter of goods and services, Croatia did so at a loss because of the unrealistic foreign exchange rates.

159

Grievances were directed specifically at the Belgrade bank monopoly that managed to maintain a privileged position throughout the period of decentralisation.

Despite these complaints, Croatians generally wanted to remain part of a federal Yugoslavia. Realistically, there was no political force capable of overthrowing the existing regimes in either Yugoslavia or Croatia. The current generation of Croatian political leaders were young, intelligent and had good prospects of successful political careers. Underneath the superficial liberalism stood a police and security apparatus that had every interest in preserving the communist regime. Consul-General Dobbs found the idea of turning Croatia into some kind of Slavic Denmark to be impractical:

> For such a solution there is neither the political tradition – Croatia has always been part of a larger political community – nor an economic urge [...] To talk of the 'disintegration' of Yugoslavia as a result of present stresses, in the sense of parts of Yugoslavia breaking off from each other, seems to me, then, to ignore objective realities.

He viewed Yugoslavia as a federal state with sovereign republics that could function similarly to a European common market.[14]

The British Ambassador to Belgrade, and Dobbs's superior, Ambassador Garvey, held much harsher views on Croatian nationalism. Although Croatian politicians assured him that no one was thinking of Croatia outside Yugoslavia's borders, he was stunned to learn how irresponsible some articles in Croatian newspapers and public statements by Croatian politicians had been – especially Miko Tripalo's. According to Garvey, they were a part of a propaganda campaign to strengthen the arguments for a better position for Croatia in the federation:

> A number of issues – the so called 'State Capital', the alleged cornering by others of Croatia's hard-won foreign exchange resources, the exploitation of Croatian industry by Belgrade 'finance capital' and the rest – themselves insubstantial or devoid of substance have been magnified out of all measure and supported by emotive clamour and the selective use of statistics [...] Some of my colleagues here express fears that past, and possible future demonstrations of Croat rapacity and self-assertion may, if

carried too far, generate a backlash which could destroy the basis of confidence on which the Yugoslav federation must rely for its survival. If other republics were all as psychologically mixed-up and nasty as the Croats sometimes show themselves, this would indeed represent quite a serious danger.

Garvey added:

> Fortunately, however, Serbia is now led by, and for the pres-ent at least firmly under the control of, a group headed by its Party chairman, Mr. Marko Nikezić, who combines firmness and political skill with an inflexible determination to make the Yugoslav federation work. He is ably abetted by the Slovene leadership under Mr. Stane Kavčič. Slovenia, as one of the chief gainers from the single market, well knows that its future depends upon close understanding and collaboration with all the republics and especially with Serbia.[15]

The Foreign Office (FCO) believed that the position of Croatia was the key for the survival of Yugoslavia, and there were reasonable hopes that the renewed state structure would satisfy her demands. Brian Sparrow, of the FCO's Eastern Europe desk, wrote in a letter to his colleague J.L. Bullard:

> The attitude of Croatia is crucial to the continual existence of Yugoslavia, and there seems to be reasonable hope that the new structure will make her more satisfied with her position within a united Yugoslavia. It is certainly better that Croat nationalism should find expression, within reasonable bounds, in the press and in open discussion, rather than it should be supressed and allowed to ferment until an explosion is inevitable [...] There are, however, two necessary preconditions for the continuance of a united Yugoslavia. Firstly all the nationalities, but particu-larly the Croats and the Serbs, must show considerable political subtlety and finesse and not allow their common interests to be obscured by nationalist irrelevancies [...] The second condition is that there should be no interference from outside Yugoslavia.[16]

In the same year, American diplomats also paid close attention to Croatian nationalism. Their May report reflected on the Croatian myths that played a strong role in the revival of Croatian national feelings. These myths

Figure 8.1 *The Arrival of Croats at the Adriatic Sea*, Oton Iveković (1905).

were promoted in the nationalist art of Oton Iveković (1869–1939), which included the mythic medieval arrival of heroic Croat knights at the Adriatic; the siege of Siget and death of Nikola Šubić Zrinski; and the execution of the Croatian noblemen Zrinski and Frankopan by the Habsburgs for their attempt to create a Croatian independent state.

Consul-General Orme Wilson observed that the Croatian intelligentsia was reviving these myths, but the common Croat was also eager to subscribe to these myths in support of Croatian statehood. The Croatian political leaders recognised and supported these trends:

> The red and white checkerboard can be seen everywhere in Croatia today, on automobile windshields, shoulder or arm patches sported by young persons on leather jackets, overcoats, and berets, lapel pins, rings, a new 'cognac' produced under the label 'Zrinski' and on phonograph records of the Croatian national anthem 'How Beautiful our Homeland' (Lijepa Nasa Domovina). The local Zagreb soccer team, whose colors have traditionally been blue and white, has introduced a new badge featuring the checkerboard. The symbol featuring part of the escutcheon of the Triune Kingdom (Croatia, Dalmatia and Slavonia) of Austro-Hungarian times gleams from the

brilliantly tiled roof of St. Mark's church in Zagreb's Old Town, a 'national monument' now undergoing extensive restoration by the Republican government.[17]

The Croatian tricolour flag was a part of everyday decoration. It could be seen on chocolate boxes and at weddings and it was regularly positioned alongside Yugoslav and party flags. During the May Day celebration of 1971, Wilson counted double the number of Croatian to Yugoslav flags. It was even more obvious that the Yugoslav flags would be paired with the Croatian one, while Croatian flags were presented on their own ten times more frequently.

> No one knows for certain when or how the first Croatians reached the Adriatic coast, but the standard image is reproduced in a local painting to be seen in Croatian homes. It depicts a mighty column of medieval knights, led by an heroic Zrinski clad in shining checker-board armor bestriding a cliff overlooking the Adriatic, claiming the sea for Croatiandom much as Columbus stepping ashore in the New World.

Wilson also mentioned that the reconstruction of the medieval town of Nin was under way, with slightly more historical accuracy than the national myths. Nin was the first centre of the autonomous Croatian branch of the Catholic Church, and the church exhibition of gold and silver from the Zadar cathedral was well received by both officials and public in Zagreb.

The opera *Nikola Šubić Zrinski* was regularly performed in the Zagreb theatre to popular acclaim. The audience's reaction to the waving of the Croatian flag in the dramatic final scene was so strong that the party considered banning the scene.

> No more. In fact an attempt in 1970 by a Croatian playwright and LC member Marijan Matkovic to portray Nikola Subic Zrinski as a megalomaniac along Dr. Strangelove lines so enraged the Croatian public that the play was withdrawn from the repertory after only three performances. A few years ago, however, Zrinskis and Frankopans were officially in the 'Feudalist' category.[18]

The 300th anniversary of the anti-Habsburg conspiracy led by Krsto Frankopan and Petar Zrinski was celebrated with press supplements and the release of a popular new LP. The historical fact that these men were willing to cooperate with the Turks to gain Croatian independence did not affect their status as Croatian heroes. On the anniversary of their execution on 30 April, the Croatian Archbishop Kuharić celebrated their memory in Zagreb Cathedral, along with a number of Croatian intellectuals and public officials. Their speeches were extremely nationalist in tone, and for the first time in 25 years, the Croatian anthem was performed in the cathedral.[19]

The opera *Nikola Šubić Zrinski* opened the theatre season on 2 October 1971. Wilson noted that the opera revealed how open expressions of nationalism had become:

> Prolonged and often rhythmic clapping interrupted the performance and led to repeated curtain calls. When Zrinjski kissed the Croatian red and white checkerboard banner at the close of the final scene just before he and his assembled nobles sally forth from Siget for a last stand against the Turks, applause was so great and prolonged that even those in the first row could no longer hear the music, leave alone the singers' voices, for the remainder of the scene. Then, after many curtain calls marked by continuous, enthusiastic, and rhythmic clapping, the opening strains of Croatia's anthem 'Lijepa Nasa Domovina' ('Our Beautiful Homeland') began to peal forth from the galleries. Soon almost the whole audience was in voice. Some members of the orchestra sat in the pit looking upward with moist eyes. Almost all in the theatre seemed carried away by the moment except for a few in boxes who may well have been connected with organs of public administration. There was no radiance in their faces, and their lips were still.

He observed that the enthusiasm of the audience could be partially attributed to an excellent performance, but the reaction would probably be the same even if the performance wasn't good. It was about expressing national feelings, although one regular opera attendee privately conceded to Wilson that the overenthusiastic manifestation of nationalism could invite negative reactions.[20]

The new British ambassador to Belgrade, Dugald Stewart, had replaced Terence Garvey in April 1971. He visited Croatia and Slovenia in June and was surprised by how developed these two republics were. He gave examples of successful businesses: INA, Agrokombinat and the Slovenian Iskra. The Croatian oil company INA had become the largest business in Yugoslavia, and it did not have enough capacity to meet national demand, which had doubled every three years. Agrokombinat, which cultivated 400 acres of land in 1960, controlled 40,000 acres and 400 shops by 1971. The ambassador was stunned by the claim that the company was the largest producer of eggs in Europe. Stewart added, however, that 'unless there has been some total suspension of the normal laws of farm economics I would guess that it had also one of the largest bank overdrafts in Europe.' The Slovenian kitchen appliance company Iskra covered a radius of 600 km with its products, which also included Milan, and ended at the gates of Siemens.

Stewart also noted different a different attitude towards management. Most enterprises had been led by cadres whose only qualification was their participation in the war and who had only recently retired. Most new managers were university-educated and had at least ten years experience in industry and trade. Management and productivity, however, still did not reach Western European standards. Stewart had the impression that this part of Yugoslavia was developing entirely in line with membership of the European Economic Community (EEC). Although nobody formally confirmed this, such an atmosphere was omnipresent. Such ambitions were usually packaged as part of an effort to increase quality and value in order to reach Western and world markets, while the management of Iskra was already including EEC membership in its long-term planning.

Stewart spoke to Savka Dabčević-Kučar and Miko Tripalo, who were without question the most influential Croatian leaders. His impression was that the Croats were eager to educate new ambassadors. He believed that these politicians followed the party line while rejecting the claim that they were weakening Yugoslav unity. This all sounded well and good to Stewart, especially since Savka and Tripalo belonged to a new type of politician: intelligent, persuasive, and unburdened by ideological dogma. In informal talks, however, the ambassador wasn't so easily convinced that Croatia was on the right course.[21]

Stewart visited an acquaintance of his wife in Zagreb, an unnamed retired General, together with Ivan Šibl, the president of the Veterans Association of Croatia. The General was very angry, blaming the centralists in Belgrade for everything that was wrong with Croatia, including the previous year's poor potato harvest. He was particularly angry at Ranković's agents, who he claimed were still in control. Šibl was more moderate. He pointed out that he had fought for Yugoslavia, and twelve years ago he would not regard himself first as a Croat, but as a Yugoslav. He was still in favour of a federal Yugoslavia, but 'only if it is the kind of Yugoslavia I want.'

A third example of the national mood that Stewart reported on was the ban on a cartoon in Belgrade newspapers *Vecernje novosti* that was allegedly insulting to Croatia. None of Stewart's sources could understand what the cartoon meant, but all insisted that it was offensive.[22] The American diplomats interpreted it as an allusion to Tito's speech in Sarajevo, in which he attacked 'café plotters' within the Croatian leadership.[23]

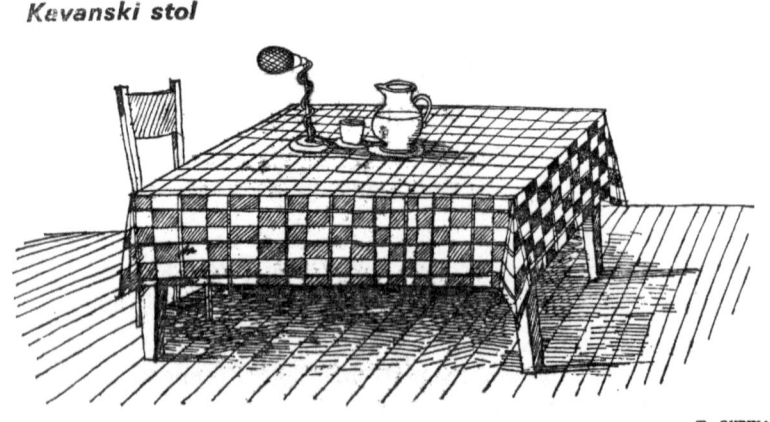

Figure 8.2 'Kavanski stol' ('Coffeehouse table') in the Belgrade newspaper *Vecernje Novosti* on 25 May 1971, a cartoon few understood, but everyone in Croatia agreed was offensive. The table has the chequered pattern of the Croatian flag, a cup of coffee, and a microphone. The 'café plotters' were an invisible force, according to Tito.

Stewart could not understand the transfer of authority from the federation to the republics with regard to foreign affairs, especially in the establishment of foreign affairs at the republic level. It was similar with defence, which along with foreign affairs, witnessed the development of parallel defence structures in the implementation of the 'Total People's Defence' concept. These included separate arms stockpiles under civilian control in the republics that would play a key role in the 1990s wars. For Stewart, however, the greatest problem remained in the economic sphere and the functioning of the common market.

The only thing that Zagreb and Belgrade had in common was anti-Russian feeling, although this was also subjected to different national perspectives:

> Even this piece of entirely common ground between Croats and Serbs is distorted by the nationalities question since in the more myopic Croat eyes centralist Ranković agents are all plotting to deliver Yugoslavia to the Russians and the equivalent Serbs see Jelić as linked with the Russians and the Croat Central Committee.[24]

University and Students

The British and American diplomats were very interested in the Čičak affair, at the beginning of 1971. In December 1970 Zagreb University organised elections to elect a new Chancellor, a Vice Chancellor and, for the first time, a Student Vice Chancellor, who would represent students on university bodies. The creation of this position was proposed by the Student Union, the only such organisation at the student level established with party and state support. This initiative was part of an agreement between student leaders and Chancellor Ivan Supek to support his re-election.

The day before the election, the Zagreb Student Union elected Slobodan Lang as their new president, while supporting Damir Grubiša as their candidate for Student Vice Chancellor. They both had immaculate political pedigrees and the unreserved support of the party and media. Unexpectedly, Ivan Zvonimir Čičak, a comparative literature and law student, was elected by students and faculty. Few people had expected that an outsider and a person who already had problems with the regime for his nationalism had managed to defeat the official candidate. His success was a clear sign of revolt against the common practice of staging rigged elections. It was also a slap in the face of communist one-party rule.[25]

In January 1971, British diplomats spoke to several students about Čičak. Ivo Bičanić, a member of the Student Union's leadership, said that Čičak could not remain Student Vice Chancellor because he was an anti-regime candidate. Bičanić further complained that Čičak was elected not by students but with the support of university lecturers, who wanted to protest against the party practice of rigging university leadership elections. He admitted that he would also like to express his dissatisfaction with official behaviour, but only a political ignoramus could vote for Čičak considering what he represented. According to Bičanić, a few months earlier Čičak had stated that Croatia should leave the federation.

As an excellent speaker, Čičak managed to gain student support as an opposition candidate. On the other side, Damir Grubiša was a less impressive personality. The public received Čičak's election as a sign of greater freedom, while the party-controlled media refrained from mentioning that he was not the party's preferred candidate.[26]

The Economist headlined its article on Čičak's election 'Zagreb's Cicero', noting that a student had been elected for the first time as university vice chancellor and that the election had caused controversy. Despite the election being a fair one, Čičak did not enjoy the support of the official student organisation. Other student leaders sought to undermine Čičak's success, arguing that he was a bad student, a practising Catholic, an extreme Croatian nationalist, that he was in touch with leading opposition intellectuals, and similar crimes. Although they tried to boycott him and organise his removal, he had the support of both the majority of the students and faculty. The London weekly commented that it was ironic that this had happened to student leaders who were moderate and progressive in their own right but had failed to gain popular support, when the tide was turning against the one-party system. Most students were dissatisfied with the slow progress of political and economic reform in Croatia. The best sign of this was the emigration of thousands of people to the West in search of jobs. *The Economist* concluded that with the attempt to remove Čičak, the student leadership had missed the opportunity to show that they were not the manipulators that Čičak portrayed them to be.[27]

The American consulate in Zagreb was following the university drama even more eagerly.[28] The American consul-general Orme Wilson commented that the 'establishment' of the official youth and student organisations in Zagreb and Croatia had lost one of the most important and freest elections they had ever participated in. The election seriously shook the morale of young careerist communists, when to their huge surprise the party candidate Damir Grubiša was defeated in the second round. The president of the Zagreb Student Union, Slobodan Lang, immediately started campaigning against Čičak by denouncing him as a self-proclaimed extreme nationalist who did not participate in the fight for university reform. The worst accusation was that Čičak regularly attended lectures at the Faculty of Theology.

Shortly afterwards, lively discussions on Čičak's election spread from the university to the Croatian press, party officials and public. On behalf of the Central Committee of the Croatian party, Ema Derossi-Bjelajac tried to give support to the Student Union, while the president of the Zagreb party organisation, Srećko Bijelić, told Wilson that the whole thing was overblown, that 'if there is an election between two candidates, one will win. The Student Union has to accept this.' With these words he implicitly conceded the party's acceptance of Čičak's election.[29]

Čičak's attendance of lectures at the Catholic University's Faculty of Theology provoked a reaction from their dean, Dr Tomislava Šagi Bunić, who characterised the attacks on Čičak as attacks on the Catholic Church. Chancellor Ivan Supek was also irritated by the attacks, because Čičak's removal would call his own election into question.[30]

The attempts to discredit Čičak eventually failed, and the media exposure made Čičak even more popular among the student body and the public.[31] As a consequence, the president of the Zagreb Student Union Slobodan Lang resigned on 2 February 1971. The official student leadership was completely discredited by this attempt and especially by the claim that Čičak was an extreme nationalist. On 18 January, Chancellor Supek confirmed Čičak's election, which affirmed Čičak's legitimacy but also the legitimacy of his political platform.

The elections for the new leadership of the Zagreb student union were postponed until April 1971; a new nationalist leadership took over on 4 April. The newly elected president was Dražen Budiša, with two vice presidents, Goran Dodig and Muje Krasnići. The formation of the new student leadership was completed with the election of Ante Paradžik as the president of the national Croatian Student Union on 18 May.[32]

Consul-General Wilson met Čičak at a dinner organised by the Institute for Research and Treatment of Alcoholism, where Chancellor Supek was also present. Having pursued their own research into alcohol together, Wilson observed that Čičak was the 'lion of the evening':

> A rather gaunt five feet nine, Cicak wore a tweed jacket over a red and white striped shirt open at the neck. His hair is dark and short. He has long, well-trimmed sideburns and a well-tended goatee. He has dark, flashing eyes. His long, bony fingers strum the table. He speaks excellent Italian and very useful English. He gives the definite impression of being a bright young man.

A director of Zagreb's *Vinogradska* hospital, Dr Bogdan Srdar, told Wilson that Čičak had the character of an old-style Croatian politician: 'strong intellectually, energetic, active, not divorced from the people and the land.'

Čičak and Wilson spoke about several topics relating to his personal, academic and political life. Čičak was adamant that he didn't want to become a priest, despite his studies in theology. He spoke with admiration of Cardinal Kuharić, then Archbishop of Zagreb, whom he regarded as a saint too good for politics and cloak-and-dagger games. Čičak believed that since 1919 two generations of intellectuals had failed to have a meaningful role in shaping Croatia. Now was the moment to change this. Supek added that the University of Zagreb would be renamed the 'Croatian University'. (This never happened.) On this, Čičak replied:

> For 49 years Croatia's wealth has flowed down the Sava to Belgrade. Now that will end. Soon, sooner than one thinks, Yugoslavia will be a confederation.

Wilson was also interested in knowing Čičak's views on Serbian leaders, especially Marko Nikezić and Latinka Perović, whom Čičak considered to be moderate politicians. He characterised the overall Yugoslav student scene as divided between 'inactive Slovenes' and 'disunited Belgrade students', who were further subdivided as unitarists, Maoists, communists and so on.

Analysing information about Čičak's health, Wilson believed him to be a hypochondriac. Dr Srdrar told Wilson that Čičak's health was fine, apart from minor problems with his neck. Dr Srdrar also mentioned the newly-elected student president Budiša, whom he likened to Čičak, while characterising the previous president Lang as self-confident, inactive and out of touch with reality. Wilson concluded his report with the observation:

> While Cicak may be but a fleeting comet in the local heavens, he is evidently held in respect by many. A lot is expected of him. As one of the first non-party men to appear prominently in many years, he seems likely to attract much sympathy and support. While he is outspokenly 200 per cent a Croat, his favourable remarks about Serbian leaders Nikezic and Perovic suggest some readiness and desire for understanding.[33]

The Return of the Language Question

The language question resurfaced again at the beginning of 1971, when *Matica Hrvatska* stopped cooperating with *Matica Sprska* on the common project of publishing a joint dictionary in two versions, in Serbian-Croatian and Croatian-Serbian. The American consul-general Orme Wilson assumed that the initiative came from the newly elected leadership of *Matrica Hrvatska*, which was composed to a great extent by rehabilitated members who had been punished for their involvement in the 1967 language declaration. On 19 January 1971, *Matica Hrvatska* publicly rejected the conclusions of the 1954 Novi Sad agreement, which had called for the creation of a compromise version of the Serbo-Croatian language. *Matica Hrvatska* explained their decision by the inability to find common ground with *Matica Srpska* over *Srpska's* attempts to 'diminish the culture and the value of the national individuality and integrity of the Croatian linguistic expression.'[34] Wilson commented that:

> The dispute over the dictionary is a continuation of a bitter quarrel which has bedevilled Serbian-Croatian relations since Versailles. Its newest manifestation points up the current surge of nationalism in Croatia which has resulted in the

'rehabilitation' of a member of a number of party intellectuals and other leaders who were severely punished for alleged
'extreme nationalist' behaviour only a few years before.[35]

The American consulate noted on this occasion that writers from Dalmatia
supported the decision, but they complained that the Dalmatian dialect was
discriminated against compared to other Croatian dialects. In Montenegro,
the supporters of the Montenegrin language clashed with the Montenegrin
Society of Writers because they disputed *Matica Hrvatska's* claim that
Croatian and Serbian were different languages. Wilson commented:

> A sign of times in Yugoslavia [...] To many educated people
> the whole episode smacks of typical Balkan particularism.
> Unfortunately, to many others such shrill exchanges serve to
> awaken old ethnic antagonisms.[36]

On 23 April 1971 *Matica Hrvatska* formally withdrew from the Novi Sad
agreement, joined by the Croatian Philological Society and the Institute
for Language of the Yugoslav Academy of Sciences. In their statements, all
three institutions claimed that in 1954 they accepted the Novi Sad agreement despite their fears, believing that this would contribute to better relations between the nations. This had not happened, however, and the Novi
Sad agreement had become a 'tool for enforcing the Serbian literary language of the *ekavian* type.'[37]

The Stormy Spring of 1971

April 1971 was a particularly important month in Yugoslav and Croatian
political life. It started with a new census of the whole country, which
like every major political event of that year, would not proceed without
incident. The census exacerbated the conflicts between the republics and
nations. Immediately afterwards, the Yugoslav Ambassador to Sweden,
Vladimir Rolović, was assassinated by a Croatian immigrant, Miro
Barešić. At the same, the Central Committee of the Croatian party publicly accused individuals within the federal administration of organising
conspiracies in order to link the Croatian leadership to the remnants of
the *Ustaša* movement abroad. These simultaneous events marked the cli-
max of a crisis that had already been simmering for months, ever since the

exiled Croatian nationalist activist Branko Jelić sent a letter to Vladimir Bakarić. Finally, at the end of April, the federal party leadership held a meeting at Brijuni which would only temporarily and partially relieve political tensions.

The Census

The census caused an unexpected political crisis after the Socialist Alliance of the Working People of Croatia complained about the instructions issued by the Federal Institute of Statistics about how to declare the nationality of a citizen. The institute classified four categories: a member of one of the Yugoslav nations, nationalities, or minorities. And those who did not wish to declare one of these categories had the right to refuse to answer and declare themselves 'Yugoslavs' or as members of a particular region (Dalmatian, Bosniak, Herzegovinian, etc).

According to the British diplomatic reports, the most contentious issue was the regional category. A direct cause was a press conference organised by the Federal Institute of Statistics, in which its director Ibrahim Latifić informed the public about the census. Immediately afterwards, *Matica Hrvatska* protested to the socialist alliance that the institute had used the regional category, instead of the national, 'under the influence of reactionary forces' who were trying to 'dilute the Croatian national corpus'. They complained that the census instructions only mentioned Croatian regions as examples.[38]

In a slightly less dramatic tone, *Matica* was supported by the Croatian Academy of Sciences, the Croatian Society of Writers and others.[39] The Institute for Statistics replied that in a trial conducted in 1969 only 0.2 per cent of those polled declared themselves according to region. The instructions were agreed between the highest bodies of the LCY and the Socialist Alliance, and the institute only followed their instructions. Meanwhile, the Croatian Executive Council made a request to the federal Executive Council to change the instructions. The federal Executive Council took the position that every citizen should have the liberty to declare themselves in any way they wished, including by region. In this sense, the Croatian complaint was overruled. Trpe Jakovlevski stated on behalf of the federal government that a citizen could even declare themselves to be 'Europeans' or 'cosmopolitan'. But it would be another matter how these results would be treated later. The federal Socialist Alliance, however, decided to concede to the Croatian complaint with the conclusion that regional attachments were of no special importance to the federation. Therefore, the republics and autonomous provinces were free to adjust the instructions in accordance with their specific needs. The regional and local category was omitted from the instructions, and republican institutes for statistics were authorised to draft their own instructions in the fourth category.[40]

The Serbian reaction to the Croatian request was particularly harsh. On 14 February 1971, *Nin* published an excerpt from the transcript of an LCY Executive Bureau meeting in which census instructions were defined. Criticisms were directed at the Croatian representatives in the Executive Bureau, who had reacted neither to the agreed census instructions nor to the later scapegoating of the Federal Institute of Statistics. In a discussion of this issue on 22 February, the Serbian assembly accepted the changes, but also added that it 'doesn't see any social or political need for such change.'[41] The Croatian claims did not convince Consul-General Wilson, who couldn't understand why Croatia should be more sensitive to this sort of regionalisation than other republics.[42]

The results of the census revealed that the number of people working abroad was slightly smaller than previously believed. While one million had been estimated, the figure was only around 700,000. Croats made up about 33 per cent of this number, Serbs 30 per cent, Bosniaks around 20 per cent, while only 7.3 per cent of Yugoslavs abroad were Slovenian. The nationality of workers from Bosnia-Herzegovina, however, was not defined, even though they were traditionally largely Bosnian Croats. The American report acknowledged that the statistical methods used were inadequate and that some revisions would be needed. Another surprise was a decrease in the Croatian population. It had the lowest birth rate of all the Yugoslav republics.[43]

A report by *Washington Post* journalist Dan Morgan on 24 April was headlined 'Yugoslav census reflects national tensions'. He wrote that 'Yugoslav' was not a special category any more, but the individuals who declared themselves as such would be registered as not having declared their nationality. As a sign of protest against the omission of the 'Yugoslav' category, some Belgrade students declared themselves as 'eskimos'. The

Croatians rejected the regional identification, although they eventually accepted three regional groups: Dalmatia, Kordun, and Lika, where a large number of Croatian Serbs lived.[44]

The Spy Affair

The 'spy affair' became public when the Croatian leadership made a statement on 7 April about the 19th meeting of the CC LCC, in which they stated their dissatisfaction with the conclusions of the meeting of the Executive Bureau of the LCY of 23 March. This concerned the role of the federal security services in discrediting the Croatian leadership and linking them to the *Ustaši* movement abroad. After the war, most *Ustaši* members fled to Germany, Spain and Latin America. It was never a unified political movement in exile, and very few of them remained 'true believing' fascists, but many were nationalists who believed in an independent Croatian state. Their activities were mostly limited to protests and publishing pamphlets. The Yugoslav authorities had a tendency to declare as *Ustašis* any Croatian organisation or individual abroad opposed to the communist regimes or the Yugoslav state. The main protagonist in the spy affair was a relatively unimportant Croatian exile named Dr Branko Jelić. He was a medical doctor, a Croatian nationalist associated with the Ante Pavelić *Ustaši* movement before the war, interned by the British during the war, who lived in West Berlin from 1949 until his sudden death in 1972. He was active in West Berlin, where he published a newsletter *Hrvatska Država*, or 'Croatian state' that was banned in Yugoslavia. His subscribers were only Croat émigrés.[45]

A direct cause of the decision to go public with this statement was the assassination of Ambassador Rolović in Sweden, and the upcoming 30th anniversary of the establishment of the 'Independent State of Croatia', as the *Ustašis* had called it. By making this information public, the Croatian central committee shook the Yugoslav political scene, further worsening the situation in the country. As usual, the statement was received particularly badly in Serbia where many took it personally.[46]

The affair, however, started a year earlier, in October 1970, when the head of the Yugoslav military mission in Berlin, Ante Kolendić, came to the Central Committee headquarters in Zagreb to warn the Croatian leadership about the unacceptable treatment of Croatian workers abroad by Yugoslav diplomatic staff. He also warned about open rumours that the Croatian leadership was working with *Ustašis* in exile. In August 1970, the Yugoslav military mission in Berlin despatched a report to Belgrade with information that the Croatian communist leadership had contacts with the Croatian political exile, Dr Branko Jelić, and that there was a secret plan for Croatia to secede from Yugoslavia to form an independent state under Soviet protection. This report was not taken seriously at the time, because the report specified that the rumour was probably a 'provocation' by Jelić designed to elicit a response. The real affair started when Milovan Baletić, the editor of *Vjesnik*, returned from Berlin with information obtained from Đuro Pintarić the *chargé d'affaires* of the Yugoslav military mission, confirming the rumour. In addition, in October 1970, Pintarić sent a new report to Belgrade, this time qualifying it as true and verified. The Croatian communist leadership was particularly disturbed that the foreign ministry was spreading this information to a number of federal institutions. As a result, Zagreb concluded that there was a conspiracy in the federal administration with the aim of politically discrediting the Croatian leadership and their policies. Message number 151 was sent from Berlin to the foreign ministry on 20 October 1970:

> According to Tomulić, who calls himself a Marxist, the main news about the political aim of the Croatian People's Committee, led by Dr Jelić is the creation of an independent communist Croatia integrated into the socialist bloc with Soviet-style socialism. This goal can be achieved with Soviet support and some contacts are already being established between the Russians and some leading communists in Zagreb. In return for their help, the Soviets would gain two military bases in Mostar and Rijeka. Such a communist Croatia, integrated into the *Lager*, would stretch from the Drina river to Trieste.[47]

The research department of the foreign ministry replied with the following message:

> Please, in the future, send any messages on the question of emigrant activities, on the protection of our workers and similar, directly to the foreign ministry services in charge of these

matters, the Consular Department, the Workforce Department, the interior minister and other institutions. We did the same with your messages 149 and 151.

At a meeting with Tito, Miko Tripalo, Savka Dabčević-Kučar and Pero Pirker requested an immediate investigation into these allegations. Tito established a party commission with the goal of investigating the work of the security services in the foreign ministry, and determining the responsibility of federal bodies participating in this alleged conspiracy. The president of the Croatian government, Dragutin Haramija, sent a similar request to the president of the federal government, Mitja Ribičič. The party commission, comprised of Stane Dolanc, Trpe Jakovlevski, Maks Baće and Žiga Vodušek, set out to investigate the allegations. Among others, the commission spoke to the Federal Secretary of Internal Affairs, Radovan Stijačić; the head of the federal Udba, Borče Samonikov; the Assistant Secretary for Foreign Affairs, Josip Drndić; the head and the *chargé d'affaires* of the military mission in Berlin, Ante Kolendić and Đuro Pintarić; and with the military attaché to the mission, Lieut Col Cerović.[48] The commission concluded that there had been attempts to compromise the Croatian leadership, and that the Yugoslav diplomatic services had not reacted appropriately. The key protagonist of these attempts was Dr Jelić, who had spread rumours about his alleged connections to the Croatian leadership ever since the 1967 language declaration. There were rumours among the Croatian political diaspora about Jelić's ties to the Soviet secret services and the idea of creating an independent communist Croatia under Soviet patronage.

The commission, however, could not determine who signed the ministry's response to message 151, because the signature was illegible. Messages 149 and 151 had been received by 50 individuals and institutions, so this unverified information from the diplomatic services came into too many people's hands, including the security services. The commission also acknowledged that the security services had not paid sufficient attention to analysing this information, nor had they asked political bodies for an opinion. The commission concluded that the security services should not act upon unreliable information without designating it as such. It is clear from the commission's report that there was no verifiable evidence that

Jelić was cooperating with the Soviets, nor that the Yugoslav secret services made any effort to verify this.

The commission had information that the American security services were following the activities of Branko Jelić, and the Soviet embassy in East Berlin had sent a letter from Dr Jelić to the Yugoslav embassy, in which he authorised Velimir Tomulić to negotiate with the Soviet embassy. The Soviet embassy allegedly asked the Yugoslav embassy to translate the letter, because the Soviets didn't have a translator, and the Yugoslavs returned it untranslated without comment.

At that particular time there were 13 Yugoslav intelligence services active abroad, of which six belonged to republics, two to autonomous provinces, two military, two attached to the foreign ministry and one attached to the federal ministry of the interior. Considering these numbers, lack of coordination, collisions and misunderstandings were part of everyday business. The commission concluded that so many operatives, agents and informants active among the Yugoslav diaspora did more harm than good. The foreign ministry's intelligence arm, and its head Ante Drndić, were particularly criticised for neglecting the importance of this information.[49]

The information on the link between Jelić and the Croatian leadership was primarily obtained from three informants. One of them worked for the intelligence services of four different countries: they included the West Germans and the Americans, which he did with the consent of the Yugoslav secret service, while also working with the Italians without Yugoslav consent. Jelić knew about the attachment of these three informants to the Yugoslav services, and used them in his amateur counter-intelligence capacity to forward selected information to his Yugoslav controllers. His close associate Tomulić had already been recruited by the Croatian Udba in 1964, but they stopped using him as an asset in 1968. The commission also determined that he continued to maintain contact with the head of the military mission in Berlin, Đuro Pintarić, and that he had visited Yugoslavia with a valid passport a year earlier.[50]

A meeting of the Executive Bureau of the LCY on the 23 March 1971 resulted in the establishment of a new state commission to investigate the Jelić spy affair, with Marko Bulc as its head. Unlike the party commission, the Bulc commission did not find any irregularities in the work of the intelligence services. It determined that there was no organised conspiracy by the federation, but there were merely some shortcomings that needed to be addressed. The report concluded that the 'federal institutions, its services and individuals, did not participate in any kind of conspiracy or in initiating the spread of intrigues about alleged links between enemy diaspora and the Croatian political diaspora.'[51]

The US State Department passed to British diplomats a letter that Jelić had sent to President Nixon in May 1970 on behalf of the 'Croatian People's Committee' and other émigré organisations. In his letter to Nixon was also included a letter that Jelić had sent to Vladimir Bakarić. To Nixon Jelić wrote that the Croatian emigrants got information 'from reliable sources' and that the Soviets, as a part of their long-term interests, were actively considering how to solve the 'Croatian question' after the collapse of Yugoslavia. In this vein, the Soviets had 'suggested' to Croatian emigrants the establishment of an independent Croatian state, which could be neutral like Austria or Finland. Jelić explained that he was not keen on the Soviet suggestion but if the United States and the West failed to take any initiatives, then Croatians abroad would be forced to seriously consider the Soviet offer in the interest of the Croatian people.

The letter that Jelić sent to Vladimir Bakarić, unlike the letter to Nixon, had the characteristics of a pamphlet. The British diplomats assumed that it was intended for wider distribution. In this letter, Jelić explained to Bakarić that the views expressed at the 10th meeting of the LCC in 1970 were received favourably among Croatians in exile, and that they were ready to establish coordination with the Croatian communist leadership in the interest of the Croatian state. On the one hand, this letter was very critical of Bakarić, and accused him of involvement in the mass execution of *Ustašis* at Bleiburg at the end of the war, and of the murder of Andrija Hebrang in 1949; on the other hand, Jelić spoke very favourably of the new generation of Croatian politicians and journalists. He specifically named Savka Dabčević-Kučar, Miko Tripalo, Neda Krmpotić, Ivo Bojanić, Srećko Bijelić, Stipan Marušić, Branko Mikulić and Munir Mešihović. Interestingly, there was also reference to Tito's pre-war activities when he allegedly participated in the Comintern purges of Croatian and Serbian communists in Moscow between 1934 and 1936. In the letter, Jelić claimed that the Yugoslavs attempted to kidnap him and transfer him via East Germany and Hungary back to Yugoslavia. A representative of a socialist country, however, had warned him of this plot. He also dismissed the involvement of Croatian *émigrés* in terrorist activities, but he did accuse Yugoslav secret services of such involvement.

While Branko Jelić may have thought of himself as an important political leader in exile, his activities carried little real weight. Nonetheless, these letters did cause a big stir in Yugoslavia. It is interesting that Jelić's insinuations were very similar to the accusations that the Croats had made against individuals in the federal administration. In his letter to Bakarić, he did not mention the Soviet 'offer' to help create a Soviet-style Croatia. While Croatian leaders did not take Jelić seriously, his letters and private counter-espionage did seem to have the effect of further antagonising the Croatian leadership and the federal government in an already tense year.

The British diplomats did not think believe that the Soviets had made any such offer, but they did not exclude the possibility that as part of *their* counter-intelligence activities the Soviets were spreading such rumours. The rumours, after all, could not be directly linked to the Soviets.[52] The Soviet deputy consul-general in Zagreb, Anatoly Stepanyuk, spoke to American diplomat Gilber Callaway about the Croatian leadership's denial of the conspiracy. Stepanyuk complained that no one in Croatia wanted to talk to him about this. He also couldn't find anything about it in the newspapers. He interpreted the Croatian move as a sign of bad relations between Zagreb and Belgrade. He also hinted that there were rumours that Nixon's visit to Zagreb and the *Ustaši* activities in the US were all part of an American plot to split Yugoslavia. Callaway responded that Nixon's visit was a sign of American support of Yugoslav federalism and a united Yugoslavia composed of six constitutional republics. Consul-General Orme Wilson remarked on this conversation:

> Given reports of Soviet encouragement of Croat separatist elements, Stjepanjuk's eager and aggressive interest in the CC LCC communiqué is predictable. Under the circumstance, it seems equally predictable that he will not seek to dampen false rumors of official American interest in promoting Croat separatism.[53]

In April 1971, the Yugoslav press agency *Tanjug* published a report that Branko Jelić had delivered a speech in West Berlin in which he mentioned the Soviet offer about creating an independent Croatian state. This was the first time that Yugoslavia publicly linked the Croatian diaspora to Moscow. The Yugoslav media were quick to attack an article published in the Polish union newspaper *Głos Pracy* which implied that the influence of the Croatian diaspora was getting stronger within Yugoslavia and abroad. The Radio Zagreb commentator Milika Šundić accused the Soviets of undermining the Yugoslav state by calling the viability of Yugoslavia into question at the 24th Soviet party congress, by initiating this Polish rumour, and by the pessimistic commentaries in *Pravda* about the forthcoming 17th meeting of the Executive Bureau of the LCY.[54]

The CIA's report of July 1971 hinted, without specifying anything, that there was evidence for the Yugoslav claim that the Soviets were behind the recent increase in Croatian nationalism, especially abroad. The bare fact that Soviet official circles publicly denounced such accusations – twice – only emphasised their sensitivity on this matter. In the beginning of 1970, the right-wing Italian newspaper *Borghese* reported that Jelić had met with several high Soviet officials in West Berlin, which Moscow's *Pravda* strongly denied. The fact is, however, that after this alleged meeting Jelić changed his anti-communist and anti-Soviet position and became an advocate of cooperation with the Soviet Union.

In April 1971 the Swedish newspaper *Dagens Nyheter* similarly linked Croatian émigrés to the Soviets. On this occasion, the Soviets were quick to deny any such allegations, especially in light of the recent assassination of the Yugoslav Ambassador Rolović in Stockholm. The *chargé d'affaires* at the Soviet embassy in Belgrade requested a meeting with Tito, in order to officially deny any Soviet support for *Ustašis* in exile. Tito benevolently accepted the explanation, adding that Yugoslav authorities did not believe such rumours.[55] Considering Tito's constant warnings about Soviet interference in Yugoslav internal affairs, we can only assume that this was a case of diplomatic courtesy by the Yugoslav president, especially in this case of unverified rumours.

American intelligence services had obtained information from Belgrade that the Soviets allegedly had contacts with certain elements within Yugoslavia. Their source made an implausible claim: the Soviets had gained information on certain Yugoslav officials who had cooperated with the Gestapo during the war, and were using this information to blackmail them.

The fact was that Jelić's monthly newsletter *Hrvatska Država* started to publish a series of articles in early 1971 about Soviet alleged interest in the Croatian question. In the February edition of *Hrvatska Država* it was reported that the recent Warsaw Pact meeting designated Croatia as important for the defence of the Warsaw Pact. *Hrvatska Država* also claimed that Yugoslav émigrés in the Soviet Union (i.e., pro-Stalinist Yugoslavians who fled after 1948) had allegedly been given the task of spreading propaganda among Yugoslav workers abroad. A Yugoslav colonel, the Montenegrin Vlado Dabčević who fled Yugoslavia in 1948, was sent to West Germany, where he coordinated anti-Tito activities. The CIA report mentions that Zagreb sources confirmed that the Croatian leadership perceived Jelić's activities as a dangerous game directed against them. The CIA confirmed that the Soviets had not succeeded in infiltrating the Croatian communists and instead had turned to Croatian émigrés.[56]

A letter that Velimir Tomović sent to Savka Dabčević-Kučar in 1990 might shed additional light on the puzzle of what really happened. In it, he confirmed that Jelić did have contacts with Soviet officials in East Berlin, and had travelled to Leningrad and Moscow, where he met with the vice president of the Soviet government Vladimir Novikov. Tomović also mentioned that the Soviets had simply overestimated the potential influence of political émigrés on Yugoslav workers abroad as a form of influence or pressure on Yugoslavia.[57] It is, however, impossible to verify these claims without an insight into Soviet archives.

The spy affair entertained the Yugoslav public throughout April 1971. Croatian politicians Savka Dabčević-Kučar, Pero Pirker and Srećko Bijelić were particularly active in issuing vociferous public denials.[58] Although the spy affair never really came to a conclusion in terms of establishing the facts among all these actors, it formally ended when the Federal Executive Council published parts of the Bulc commission's report on 28 April, which concluded that the 'Croatian accusations were false, and federal intelligence services were not involved in any conspiracy.'[59] But this was only the beginning of fiercer political clashes that would occur at the 17th meeting of the Executive Bureau in Brijuni that also started on 28 April.

The Brijuni Meeting and Brezhnev's Call

The 17th meeting of the Presidency of the Executive Bureau, held on 28–30 April 1971 in Brijuni, revealed the true depth of the political crisis. The key topic was a discussion on the CC LCC's public pronouncement regarding the spy affair, but the meeting would be primarily remembered for the telephone call from Leonid Brezhnev to Tito. According to Tito's words, Brezhnev offered help in solving the Yugoslav crisis.[60] Brezhnev reportedly said that he had heard that Yugoslavia was in a serious situation and that he had information about army movements towards Belgrade. Tito politely declined Brezhnev's offer of support, confirming that there was an ongoing meeting intended to solve the problems in the party.[61]

The CIA report of August 1971 confirmed that the story of Brezhnev's call had been circulating in Croatian party circles since early May. Two Croatian representatives allegedly overheard Tito's conversation with the Soviet leader. Throughout May and June, some members of the Croatian central committee likened Brezhnev's offers to the offer made to the Czechoslovak leadership in 1968. Some argued that Tito probably invented the call in order to use the threat of a potential Soviet intervention to strengthen national unity and force the party leaders to compromise. Tito called for another meeting of the Croatian central committee on 4 July to confront and suppress such rumours. According to the same CIA report, Tito spoke only for eight minutes, and he was so angry that he almost lost his temper. He reiterated his talk with Brezhnev and warned of the real danger of Soviet intervention. He also emphasised that he was ready to become a dictator if that is what it took to resolve this situation.[62]

Despite Tito's dramatic appeal, the CIA's July report actually minimised the Soviet threat, emphasising that Brezhnev was far less interested in Yugoslavia compared to his predecessors Stalin and Khrushchev. It appeared that the Soviets had come to accept that they would not be able to increase their influence in Yugoslavia as long as Tito was firmly in control. An additional problem was that there were no political or social avenues to support a movement for a more pro-Soviet policy in Yugoslavia. As early as 1948 it had been apparent that not even Soviet economic pressure would do much harm as long as the West was ready to aid Yugoslavia economically.

Moscow was eager to maintain relatively amicable relations with Belgrade, but the CIA report pointed out that the Soviets were nonetheless involved in petty diversions, semi-diplomatic activities, and the spread of propaganda against Tito's regime. The Yugoslav ambassador to Moscow,

Veljko Mićunović, sent a report to Belgrade in January 1970 that described Yugoslav–Soviet relations in similarly negative terms. He analysed the policy of Moscow towards Yugoslavia as being publicly friendly while at the same time pursuing a policy of subversion. He concluded the report with the following words: 'The Russians are linking the increase in their influence with the increase of our internal problems and our potential difficulties in foreign affairs.'[63]

Although the Yugoslav claims were often overstated, with the purpose of strengthening Tito's regime, there were some indications that the Soviets were pursuing greater influence in Yugoslavia. Although they lacked firm evidence, the Yugoslavs suspected that the Soviets had been involved in the 1968 Kosovo riots, and that they had links to the Yugoslav political émigrés. But it was common knowledge that the Soviets supported Bulgarian territorial pretensions towards Yugoslav Macedonia.[64] In January 1970 Tito accused the Soviet embassy, and Ambassador Benediktov, of semi-officially offering financial and technical aid to Yugoslav enterprises in financial difficulty. Despite Yugoslav protests, the Soviets continued their informal activities, forcing Belgrade to protest officially. The Soviets continued to distribute propaganda materials, such as books and films, which was in sharp contrast to relatively modest Yugoslav activity in the Soviet Union. In June 1971 Yugoslav diplomats warned that the activities of Soviet cultural and information centres in Yugoslavia contradicted the principles of good faith and reciprocity.

Equally worrying was the distribution of printed material in the Soviet Union and abroad and Soviet radio broadcasts to Yugoslavia that criticised the Yugoslav political system. Some parts of important Yugoslav documents, including Tito's political speeches, were deliberately misinterpreted. According to Yugoslav complaints, the Soviet authorities even recruited Yugoslav émigrés to publicly discuss their negative experiences with Tito's regime.[65] The CIA emphasised the importance of the spying affair in these activities. Allegedly Eastern bloc diplomats in Belgrade were particularly active in spreading such rumours.[66] In his conversation with Richard Nixon and Zhou en Lai in Beijing in 1972, even Henry Kissinger confirmed that the Soviets were active in subversive activities in Yugoslavia.[67]

Although the meeting with the Croatian party Central Committee was not public, and no minutes were taken, American diplomats managed to obtain good information about it. A diplomatic source and the CIA report agree with contemporaneous memoirs. Savka Dabčević-Kučar noted in her memoirs that Tito did indeed threaten military intervention if the situation did not change. He was primarily referring to the increase in nationalism, accusing *Matica Hrvatska* and the student organisation, and specifically singling out the nationalist economists Šime Đodan and Marko Veselica. Tito added that Brezhnev's call did indeed occur, and that the Soviets had held a meeting in which they agreed to intervene but had not yet decided when. In his memoirs, the Croatian politician Jure Bilić wrote that immediately before Tito's arrival he spoke to Vladimir Bakarić about the situation in Croatia. Bakarić warned Tito about the difficult situation and the increased danger of nationalism. The meeting revealed that two opposing camps were already forming within the Croatian party.[68]

The Yugoslav ambassador to Moscow, Veljko Mićunović, confirmed that the phone call did occur. At a reception at the Canadian embassy in Moscow on 19 May, the Soviet Deputy Prime Minister Dmitry Polyansky mentioned that the conversation had taken place. Soviet officials were unusually interested in the situation in Yugoslavia, including Prime Minister Alexei Kosygin, and Deputy Prime Ministers Lesechky, Novikov and Baibakov, as well as Foreign Minister Andrei Gromyko. This information came as a surprise to Ambassador Mićunović, and he complained to Belgrade of not having been informed. With Tito's approval, the foreign ministry did send a report of the phone conversation.[69]

Tito once again warned against Soviet threats at the 83rd meeting of the Executive Bureau on 9 June 1971. He pointed out that former partisans were giving speeches in the Soviet Union against Yugoslavia, which had not happened since 1948. He also complained about economic pressures and delays as a form of political coercion. Tito received a visit from the Soviet ambassador to request the approval for 14 Soviet planes to fly over Yugoslav territory in order to reach the Mediterranean. The Soviet request was promptly denied, and Tito interpreted it as a test designed to show the Americans that the Soviets could reach the Mediterranean with their aircraft. He warned that such action would compromise Yugoslavia internationally and worsen relations with Albania and Romania. He also warned that the Soviets already had their people in the country. He also mentioned a conversation with an Italian general who confirmed that Italy did not have any territorial demands upon Yugoslavia, unless they agreed with the Soviets to return certain parts of Yugoslavia to Italy – implying that this might occur if Yugoslavia broke up. Tito warned about the threat of nationalism, and specifically about verbal abuse of Yugoslav army officers in Zagreb and Ljubljana. He concluded his speech with the ominous warning: 'We must find a way to isolate these groups. If all else fails, we will lock them up. We have plenty of uninhabited islands.'[70] This last remark was a reference to Goli Otok ('Barren island'), which was a labour camp for Informbiro suspects during the rift with Stalin.

In her speech at the same meeting, Savka Dabčević-Kučar tried to downplay the danger of nationalism with a lot of ideological jargon. She emphasised that after the Brijuni meeting the 'enemies of the party line' were brought under control. She characterised two groups of Croatian opposition: the 'Croatian chauvinists', who used public events and the press (like *Matica Hrvatska* and its paper *Kolo*); and the other group that consisted of 'Informbiro, remnants of Ranković's people and unitarists', who were removed from the system, and used anonymous letters, rumours and telephone threats. She also tried to contradict Tito's remark about the abuse a Yugoslav colonel had received in Zagreb. Tito sharply replied: 'Your interior ministry is worthless. Replace Krpan. That's enough.'[71]

Despite this brief verbal exchange, Savka tried to emphasise the Informbiro's activities and link them to the Soviets, in order to exploit Tito's sensitivity and minimise nationalism. She mentioned the problems of foreign trade and the currency regime, adding that the nationalist problem would diminish if these issues could be resolved. Finally, she pointed out that the Croatian nationalists presented a smaller problem than unitarists, because at least the nationalists operated openly which made them easier to control. The unitarists, on the other hand, worked predominantly in the shadows of the party structure. She mentioned 'some retired individuals', referring to former officers who were visiting parts of Croatia to incite the Serbs who lived there.[72]

The American consulate in Zagreb commented on the 17th Brijuni meeting in April 1971:

> Croatians in general within and without the party-government establishment seem relieved that political tensions, which had

been building over the past several months, have not yet led to crisis involving arrests and purges, as had been widely rumored in rumor-prone Zagreb in late April.[73]

Rumours were circulating that the Zagreb military district did not support the policy of the Croatian leadership, and that they were ready to remove it.[74] Consul-General Wilson reported that such fears prevailed in Croatia before the 17th meeting, which helped avert this worst-case scenario. On the anniversary of the liberation of Zagreb on 7 May 1971 the entire Croatian leadership was present at a mass gathering in Zagreb Republic Square. The leaders could show the Croatian public that they had survived the 17th meeting with their heads still on their shoulders.

The 20th Plenum of the CC LCC later in May 1971 sent a similar message: the party leaders had managed to emerge successfully from the crisis. According to Consul-General Wilson, however, unlike the optimistic message projected to the public, party members were not convinced that the worst was over. After the Brijuni April meeting, the pressure on the Croatian liberal leadership started to mount, and this was visible at the 20th Plenum of the LCC. The American consulate noted a public statement by General Rade Bulat, who was a Croatian Serb, a parliamentarian from Vrginmost, and a member of the Croatian central committee:

> In free paraphrase what Bulat is saying 'You Croats accuse us Serbs of monopolizing positions within the Army and Security Services, so what if we do? The reason is (a) after the war we Serbs constituted the only reliable political element within Croatia, for well known and irrefutable historical reasons; and (b) now, while this may no longer be true, you Croats show no interest in these demanding professions, which appeal most to the poor boys from the village who are more likely than not to be Serbs. If you really do not want us in the party, well then throw us out – but this will mean the end of the communist party in Croatia and a return to Croatian chauvinistic reaction, which I, for one, will continue to resist with all my strength.'

In this context the consulate also took an interest in a statement by Vladimir Bakarić, who expressed a fear that the Croatian League of Communists was beginning to show cracks and dividing into two camps of liberals and ideologues.[75]

Figure 8.3 Savka addresses the crowd. The banner reads, 'A sovereign state is the right of Croatia and all other nations in Yugoslavia'.

At the public mass gathering of 7 May, Savka Dabčević-Kučar and the president of Zagreb's Socialist Alliance, Drago Božić, delivered speeches to a crowd of 200,000. Savka spoke about the Brijuni meeting and nationalism. She insisted that fears of purges or the reversal of political and economic reforms were unfounded. The American diplomats were puzzled by the emotional charge and enthusiasm of the crowd. Some wept when the Croatian anthem was played and Savka's speech was interrupted by applause and cheers nearly 40 times. Their report concluded that the masses were not cheering the party but the Croatian leader. Such genuine popularity was not matched by any other high official. Although Savka devoted equal time to the problems of nationalism, or 'chauvinist extremism', and to the role of the Croatian League of Communists as the only force that could give Croatia an acceptable level of autonomy, the American diplomats did not fail to notice the crowd's reaction:

> While the crowd listened with unusual attention, its cheers were triggered more by catch-phrases than by content; when she castigated 'deaf and blind nationalists' for endangering the Reform by their extremism, the crowd listened politely but by and large in silence. Her vigorous attacks on 'provocateurs', 'informbiroists', 'statists', and 'Serbian great state hegemonists' were, however, signals for frantic cheers, applause and chants.

The stage was decorated with a large Croatian tricolour and the chequered coat-of-arms, along with the words of the 20th constitutional amendment that defined Croatian autonomy within the federation. Despite the constant cheers of 'Savka!' and 'Tripalo!', Wilson noticed that Miko Tripalo was absent, because he was in the Croatian region of Lika at the time. Rumours were spreading that at Brijuni Tripalo was ordered to decrease his visibility.[76] But this was not true. From 1 May Tripalo devoted his time to visiting predominantly Serbian areas in Lika, Dalmatia and Slavonia. In his native Dalmatia, he encountered a degree of popularity that had hitherto only been permitted to Tito. The high point was a three-day visit to Zadar, where he was welcomed by a public gathering of over 30,000 people – an impressive number for such a small city.[77]

The Western Press in 1971

The Western press reported extensively on the spring events in Yugoslavia. *The Economist*'s correspondent, the Croatian–British Chris Cviić, published an article on 1 May 1971 headlined: 'Will he make it?' He summarised the events of 1971, especially the conflict between the Croatian and Serbian party leaderships about the status of the autonomous regions Kosovo and Vojvodina, as well as the Croatian spy affair. According to *The Economist*, Tito was aware that Yugoslavia would find itself under increased Soviet pressure after he was gone. That was his main motive for resolving the national question. With federal responsibilities limited only to the areas of defence, foreign affairs, the single market and the underdeveloped regions, Tito hoped to make the idea of Yugoslavia more acceptable to the non-Serbian nations. This process, however, had not been simple considering the resistance coming primarily from Serbia where party leaders had difficulty convincing their more conservative and nationalist colleagues to accept changes. The greatest challenge to the conservatives, however, was the democratisation of society. This was particularly obvious in Croatia, whose leaders enjoyed genuine popularity. This was also reflected in the election of the non-party student leadership at Zagreb University, and the freedom of the press. A similar combination of progressive leadership and press freedom prevailed in both Slovenia and Serbia. Tito's efforts to stabilise the country with the liberal and decentralising movements had been supported by President Nixon, President Pompidou and Chancellor Brandt. *The Economist* pointed out, however, that Western leaders supported this process not because they hoped to establish capitalism after

189

Tito's death but because there was no attractive alternative to the existing stable and independent Yugoslavia.[78]

The *Christian Science Monitor* published an article on 11 May, headlined 'Drama in the Balkans', which raised the key question: what would happen to Yugoslavia after Tito died? It emphasised that his efforts to preserve Yugoslavia were weakened by problems rooted in the past but also by external influences. The most obvious conflict was between the Serbs and Croatians, but the article made interesting broader cultural and historical comparisons in the attributes used to describe the conflict between the two nations. The Serbs were characterised as a proud and fierce nation that believed itself superior to other Slavic tribes. The Croats, on the other hand, were the first among the south Slavs to adapt to urban and industrial society. Croatia and Serbia were modernised in completely different ways. Serbia had been under Turkish influence for a long time, whereas Croatia had long been a part of the Austro-Hungarian Empire. Serbia was culturally a part of the Eastern Mediterranean, while Croatia was under strong Central European influence. Belgrade still had the character of an oriental city, while Zagreb was similar to any other city in Austria or southern Germany. The article speculated about the links between the Croatian diaspora and the Soviets as part of Moscow's attempts to break up Yugoslavia, probably its last opportunity to do so.[79]

On 26 April, the Washington-based *Evening Star* reported on the assassination of Ambassador Rolović and linked this to the conflicts between the industrialised north and the backward Yugoslav south. It emphasised that the 'rebalkanisation' of Yugoslavia could lead to chaos, which the Soviets could exploit: 'The Yugoslavs, who were able to raise their heads after centuries of tyranny, should understand this better than anyone. Let's hope they decide to hang together, rather than go separately to the Soviet gibbets.'

The *Washington Post* and the *New York Times* each published an article on 2 May with the headlines 'All Tito Wants is a Little Bit of Unity' and 'Tito Says Party Will Keep Unity'.[80] Both reported in a similar vein about the conflicts within the party leadership and the mutual recriminations between the media in Zagreb and Belgrade. The *New York Times*, however, considered the economic conflict between Zagreb and Belgrade to be the country's most fundamental problem.

The Veselica-Đodan Case

American diplomats continued to follow events in Croatia. The summer of 1971 started with a 'mini-Žanko affair', when a parliamentarian from the city of Sinj was removed for his opposition to the policy of the Croatian liberal leadership. Soon after, another scandal caught the public's attention and led to calls for the resignation of Ivan Šibl as president of the Croatian Veterans Association. This initiative was started by the retired General Nikola Vidović, of the veterans association's branch in Vrginmost. In April and June, General Vidović had accused Croatian nationalists of spreading fear with their rhetoric among the Serbian population of the Croatian region of Kordun in such a way that 'the veterans are saying that they are sorry for giving up their weapons in 1945.' He specifically accused two Croatian economists and academics, Marko Veselica and Šime Đodan, of assisting the development of the 'Greater Serbia' Četnik movement in Kordun. Vidović also linked *Matica Hrvatska* with *Ustaši* elements and *Matica Srpska* with the Četniks. The presidency of the veterans association rejected these accusations, and reprimanded Vidović for his behaviour.[81]

The Croatian party leadership was forced to act, caught between sustained public pressure and Tito's earlier warnings relating to Đodan and Veselica's actions. They were first ejected from the LCC on 23 July at the 6th Conference of the Zagreb's branch. President Srećko Bijelić explained that they were forced to do this because Đodan and Veselica had implied that Croatia should be an independent state and sought to portray these activities as being supported by the LCC. By doing so, they invited attacks on the LCC leadership and made the fight against unitarist forces *more* difficult.[82] American diplomats assumed that the order to remove them came directly from Tito at his meeting with the Croatian leadership on 4 July. According to Consul-General Wilson, Veselica and Đodan were very popular among students and young intellectuals. They were both promising writers who pointed out the injustice of Croatia's economic position and the need to change the banking and foreign currency systems. Veselica was also a close associate of Savka Dabčević-Kučar, and therefore his fall was interpreted as diminishing her stature. There were, however, no indications that she was truly affected.

Wilson noticed that the atmosphere at the celebration of the 30th anniversary of the 1941 popular uprising against fascism in Srb was very serious.

Although Savka was present, she did not give a speech. She also cancelled her speech at the public gathering in Vodice on 18 July. A member of the Croatian government, Agata Pavlinić, told Wilson on 26 July that Savka worked too much, and she wouldn't be surprised if she suffered from mental exhaustion.[83] The pressures on the Croatian leadership were increasing. On the one hand, *Matica Hrvatska* and the student leadership were accusing the leaders of being too soft on unitarists, while on the other hand, the faction of the Croatian party leadership led by Vladimir Bakarić blamed Savka and her circle of being too soft on nationalism. In speeches in Srb and Plitvice, Vladimir Bakarić and Jakov Blažević directly mentioned Đodan and Veselica. Bakarić warned that the 'Zagreb incidents surrounding their activities and expulsion, are not isolated. There are many other party bodies that allowed nationalists to go too far.' In a similar tone, Blažević characterised Đodan and Veselica as 'counter-revolutionaries' who were 'linked to enemy forces'.

On 28 July, the student leaders Ivan Zvonimir Čičak, Dražen Budiša and Ante Paradžik met in Split and released a statement on behalf of the Croatian Student Association opposing the removal of Veselica and Đodan from the LCC. The leadership of the University of Rjeka's student association, however, did not support this statement. This was the beginning of a rift in the student movement.[84] In order to mitigate the negative impact of the Split statement, Miko Tripalo and Maks Baće, LCC Secretary for Dalmatia, met with Dražen Budiša in Split and tried to explain to him that his activities were damaging the political position of the LCC leadership. According to others present, Budiša was not persuaded to back down. As a consequence, the party leadership distanced itself from the student movements. At a mass gathering in Hvar, Tripalo stated publicly, 'We will not allow a different programme opposed to the official party line to be pursued under the banner of the student association. There can be only one student association that supports and adopts the position and policies of the LCC.' The presidency of the Zagreb LCC branch also denounced the methods pursued by the student movement.[85]

The conflict surrounding Đodan and Veselica would become the first serious clash between the Croatian liberal politicians and the newly elected student leadership that was supported by *Matica Hrvatska*. In an atmosphere of intensifying student support for the national and economic autonomy of Croatia, and their confrontation with the party leadership, American diplomats were increasingly reluctant to justify such behaviour.

On the Fourth of July the consulate received a delegation of student representatives who praised American independence. The Americans were intrigued by the students' pro-American and anti-Soviet attitudes, as well their views on the democratic changes in the student movement. The diplomats noticed the students' obvious nationalism and isolation from similar student movements in Belgrade and Ljubljana.[86]

The weekly *Hrvatski Tjednik* published fragments from the speeches by Bakarić and Blažević in its 30 July edition with the front cover headline 'A dramatic moment for Croatia', and joined *Matica Hrvatska* and the student movement in denouncing the expulsion of Đodan and Veselica.[87] The Zagreb public prosecutor banned the issue, but the Zagreb district court repealed this order on 3 August, with the explanation that 'this allegedly offensive material has already been published in other media.' The Supreme Court of the Socialist Republic of Croatia next overturned the repeal by the district court, reinstating the ban on 16 August. As only the front cover was banned, the editors replaced it with a blank cover with the text of the court decision written within a thin black frame – as if it were an envelope announcing a bereavement.

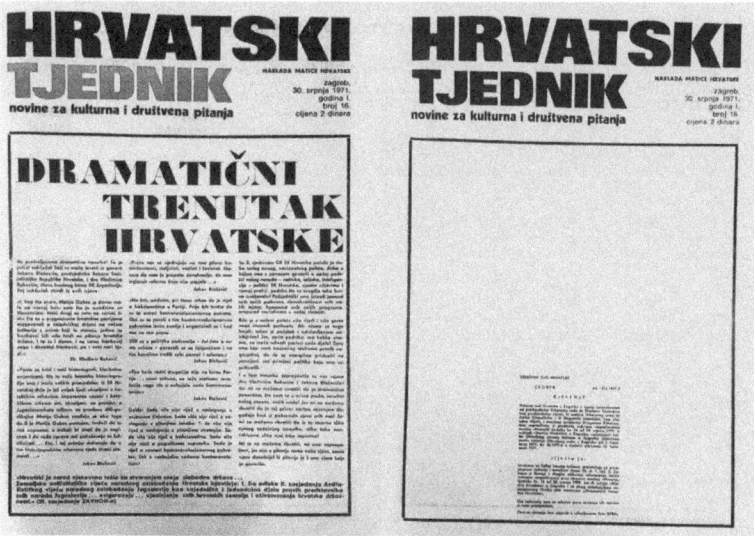

Figure 8.4   Two versions of the *Hrvatski Tjednik* of 30 July 1971. On the left the banned edition with the leading headline, 'Dramatic moment for Croatia'; on the right, the new edition with a 'mourning envelope' cover that included a miniature reproduction of the court order banning the original cover.

On 2 September, however, original copies of the magazine with the original cover, but camouflaged with the new cover, started to circulate. It was not clear who did this, but it was certainly aimed to provoke the regime. Consul-General Wilson suspected that someone who wanted the magazine to be banned might be behind it.[88]

The consulate noted a statement by a member of the Executive Committee of the Croatian Workers Alliance, Zdravko Tomac, that he had the impression from his contacts with student leaders that they disagreed with the policy of the LCC and the decision to expel Veselica and Đodan. He complained that a small group of individuals within the student organisation had abused their mandate to represent all students to create the false impression that students did not support the policy and decisions of the LCC. For this reason it was necessary to activate the 'passive members' of the student movement, which could have been interpreted as a call to remove the democratically elected student leaders. Miko Tripalo was also critical of the student leaders. In a speech in Hvar on 22 August, he made the circular argument that the LCC could not agree with the position of certain individuals, groups, and even student leaders who didn't agree with the LCC. Consul-General Wilson concluded that the opposition towards official party positions was still very strong and he foresaw a 'hot political autumn' for Croatia.[89]

9

Two Visits

The autumn of 1971 witnessed two state visits: Brezhnev to Yugoslavia and Tito to the United States. Although Tito's visit to Washington in November 1971 was the most spectacular part of his activities that year, Brezhnev's visit to Yugoslavia from 22–25 September 1971 was more decisive for internal Yugoslav developments.

The challenge of preserving Yugoslavia's non-alignment was a delicate balancing act for Tito. The fear of Soviet intervention and interference was an important centripetal force for a federal Yugoslavia. Good relations with the West and promoting liberalism would invite Soviet accusations of bowing to 'imperialism' and amplify Soviet attempts to interfere in both Yugoslav foreign and domestic policy. These attempts were resisted, but on the other hand the looming Soviet threat was always a useful tool in Yugoslavia's dealings with the West. It remains an open question to what extent Brezhnev's visit contributed to Tito's decision to initiate the purge of liberals in Croatia and across Yugoslavia.

Comrade Brezhnev Comes to Belgrade

Brezhnev's visit was prepared amidst tense relations between the two countries in the shadow of Czechoslovakia and allegations of Soviet meddling.[1]

The Yugoslav political leadership discussed Brezhnev's visit at the meeting of the Executive Bureau on 14 September 1971. Tito warned that the Soviets would try to limit the purpose of the visit to concern only party matters, although it was a formal state visit. Tito's fear was that inter-party negotiations might put ideology and party relations before national sovereignty. He added that the Soviets would attempt to pursue their strategic interest of accessing the Middle East via a Balkan-Mediterranean route.[2]

The Secretary of the Executive Bureau's Presidium, Stane Dolanc, predicted that Brezhnev would try to interfere with internal developments, compete with the Chinese in Europe and the Balkans, and legalise Soviet geostrategic interests over Yugoslavia such as use of airspace, overland and naval access. He also suspected that the Soviets would try to use Yugoslavia to improve relations with Romania and Albania.

Based on a conversation with a Soviet diplomat, Dolanc suspected that the Soviets believed that the situation in Yugoslavia would get worse. The diplomat had suggested a 'friendship agreement' comparable to the agreements that the Soviet Union had signed with India and Egypt to increase its influence over the non-aligned nations. According to the Soviet diplomat,

> Such an agreement would guarantee long-term friendly relations with the Soviet Union, even after Tito's departure. This would be a binding document for future Yugoslav leaders, because among them there are some who do not sympathise with the Soviet Union and who boycott the supporters of good Soviet-Yugoslav relations.

Dolanc therefore suspected that Brezhnev would try to initiate the signing of such a document in order to divide the Yugoslav leadership. The Presidium decided that a friendship agreement should not be signed, because of its negative consequences for Yugoslavia. They also decided that the final communiqué should reaffirm the values of the 1955 Belgrade Declaration that Brezhnev should sign as a pledge of Soviet respect for Yugoslav neutrality and independence.

Edvard Kardelj agreed that a friendship agreement should not be signed because it would compromise Yugoslav non-alignment and was not comparable with India and Egypt. Kardelj believed that the Soviets were also aware that China could not 'save' Albania, Romania or Yugoslavia from Soviet pressures or attack. This was the reason that the Soviets had begun to promote a story about Chinese influence in the Balkans. More worried about Soviet intentions than Chinese hordes at the gates, the foreign minister, Mirko Tepavac, dismissed a pact between Bucharest, Belgrade and Tirana as nonsense. He interpreted this attempt as a Soviet tactic to weaken the relations of Balkan countries with China, in order to strengthen Soviet influence and limit the independence of the communist countries in the region.[3]

Tito's report on Brezhnev's visit to the Executive Bureau of 3 October 1971 showed that the Yugoslav predictions had been correct. Brezhnev indeed demanded that Tito sign a friendship agreement. In a private conversation, Tito told him that this suggestion would not be accepted at official negotiations, but Brezhnev nevertheless raised it again between the two formal meetings of the delegations. Brezhnev next urged Tito to suggest to Nixon (as Tito's idea) that it was necessary to settle both the Middle East and Far East crises with negotiated deals.[4]

Brezhnev also complained about the enormous and irretrievable Soviet costs in Vietnam, Cuba and the Middle East. These poor investments had brought few economic, strategic or political returns. He added that the Soviet Union had no long-term military interest in the Middle East and suggested that Tito use his influence with Arab leaders to deal with the Middle East crisis. Tito would pass this information to Egypt's President Sadat, whom he would also inform that he would discuss the Yugoslav position on the Middle East with Nixon. According to Tito, Brezhnev was equally tense in private conversation as he was in the official negotiations, banging his fist on the table and swearing vociferously that the Soviet Union had no intention of attacking Yugoslavia. He was upset by the accusation that a Warsaw Pact exercise close to the Yugoslav border could be interpreted as a threat to Yugoslavia. He allegedly told Tito, 'I am ready to sacrifice my family and myself if this occurred. I am ready to sacrifice all that is dear to me not to allow this to happen.'

Brezhnev reacted similarly in the official meetings with Yugoslav officials: he criticised the liberal attitudes of the Yugoslav press and softness on 'imperialism' as the key disadvantages of Yugoslav internal and foreign policy. Tito replied with accusations of Informbiro activities in the Soviet Union. He was clear that Yugoslavia would prohibit entry to all who were involved in anti-Yugoslav activities, including Soviet citizens. Brezhnev denied knowing anything about this and promised to investigate.

In the final communiqué, it was very important to avoid any appearance of Yugoslavia moving closer to the Eastern bloc. The Soviet suggestion of a friendship agreement was immediately rejected, and the Yugoslavs insisted on affirming the Belgrade Declaration with a sentence that would clarify that this was a negotiation between two sovereign states. The Yugoslav leadership also wanted to define the character of the Non-Aligned Movement to be more than just 'anti-imperialist', as the Soviets perceived it.

Brezhnev also inquired about the possibility of a new Balkan pact between Yugoslavia, Albania, Romania and Greece. Although Tito immediately dismissed the idea, he was surprised that the Soviets even considered it to be realistic, especially the inclusion of Greece.

The president of the Federal Assembly, Mijalko Todorović, was far more critical in his analysis of Soviet attitudes. He pragmatically concluded that the Soviets had not changed their strategy towards Yugoslavia, and that Brezhnev had not come for bilateral negotiations between two independent states but merely to present the Soviet position. In this sense there was no real dialogue between the two delegations. The Executive Bureau concluded, however, that the meeting went well, successfully resisting Soviet efforts to interfere in Yugoslavia while affirming Yugoslav positions and long-term policy towards the Soviet Union.

Mr Tito Goes to Washington

ROGERS: *And he said: 'I want you to know, for your own ears, and your*
            ears only, the meeting with Brezhnev did not go well.'
NIXON: *Ha.*[5]

Tito had officially visited the United States four times: to meet President Eisenhower in 1960, President Kennedy in October 1963 (a month before his assassination), President Nixon from 27 to 30 October 1971, and President Carter from 6 to 9 March 1978. On his 1971 visit to the United States and Canada, Tito sought to balance the Brezhnev meeting by securing American economic and political support, investment and military cooperation.

In September 1971, Yugoslavia's ambassador to the US, Bogdan Crnobrnja, met Henry Kissinger to prepare for Tito's visit to Washington the following month. Crnobrnja emphasised that Tito was particularly sensitive about the activities of émigré groups, and, he requested that the US curb them as well as any protests they might hold. Crnobrnja also complained about a US Congressman referring to Croats and Serbs as 'captive nations'. Tito would also like to spend a night at Camp David. Kissinger responded that he would see what could be done. A private meeting would be arranged.[6]

Tito flew into America from Canada, first to Camp David on 27 October, then on to Washington for the official visit. Arriving in Washington in the morning of the 28th, Tito was received with a very elaborate military reception that included a marching band in colonial red coats. The garden ceremony in all its pomp was filmed from every angle and broadcast on Yugoslav television, accompanied by an orchestral rendition of the Beatles' 'Yesterday'.[7] The first formal meeting between the presidents, accompanied by Kissinger and Presidium member Vidoje Zarković, commenced at 11:30.

The meeting resumed discussion of a range of international themes raised at their last meeting in Belgrade on 1 October 1970. In Belgrade, the discussion had touched on the Middle East, Africa and Vietnam – and in each of these regions, Tito advocated third-way solutions and diplomacy.[8] In the Washington meeting a year later, Tito continued to show his international value as a mediator between non-aligned states in crisis, and filled Nixon and Kissinger in about his meetings with President Sadat, India's leader Mrs Indira Gandhi and President Yahya Khan of Pakistan, regarding the crisis in East Pakistan/Bangladesh. Tito had tried to persuade both sides to prevent escalation to war. Tito also noted that he understood from his meeting with Brezhnev that the Soviets did not want to see a war over East Pakistan.

Concerning Soviet intentions towards Yugoslavia, Tito noted that the draft declaration that Brezhnev had brought with him clearly reaffirmed Yugoslav sovereignty and independence, upholding the principles of the 1955 declaration. 'The final text as it emerged from the talks made clear that the USSR and Yugoslavia were dealing with each other as two sovereign states and that Yugoslavia had the right to develop its own social system.' Tito commented of Soviet manoeuvres in Eastern Europe that 'the Yugoslavs were not afraid of them,' and that Yugoslav manoeuvres had been 'very successful', having tested the new doctrine of 'combined operations by both regular troops and territorial defence units.'[9]

On this upbeat note, the meeting adjourned for lunch, and Tito had other activities for the rest of the afternoon. That evening there was a reception in Tito's honour, and foreign minister Mirko Tepavac seized the opportunity to catch Secretary of State William Rogers and speak with him in private without his translator present. Rogers called Nixon the following morning to recount the conversation.

ROGERS: *He doesn't speak English very well, but he didn't want the interpreter there. And he said: 'I want you to know, for your own ears, and your ears only, the meeting with Brezhnev did not go well.'*

NIXON: *Ha.*

ROGERS: *And then I said to him to say it again and he said: 'The meeting with Brezhnev did not go well.' He said: 'You should know that.' And he said: 'You're the only one I have told it to.' And, I said, 'Well, of course, I want to tell President Nixon.' He said, 'Yes, President Tito told me to tell you so you could tell President Nixon.'*

NIXON: *Isn't it interesting that Tito, of course, he's a little gingerly, but he did not indicate that much. He said it did not go well?*

ROGERS: *That's right.*

NIXON: *Very interesting.*

Via Rogers, Tito and Tepavac succeeded in informing Nixon about the fear of the Soviets at the highest level in Yugoslavia, despite the positive words exchanged at the official meetings in both Belgrade and Washington. Nixon replied that Tito's interpreter had similarly told him that Yugoslavia 'may face some very great problems'.

> He said that 'President Tito is a very old man and when he dies, when he goes, I mean when he retires, then we may be confronted with the attempts of some of our neighbors to capitalize on that.'

Whatever Tito's reasons were for instructing Tepavac and his interpreter to take this approach, Rogers' anecdote matched his (Nixon's) brief exchange with the interpreter, 'but now I see the two conversations fit together like a glove'. These personal interventions from two directions confirmed in Nixon's mind the impression of 'how scared they are' of the Soviets intervening in response to domestic unrest or Tito's death. So scared, in fact, that they could never speak of it in public.[10]

Yugoslav military officials would later use similar tactics in their dealings with NATO (see Chapter 11), so these moves in Washington were probably coordinated to invite greater support from the West. The fear of Russia was real, but these coordinated messages succeeded if Tito's purpose was to invite increased Western support.

The following morning, 30 October, Nixon and Tito met for an hour with only an interpreter present. The meeting addressed the United Nations and the Group of 77, Vietnam, and issues surrounding the difficulties of US trade with and investment in Yugoslavia. Sensitive to Yugoslavia's position, Nixon first noted the 'strictly private nature' of his remarks, which should be 'issued only to the two Presidents and not distributed further'.

> While he did not know Brezhnev or Kosygin personally, there was no question in his mind that, because of its self-interest, the USSR would continue its efforts to bring its neighbors under increased influence. The independence of Yugoslavia and Romania, regardless of these two countries' internal systems, was consistent with U.S. interests but was not consistent with Soviet interests.

The challenge for the Eastern bloc was to have good relations with the United States without provoking the Soviets to intervene. Referring to the case of Hungary, 'liberation meant suicide.'

> However, the President stressed, his position would be to avoid any kind of understanding with Moscow that would give the Soviets encouragement to fish in troubled waters in Yugoslavia or elsewhere. He felt that he did not have to say more than that. President Tito said he fully understood what the President had in mind.[11]

In this manner, the presidents understood each other quite well – and Tito had achieved his objectives for the visit. After Washington, Tito visited Houston, Palm Springs and Los Angeles, and departed for Yugoslavia on

2 November. Neither of the meetings with Brezhnev and Nixon dwelt much on the internal situation in Yugoslavia, or on questions of democratisation and liberalism. On the heels of a hot political autumn in Croatia, Tito called the Croatian leadership to a meeting in Karađorđevo in late November.

10

Purge

'The Croatian leadership simply overplayed a hand which was virtually won'.[1]

The Hot Political Autumn

The autumn of 1971 started with the drafting and adoption of amendments to the Croatian constitution. American diplomats reported that the most contentious and publicly discussed issue was the first draft of the first amendment that defined the Socialist Republic of Croatia as,

> A sovereign national state of the Croatian nation, a state of the Serbian nation in Croatia, and a state of nationalities that live in Croatia, based on the sovereignty of nations and on the authority and the self-management of the working class and all working people, and socialist self-managed democratic community of working people, and citizens, and equal nations, and nationalities.[2]

The *Hrvatski Tjednik* was particularly critical of this formulation on nationalist grounds, claiming that it was contradictory. If the Socialist Republic of Croatia was the state of the Croatian nation, then Croatian sovereignty was the exclusive right of Croats. They complained that the proposed formulation meant that Croatia was a national state of not only Croats, but of all nationalities that lived there, which automatically diminished the value of Croatian sovereignty.

General Rade Bulat again caused a stir with a proposal to change the fourth amendment, which involved the establishment of a committee to manage the relations between the nationalities. The original amendment determined that the committee should have an equal number of Croats and Serbs, and a certain number of minorities. Bulat challenged the adequacy of such a proportion, suggesting that the committee should represent all nationalities equally and pass decisions only unanimously rather than by a majority. In practical terms, he was suggesting the establishment of a republican version of the federal Chamber of Nationalities. In his opinion, the committee would otherwise not guarantee complete protection to the Serb minority in Croatia. The Croatian party immediately accused Bulat of Serb chauvinism that wished to turn Croatia into a miniature federation of nations, and that he was challenging the ability of the LCC to secure equality for all nationalist living in Croatia. Simultaneously, the Croatian party strongly reprimanded Croatian 'chauvinists' who portrayed the LCC as traitors and promoted *Matica Hrvatska* as a political organisation and a substitute for the League of Communists.[3]

The British consul-general in Zagreb, Geoffrey Baker, reported on Bakarić's speech of 30 September in Topusko. Bakarić supported the draft of the first amendment, arguing that it was absurd to treat Serbs in Croatia as a national minority and that the key goal of this amendment was not to establish an independent Croatian state but to 'allow for the self-determination of nations.' Constitutions of multi-national states recognised *citizens*, rather than nations, as the guarantor of statehood. According to Bakarić, a similar model should be applied to multi-national Croatia. He also mentioned the language question, noting that Croats and Serbs spoke the same language. If some nationalities in Croatia wished to keep certain features of their dialects and literal language, they should be free to do so and the state should guarantee this right. Multi-lingual schools, however, should not be permitted, but pupils should learn of the language differences between Serbia and Croatia, and be permitted to use any of those variants. He also reprimanded *Matica Hrvatska* for its attempts to introduce a new Croatian orthography in schools. Later in December, after the removal of the Croatian liberal leadership, most of the 40,000 copies of the new Croatian orthography would be destroyed. The party would then conclude that the orthography 'does not satisfy basic political criteria.'[4] A copy was smuggled out of Croatia and it was republished in London, aimed at the 2 million Croats living abroad. Its preface complained:

> As part of a drastic political purge in Croatia, all 40,000 copies of the new Orthography, 'a mere orthographic rulebook' (Dr Dalibor Brozović) were destroyed. This happened despite the authors' great efforts, evident from their choice of examples in the book, to avoid a head-on clash with existing political concepts in Yugoslavia. Nevertheless, the new regime called the new book a 'nationalist act of sabotage' and ordered legal proceedings against the publishers.[5]

But Consul-General Baker remarked on the orthography: 'It was a one-sided and intolerant selection, maximising the differences between Serbian and Croat, and if officially approved would require separate schools to be set up in areas of mixed population.'[6]

The language question remained a contentious issue in 1971–2. The Croats wanted their language to be called the 'Croatian literary language' – at least in Croatia. The Serbs in Croatia, however, wished the language to be called 'Serbo-Croatian' or 'Croatian-Serbian', and wished to continue using the grammatical guidelines of the Novi Sad agreement. The Cultural Society of the Serbs in Croatia, *Prosvjeta*, objected to *Matica Hrvatska*'s attempts to separate the two languages. The fifth amendment draft regulated the use of language, stipulating that all republican laws and regulations were to be published in the Croatian and Serbian languages (the language of Serbs in Croatia), and in both Latin and Cyrillic alphabets. This was in line with recent decisions to reject the Novi Sad agreement and separate the Croatian and Serbian languages. The fourth amendment, however, defined the rights of nations and nationalities in Croatia, which included the right to education in languages of the nations and nationalities living in Croatia. Along with this, the Croatian Serbs were guaranteed the right 'to freely develop, the right to use their own language and letter, their culture, and organisation of education in their own language.'[7] Baker also reported on Croatian economic demands:

> Croatia's economic ambitions – the desire to fully control their own development, to retain and use a much greater share of the foreign currency earned in Croatia, and to prevent the alleged waste of national resources by mistaken investments in the under-developed regions – are being more freely discussed. They are the counterpart, for the industrialists and materialists, of the sentimental nationalism of intellectuals and students.

The key problem was the retention quota, the amount of foreign currency that businesses were allowed to keep, and the Croatian contribution to the fund for underdeveloped regions. Croatian politicians feared that this fund would continue with the same tradition of 'extra-budgetary funds' that were previously the instrument of the centrally planned economy.[8]

The British embassy in Belgrade believed that the greatest problem in Croatia was the position of the Serb minority, which included the issues surrounding the definitions and names of the state and language; the removal of General Bulat from his position as president of the Commission of People's Defence of the Socialist Republic of Croatia; and efforts to change the police structure, where there was a disproportionate number of Serbs. Other contentious issues were the control over the economy, the reform of the foreign currency distribution system and the Croatian contribution to the federal budget. The open manifestation of national feelings during the period of debate on the amendments was another problem. The British diplomats assumed that the Croatian leadership, which was supposed to keep nationalism under control, had been weakened by the internal conflict between the factions led by Bakarić on one side and the liberals Tripalo and Savka on the other.

> The search for public sympathy also comprises those whose doctrinal links with communism in Yugoslavia are more formal than real, such as certain academics (e.g. the Veselicas, Marko and Vladimir), some students (e.g. Budiša) and the crankier intellectuals of Hrvatski Tjednik.[9]

The British diplomat Michael Tait summarised these problems and concluded that the principle of parity that Bulat proposed was already in use at the federal level and should also be applied to the republics in order to prevent the majorities from outvoting the minorities. He mentioned that similar requests had been voiced in Serbia and other republics. The issue of foreign currency distribution, under the motto, 'Our foreign currency for us', did not hold ground because it contradicted the principle of the single market. He added that other republics supported Croatia with investments, raw materials, food and labour in order to earn foreign currency through both tourism and exports. Tait correctly assessed that the Croatian leadership had to take into serious consideration some radical demands in order to preserve its political influence. But as a consequence, this would increase tensions within the federation.

> In spite of earlier hopes that the Amendments to the Federal Constitution would take the steam out of the nationalities issue I very much doubt they will. The Amendments to the Federal Constitution are proving more of a milestone than a winning post.[10]

In November 1971, a rumour started to spread that the Croatian political leadership was divided, which had been known within the party but not to the wider public. The British reports noted that it was not likely that Tripalo would lose influence, despite recently suffering two heavy blows: his departure from the LCY Executive Council, and the expulsion of his 'poodles, Veselica and friends' from the LCY. According to this optimistic scenario, Bakarić as a spent politician would be retired to the Chamber of Federation of the Federal Assembly, while Savka Dabčević-Kučar would assume the key leading position in Croatian political life. The assumption was that Savka and Tripalo represented the new political force that would win over the 'conservatives' led by Bakarić. The British assumed that Bakarić would lose the factional battle, but that he was nevertheless a voice of reason in a fervent political environment.

> On the national issue Bakarić seems to every observer outside Croatia to represent common sense and an intention to keep Yugoslavia together; not conservative in any normal sense.[11]

Tito's visit to Croatia in September 1971 coincided with the public and parliamentary debates on the amendments to the Croatian constitution. He opened the traditional Zagreb autumn trade fair, and he visited Koprivnica, Križevci, Ludbreg, Varaždin and Kumrovec. The most important moment, however, was his meeting with the Croatian party leadership in Zagreb on 14 September 1971. He wanted to assess the situation in Croatia for himself, especially the position of the Serbian minority. The Croatian leadership, on the other hand, was eager to make Tito's visit to Zagreb as spectacular as possible, especially to counter his complaint that he was not as popular in Croatia as in other republics. The visit to Zagreb fulfilled all expectations, as Savka described it: 'You can bring people to the streets, but you cannot force a smile on their faces.'

Tito's speech at the gala dinner in the Hotel Esplanade after the meeting with the Croatian leaders had a tremendous impact on wider Yugoslav political life. He said that the stories about 'flourishing Croatian chauvinism' were absurd. The cheerful atmosphere surrounding his visit must have helped. He also emphasised that Croatian demands on the foreign currency and banking needed to be resolved, but he also made it clear that he would not permit the fragmentation of the republics. This was a message to everybody in Yugoslavia that the regime would not allow the dissolution of the Yugoslav state.[12]

The discussion on the amendments was a good opportunity to promote different political platforms. The student movement and *Matica Hrvatska* went the furthest in promoting their positions about the future of Croatia within the federation. While they also held less controversial positions on foreign currency and foreign trade, more in line with official LCC policy, the student leaders Budiša and Čičak also loudly promoted the definition of Croatia as the national state of the Croatian nation. The amendments were one of the key reasons for the student protest and occupation of administrative buildings in November. Some statements made at public gatherings organised at Zagreb faculties were particularly bold for their time, and would later be used to persecute the speakers. At a protest gathering at the faculty of philosophy on 29 October 1971, the economist Hrvoje Šošić proposed that Croatia should be accepted into the United Nations, similarly to the status of Belarus and Ukraine at the time. He also argued that Croatia should establish its own central bank, elect a governor, and send him or her to the United States to obtain loans. Although these statements may have been made speculatively, they further inflamed the political and public atmosphere.[13]

In September 1971, Ivan Zvonimir Čičak and his brother Neno visited the American consulate to discuss opportunities for exchanges with American universities. Čičak suggested that a delegation of American students could attend a student gathering in Dubrovnik in October, which was organised by the Croatian and Zagreb student organisations. He also proposed a visit of Croatian students to the United States. But because of lack of time and information about the Dubrovnik event, and political sensitivities, the consulate politely declined the invitation. They were extra careful about the Čičaks' plan to promote independent relations between Croatian and foreign universities without the participation of the Yugoslav student organisation.[14] The Dubrovnik gathering, known as 'University Today', was the forum where the ideas for the student protests took shape, which would set in motion a chain of events that contributed to the collapse of the spring movement.[15]

The British embassy commented on an article in *Borba* that reported on the Dubrovnik student gathering. They were puzzled by Budiša's statement that Croatia was 'exploited by the federal bureaucracy, banks and foreign exporters.' Accordingly, he had invited foreign student organisations to promote the truth about the situation in Yugoslavia. He also made clear the Croatian student organisation would independently start to establish relations with foreign student organisations. The embassy reported that Budiša's speech was badly received at the headquarters of the Yugoslav student organisation in Belgrade, where the majority of republican student organisations opposed the Croatian initiative, considering the international nature of the gathering and the fact that Budiša only represented the Zagreb branch of the student organisation.[16]

At the party level, the confrontation between liberal reformists and communist conservatives had already escalated by the 22nd plenum of the CC LCC in early November 1971. At the plenum, Savka Dabčević-Kučar once again drew attention to the foreign currency issue. Consul-General Wilson focused on this part of her speech:

> If the present system should be continued, with this degree of centralization, administrative management and [favouritism] of importers (over exporters), then the only alternative – which does not seem a reasonable (*razumnom*) one – would be to impose a complete decentralization of the foreign currency system and regime among the Republics.

With such sharp words, Savka tried to express her dissatisfaction with the slow pace of economic reform and the foreign currency regime, which were Croatia's most important demands. According to Savka, it was also a test for other republics, primarily Serbia, to show their support for reforms and the implementation of constitutional amendments. Savka pointed out that Croatia earned 28 per cent of Yugoslavia's foreign currency from exports, 59 per cent from transport, 72 per cent from tourism, and 34 per cent from workers abroad. She also made clear that only Croatia and Montenegro had a positive foreign trade balance, while all other republics, including Slovenia, had negative foreign trade balances. Hence, the foreign currency that remained in Croatia was disproportionately low. Another problem was how to treat remittances from workers abroad. Remittances sent by workers to their families were treated just like foreign currency income from other sources, with a large portion confiscated by the federal state.

Savka's key complaint was that the existing system was not in line with the constitutional principles of the single market, and that the burden of economic relations with the world was disproportionately distributed among the republics, at Croatia's expense. Another request was that the foreign currency should be kept in republican banks and not in Belgrade, which was a direct attack on the privileged position of the Belgrade banks.[17] Savka also pointed out a problem with military contracts, which only certain republics could obtain. This criticism was particularly distressing to military circles across Yugoslavia.

Despite the clash with their adversaries in the Central Committee, the reformists got the upper hand at the 22nd meeting of the CC LCC. At this meeting, the Croatian Serb Dušan Dragosavac was the most visible opponent of the reformist line and the fiercest critic of nationalism in Croatia. Although the impression was that he did not manage to discredit the circle around Savka and Tripalo, preparations had already quietly been started to remove the Croatian leadership. Dragosavac's greatest complaint about Savka's speech was her affirmation rather than criticism of the 'mass movement' and the uncustomary adoption of her speech as an official plenum document and programme of the Croatian party. Dragosavac's fierce criticism of the Croatian leadership's recent moves publicly brought to the surface the brewing conflict between the two opposing camps in the Croatian party.

After the 22nd plenum, Dragosavac requested a meeting with Tito to inform him about the events in Croatia, in agreement with the conservative faction of the Croatian leadership. In his meeting with Tito on 14 November in Bugojno, Bosnia, he accused some of the Croatian leadership of favouring Croatian nationalism. Tito was already concerned about the events in Croatia and his decision to intervene in its political life was probably influenced by Dragosavac's intervention. The only question that remains today is whether Tito was already prepared to intervene, or whether the student protests that started late November tipped the scales.[18]

The student protests started on 22 November 1971 and lasted for twelve days until 3 December. The formal reason to boycott classes at most Zagreb faculties, as well as at some faculties in other Croatian universities in Split, Rijeka and Osijek, had nothing to do with the university. It was about the conflict between Jure Sarić, the 'liberal' vice president of the Association of Trade Unions of Croatia, and its 'unitarist' president, Milutin Baltić. The cause of the conflict was the expulsion of Marko Veselica from its executive council, at Baltić's initiative. The student movement used this incident to show their support for the liberal Croatian leadership and their demands for economic fairness and transparency. Very soon the protests became a platform to promote policies of reform of the foreign currency, banking and foreign trade systems – in line with Savka's most recent speech.

Miko Tripalo and Pero Pirker tried to mitigate the damage and reprimanded the students for boycotting classes, as an attempt to discredit the LCC's official policy. Although Tripalo and Pirker supported the substance of the protests, they opposed the methods. In a speech to the workers of the Tvorpam factory in Zagreb, Tripalo warned that the consequences could be tragic for the LCC and its leadership. He also warned that the protest endangered the ability of the Croatian leadership to renegotiate the foreign currency system.

The student protests were the final straw that irreversibly divided the Croatian leadership, as well as the student movement. In a letter to Tito on 23 November, Pero Pirker sharply attacked the student leaders and with some exaggeration accused them of calling for the break-up of the Yugoslav army. Pirker summarised the efforts by the Zagreb party committee in mitigating the damage done by the student protests, but he also warned about 'potentially more dangerous consequences, if the public finds out about the recommendations of the Parity Commission which doesn't change anything with regard to the foreign currency regime.'[19]

The party leadership was opposed to the student protests from the very beginning, and this represented the most obvious conflict between the two opposing factions of the Croatian national movement. The party leaders pragmatically understood that the student protests, in an already heated atmosphere, would only aggravate the relationship with Tito and other political players in Croatian and Yugoslavia. But despite pressures to end the protests, the Croatian party respected the students' decision to boycott classes until 3 December.

British diplomats observed that the protests caused a small sensation across Yugoslavia. The key demand was to obtain firm assurances that a foreign currency reform would be carried out. Along with this, the president of the Croatian student organisation, Ante Paradžik, presented additional demands that the British considered to be openly nationalistic. The Belgrade embassy pointed out that Paradžik justified these demands by claiming he supported the LCC's official line, whereas the LCC had only paid lip service to the students.

At the British Embassy in Belgrade, Michael Tait emphasised that the student demands differed significantly from the official party line. On 22 November, Paradžik had demanded the exclusive use of the Croatian language in Croatia, and generously added that translators should be hired to help those Yugoslav citizens who had difficulty understanding it. He also suggested that the headquarters of the Yugoslav navy should be moved from Belgrade to Split; that Croat conscripts should only serve in Croatia; and that the official language in the army units based in Croatia should only be Croatian.[20]

Tait did mention that this was not the first time that Croatian students had presented these demands, but it was the first time that they had done so publicly. The reaction to the protests was mixed. Although the Zagreb faculties mainly supported the strikes, this was not the case with other universities. Students from Osijek and Rijeka universities opposed the protests, although they supported reforms of the foreign currency regime. Similarly, a majority of Zagreb manufacturing businesses also opposed the protests.[21]

Tait concluded that it was unusual for student organisations to organise protests about these particular issues. He acknowledged, however, that the foreign currency and foreign trade issues were becoming a matter of great discontent in the whole of Croatia. In a more democratic society, the protests and their demands could be acknowledged as a normal part of public debate, but given the firm position the students had taken against both the federal government and other republics, the regime had to act.[22]

The Karađorđevo Meeting and the Purge

> *It was good that the comrades in their speeches were primarily turned towards themselves, and then, naturally, towards these events in Zagreb, which do not represent an isolated case. This is not the first time that a strike has taken place. Here, during these discussions we saw a good number of reasons which had led to such a development as a massive strike of students, a strike which had a tendency towards growing into a general strike, not only of students, but also of the working class, a tendency towards bringing our whole life to a standstill. The very hint at the possibility of organising such a general strike is a counter-revolutionary development.*
>
> Tito's concluding speech at Karađorđevo
> 2 December 1971.[23]

The December 1971 events represented the height of the political crisis and the end of the Croatian liberal leadership. Immediately before the 21st meeting of the Presidency of the LCY at Tito's country residence in Karađorđevo on 31 November and 1 December, Tito called a meeting with the Croatian leadership. He invited both factions and gave them the opportunity to present their arguments, which he moderated in an ostensibly impartial manner. But his real goal was to prepare the ground for a political purge. It was obvious from Tito's final speech that he no longer supported the liberal wing of the Croatian party. He clearly criticised the actions of *Matica Hrvatska*, the media, the student movement, the efforts to counter the dangers of 'unitarism' and tolerating Croatian nationalism. He made it clear that he did not support the current policy of the Croatian leadership, because this policy was leading to civil war.

Despite general acknowledgement that some people would have to go, no names were mentioned at this first meeting with the Croatians, nor was it clear what actions would be taken.[24] Tito repeated his views at the meeting with the LCY presidency, and these were later published all over the Yugoslav press. Even then, there were no specific demands or requests for the departure of individual Croatian leaders, but only general criticisms about the situation in Croatia.[25]

The week after Karađorđevo was a period of transition, when there was still hope in Croatia that the purges would not be severe. Immediately after the meeting, the LCC and Savka Dabčević-Kučar were cheered all over Croatia, except by the workers of the steel mill in Sisak, who on 3 December publicly refused to support the Croatian leadership unless they fell into line with Tito. Consul-General Baker was told that many of these workers were Serbs. Savka's name was mentioned less and less in the press until 8 December, when a member of the conservative faction, Milka Planinc, declared that only Tito's name could be celebrated. It then became clear that Savka and Tripalo would have to go.[26]

The first sign that the compromised faction would be removed was Bakarić's speech on 7 December, when he openly attacked Savka for the first time. It seems that not even she was aware that her removal was imminent.[27] On 8 December the Executive Bureau of the LCY formally decided in Karađorđevo that Savka Dabčević-Kučar and Pero Pirker would have to resign from their party positions. Although Miko Tripalo wasn't mentioned specifically, he also resigned along with other liberal Croatian officials at the 23rd meeting of the Central Committee LCC on 12 December.[28]

The American report compiled immediately after the first Karađorđevo meeting acknowledged part of the blame lay with Tito, because for several months he had been preoccupied with foreign policy. The signs that nationalism was on the rise were present in all the republics, most of all in Croatia, where the communist leadership had tolerated such activities. It had ignored Tito's warnings from April and September, and the reactions to the situation in Croatia could best be interpreted by two articles in the magazine *Komunist* on 4 and 25 November which sharply criticised the mild reactions of Croatian leaders to nationalism.

> It is unclear whether Tito has any concrete evidence of outside hostile forces or whether he merely felt it politic to allude to their involvement. However, his use of epithet 'counter-revolutionary' had clear-cut purpose in mind. Tito obviously

feared linkage between students and workers which might have produced violent action in streets to damage of Yugoslavia's image abroad as socialist country while providing fuel for Soviets to claim, in harmony with Brezhnev Doctrine, that counter-revolutionists threatened socialism in Yugoslavia and required outside intervention. By labelling students' actions and other nationalist manifestations as 'counter-revolutionary', and by giving instructions for sharp and immediate retaliation, Tito provided evidence that the LCY recognized the threat and was moving quickly to crush it. That this tactic is instructive to other republican parties in highlighting threat to Yugoslavia unity is indicated by their careful efforts to avoid public criticism of Croatian party, while at same time taking steps to put their own houses in order lest virus spread to their republics. The Serbian party in particular, while admitting to considerable anti-Croatian feeling in Serbia, has made clear its awareness that nationalism within Serbia (e.g. Kosovo) also poses potential for trouble.

The American diplomats assumed in December that *Matica Hrvatska*, the university professors, the student leadership and the media would be the first targets of a purge. Their contacts believed that purges within the Croatian party were also imminent.[29]

The officials at the American consulate in Zagreb felt that the majority of the population in predominantly Croat areas were still loyal to the Croatian leadership. A member of the Executive Committee of the Central Committee of the LCC told Wilson on 9 December that the next meeting of the Central Committee would have to decide about the removal of some of its officials. He mentioned that he had warned Savka and Tripalo to stick to the facts, instead of spreading unsubstantiated accusation about the economic exploitation of Croatia. Wilson added that the source was a member of the liberal faction and a strong supporter of Croatian interests. The student leadership kept quiet until 3 December, but the instigators of the protests came under strong pressure. Some faculty members told the Americans that the protests had been counter-productive and damaging.[30]

The 23rd meeting of the CC LCC held on 12 December revealed the depth of the political purge in Croatia. The Central Committee accepted the resignations of Miko Tripalo, Savka Dabčević-Kučar, Pero Pirker and

Marko Koprtla. Srećko Bijelić resigned as president of the Zagreb party branch, Ivan Šibl announced his resignation from the veterans association, and the Deputy Commander of the 5th JNA district, General Janko Bobetko, resigned from his membership of the Central Committee and all his military duties.[31] At the same meeting, Milka Planinc was elected as the new president of the Central Committee, instead of Savka Dabčević-Kučar; and Josip Vrhovec replaced Pero Pirker as the new secretary of the Executive Committee of the Central Committee. Milan Mišković replaced Marko Koprtla as the new member of the Executive Committee. Resignations from all parts of Croatia then started pouring into Zagreb.[32]

The election of Milan Mišković drew special attention from the US Embassy, for his past in the security services. He was the Croatian Minister of the Interior for ten years (1953–63), and his election was noteworthy considering the purge of political rivals that followed. The American diplomats did not fail to notice that Belgrade newspapers published extensive biographies of Josip Vrhovec and Milka Planinc, but omitted Mišković's association with the security services.[33] The entire leadership of *Matica Hrvatska* resigned and the student leaders Ivan Zvonimir Čičak, Dražen Budiša and Goran Dodig were arrested on 12 December along with ten other students, while the police continued to search for Ante Paradžik. Rumours were circulating that preparations for new student protests were under way, to coincide with the 23rd meeting of the Central Committee.

The student protest planned for 12 December was prohibited, and the party headquarters were surrounded with police and armoured vehicles. Despite this, 400 students were arrested, although the police was not overly harsh with them. The police apologised to passers-by for any random injuries, while many protesters were simply driven 20 km out of town and dumped there to walk back. On the following day, around 400 students gathered on Republic Square on 13 December in support of the Croatian party leadership. In the ensuing unrest, the police arrested 76 of them.

The Zagreb consulate reported on 14 December that the situation was quiet and that classes had resumed.[34] The American diplomats believed that such drastic measures were the consequence of the criticisms made at the 22nd meeting of the presidency of the LCY, about the reluctance to carry out the decision of the 21st meeting (when Tito had hinted at necessary removals without naming anyone). Tito's meeting with the military leadership in Karađorđevo on 11 December was believed to be a precautionary measure, similar to the move he made in 1948 during the conflict with the Cominform.[35]

It was expected that the Croatian prime minister Dragutin Haramija would resign for defending Savka and Tripalo, and for warning the police to respect the law. The public prosecutor Slobodan Budak also resigned on 14 December over criticism that he was not aggressive enough in suppressing Croatian nationalism and 'chauvinism'. There was a heavy police presence all over town, and Wilson personally saw them beating students during the arrests on the 13th. Posters were put up across the university against the 'imposed dictators' of the new party leadership. There were rumours that Čičak and Budiša were injured during their arrests, and that the workers of the *Končar* factory were considering a Christmas strike if the foreign currency system was not fixed.[36] The British Consul General Geoffrey Baker reported in a similar vein:

> It is worth noting in fact how non-violent the 'opposition' has been. When the students boycotted their lecturers, they did not accept to march in the streets; in clashing with the police since 12 December they have not even resorted to stone-throwing. Slogans and songs are their weapon, so far. The show of force has all been on the other side. There have been no reports of fatalities; but I would not be surprised to learn that a few students did not survive the clubbing they received.

The largest group of protesters gathered on Republic Square on 15 December, but this time the police were less violent. A member of the Central Committee confirmed to Wilson that Haramija's speech at the 23rd meeting was not in line with other speeches, because he called for an end to the witch-hunt and Stalinist practices. He also defended the sacked Croatian politicians. This compromised his prime ministership and he would resign on 22 December. A doctor confirmed that the arrested student leaders were well and that the people of Zagreb were comparing the situation in Croatia to Czechoslovakia. A police source told Wilson that 'the situation is hard to repair, because the key to the solution is elsewhere.'[37]

On 15 December, a US Embassy official spoke to the chief editor of *Komunist*, Gavro Altman, about the situation in Croatia. Altman told him that the federal party leadership feared that events would get out of control after the removal of Savka and Tripalo. He also mentioned that Jakov Blažević, a Croatian member of the CK, had warned Tito about the grave situation in Croatia before the student protests began. The Yugoslav League of Communists leadership were shocked by the events in Croatia because they realised what the consequences would be if Tito had not decided to intervene. According to Altman, Blažević and others believed that 'foreign intelligence services' were behind the student protests.[38] Blažević repeated his view at the 23rd plenum when he linked the student leaders, *Matica Hrvatska* and *Prosvjeta* to an 'international conspiracy against socialism.'[39]

The *New York Times* and *The Times* of London reported on 3 December that Tito had accused the Croatian leadership of not putting an end to the student protests.[40] David Binder, the *New York Times* correspondent in Belgrade (1963–6), returned to Zagreb in 1971 to follow the unfolding event in Croatia. He recalled to the author that,

> All I can remember is that Zagreb was cold, dark and grim. [...] The shock of the demonstrations was profound, partly because life had begun to become more pleasant in the late '60s, making Croats better off than, for instance, Serbs. Nationalism was not a surprise in Kosovo [...], but it was in Croatia because the Croats were considered more docile than the Serbs. After all, Tito was a Croat! The Croatians I met at that time were all profoundly depressed over the events and to find themselves under the thumb of that cross-eyed and narrow-minded dogmatist, Josip Vrhovec. I didn't blame them.[41]

On 16 December, Binder reported that Zagreb was quiet after several days of unrest. The key reason for the protests were the resignations of Savka Dabčević-Kučar, Miko Tripalo and Pero Pirker, who were considered to be Yugoslavia's most intelligent and progressive politicians. The Croatian leadership was removed because they hadn't put an end to the student protests. Their main criticisms had been directed at the foreign currency regime, which confiscated most of Croatia's earnings from tourism. Binder also added that despite this, the quality of life in Croatia was much better than in Serbia or other parts of the country. A young Croatian business-man complained to Binder: 'It is a tragedy. Our best leaders were sacrificed to stupid student extremism. Those leaders, Mika and Savka, lost control and maybe that is the lesson – when you lose control of something progressive, it can be the opposite of progressive.'[42]

On 17 December Binder reported on Josip Vrhovec's comment that 'nationalist forces' were planning Croatia's secession from Yugoslavia. He spoke to a *Vjesnik* employee who told him that the situation inside its offices was becoming unbearable because of nationalist sentiment, and that if Tito hadn't intervened, the nationalists would start 'to open camps for those who thought differently.' One Croatian Serb compared the situation in Croatia to Bangladesh, and the secession of East Pakistan from Pakistan with the support of the Soviet Union and India.[43] The link to Bangladesh was not merely a metaphor. The Yugoslav ambassador to the United Nations, the Macedonian Lazar Mojsov, reported to Belgrade in December 1971 that he had a conversation with the Pakistani ambassador, who said he planned to comment on the bad American press Yugoslavia was receiving on Croatian separatism and the possibility of foreign intervention. This was Pakistan's reprimand for Yugoslavia's decision to support Bangladeshi independence. Ambassador Mojsov managed to convince his Pakistani colleague to refrain from this, but the Pakistani ambassador added that a similar situation could occur in other parts of the world, alluding to Croatia.[44]

Two days later Binder reported that the crisis in Croatia was more severe than previously thought. New information revealed that the removed leadership not only tolerated but had encouraged nationalists. This was confirmed to Binder by an established Zagreb journalist, who singled out Savka and Tripalo. Sources in Zagreb and Belgrade also told Binder that the 'movement' had contaminated all aspects of Yugoslav life, the economy and the morale of the armed forces. One example was the unwillingness of Croatian enterprises to do business with other republics, including the refusal to distribute Belgrade newspapers in Croatia.[45]

Croatian Prime Minister Haramija resigned on 22 December, along with his deputy Vjekoslav Prpić and two deputy speakers of the Croatian parliament, Maks Baće and Milivoj Rukavina. Despite this, Haramija was in a better position than the party leadership, because he was more of a technocrat than a politician. But he still had to resign, not for any failures as prime minister, but for his sympathy with the reformers.[46]

On 20 December Wilson reported that the situation in Zagreb was calm. Thousands of workers returning from abroad for Christmas were searched and placed under surveillance. Radio stations warned the population not to succumb to 'false propaganda'. Midnight Mass at Zagreb Cathedral was cancelled, and a 'good source' confirmed that the Archbishop of Zagreb, Cardinal Kuharić, was very depressed, while church newspapers were also placed under surveillance. Interestingly, all tickets for the 'nationalist' opera *Nikola Šubić Zrinski* were sold out, and the performance was not banned.[47]

Christmas in Zagreb was cold and foggy, while the Mass celebrations were unusually well attended. Wilson feared that the Archbishop's Christmas message, where he emphasised the rights of the Croatian people and the importance of Croatian traditions, could provoke the authorities. In his message, Archbishop Kuharić declared that everyone had the right to their own home, language, life and freedom, reminding worshippers that patriotism had Christ's blessing. Wilson added:

> While under more normal conditions the Christmas message of Archbishop-Metropolitan Franjo Kuharić of Zagreb would in all probability be considered moderate, in the current atmosphere it seems likely to be interpreted as a strong reaffirmation of the Croatian people's right to cherish their national heritage. It may, therefore, evoke a negative official reaction.

The Belgrade weekly *Nin* did attack the Cardinal's message, calling him the 'confidante of counter-revolution'.[48]

On 27 December, American diplomats spoke to Stane Dolanc, a member of the LCY Presidium, who believed that the Croatian affair was the worst crisis in postwar Yugoslavia. He confirmed that the Croatian leaders would not be imprisoned, because there was no proof that they were connected to either the *Ustaša* or the Cominform. He singled out Tripalo as the main culprit behind the events in Croatia.[49] Dolanc also told the Swiss ambassador that the Croatian leadership did have a point when speaking about economic problems, as Croatian industry was in a bad state and required investment for modernisation.[50] American diplomats reported on the rumours that were circulating in Belgrade:

> Ranković will return: many of his former agents have been 'rehabilitated' and dispatched to Croatia; Steps have been taken to tighten Yugoslavia's borders with Western countries; Both Yugoslav and local Serbian authorities seriously worried over large-scale smuggling into Kosovo of small arms by Slavs and Shiptars [Albanians] alike; Serbian LC leadership in trouble with Tito because of public statements early in the Croatian crisis; Kardelj and Crvenkovski could have called halt to trend of developments in Croatia in absence of Tito but refused to do so.[51]

Immediately after Karađorđevo purges started in the Croatian media, and the tone of their reporting changed abruptly. All 'nationalist' media disappeared from kiosks, including *Hrvatski Tjednik, Hrvatsko Sveučilište, Hrvatski Gospodarski Glasnik, Telegram, Omladinski Tjednik* and *Studentski List.* The director of *Vjesnik,* Božidar Novak; the director of Radio-television Zagreb, Ivo Bojanić; the editor-in-chief of *Vjesnik,* Milovan Baletić; and the editor-in-chief of *Vjesnik on Wednesday,* Krešimir Džeb, all resigned. The American contacts believed that the media purge would continue and that only Tito would be able to put a stop to it. But they did not expect that this was going to happen any time soon.

Opinion in Croatia was divided. Many believed that the media had been promoting harmful trends over the past several months, but others thought that the desire for freedom of information was so strong in Croatia that the Western style of free media would eventually prevail.[52]

American diplomats also noted the conspiratorial statement by the new secretary of the Croatian party, Josip Vrhovec, about plans to divide Yugoslavia along Yalta lines. He added that the 'counterrevolutionaries' had tried to draw Croatia into the Western camp, which would inevitably provoke a Soviet intervention. The Americans noted that Vrhovec's statement was published only by *Tanjug,* the Yugoslav news agency. *Borba* and *Politika* did not mention it, so it was probably aimed at international rather than domestic readers.[53]

At the end of December and in early January 1972, embassies were dispatching analyses explaining the causes and developments of the crisis in Croatia. The western diplomats identified the weakness of the Yugoslav party as the key reason, as well as the complacency that followed the sharp rise in party membership after the invasion of Czechoslovakia. Before the crisis Tito neglected his role in the party, while other leaders were preoccupied with drafting and adopting constitutional amendments. The party was traditionally unpopular in Croatia and represented a political ideological apparatus imposed from the outside, primarily from Belgrade. As such it wasn't seen as a protector of local interests. In order to overcome this animosity, the Croatian leadership turned to nationalism as a source of support.

Another cause of the crisis the diplomats identified was Croatian nationalism, which had posed a problem ever since the Yugoslav state was established after World War I. The Croats perceived the central authorities in Belgrade to be the extended arm of Serbian hegemony. The fall of Ranković and the constitutional reforms increased media freedoms, freedom of speech and Western influence. They also brought greater autonomy to the republics, increasing nationalist sentiment. The key players were *Matica Hrvatska*, the press, the students and professors, but also 'primitive elements' of poorer regions of Croatia. Nationalism became a central instrument by which the Croatian party sought to gain concessions from Belgrade – and protect itself against negative reactions.

The economic factor was equally important, in the diplomats' view. The key issues were the problem of the Belgrade banks, assistance to the underdeveloped areas and the foreign currency system. Croatia demanded a larger share of foreign currency reserves in order to import Western technology for its industry.

Lastly, it was difficult to assess to what extent international factors influenced the situation in Croatia. There was no evidence of a link between the Soviets and *Ustaši* émigrés. The Americans concluded that the crisis would not increase separatist and terrorist activities.[54]

> Until the end of November I would have endorsed my predecessor's conclusion that this nationalism would not develop separatist tendencies that would weaken the cohesion of Yugoslavia.

With this observation, the British consul-general Geoffrey Baker started his report on the December crisis. He concluded that the amendments adopted in June did not help to alleviate the situation, but on the contrary led to an increase in nationalism demands for greater autonomy. The key issue were the amendments on the Croatian constitution and the Yugoslav financial system. Baker noted that the Croatian party on one side, and *Matica Hrvatska* with the students on the other, were the two leading forces articulating and pursuing these demands. In mid-December Baker observed:

> Nevertheless they are, with few exceptions, Croats at heart, and welcome the opportunity now – at last – afforded by the changes in the Federal constitution for Croatia to become largely self-governing. By the same token they are not perturbed at the growing freedom of discussion and debate, and of comment by the communications media, which has in recent years been evidence of the liberalisation of political life in Yugoslavia … Lastly, if I may dare a generalisation, it seems to me that the lust for debate springs from an innate liveliness of the Croatian mentality; Croats appear to be naturally more analytical and argumentative than Serbs or even Slovenes. Better perhaps that this be given scope for expression in words, rather than in conspiracy and bloody violence.

The position of the Croatian Serbs was also of particular interest to the British. The 'sentimental nationalists' believed that giving the status of 'nation' to the Croatian Serbs diminished Croatian sovereignty by declaring Croatia a multinational state.

> They, and the generations that begat them, have so keenly aspired to the full realization of their essential 'Croatianism' that in the formal definition of their own Republic they are unwilling to share it with the Serbian minority. Thus moreover their language should be called 'Croat' and the differences between it and 'ekavski' variant of Serbo-Croat should be cultivated; and their University should be the 'Croatian university', not merely that of Zagreb. This 'sentimental' nationalism has been nurtured through long centuries of alien imperialist rule, and has persisted hardly weakened by the 'Act of Union' after the First World War which created the Kingdom of the

Southern Slavs. The single generation that elapsed since the Second World War is not sufficient to defuse it. No wonder that this issue should attract such wide attention, and considerable public support. I do not however see in this polemic any serious threat to long-term inter-Republican cohesion in Yugoslavia, or to the Communist leadership.

Baker noted, however, that the Serbian question was not the most important aspect of the crisis. He was clear that the Croatian political leadership, despite pressures, was determined to guarantee national rights to the Serbian minority. And apart from the Karin case,[55] there were no significant conflicts between Croats and Serbs. Even in cases where Serbs were relieved of their jobs, the reasons were mainly related to the removal of unqualified political appointees who were often former veterans. The most controversial demands were limited to student leaders, including Croatian UN and IMF membership, the right to serve in the Yugoslav army in Croatia, and the demand to move the Navy headquarters from Belgrade to Split. Apart from the students, no one went so far as to demand the exercise of the new Yugoslav constitutional right to secession. Baker added that the Croatian leadership was never so popular as now that it had been deposed, and continued:

> The large number of helmeted militia-men in the streets and the tanks guarding the Party headquarters over the weekend appear to the populace of Zagreb as evidence of re-assertion of authoritarian rule, imposed moreover from the centre – Belgrade. [...] The people of Zagreb are profoundly distressed by these developments, and wear uniformly long faces. [...] A chance acquaintance – a young musician met in a public park – told me, when he learnt who I was, that he and his like equated the downfall of the LCC leadership with events in Czechoslovakia in 1968; for Dubček read Dabčević. There are indeed certain parallels, on the plane of general political life; but in Croatia the decisive issue was of course the apprehended rise of the nationalists.

Finally, Baker concluded his report with prophetic words: 'It will be a sad irony if future historians have to date from 2 December 1971 a growing belief among thinking Croats that some form of separatism, however materially disadvantageous, may be the only way of escaping from Serb hegemony.'[56]

It was already clear that many people would be thrown out of political and public life. The British consul-general expressed hope, however, that the new Croatian leadership would regain the trust of the Croatian people. The adoption of some of the Croatian demands would certainly alleviate the situation.[57]

Tito's main criticism of the Croatian leadership concerned their benevolence towards nationalism, not their direct cooperation with the nationalists. Baker added, 'All this is true, but neither the outgoing leaders nor general Croatian opinion have seen anything wicked or dangerous in it.' The British ambassador to Belgrade, Dugald Stewart, disagreed with Baker's view that Tito had overreacted to events that were 'natural and harmless'.

> As the veil lifts we are beginning to get convincing evidence that some ugly and dangerous things have been happening in Croatia in the last few months. Perhaps the most direct expression of the Croat case which I have recently seen in print, i.e. *The Economist* article entitled 'Old man in panic', is certainly a long way off beam.[58]

We return to 'An old man in a panic' in the next chapter, and how the FCO operated to bring the British press 'on message'. It seems here, however, that Stewart's remarks about 'ugly and dangerous' things were related to the conversation that his colleague Michael Tait had with the former student leader Slobodan Lang, and with Novak Pribićević, a member of the Croatian government. He got a similar impression from his Croat friends in Belgrade, 'as well as, I need hardly say, from everyone I know in Belgrade who is not a Croat.'[59]

On 19 December Tait spoke to Slobodan Lang, whom he described as a 'twenty-year-old medical student'.[60] His father was Jewish, while his mother was a member of a middle-class Dubrovnik family. Lang was very depressed by the situation and was considering emigrating. As a Jew he was very sensitive to extremism, and he asked Tait to take this into consideration. He described Budiša, who was imprisoned at the time, as a hardline nationalist preoccupied with the idea of the nation, at the expense of the well-being or wishes of the individual. According to Lang, in one of his speeches, Budiša told his fellow students that they need to 'act and not think', while Budiša would assume responsibility for the 'thinking'. He adored the idea of being a leader. When Lang asked Budiša whether he saw any resemblance between himself and the *Ustaša* leader Pavelić, Budiša replied that his positions were firm and that others should adapt to him.

He accused Budiša of physical violence, throwing Serb students out of dormitories. One of Lang's associates was threatened with being thrown out of a window if he were to stand for the student leadership. Many students carried Croatian coats of arms on their sleeves, and once a girl was attacked who was a moderate member of the student organisation. She had described the coats of arms as an *Ustaši* symbol. Lang believed that the students in dormitories were armed, and he feared for his safety. Someone had drawn a Star of David and a swastika on his house. He also told the British diplomat that one of his Serb associates was driven to suicide by the pressure from Croat students.

Lang and Čičak were called to the chancellor's office to explain this incident, and Čičak blamed himself and others. But when Čičak learned that the student was not dead, but severely injured, he turned around and blamed the suicide attempt on a Serb conspiracy. Later Lang was present at a meeting in which Croatian students discussed how to take political advantage of this incident.

Čičak and Lang had many disagreements, and once Čičak told him he despised people, but he would tell them what they wanted to hear so he could achieve his aims. When Lang asked him what he would do if he failed to deliver on his promises, Čičak answered that he would simply blame somebody else. Lang also described the case of a Serb student who did not support Budiša, and he could not get a place in a dormitory. Something similar had happened to the Serb student who attempted suicide, and remained disabled.[61]

Lang was in a difficult situation because he was accused of 'unitarism' for his disagreements with Budiša and other student leaders. On the other hand, he was characterised as a nationalist by the regime because he opposed the harsh treatments in the December purge. Until February 1971, Lang believed that Tripalo was not really a nationalist but he later changed and became a weapon in the hands of extreme nationalists. Tait had the impression that Lang was honest and moderate, and Joseph Dobbs, the previous consul-general in Zagreb and a good friend of Lang's father, shared his view.[62]

The following day Tait spoke with Novak Pribičević, a Croatian Serb who was the son of the former Yugoslav ambassador to Canada and a cousin of Branko Pribičević, a member of the Central Committee of the Serbian party. Tait reached out to Novak Pribičević through a mutual friend, and wrote in his diplomatic report that he wished to speak privately and informally.

Pribičević said that the only reaction to Tito's July warning was the expulsion of Professors Veselica and Đodan. During his second visit to Croatia in September, Tito declared that there was no danger of Croatian nationalism. According to Pribičević, the only explanation for Tito's pro-nouncement was an attempt to protect the Croatian leadership from attacks from other republics, and to give them an opportunity to honour their July promises. Another more personal explanation was that Tito sim-ply underestimated the dangers of nationalism.

Pribičević believed that Tito reacted because he wanted to prevent the removal of Bakarić and Vrhovec from the Croatian leadership. Bakarić par-ticularly influenced Tito's decision by pointing out the possibility that the Croatian leadership could shift blame and remove opponents of national-ism. Another risk was the possibility that student protests could turn into bloody street violence.

The new Croatian leadership was in a difficult position and had to gain early legitimacy. The foreign currency issue needed to be resolved quickly in order to prevent the impression of an anti-Croat policy being imposed by Belgrade. The goal was to dissuade the Croatian population from thinking that the clock would turn back to pre-1966 authoritarianism. According to Pribičević, Tito might have overreacted with the purge, and his statement that the judiciary and public prosecutors should not cling to the letter of the law like 'drunks to a fence' was unhelpful.

Finally, Pribičević mentioned *Matica Hrvatska* and the students, link-ing them to threats and violence. Budiša's supporters controlled three of seven Zagreb dormitories, where no one was allowed to live who was not a

Croat and a follower. *Matica* was very successful in promoting its goals via the media. Pribičević was close to Savka and Tripalo, and he did not believe that they were nationalists. But by September, Pribičević concluded that he couldn't continue to support their line.[63]

Ambassador Stewart spoke to Sonja Bičanić, a professor in English at the Zagreb university faculty of philosophy. She agreed that an ugly side of Croatian nationalism had gained momentum and its tide swept up even reasonable and moderate people. At the time, she was in no doubt that the situation would have worsened if Tito had not put an end to it.[64]

It is ironic that the purge helped solve the foreign currency problem. On 27 December the republics agreed to an increase in the retention quota, with companies allowed to keep 20 per cent of their foreign currency incomes, and tourist enterprises 40 per cent.[65] This measure was doubtless a direct consequence of the December crisis, and had two goals: it was supposed to secure some degree of popularity among Croatians by creating the impression that the new leadership was devoted to Croatian economic interests. Secondly, the measures had to demonstrate that the federation was capable of solving national and regional problems. In this way, they could blame the ousted Croatian leadership for instigating conflicts between the republics with unrealistic demands.

The British diplomats believed that the regime would strengthen repression after a bomb exploded in the *Borba* headquarters in Belgrade on 5 January 1972, but harsh measures served no one's interest. The leaders of all the republics feared that crises similar to Croatia's might spill over into other parts of the country. The president of the Serbian party, Marko Nikezić, told Stewart: 'You cannot have a tough police regime in Croatia without regrettable consequences in other republics.'[66]

After the New Year celebrations of 1972 concluded, the purge resumed. Leaders and members of *Matica*'s branches across Croatia resigned in large numbers. The press also reported on resignations from the Croatian-Serb organisation *Prosvjeta*. Ivan Supek, the chancellor of Zagreb University, was attacked because he was abroad and failed to return to Croatia at the height of the student protests. At the same time, student leaders ended up in prison. On 12 January, the Zagreb public prosecutor charged eleven people with 'counterrevolutionary activities' and the 'misuse of institutions'. This was primarily related to *Matica Hrvatska*, the student organisation, the student protests, and the alleged coordination of activities with *Ustašis* abroad and foreign intelligence agencies – with the goal of detaching Croatia from Yugoslavia.[67]

The British diplomats assessed that the new party and government leaders would have a difficult task in gaining public confidence, considering the popularity of their predecessors. As the British were primarily interested in the integrity of the Yugoslav federation, and had no sympathy for Croatian demands, the diplomats put a positive spin on the new leaders. The new party president, Milka Planinc, was characterised a 'solid and reliable person' with long-standing party membership, while Vrhovec was described as a 'man with great potential'. He used to be the *Vjesnik* correspondent in New York and London, and later editor of *Vjesnik*. But the last word about the new leadership was, whatever they did, they were not Savka and Tripalo:

> In general however the present leadership still have a long way
> to go before they can expect to have much popular support
> at grass roots level and it is very doubtful that they will ever
> achieve the sort of popularity enjoyed by Tripalo and Savka
> Dabčević-Kučar.[68]

To avoid the impression that Croatia was being singled out for persecution, the Yugoslav leadership ecumenically pursued Serbians and the Orthodox Church as well with similar measures. Nikola Rundić, the editor of the satirical magazine *Jež* ('The Hedgehog'), was removed. *Jež* was often criticised by the regime for publishing anti-Croat content. The authorities also turned against extreme left-wing (Maoist) student circles. They announced their intention to arrest Slobodan Subotić, chairman of the Serbian-Montenegrin bar association, who was accused of distributing leaflets with nationalist and anti-communist content in Serbia and Croatia. The Serbian Orthodox Episcopus Vasilije Kostić was also arrested for promoting Serbian nationalism.[69]

Ambassador Stewart spoke to the president of the Serbian party, Marko Nikezić, about the situation in Croatia. Nikezić admitted that the Croatian party had played a very useful role in postwar Yugoslavia, 'having again and again pressed for a relaxation of repression and an expansion of democracy with results that have benefited every Republic.' But in the past two years, the Croatian leadership had begun to pursue exclusionary policies without considering the positions and interests of other republics. He had warned Croatian leaders not to play the nationalist card in promoting their goals, because they would not be able to control these forces after they were unleashed.[70]

Despite these warnings, he had not thought that such a drastic intervention could occur, nor did he consider it to have been necessary. Nikezić believed that Croatia would need help to face the challenges and frustrations that would inevitably occur after such a deep political crisis. This could have a positive effect on democratic processes in Serbia and Yugoslavia. He added that was very hard to manage a country that had no democratic tradition.[71] The FCO's desk for Eastern Europe and the Soviet Union made an interesting note. A memo was circulated among the British Foreign Service to identify which countries or regions might require urgent action and priority for the highest levels of government during the next 12 months. Yugoslavia was the only country that the department identified, suggesting the importance of the Balkans for British interests.[72]

Additional details about the events in Croatia started to come to the surface, the most important of which was Tito's assessment that the situation had reached such a point that any further delay starting action was impossible. The animosities between political factions in Croatia, and between the leaderships of Croatia and other republics, had become so strong that the fear of disintegration outweighed the fear of authoritarian measures to hold the country together. In that sense both Tito and Kardelj stated in December 1971 that it would be much harder to press these issues a few months earlier – now they had an excuse to intervene harshly without causing unmanageable public outrage.[73] Ambassador Stewart observed:

> As with Đilas there was a fundamental error of political judgement, this time on the part of what is called 'the leadership' in Croatia. Since 1969 this had come increasingly to mean a triumvirate: Miko Tripalo, one of the Croatian representatives on the Executive Bureau of the Presidium of LCY; Dr Savka Dabčević-Kučar, President of the Republican League

of Communists; and Pero Pirker, its Secretary. All are in their
40s and though Pirker was an administrator the other two
were outstanding examples of new style Yugoslav politicians.
Dr Dabčević-Kučar, a red-headed economist, has always been
described by British correspondents as the Barbara Castle of
Yugoslavia and with much more justice than such comparisons
usually have. My own strongest personal impression of Tripalo
was that if born into a British political ambience he would
undoubtedly have won a seat in Parliament after a career in
public relations, but I was not al all certain whether he would
have chosen the Conservative or Labour interests. Both set out
to be popular politicians in a sense unknown in Yugoslavia
since the last war. Both proved to have real talent for Western-
type public political meetings and the ability to draw crowds
of a size normally seen only at football matches. Up to a point,
perhaps it would be more accurate to say at first, they were a
most encouraging phenomenon.

Yugoslav politicians with whom Stewart spoke could not confirm with cer-
tainty whether Tito should have reacted so harshly in Croatia to prevent
violence and civil war. Stewart believed that Tito was right, at least when
violence was concerned:

> There have always been two opposite strains in Croatian nation-
> alism. One is highly respectable, represented in its purest form
> by the charming and civilised if slightly potty retired professors
> who abound on the Dalmatian coast and in the pages of Miss
> Rebecca West. The other is an exceedingly ugly form of extreme
> racialism represented by the genocidal *Ustaše* of 30 years ago
> and by some of their modern descendants in exile. There were
> already signs that the second strain was reappearing and dis-
> crimination against the Serb minority in such matters as jobs
> and housing was clearly on the way. Another six months on
> the same road might I think very easily have produced serious
> clashes.

Stewart added that the claim about the conflict between the 'progressives'
and 'conservatives' was superficial. Leading Croatian politicians did indeed
enjoy public support and were a good example of a progressive force, but
it would be 'grotesque' to refer to Šibl or Bobetko as 'progressives'. 'The

trouble was that the shortest road to popular support in Croatia is through nationalism and it is a very dangerous road indeed.' Lastly, Stewart added an epitaph to the events in Croatia with the words of Marko Nikezić, whom he characterised as the most moderate and the most sophisticated Yugoslav politician, who identified the lack of democratic traditions as a key problem for Yugoslavia.[74]

11

1972: Aftermath

'It would be a sad irony if future historians had to acknowledge that from 2 December 1971 an increasing number of reputable Croatians started to think that some kind of separatism, regardless of how materially unprofitable, was the only way to escape from Serbian hegemony'.[1]

'I came to the conclusion that Tito had made the greatest single political mistake he could possibly make'.[2]

The purge led to the removal or resignation of the top two layers of Croatian leadership, altogether around 2,000 people, which was the entire political and administrative class, as well as many figures from cultural life. To try to avoid the appearance of anti-Croatian oppression, liberal and religious leaders in Slovenia and Serbia were also targeted and removed. The aftermath throughout 1972 included political trials in Croatia and Serbia, while Tito moved to place allies in key positions, suppressing both national and individual liberties. These moves were quietly supported by British and American diplomats, who ultimately stuck with the official line of prioritising the integrity of the Yugoslav state over the rights of nationalities or individuals. What is remarkable about this moment is the manner in which the FCO worked to get the British press 'on message'; an effort, it must be said, which was resisted by *The Economist* and the *Observer*, while the *Financial Times* gradually reported more in line with the FCO's diplomatic aims and *The Times* was co-opted most fully. The Soviets were very happy with the purge that continued throughout 1972, and it would lead to deeper penetration of Soviet influence in Yugoslavia in the 1970s.

Trials in Croatia and Serbia

Croatian public life of 1972 was marked by the trials of the leaders of the student movement and *Matica Hrvatska*, accompanied by a wave of resignations by individuals who were in any way involved in Croatian political life.[3] Ambassador Stewart's assessment was that the measures were not necessarily for the worse:

> Immediate consequence, particularly for personal freedom, may be unfortunate but should not go too far. They will not wholly be bad, for a return to discipline and common sense was overdue.[4]

The fate of the removed Croatian politicians was understandably of great importance to foreign diplomats. A member of the Croatian executive committee told British diplomats that fewer than 100 remained in custody, and it was obvious that the authorities did not want to draw too much attention to their trials and incarceration. This was particularly important for Savka and Tripalo, who had quietly retreated into private life. Novak Pribičević confirmed to Stewart and Tait that these Croatian leaders were under informal surveillance and self-imposed exile. The diplomats recorded his ironic observation that no one was applauded and cheered any more when they visited friends.[5]

Ambassador Stewart predicted that in six months the political repression would subside. Stewart was more afraid of the possibility that several well-placed bombs might lead to increased power for the security services. But even if this kind of tactic was used, Yugoslavia would still remain more liberal than any other Eastern European country.

Tito visited Zagreb from 19 to 24 April 1972, when he spent most of his time with the new Croatian leadership. Consul-General Baker noticed that Tito's advisers were realistic when they assessed that excessive public exposure would not be good after he had removed virtually the entire Croatian leadership as recently as December. Even if they did try to put on a grand spectacle, it would diminish his prestige. Baker formed the impression that Tito had lost some of his 'magic and popular appeal' with the public.

> The President is still widely respected, even revered; and the prospect of his eventual departure is regarded with misgiving or dismay. But there is not, at present, the same warmth of feeling towards him, the same keen interest in his every word and action, as there used to be. The scene of last September, when arm-in-arm with Dr Savka Dabčević-Kučar, he walked several hundred yards along Ilica amid an excitedly cheering crowd, is in the foreseeable future unlikely to be repeated.[6]

On 1 June 1972 Ambassador Stewart reported on the conclusions by the Special Commission of the LCC that had investigated the events in Croatia. Back at the Karađorđevo meeting, Tito had referred to a shadowy 'revolutionary committee of 50', which was supposedly plotting to destroy Yugoslavia. But he never identified who the 50 might be. After the Special Commission report was published and failed to refer to this mysterious committee, however, *Borba* helpfully fabricated a list of 50 names for the occasion. There was no evidence that this committee actually existed. Commenting on these developments, Stewart speculated what could have happened had Tito not intervened in Karađorđevo: *Matica Hrvatska* would become a serious political force by the time of the 1973 elections, which would consequently lead Yugoslavia back to pre-war instabilities. He concluded:

> It would be nice to think that Yugoslavia deserved something better than a one party Government. Unfortunately it is still impossible to envisage a second party emerging on any basis except one or other of the regional nationalisms. Even the existing single party has found it hard enough to maintain a cohesive all-Yugoslav basis; at present no other party would stand a chance of doing so.[7]

The British diplomats feared that the trials might worsen already fragile relations between the nationalities. In August Michael Tate reported that the authorities were desperate to incriminate the 'Mass movement' (*Maspok*), which was the term used after the December 1971 purges to defame the 'Spring movement'. The term 'Croatian Spring' (*Hrvatsko Proljeće*) was also coined only after it was suppressed in December 1971 – and would be banned from Yugoslav discourse until 1989.

The courts, however, had great difficulty in producing substantive and incriminating evidence. The student leaders refused to answer the public prosecutor's questions, and were using the courthouse as a podium to publicly vent their criticisms of the regime. Tait concluded with characteristic British understatement that the accused did not make the public prosecutor's job any easier. He finally remarked that the fact that students were allowed to express their opinions freely was probably the best thing that came out of these trials.[8]

Along with the diplomatic corps, the Western media were equally active in following the events in Croatia. *The Economist* devoted most space to highlight *Maspok*'s links with foreign circles of émigrés and others. Most attention was devoted to the unsuccessful attempt by Croatian émigrés to infiltrate Yugoslavia and to mount a guerrilla campaign against the regime from the mountains of western Bosnia. This was the so-called *Bugojno* group of 19 who entered Yugoslavia on 20 June 1972 with the intention of instigating a broader rebellion against the federal regime. This was another in a series of unfortunate events that the Yugoslav authorities wanted to attribute to a broad conspiracy of Croatian émigrés. Other events included a Yugoslav plane crash over Czechoslovakia, a bomb on a train between Zagreb and Vienna, and the assassination of Ambassador Rolović. While these attacks were blamed on Croatian nationalists, only the assassination could be properly attributed to them. Considering the weaknesses and disunity of the extremist Croatian underground, there was little chance of an 'IRA-like' campaign of terror.

There was also no chance of support for the cause of Croatian independence from the West, whether the particular movement was liberal or extremist. Western governments supported Tito's regime and the Soviet Union had already distanced itself from Croatian émigrés. The Soviets preferred a strategy of gradual political and economic penetration, and cooperation with Croatian or other Yugoslav extremists would only harm this approach. *The Economist,* however, believed that lower-ranking East German and Soviet agents probably did support the efforts of the private Croatian nationalist-spy Branko Jelić in Berlin. In pursuit of his quixotic crusade for Croatian independence he attempted to compromise the Croatian leadership and to incite a conflict between Croats and Serbs. After the Croatian leadership was removed, the Soviets simply had no more use for him.[9]

In August 1972 a new crisis in Serbia would overshadow the trials in Croatia, when Tito decided to remove the Serbian leadership. Relations between Tito and the Serbian leadership had started to worsen gradually since the spring of 1972, when the Serbians declined to support Tito's policy of harsh measures against the Croatians. Denying that Serbia had a similar nationalism problem, the Serbian leadership refused to support political trials, but Tito doubled down.

In October 1972, Tito organised a political coup with the help of Petar Stambolić, the former prime minister of Yugoslavia (1963–7) and an influential member of the Serbian party, along with Draža Marković, the president of the Serbian Assembly. With their support, Tito forced the resignation of Marko Nikezić and Latinka Perović, two leading personalities in the Serbian party. Nikezić and Latinka were a popular liberal double act in Serbian political life comparable to Tripalo and Savka, but unlike their Croatian counterparts they could not be accused of 'tolerating nationalism'. Michael Tait described Nikezić as an intelligent and sophisticated man who personified the most progressive of political forces across Yugoslavia. With regard to nationalism, he acted like a rational statesman; and before the crisis in Croatia, he refrained from joining the rhetoric surrounding Croatian nationalism. After Karađorđevo, he used his authority to soften the regime's negative reactions and measures. He had been under suspicion for his pro-Western views that manifested themselves during the 1967 Middle East crisis, when he was foreign minister. This pro-Western orientation and his refusal to agree to political trials in Serbia led to his removal.[10]

Unlike in Croatia, the British diplomats believed that the removal of the Serbian liberal leadership was a mistake. Despite this, good relations with Tito were prioritised over political sympathies for ousted officials.

Ambassador Stewart reported that most people in Serbia did not understand why Nikezić had to resign: 'Although we do not drop friends in trouble I do not think it pays to try to see them too soon after such events.'[11]

The Nixon administration took a similar view. In the autumn of 1972, in response to a request for diplomatic intervention on behalf of a Serbian dissident, Henry Kissinger was warned that this might draw the American government into a conflict between Croats and Serbs because there had been no American response to the removal of the Croatian leadership after Karađorđevo.[12]

Despite their personal and political sympathies, British and American diplomats quietly supported the removal of the Croatian leadership because they agreed that the threat of Croatian nationalism could tear the country apart. On the other hand, the Serbian leadership never took a nationalist line and limited themselves to focus on economic affairs and controlled liberalisation of social and political life. When the Serbian leadership was removed, however, the British and Americans did not support the removal but also failed to react.

Western diplomats were quite aware of the 'imperfections' of the Yugoslav political system but tolerated them nonetheless, because they knew that in the Cold War climate this was the only practical and sustainable political option. Western policy towards the events in Croatia and Serbia accommodated a little too quickly Tito's relatively easy purge of leaders accused of nationalism and 'rotten liberalism'. In his famous article 'An old man in a panic', Chris Cviić of *The Economist* described Tito's confrontation with the Croatian leaders and their subsequent resignations that had occurred 'without any fuss':

> It did not prove necessary even to use the tanks and troops that had surrounded Zagreb. [...] The arrest of intellectuals and other 'undesirable elements' identified with the sacked leaders went just as smoothly. Not one, out of more than a hundred, apparently slipped through the net. [...] It was, as Lloyd George once said about another country, a rape, but only a little one; and everything was over before you could say 'Long live the self-managing, socialist, federative republic of Jugoslavia.'[13]

'An Old Man in a Panic': The FCO Helps the British Press

> *Since I have a despatch of my own on the stocks I will make only one comment; that I certainly do not accept the general Croat line that Tito's intervention was a gross over-reaction to the developments which were in reality natural and harmless. As the veil lifts we are beginning to get convincing evidence that some ugly and dangerous things have been happening in Croatia in the last few months. Perhaps the most direct expression of the Croat case, which I have recently seen in print, i.e. The Economist article entitled 'Old Man in a Panic', is certainly a long way off beam. To judge from Tito's demeanour when he had Heads of Missions to Karadjordjevo on 10 December and on numerous subsequent appearances on the television 'Old Man at a Picnic' would be nearer the mark.*[14]
>
> – Letter from Ambassador Dugald Stewart,
> 31 December 1971

In early 1972 the Foreign Office was alarmed by the coverage of the situation in Croatia by the British press, which was reporting very critically on the ongoing purge that had started at the Karađorđevo meeting. In particular, *The Economist*, the *Observer* and the *Financial Times* wrote critically of this period, and Michael Tait wrote a series of dispatches from Belgrade complaining about the 'sensationalist tone' of some journalists. Yugoslav officials and diplomats complained frequently about the British press, and repeatedly had to be reminded of the concept of press freedom, but the concern over a deterioration of British–Yugoslav relations was real. It was the beginning of the FCO's broader strategy to get the British press to project the right message.

In January 1972 Tait singled out the articles 'Tito losing grip on his country' by Lajos Lederer of the *Observer*, and Chris Cviić's 'An old man in a panic' in *The Economist*.[15] Tait echoed Stewart's wording that *The Economist* was 'pretty consistently off beam, but it did have the decency to publish in its correspondence column of 1 January a letter commenting critically on this bias.'[16]

Lederer had described the Yugoslav Communist party as 'disintegrating', with 'Tito himself losing control of the country.'

His authority, which he used successfully in the last spring to prevent a split in the party and to save the unity of Yugoslavia, is apparently on the wane. Tito, who is 79, admits that there is a renewed struggle for ideological supremacy within the party. He has called on the nation and the party to stem 'the counterrevolutionary phenomenon.' [...] In Croatia, where the movement is most powerful, the leading positions in the party have been taken by young people who, he says, have no connection with the workers' ideals or interests. [...] The old faithful of the centralised Communist bureaucracy have gone. The young, on whom Tito counted to establish a system of Marxism without tears, have turned their backs on their conventional Communist ideology, which they see as a dead hand from the past.[17]

Six days later, Chris Cviić described Tito's purge as a 'colossal blunder committed by an ageing ruler acting in a panic on bad advice.' Cviić noted that the Croatian leaders had 'gained popularity by their spirited fight to win a better economic deal for Croatia,' and in so doing they had

brought into the party more intellectuals and young people. But this pressure for economic change had 'certainly made them unpopular with some people – in particular, with the big banks and trading corporations in Belgrade which had grown fat on the old centralised system. But this was not the main cause of the Croat leaders' downfall. Nor was it their alleged 'nationalism' and 'separatism'; it was only autonomy, not national independence that they were after. [...] In fact, under the now evicted leaders, hopes for full independence for Croatia had waned rather than increased.

He made it clear that the key reasons for the fall of the Croatian leadership were not their demands for economic changes, nor growing nationalism or separatism. The main reason why Tito removed them, according to Cviić, was his fear that Croatia would become too liberal, which might endanger party monopoly:

So why did President Tito order this purge? He may have feared that the forming of a coalition of radical students and disgruntled workers, of which there were some signs during the recent student strike in Croatia, could set a dangerous precedent at a time when the whole of Jugoslavia is experiencing a wave of social discontent. He may have been afraid of going the way of Mr Gomulka, who was brought down a year ago by the Polish workers even though they did not have much support from students and intellectuals. But it is more likely that he decided to ditch the Croat leaders because he feared that Croatia had become too liberal and that the party's monopoly of power was in danger.

But who convinced Tito to suddenly change his mind and to revert to centralism? Cviić wonders, 'Did someone at last convince him that he risked losing his own grip on the country by tolerating all sorts of dangerous "pro-Western" liberals?' He speculates that Tito succumbed to pressures not only from conservative circles, but also from Brezhnev and Romania's leader Nicolae Ceaușescu, whom Tito had met shortly before Karađorđevo.[18]

> No doubt Mr Brezhnev's was one of the foreign voices that bombarded him with such thoughts. President Ceausescu's of Rumania may have been another; he talked to Tito only a few days before the fateful party meeting on December 1st and 2nd that sealed the fate of the Croat leaders.

The article concluded that Tito's intervention did not solve the problems of the multinational federation but only made the co-habitation between Croats and Serbs more difficult.

> There is in the air a new whiff of his 1968 doctrine of limited sovereignty for socialist countries. And for the first time it is not coming from Mr. Brezhnev. It is President Tito, of all people, who is applying it to a part of his own country.[19]

Following the mass arrests of students in December, Paul Lendvai of the *Financial Times* quoted a speech by Jakov Blažević, the president of the Croatian parliament, a member of the Presidium, and a close associate of Tito since the Partisan days. He had worked with the modernisers in the past, but dropped them after Karađorđevo. In his 15 December 1971 article, Lendvai quoted Blažević's conspiracy theory:

Nothing could illustrate the tense situation better than the long emotional speech made last night by Mr. Jakov Blazevic, President of the Croatian Parliament and member of the all-Yugoslav Party Presidium. He accused the nationalists of having planned to seize power with their friends in the Communist Party.

He said: 'The counter revolution has already started and it (the Nationalist movement) wanted to provoke a civil war which should have given a pretext for a brotherly intervention and help from the outside. Had we not carried out the changes in the leadership, we would have had to fight on the streets.'[20]

Ambassador Stewart reported on 26 January 1972 that he had received a stream of complaints from Yugoslav authorities about the British press, and that such reporting might affect British–Yugoslav relations. On his visit to Zagreb to meet the new Croatian leadership, including Blažević, he heard more complaints about the British press. Stewart told Blažević that he had heard similar complaints about the British media in June 1971, when the press emphasised the dangers of nationalism. He also discovered that Blažević had made similar objections about the free press to the Italian ambassador. Blažević added a new flourish to his perceived conspiracy that the 'counter-revolutionaries' had support from abroad, from *both* the Soviet Union and the Western media.

When speaking to Stewart in January, Blažević specifically referred to a column by C.L. Sulzberger in the *International Herald Tribune*[21] that discussed scenarios of the Soviet Union's efforts to consolidate control over socialist states. Earlier, in a column of 3 December 1971, Sulzberger wrote:

But Tito is now an elderly Diocletian living on an isolated Adriatic pleasure dome from which he rarely ventures except for grand diplomatic forays. The moment of change approaches in Yugoslavia. The marshal has sought to prepare for this by naming a ruling collegium as well as a secret council of elders representing all peoples of that multinational state.

But the Russians are making their own quiet preparations to stir centrifugal Yugoslav forces when the marshal dies. Should that strategy succeed, it is but a step to put the squeeze on

Ceausescu's stubborn Romania and press against tiny Albania, China's impoverished European satellite.[22]

Sulzberger continued in a similar vein in 'Reading Soviet Tea Leaves', on 17 January 1972:

> The only European danger point is Yugoslavia where Tito has been having trouble with nationalist movements. Tito is almost 80 and, when his prestigious voice disappears, centrifugal forces may become uncontrollable. In such a case the Kremlin, under its muted but still operative Brezhnev Doctrine, is likely to back its own adherents. There is little likelihood of more than verbal protest from the West.[23]

Blažević, however, interpreted this hypothetical scenario as the coded announcement of a conspiracy between the Soviets and the Western press to support separatist movements, break up Yugoslavia, and hand the country to the Soviets. Ambassador Stewart was also told that Blažević would raise the question of the problem of the British press in the Federal Assembly.

The ambassador replied that this was due to the fact that the Croatians were so skilled in propaganda that until Karađorđevo they had succeeded in convincing some correspondents of the British press to write favourably about the situation in Croatia. It would take time time to 're-educate' those reporters. Stewart was also convinced that the trials would also establish a link between *Matica Hrvatska* and the *Ustaši* émigrés and that the Yugoslav authorities would try to use this to balance East and West.[24]

Back in Belgrade, Michael Tait was also alarmed by the reporting in the *Financial Times*, whose Vienna correspondent Paul Lendvai visited Zagreb in December and dashed off six articles that month alone.[25] In addition, the *FT*'s Belgrade correspondent Aleksander Lebl and East European correspondent Michael Simmons reported the purge very critically.[26] Tait allowed that Lendvai's articles

> are nowhere near as bad as *The Economist* articles but they by no means present a balanced picture of the politics and interwoven economic problems of Yugoslavia. It would not matter very much what these long range Hungarians and Yugoslavs said if people took Mr Harold Wilson's advice and did not believe all they read in the newspapers.[27]

But something needed to be done about 'these long range Hungarians and Yugoslavs' in the British press, who were causing damage by their undue influence on British and Western public opinion. He suggested that the FCO's information department approach the matter by releasing a selection of first-hand diplomatic reports from the Belgrade embassy to 'reliable' journalists. The diplomatic correspondent of *The Times*, Alexander 'Sandy' Rendel, was briefed regularly in this way, and was also granted access to the annual reports on Yugoslavia, which would be reflected in his writings. Brian Sparrow of the FCO's Eastern Europe desk was also in contact with the *FT* journalist Michael Simmons, whose tone would change in the course of the year.

The Times of London had published a number of balanced and critical reports on the major developments of the purge in December and January,[28] but Sparrow's contact with Sandy Rendel would lead to two unsigned editorials that the diplomats describe as authored by Rendel.

On 24 January, *The Times* published an editorial 'The way forward for Yugoslavia', which opened by questioning the 'whole nature of the Yugoslav experiment in decentralisation and democratisation.' And while the 'handling of the Croat problem has reminded people of past methods,' the purge was in response to Croatians who 'found themselves carried away by a mixture of reasonable grievances and ancient passions.' When one demand on foreign exchange rates had been met, 'absurdity set in, and students were demanding Croatian membership of the United Nations. The Croatian party leaders were carried along on the tide, trying sincerely to control it but not able or determined enough to stop it.' With the rumour of Russian meddling in the 'dangerous waters of Croatian extremism', Tito decided that the 'state was in danger and struck hard.' Following this justification, Rendel wrote that the wisdom of this move would emerge over time, that the question of the best way to handle nationalism remained open, and concluded that it would be unwise to make martyrs of the Croats in prison.[29]

But he also suggested that ending the process of decentralisation and democratisation would be a mistake. In this subtle and indirect way, the British government leveraged public opinion to communicate its view to the Yugoslav regime. Ambassador Stewart felt that Rendel's article had the desired effect of preventing a worsening in British–Yugoslav relations, especially at the sensitive time of an airline accident over Czechoslovakia and a train explosion that occurred within twelve hours of each other on 26 and 27 January. The Yugoslav plane and the Vienna–Zagreb train were struck by bombs, which remain unattributed to this day, but the Yugoslav authorities blamed them on Croatian *Ustaši* terrorists.

In the next unsigned editorial 'Shadows over Croatia', published on 28 January immediately after these accidents, Rendel warned that harsher measures in Croatia could only serve terrorists to elevate their propaganda and activities among the 800,000 Yugoslav workers abroad. He added that nobody, apart from the Russians, could benefit from increased repression in Yugoslavia. Rendel concluded that this was not only a Yugoslav internal matter, because of Yugoslavia's political and geostrategic importance, the activities of militant émigrés and the dangers for to international transport. Above all, Rendel called for reconciliation after the purge. He closed with these qualifications:

> President Tito may have overreacted to the Croatian situation at first. He has certainly caused some bitterness in Croatia that will take time to heal. But calmer policies are now emerging, and it would be a great pity if they were to be abandoned or inter-rupted because of the real or alleged activities of terrorists.[30]

In name of stability there was little sympathy left in the British diplomatic corps for matters of democracy or liberty, but the economy and industry of Yugoslavia had to be helped. Less than a week later on 2 February, *The Times* published a three-page special report on Yugoslav trade and indus-try. It carried articles written by academics of the University of Bradford Postgraduate School of Yugoslav Studies and by journalists, with headlines such as, 'Bank mergers point way to efficient financing', 'Construction gets international boost', 'Plans for petrochemical expansion', 'Bright outlook for car output' praising the CZC-101: 'the first all-Yugoslav car', and an article with the headline 'Chauvinism hinders foreign investment'. These economic puff pieces were surrounded by advertisements for Yugobanka, the Yugoslav Export & Credit Bank, the Yugoslav Agricultural Bank and various manufacturers. But the leading article, 'Three steps to self-man-agement within an economic commonwealth', did allude to the purge in its opening paragraph:

Behind the eruption of anger by the Croat students – whose slo-
gans were concerned with what they believed to be the economic
plunder of Croatia – lie fundamental economic and political
issues which strike at the heart of socialist Yugoslavia's existence.

The article ended with the prophetic words:

The recent troubles in Croatia suggest that too many Yugoslavs
the ideology of nationalism – in its economic, political and cultural manifestations – may be more powerful as a divisive force.
One can only hope that the present troubles are nothing more
than a painful readjustment to a new situation, and not the first
signs of disintegration.

Other reports on Yugoslavia in *The Times* for the remainder of 1972
remained largely positive about Tito and the Yugoslav economy. Michael
Tait commended the writings of Dessa Trevisan for *The Times* and Noel
Clarke of the BBC, who were in his view 'more objective' about the Croatian
situation.[31] Sandy Rendel wouldn't write about Yugoslavia in his own name
until November 1972, when he cited justifications of the purge because the
'basic nationalism of the Croats would rapidly get out of hand in a recently
decentralised economy.' Rendel expressed surprise, however, at the 'harsh-
ness and haste' with which Tito turned against the Serbian liberal leaders.
While 'some stern measures were justified,' Rendel did conclude presciently
that 'paradoxically in cutting down the leaders in Croatia and Serbia to foster
unity, President Tito could end up driving the republics apart.'[32]

The FCO also tried to influence the reporting of the *Financial Times* and
The Economist, but while the *FT* would eventually moderate its tone, they
would not be co-opted as thoroughly as *The Times*. On 29 March 1972, the
FT's three main correspondents on Eastern Europe, Paul Lendvai, Michael
Simmons and Alexander Lebl, each wrote lengthy and critical articles
about the climate of political and economic uncertainty in Yugoslavia.[33]
But in the course of the year the tone moderated. On 6 May 1972, a month
after a smallpox outbreak in Yugoslavia, the first positive lifestyle article
appeared extolling the stimulating experience of new golf courses on the
Adriatic coast.[34] Later that month an article by Michael Simmons had a
drastically different tone from his earlier reports, opening with the words:

It can be taken for granted that almost all Yugoslavs, except those who are separatists and still smouldering with resentment following the suppression of nationalist outbursts last year, will this week join forces to celebrate the 80th birthday of their indefatigable President Josip Broz Tito.[35]

In the same period, Michael Tait in Belgrade and Brian Sparrow at the FCO had an interesting correspondence regarding the problem of *The Economist*'s Chris Cviić and his criticisms of Tito. Tait believed that Cviić represented a 'typical Croatian lack of understanding' about the impact of a revived Croatian nationalism on the rest of the country. Manifestations of nationalism that were normal in other countries were a particularly sensitive matter in Yugoslavia, not just because of the integrity of the federal state, but also because they were a nightmare for people who remembered the effect of Croatian nationalism during the war. Branko Jelić and others served as constant reminders of this.

When the Cviić line is pursued so often and at such length in the highly dogmatic style of *The Economist* and with the embellishments which that style demands, it seems to us to produce a result far removed from objectivity.[36]

On 27 January, Sparrow replied to Tait in a similar vein. He believed that Cviić was not responsible for all the articles in *The Economist* and that he did not represent a 'typical *émigré* journalist', a refugee who hated the government of his country of origin. He was still in close contact with many people in Yugoslavia and Sparrow had the impression that Cviić was very sensible and not entirely happy with developments in Croatia.

After December's 'An old man in a panic', Cviić wrote an article headlined 'The only ally' for *The Economist* on 22 January 1972, arguing that while nationalism was discredited in the liberal west, it was in fact the only ally of liberalism in Eastern Europe. Sparrow felt that Cviić had gone too far, and the FCO tried to warn *The Economist* that such reporting was not helpful. The article began ominously,

President Tito's policemen, who have led rather frustrated lives in recent years, are happy again. He has told them that Jugoslavia has an official and easily identifiable internal enemy which must be ferreted out and destroyed. That enemy is nationalism – and particularly the nationalism of the Croats, the country's second biggest nation, who are now getting it in the neck.

Cviić continued that 112 Croats 'are to be tried on charges of counter-revolutionary nationalism and separatism'. Hundreds of others were victim to 'administrative measures' as a part of the campaign to solve the 'Croat question'. He conceded that nationalist aspirations generally had little sympathy in the West, especially in the UK, where the Northern Irish Troubles had started to escalate to greater violence. He added, however, that nationalism in Eastern Europe could not be compared to the despised nationalism of Western Europe because in the East it represented the only way to express freedom for peoples who could not do so through open elections. Without nationalism the Albanians and Romanians would not have stood up to Moscow, and added that while such an assertion of independence had not automatically brought more liberalism, there were two important exceptions to this:

> But liberalism and nationalism did march in step on two important occasions in the recent past. One was Czechoslovakia's liberalisation between 1966 and 1968. The other was Jugoslavia's between 1966 and 1971. Neither could have taken place if the reformers had not been joined by 'impure' nationalists.

In the case of Czechoslovakia, the liberalisation really took off with support from Slovak nationalism. Therefore he didn't see anything wrong with nationalism as such, but he blamed the communist regimes of multinational states, such as the Soviet Union and Yugoslavia, who were afraid that their nations might realise that their national interests were more important than the preservation of the artificial constructs ruling over them. This was a critique of both Russian and Serbian hegemonism whose supporters justified their reign with propaganda about the necessary fight against 'bourgeois nationalism'. Cviić concluded that,

> Sooner or later, the communist party's rule in the 'motherland of socialism' itself may be questioned because many Ukrainians and other non-Russians will have discovered that they will like their own motherlands more. No wonder the spectre of nationalism has got the present rulers of both the Soviet Union and Jugoslavia worried.[37]

Ambassador Stewart saw the danger in Cviić's articles in *The Economist*, and moved to warn the magazine:

> If at the same time a paper of the standing of *The Economist* has an article every two or three weeks expressing almost unqualified support for Croatian nationalism quite a number of Yugoslavs put two and two together and make nine.[38]

The FCO's interventions, however, ultimately did not persuade *The Economist* to change its tone about Yugoslavia.

On 19 February 1972, the magazine reported that Tito's rhetoric had changed and he was calling for moderation, but the hardliners had grown stronger. The Yugoslav authorities began to describe the Croatian crisis as a minor local affair, 'grossly exaggerated by the foreign press.' The article quoted Savka Dabčević-Kučar, who summarised the dilemma the modernisers found themselves in:

> The unitarists and pan-Serbian chauvinists offer us a kind of Jugoslavia we do not want. The Croatian chauvinists want to destroy the kind of Jugoslavia we do want.

The ousted liberal leaders 'cannot now explain what they hoped they would be allowed to do, for they have been silenced.' But had they had their way, then contending factions would be legally and openly permitted, 'almost like a government and opposition.' The moves towards pluralism, however, had been met with accusations of nationalism and excessive liberalism, of which 'the accusation of liberalism is the true one.' The article concluded that while Tito had asked his Croatian supporters not to engage in witch-hunts, any march towards a more liberal communism would be halted unless the jailed intellectuals and students received fair trials. 'But the very fact that all this is still in doubt is a measure of the seriousness of President Tito's overreaction to the Croat challenge in December.'[39] The reporting and comment on Yugoslavia in *The Economist* remained critical of the ongoing purge and assault on liberalism throughout the year, culminating in a critical assessment in October 1972 about the Queen's visit to Yugoslavia as an undeserved honour in the wake of repression.[40]

Similarly, Lajos Lederer of the *Observer* continued delivering his scoops in his famously concise copy throughout the rest of 1972, writing about

Yugoslavia whenever Tito looked around for whom next to purge, with headlines that included, 'Tito uses army to break revolt', 'Tougher tactics in Croatia', 'Tito clamps down on millionaires', 'Tito sacks Marxist professors', and 'Tito sacks top party opponents'.[41] Lederer was also the first to report that after Tito came to terms with the Kremlin following a visit to Moscow in June 1973, the Yugoslav State security agencies re-established ties with the KGB in November.[42]

Over on television, on 27 January the BBC started to broadcast a three-part documentary on the events in Yugoslavia. The first part tackled the suppression of student protest in Zagreb in November–December 1971, which showed dramatic footage of tanks on the streets. The British diplomats had not seen tanks in Zagreb, and assumed this footage was taken from Prague. The programme editor Derek Hart next described the plane and train incidents as acts by 'Croatian rebels' fighting the Yugoslav authorities. The second part of the documentary showed footage of the Serbian film *Terrorists*, about the trial of Miljenko Hrkač, who had placed a bomb in a Belgrade cinema in 1968. Zagreb television declined to broadcast the documentary before Karađorđevo because of its anti-Croatian sentiments. The third part of the documentary focused on pirate radio operators in Croatia. The Foreign Office was not convinced that the documentary provided a realistic picture of events in Yugoslavia. In this case, the BBC's 'even-handed view' was not based on original reporting or fact-checking but on balancing opposing Serbian and Croatian propaganda. The Yugoslav embassy in London tried to prevent the broadcast, and Brian Sparrow had to explain to protesting Yugoslav diplomats that the British government could not influence the BBC.[43]

The magazine *Hrvatska Revija* (*Croatian Review*), edited in exile by the Croatian novelist Vinko Nikolić, reviewed the world media's reporting and analysis of the Croatian crisis. This is probably the best and the most comprehensive overview of global reaction, encompassing reports in European, British, North American, Australian and New Zealand media. With the exception of *The Economist*, the editors of *Hrvatska Revija* sadly concluded that most of the world media had reported negatively on the goals and policies of the ousted Croatian leadership while praising Tito's repression. *Hrvatska Revija* believed that the main cause was the acceptance of the official Yugoslav line that propagated phrases like 'brotherhood', 'unity', 'federalisation', 'liberalisation', and so on. The *Revija* concluded,

> All foreign journalists uncritically accepted the *leitmotif* of the crisis, which is the 'national chauvinism' of the Croatians. At a time of a general turn to the left [across the Western world] and fresh memories of fascism, it is easy to understand why journalists fell for well-placed slogans about 'extremist nationalism' that spreads like some Asian flu that needs to be suppressed. We can only regret that not one journalist bothered to examine whether it was really a matter of national chauvinism, what were the causes of this 'virus', what was its content, and how did it first come about?[44]

Diplomats Disagree Between Belgrade and Zagreb

The Croatian Spring was viewed very differently from Zagreb than from Belgrade, due to the fact that both journalists and diplomats were unavoidably exposed to, and influenced by, differing everyday discourse and propaganda. Although this did not influence the overall policy of the West towards Yugoslavia, informal biases began to manifest themselves among the diplomatic corps to the point that those stationed in Zagreb and Belgrade started to show interesting disagreements.

From Belgrade Michael Tait warned the FCO that Ambassador Stewart was not entirely certain about the reliability of reports coming from the British consulate in Zagreb. He believed that the reporting coming from Belgrade would be very strange if it relied *only* on the reporting by 'local staff'. He felt remorse, however, for not taking into consideration the warnings of one of the junior diplomats in Zagreb in the previous year that the Serbian minority was beginning to arm itself. This was particularly worrying because some consulate officials in Zagreb still refused to understand why Tito *had* to intervene.[45]

Among American diplomats similar differences manifested themselves. Excellent sources for this can be found in the Foreign Affairs Oral History Collections of the Association of Diplomatic Studies and Training. On the initiative of the retired diplomat Charles Stuart Kennedy, more than 2,300 former diplomats, consular staff, State Department personnel, military attachés, USAID staff, and even ambassadors' wives, have been interviewed since 1986. This collection of interview transcripts is an underused resource for historians, containing anecdotes, memories and gossip that are a valuable supplement to the declassified official diplomatic reports, and provide a window into the lives and perceptions of American diplomatic staff.[46] These include insights into the differences between those stationed in Belgrade and Zagreb. Charles Kennedy had himself served in Yugoslavia in the 1960s, and interviewed Thomas P.H. 'Harry' Dunlop in 1996, and Donald Tice in 1997.[47]

Kennedy and Dunlop had studied Serbo-Croatian together at the Foreign Service Institute in 1961–2, after which Kennedy served in the Belgrade embassy in 1962–7 under Ambassadors George Kennan and Charles Burke Elbrick. Dunlop served in Belgrade from 1963–5, in the Zagreb consulate from 1969–72, and again in Belgrade around the time of Tito's death in 1978–82. Donald Tice served as the Yugoslavia Desk Officer during the time of crisis, Tito's visit and the purge in 1970–2.

During their first language training at the Foreign Service Institute in 1961–2, Kennedy and Dunlop were taught by two Serbian brothers-in-law, former Royal Serbian Army officers who had lost everything to communist Yugoslavia and presented the budding diplomats with a 'big dose of Serbian nationalism, and despite the excesses of it, I came to believe that the Serbs were badly treated by history. [...] The degree to which I had to "unlearn" came later on.'[48]

The learning started in Dunlop's first junior officer posting in Belgrade. One of his first responsibilities was to oversee a team that translated nearly 40 articles daily from the local press, which he observed was the main way in which communists communicated indirectly with each other – both without speaking directly to each other, and through a meta-language. 'Communist prose has to be seen to be believed,' and like 'Kremlinologists', they became 'Kardeljologists' and 'Borbaologists', able to uncover the meaning behind the rhetoric. From their teachers at the FSI to the Serbs they encountered on a daily basis in Belgrade, Dunlop left his first tour in Belgrade with two impressions: that the Serbs had been treated unfairly by history; and the 'intense dislike of other Yugoslavs by the Serbs.'[49]

After a tour in Vietnam, Dunlop returned to Yugoslavia in 1969 as Number Two at the Zagreb consulate, and was impressed by real economic reforms that had been carried out, decentralising decision making from

Belgrade to the republics. But he quickly noticed that devolving economic decision making without political decision making was impossible:

> When I got to Zagreb in 1969, this process of devolution of authority was picking up momentum, on the political side as well as on the economic side. The political process of devolution was, it turned out, unacceptable to Tito.[50]

Dunlop describes the 'electricity in the air' of more than 200,000 people gathered to hear Savka's speech on 7 May 1971 and the crowds chanting her name. Dunlop recalls:

> All of us in the Consulate thought that this public support for reforms in the Croatian communist party was a good thing. In the Embassy they paid less attention to it. We thought that this was a reflection of change in a good direction, a change in which the people's will, as it were, was beginning to be listened to and responded to.
>
> What did the people of Croatia want? They wanted identity, they wanted to be thought of as Croatians, not Yugoslavs, they wanted control over their tourism earnings. They had the biggest chunk of the Adriatic Coast of Yugoslavia. They had made all of these Austrian schillings, Swedish kroner, and, above all, German Deutsche Marks, which were pouring in down there from tourist spending. They wanted what they regarded as a 'fair cut', which would probably have amounted to most of it. They wanted to be able to decide that, if they needed a new railroad or new highway, they could allocate their own resources and not have to go to Belgrade, hat in hand. We couldn't see anything particularly wrong with those desires. The same thing was happening in Slovenia, and not much less in the Serbian and in the Macedonian Communist Party.[51]

This became a source of friction between the consulate and the embassy. Like Kennedy, Dunlop's education had started with a 'total immersion in Serbdom', where the language training by Serbs had been followed by almost exclusive contact with Serbs during their first assignments in Belgrade.

> I learned of the atrocities committed by the 'Ustashi', the fascist goon squads that the Croatians employed, especially during the early years of World War II. These were horrendous atrocities

which took place against the Serbs. So I didn't arrive in Croatia with any pro-Croatian point of view.

But the differences between the embassy and consulate (which was also responsible for covering Slovenia), turned not on a sectarian difference between Serbs and Croats, but between the central communist party leadership and the republics.

> This issue began to get sharper and sharper over the years that I was in Zagreb. To some extent the Embassy tended to dismiss, or so we thought, the importance of what was happening, politically, in Croatia and in Slovenia. In the Consulate in Zagreb we said that, 'These are real people, with goals and objectives which they are working hard at. So we need to pay attention to that.' Perhaps, in this connection, I am somewhat gilding the clarity with which we expressed ourselves. However, the Embassy's view tended to be, 'Well, that is the view of the "boondocks"', that is, of the sticks. That's Croatia, and Croatians always bitch and moan about the Serbs. This is all in the realm of domestic politics. It may be interesting but it's not all that important. [...] I think that we in the Consulate in Zagreb felt that the Embassy tended not to pay enough attention to what we were reporting was going on up in Slovenia and Croatia.[52]

As the political tensions between the central government and Croatia/ Slovenia escalated, so did the differences between the embassy and the consulate. In Belgrade a personal dispute between Ambassador Leonhart and his deputy, Tom Enders, and their wives, led to both diplomats being dismissed from their posts. After an interim period, Leonhart was replaced in 1970 by Malcolm Toon, who was 'an old Russian hand and had broad experience with the old style, communist governments and ways of doing things.' Under Toon, the embassy in Belgrade attempted to impose controls and require the reports from the Zagreb consulate to be cleared before they were sent to the State Department.

The disagreements between the consulate and embassy were visible from Washington. Over at the Eastern Europe desk in the State Department, Donald C. Tice was the recipient of reports from both. He noted:

The reporting was good. Both offices were very active. The Consulate General in Zagreb at one point had 'gotten a little bit out in front of the Embassy,' not from my point of view but from the point of view of Ambassador Toon. In 1971, I guess it was, there was a political 'upheaval' in Zagreb, a belated sort of 'Prague Spring' kind of thing. [...] We had some young Political Officers who got very much involved in reporting, based on what the 'anti-Tito types' were doing in Croatia. This caused some unhappiness in Belgrade because the interpretation of these events was somewhat different from the two posts.

I remember that when Ambassador Toon was getting read into the situation in Belgrade, he was 'livid' because this report-ing was going directly to the Department from the Consulate General in Zagreb, without first going through the Embassy in Belgrade. The Embassy was just getting information copies of this reporting. When Toon went out to Belgrade, one of the first things that he did was to order all reporting from the Consulate General in Zagreb to go through the Embassy in Belgrade before going to the Department. However, I think that, by and large, the Political Officers in Zagreb were doing a good job.[53]

But this initiative contravened the Foreign Service Regulation in '3 FAM' (vol. 3 of the Foreign Affairs Manual). Dunlop recalled:

Orme Wilson, who at that time was Consul General in Zagreb, really hit the ceiling over this issue. So did I. He went down to Belgrade, clutching 3 FAM [...], and made a very strong pitch about this. This did not improve people's personal atti-tudes. There was some friction. However, we were 420 km away from Belgrade. The road was a difficult one, with a lot of potholes in it.

We still had a lot of autonomy. However, there was this sense in the Embassy in Belgrade that the folks up in the Consulate in Zagreb are saying that the political situation in Croatia is much more 'tense, important, and significant' for the future of the country than the Embassy thought it was. They said that it was an irritant to the Embassy to have its views be reported to the Department in Washington and then have this somewhat dif-ferent, or differently shaded view, also reported to Washington by the Consulate in Zagreb.[54]

While the tensions between the embassy and consulate never reached 'crisis proportions', Dunlop felt, both before and after the shock of the purge, that 'there tended to be a tendency in the Embassy to blur over Tito's deficiencies.'

NATO Reacts

Throughout 1971 NATO analysts paid close attention to internal developments in Yugoslavia through the POLADS group. This working group of foreign policy advisers operated from 1967 to 1974, and presented a series of informal advisory and discussion papers to the NATO Political Committee.[55] In the context of preserving Yugoslav independence and integrity, the worsening economic and political situation was a source of security concern. The first reports about the political crisis emerged in January 1971. The key concerns were the process of liberalisation and decentralisation, as well as exploring scenarios in the event of Tito's death. Yugoslavia presented a delicate issue, because it was an independent communist country with strong relations with the West. In the POLADS meetings, the British were particularly keen to avoid the impression that NATO was discussing a non-member country in a way that might raise suspicions in Yugoslavia of Yalta-style great power decisions being taken, such as the 'percentages agreement' between Stalin and Churchill.[56]

The FCO proposed that the Yugoslav discussions should be placed in the wider Mediterranean context, while the American delegates believed that a discussion on Yugoslav relations with the Warsaw Pact, and the position of Yugoslavia in the wider Eastern European context would create a clearer picture.[57] NATO had a very clear interest in Yugoslavia:

> Yugoslav territory includes an important slice of Mediterranean littoral and major land routes into Italy and Greece, which need to be denied to Russians in peace and war. Yugoslav are prepared, indeed resolved, to defend their territory. Their mini-deterrent (all-people's defence) is mounted to this end at no cost to Nato which (since Yugoslavia is non-aligned) is not even asked to provide an umbrella. This is excellent value for no money [...]. The most useful thing that Alliance could do would be to take note that the survival and success of an independent, non-aligned, united, prosperous and non-capitalist

Yugoslavia is a concrete interest of the West. If any of its members can afford to assist Yugoslavia's return to economic health, they will be supporting the common interest. They could also help by being a bit less sticky in selling Yugoslavia the arms she needs to defend herself. She is doing her best to diversify sources of procurement but this presupposes willing sellers.[58]

The British ambassador to Yugoslavia, Terence Garvey, was relieved when the American side accepted the British position that Yugoslavia should be treated more delicately and included in the general Mediterranean discussion. Especially important were the conversations that Western diplomats had with Yugoslav officials. The Norwegian representative in the NATO Political Committee reported on a meeting with the Yugoslav ambassador to Norway, in which the Yugoslav official highlighted the danger of the Brezhnev Doctrine to Yugoslavia, considering that the Soviets had never defined the geographic area and limits where the doctrine applied. They only stated it applied to socialist countries but not exclusively to Warsaw Pact members.

The Yugoslav ambassador to Belgium, Miloš Lalović, was known to be pro-Western and anti-Soviet. He invited three Belgian high military officials to a private dinner, in which he dropped hints about Yugoslav doubts about Soviet intentions. He was afraid that after Tito's death the Soviets would intensify their pressure on Yugoslavia – and he warned that NATO should be aware of Yugoslav fears and have a clear position in case of this scenario. Similar to the impressions left by the private exchanges during Tito's visit to Washington, there was no doubt in Brussels that Lalović had clear instructions from Belgrade to approach Western officials and reveal that a fear of a repeat of the invasion in Czechoslovakia was real at the highest level.

Yugoslavia's interest in NATO was also highlighted by a request that the Yugoslav military attaché in Vienna, Colonel Vrhovec, communicated through his Belgian counterpart. Col Vrhovec asked to gain access to NATO's analysis of the Yugoslav military position in return for Yugoslavia's military analysis of its neighbours. In response to this offer, the FCO sent a very clear message to its diplomats in Belgium: 'The Yugoslavs have certainly got plenty of cheek. I presume if you feel it necessary to do so you will make sure that the Belgians are in no danger of acceding to the Yugoslavs' request.'⁵⁹ The British assumed that Colonel Vrhovec was acting on his own initiative, but the possibility was not excluded that he was under instructions. It was not possible to verify this detail, because the former Yugoslav military archives are still restricted, and there is no record in Belgrade's foreign affairs archives. Nonetheless, it is possible that he was sent to test the waters.

The American embassy in Vienna reported that Austrian officials were worried about the current situation in Croatia:

> Among knowledgeable Austrians in official circles, there is gen-
> uine concern over the current situation in Yugoslavia. For some
> time now they have contemplated with vague uneasiness the
> prospect of turmoil and change when Tito disappears from the
> scene. More recently, however, as reports of separatist unrest
> emanate from Croatia, and the whole country seems to be in the
> throes of another economic crisis, responsible Austrians have
> begun to worry about the continued existence of a friendly gov-
> ernment to the South, and some even begun to fear lest Austria
> become involved in some sort of Soviet military intervention.
> Certainly there are those who are persuaded that the Soviets are
> busily fishing in troubled waters and only waiting for the right
> moment to invoke the Brezhnev Doctrine against the present
> leadership of Yugoslavia. And – given the geographical position
> of Austria – all Austrians believe that any Soviet interference in
> Yugoslavia cannot but have unpleasant and dangerous conse-
> quences for Austria.

The State Secretary at the Austrian Ministry of Foreign Affairs, Walter Wodak, had previously been a long-standing ambassador to Moscow and Belgrade. He was particularly worried and believed that a serious internal conflict in Yugoslavia could initiate the return of an orthodox Soviet-style regime.⁶⁰

Yugoslavia was a topic of conversation between the Austrian and Italian foreign ministers, Aldo Moro and Rudolf Kirschsläger, in July 1971. Kirschsläger told Moro that the current political situation could provoke a Soviet intervention and a new Czechoslovakia. The Italians tried to reas- sure the Yugoslavs by offering to strengthen political and military coopera- tion.⁶¹ In the spring of 1971 the Yugoslavs had offered Italy a bilateral treaty for joint defence planning. By August 1971, the Yugoslav defence minister and military attaché even proposed shared use of Yugoslav and Italian air bases for Adriatic security. But none of these mutual offers would ever bear fruit, mostly because after 1972 Yugoslavia began to strengthen her military cooperation with the Soviets.[62]

NATO intensified its attention towards Yugoslavia in the spring of 1971, especially after the LCY Presidium meeting in April. The reason was the worsening of inter-republic relations. Meanwhile, Yugoslav officials were also interested in understanding NATO's view of and position towards Yugoslavia. The Yugoslavs requested explanations from the State Department regarding NATO's public statement on the need for attention to the 'situation on Nato's flanks', and also about potential NATO discussions on Trieste. Over that bitterly contested city, the Yugoslavs were concerned about Aldo Moro's recent statement in the Camera, the Italian parliament. The State Department replied diplomatically that NATO had discussed the Soviet presence in the Mediterranean, and, thus, 'while Yugoslavia itself was not discussed, an area of obvious mutual policy interest was the subject of focus.'[63]

The American NATO delegation was the most active in initiating discussions on Yugoslavia and the Yugoslav armed forces. The American embassy in Belgrade believed that the Yugoslav leadership had removed pro-Soviet elements from the military leadership after the 1968 Czechoslovak invasion, and reoriented its military doctrine towards defending itself against an attack by the Warsaw Pact. In this context, Ambassador Leonhart reported to the State Department:

> It will be important for all of us to find ways soon to increase Nato contacts with Yugoslav military seniors and to assist their effort to diminish exclusive supply position Soviets have enjoyed since 1965.[64]

The military exercise *Sloboda '71* (Freedom '71), carried out in central Croatia from 2–9 October 1971, had a prominent place in the NATO report. It was the largest military exercise in Yugoslavia since World War II, simulating a defence against an attack from the east. The exercise was meant to show the efficiency of the Yugoslav 'Total People's Defence' that was implemented from early 1969 to keep nearly the entire population involved by creating a nation of reservists. The exercise was announced in June 1971 and NATO reported movements of heavy armaments and all army units in the August and September. Recruits who had completed their military service were ordered to remain in uniform, and around

1,500 people who worked in West Germany were called up for reserve duty. NATO experts assessed the 'Total People's Defence' and concluded that the territorial defence units had a relatively small role compared to the regular standing army. The NATO report added that the reservists in the territorial units showed 'little enthusiasm', which could be attributed to 'insufficient and diverse equipment' – referring perhaps to both humans and materiel. The final assessment was that Yugoslavia could not hold out for very long in case of a conventional Warsaw Pact attack, but *Sloboda '71* meant that the invasion of Yugoslavia would be difficult and would never completely succeed in light of guerrilla insurgencies and urban warfare.[65]

The time and place of the exercise was interpreted by many politicians – and historians – as a source of pressure on the Croatian leadership and a preparation for their removal. Contemporaneous diplomatic documents and NATO papers, however, do not place the *Sloboda '71* exercise in this context. Savka Dabčević-Kučar recalled that at the time she and her colleagues did not link the exercise to the Croatian internal situation. But in hindsight she believed that the military leadership had this in mind. Apart from 'provocations' by individuals, there were no indications that this was a policy matter, nor did Tito show any sign that the Croatian leadership had lost his support.[66]

The political crisis in Croatia was the central topic of the POLADS meeting at the NATO Political Committee on 21 December 1971. The German, French and American representatives highlighted the potential consequences for the stability of Yugoslavia. The German representative quoted a part of a conversation between a German diplomat and an unnamed 'prominent' Yugoslav, 'identified as convinced communist and well-known historian', who said that, 'Yugoslavia is experiencing a general political, organisational and economic crisis concurrently with a profound moral crisis.'

The French representative hinted at Soviet interference, and observed that 'current events are causing a re-evaluation of the possibility of subversive attempts against Yugoslavia, and we all know from where these subversive attempts come.' He also pointed out that he had suggested to the French authorities that they needed to reassess the generally accepted belief that Yugoslav unity could survive a succession crisis. The Italian representatives thought along similar lines, believing that 'Italian authorities believe that recent developments heightened threat of intervention.'[67] A Finnish diplomat in Brussels confirmed to Yugoslav diplomats that

NATO was very interested in the situation in Croatia. He informed them that the NATO Council was following the events in Yugoslavia and had formed a special group for it.[68]

Immediately after the removal of the Croatian leadership, the Political Committee discussed Yugoslavia again on 27 January 1972. NATO representatives were particularly puzzled by Brezhnev's statement that although there was no such thing as the 'doctrine of limited sovereignty' Yugoslavia was a member of the communist world, thus implying a legitimate Soviet interest in developments there. This revealed that as far as the Soviets were concerned, Yugoslavia's status as a neutral and non-aligned country would not necessarily be respected.[69]

Considering the geostrategic importance of Yugoslavia in Western defence planning, NATO's interest was not surprising. The West wanted to see an independent socialist Yugoslavia which could serve as a Trojan Horse for the Eastern bloc and a neutral buffer zone between Italy, Austria and the Warsaw Pact. Equally importantly, Yugoslav independence prevented Soviet access to the Adriatic and the Mediterranean.

From very limited NATO reports, it is obvious that NATO was concerned about the situation in Croatia, but also that it was not involved in supporting Croatian separatism. Such claims by many politicians and historians after 1971 did not have any basis in fact: the West favoured a cohesive and federal Yugoslav state. For this reason, the NATO moves were aimed at helping Yugoslavia diversify its military equipment while sending a clear signal to the Soviets not to meddle. The West and NATO were particularly concerned by the vagueness of the Soviet position, which straddled neutrality and the Brezhnev Doctrine. Tito's intervention in Croatia temporarily stopped such speculation, but fear of Yugoslav internal instability which might provoke Soviet intervention would remain a constant fear in the West. The nightmare scenario would be Yugoslavia collapsing into civil war, drawing in both NATO and the Soviets on opposite sides.

Soviet Reactions

The Soviets were undoubtedly satisfied with the course of events in Croatia after Karađorđevo. This was confirmed to American diplomats by the first secretary of the Yugoslav embassy in Moscow. He told the Americans that during a visit to Moscow in March 1972, the secretary of the Yugoslav party, Jure Bilić, met with the Soviet foreign secretary, Nikolaj Patolichev, and with Mikhail Suslov, a key Soviet ideologue. Suslov was very satisfied that Croatian nationalism had finally been brought under control, and that the party had managed to reimpose its central authority. The Americans assessed that Bilić got special treatment from the Soviets, because they believed that among the new Croatian leadership he was the most conservative. The Soviets therefore might have viewed him as a leading Croatian figure in the future, especially since Bakarić and Blažević were near the end of their careers and in poor health.[70]

The Yugoslav embassy to Moscow reported on 8 December 1971 about a conversation with the chief of the European department of the Soviet foreign ministry, Mr Zubkov. He told the Yugoslav diplomats that Tito's speech in Karađorđevo was 'received with great pleasure', because it was a 'reliable sign of a shift towards taking matters into his own hands, as liberalism in Yugoslavia was largely abused by powers that represent our mutual enemy'. Zubkov pointed out that 'the position of the Presidium of the LCY was accepted by the Soviet Union with sympathy, understanding and brotherhood'.[71] In a similar tone the embassy reported that the Soviets believed that the intervention in Croatia was long overdue, but they didn't want to be seen suggesting it directly. They also rejected any accusation of links to Croatian émigrés and warned that further measures, including administrative ones, would be needed to 'solve this situation'.[72]

The fact was that the relations between Yugoslavia and the Soviet Union improved after Tito's intervention. It is still unclear, however, to what extent Brezhnev's visit influenced Tito's decision to intervene. Certainly, the American guarantees given to Tito in Washington gave Tito more confidence to deal with internal and Soviet threats. But the years after the purge were also marked by a *rapprochement* between Yugoslavia and the Soviet Union in the last period of Tito's rule.

In 1972 the Soviet minister for the automobile industry, Nikolai Baibakov, who also headed *Gosplan* – the agency responsible for central economic planning – visited Yugoslavia. Moscow promised Belgrade $1.9 billion in loans, and Yugoslav exports to Comecon countries increased from 32.5 per cent of the country's total exports in 1970 to 46 per cent in 1980. The high point of improved relations between the two countries came with Tito's visit to Moscow in June 1972 and the visit of Soviet Prime Minister Kosygin to Belgrade in 1973. Good relations would continue until Tito's death in 1980, but as one Soviet diplomat to Yugoslavia explained, Soviet–Yugoslav relations would remain 'friendly and dishonest'.[73]

A Reflection

After three diplomatic assignments in Yugoslavia, in Thomas Dunlop's oral history interview he reflected on the purge. While it was unlikely that Yugoslavia could have been saved on the long-term, the civil war was not inevitable.

> I still firmly believe that the intercommunal conflicts in Yugoslavia could have been resolved without all of this current bloodshed in the 1990s. I think that one of the reasons why they were not was the purging of these modernizers by Tito in 1971. At that point I came to the conclusion that Tito had made the greatest single political mistake he could possibly make. That is, he not only failed to provide for his own succession, but he also beheaded those who could have modernized and Westernized the party after his death. I still think so.[74]

Conclusion

The Croatian Spring and the broader modernising movements in Yugoslavia from 1966 to 1972 were primarily internal efforts to modernise and democratise Yugoslav society and economy in line with the proclaimed goals of the Yugoslav 'self-management' system that sought to find a balance between a socialist and a capitalist economy. The process of economic decentralisation, however, could not be separated from cultural, national and political forces which were ultimately perceived as a threat to the federal system. But the purge of the modernising leadership was not only a Croatian affair: it occurred across the Yugoslav republics, as the new generation of Slovenian, Serbian and Macedonian leaders was also removed in 1972–3. The term 'Croatian Spring' was coined after the purge but we might be justified in referring to the period as the 'Yugoslav Spring', although this is not commonly done in historiography. However, liberals in different republics weren't unified allies even if they were purged in the same period.

Rather than being merely an anti-nationalist purge, it was very much an effort by Tito to restore his authority as the ultimate arbiter. After the initial removal of the Croatian liberal leadership in December 1971, Tito continued to purge critics, modernisers, religious leaders, academics and party rivals in the years that followed. And while many of the Croatian

Spring leaders' demands were implemented in the 1974 constitution, no further effort was made in the 1970s and 1980s to bring the new generation of progressive leaders back into political life.

In the long-term, Yugoslavia probably could not be saved, but like Thomas Dunlop one may argue that the Yugoslav wars of the 1990s could have been prevented. The 1971–3 purge not only removed the progressive leaderships in Croatia, Serbia, and other republics, but it irrevocably damaged relations between Croats and Serbs. The main centripetal forces holding the country together, other than Tito's personality, were the shared fear of Russia and the political force of federal communism. After Tito's death, the mechanism of a rotating presidency that was devised to keep the Federation alive worked throughout the 1980s so long as there was still only one ruling party. With the end of the Cold War and the introduction of a multi-party system, there were no more counterweights to the centrifugal forces of nationalism that won everywhere in the 1990 election, accelerating the process of Yugoslavia's disintegration. These would lead to referenda in Croatia and Slovenia, and both republics declaring independence from Yugoslavia in June 1991. The prospects of Croatia's independence led the Croatian Serbs, with the support of Serbian President Milošević to proclaim their own autonomy and start an insurgency against the newly elected Croatian authorities. This cumulative effect accelerated the path to war.

But the emergence of nationalism following the end of the Cold War should not have inevitably led to war. The breakup of the Soviet Union into the Russian Federation and 14 independent post-Soviet republics is the largest peaceful dissolution of an empire in history. Similarly, the Czech and Slovak republics separated amicably, stewarded wisely by their leaders. In the American diplomatic oral histories, Thomas Dunlop speculated how this could have succeeded in Yugoslavia:

> It seems to me now that the Serbs and the Croatians each had a non-negotiable demand, but they were not totally incompatible. Their differences could have been resolved or met with some ingenuity and some political skill. The Croatians were dead set on independence, on the recognition of a sovereign, Croatian state. That view was never articulated by the Savka and Tripalo leadership, but it was quite implicit in what they were doing and in the direction in which they were going.[1]

The most important general lesson of the Spring movement concerns the quality and wisdom of leadership that can steer the course of their nations' history to avert major crises and large-scale suffering. The more specific lessons of the period 1966–72 concern the interaction between liberalism, federalism and nationalism. In the West, modernisation and liberalism tend to be allied to federal systems, but in Eastern Europe, as the journalist Chris Cviić observed in 1972,[2] nationalism has often been its ally, and the instrument by which Eastern European nations pursued liberty and democracy to escape the yoke of communism.

Democracy, however, is not merely a political process but a way of life for a society where all matters of general and public interest can be debated freely and safely. Tito's instincts were never on the side of free debate or public criticism. The case of Yugoslavia was a continual balancing act between internal tensions and external forces during the Cold War. The irony of the history of the reformist movement is also that it led to a series of well-intended reforms that consistently failed to produce the intended results.

As a direct result of Yugoslavia's break with Stalin in 1948, a process was set in motion to differentiate Yugoslav socialism from the Soviet model of political and economic development. This process that led to greater decentralisation of the federal government and the economy, autonomy of the republics, the liberalisation of social and political life, and the revival of nationalism started in 1952 when the self-management system was introduced. Equally important for the introduction of a more liberal form of socialism was the economic, military and political cooperation with the West in the period between 1949 and 1956, which continued in a more moderate form after the end of the Soviet–Yugoslav conflict. But Tito's regime was not willing to give up the communist ideology and accept the Western democratic and capitalist system. Such an international position meant that Yugoslavia had to devise a hybrid form of self-governing economy that was aimed at reconciling the opposing features of a centralised and a free market economy.

The triangulation of a unique Yugoslav model between socialist and capitalist systems was also reflected in its foreign policy. Caught between the Cold War blocs, Tito pursued the open geopolitical space and created an entirely new track of Yugoslav foreign policy towards the Third World, leading to the establishment of the Non-Aligned Movement in 1961. While this project didn't create a cohesive third bloc comparable to the Cold War belligerents, it did elevate Yugoslavia's importance beyond her geopolitical and economic clout.

The 1960s brought the need to adopt new technologies and transform the economy, which necessarily entailed a greater economic cooperation with Western Europe and the United States. The opening of the country's economy brought problems with the foreign trade deficit and inflation, but also aggravated the already existing socio-economic differences between the developed north-western republics of Slovenia and Croatia and the rest of the country. The dismissal of Aleksandar Ranković in 1966 allowed further liberalisation of political and social life in Yugoslavia, while in Croatia, the process took on a strong nationalist component. This process led to the strengthening of hitherto suppressed inter-ethnic disputes and enhanced the political conflict over the future of Yugoslav federation.

The West

The process of decentralisation was welcomed and supported by the West with investment, aid, tourism and cultural exchange. But Western policy was reactive insofar as it followed larger trends, much as the Western nations, diplomats and press quickly accepted Tito's purge in 1972. The primary considerations for Western powers remained geopolitical balance between NATO and the Warsaw Pact, within the overall context of emerging European *détente*.

Since 1948 the West had developed a complex set of policies to provide support to Tito's communist regime, the territorial and political unity of Yugoslavia, and its international independence. At the same time, Western governments sought to alleviate the repressive side of the Yugoslav regime. Both approaches were primarily linked to the geostrategic position of Yugoslavia vis-à-vis the Soviet Union. Nonaligned Yugoslavia was an obstacle to Soviet efforts to obtain access to the Adriatic and Mediterranean, and a buffer zone between the Soviet satellites and members of the Western defence alliance, especially Italy and Austria.

In addition, Yugoslav experimentation with self-management socialism, and its liberal component, was interesting to the West not only as a test of a new and unproven socio-political system but also as a promising tool to influence further liberalisation and greater independence of the Soviet eastern European satellite states. On the Yugoslav side, investment from the West was welcomed but socialist self-management meant there was still much catching up to do with Western business practice. This dilemma between a desire to support the Yugoslav economy and awareness of the shortcomings of Yugoslav economic practice is evident in both American and British memos. Without clear ownership or accountability in enterprises to either investors or government, decisions were not necessarily made in the interest of businesses or their relationships.

The United States and its Western European allies supported the liberal atmosphere in Croatia and Yugoslavia, and the Communist Party's determination to further decentralise the country as a way to alleviate its economic and ethnic problems. But Western governments were aware that the key to Yugoslav unity lay in its strong centralised regime, and were not prepared to support the establishment of a multi-party system at the cost of destabilisation or the break-up of the country. In this sense, the West supported the process of economic and political liberalisation in Croatia and Yugoslavia only as far as it served the goal of strengthening the integrity and international independence of socialist Yugoslavia.

Dispatches by British and American diplomats reveal cautiousness with regard to the regime's controlled revival of nationalism, and resolution of inter-ethnic and inter-republican disputes that weakened party control over political and economic life. The Foreign Office and the State Department correctly assessed that partial political and economic reforms, and decentralisation of the country, could not solve the chronic problems of the Yugoslav state. In addition, the key issue was the fate of Yugoslavia after Tito's death and the possibility of internal destabilisation, which could lead to stronger Soviet influence.

This context is crucial to understanding Western reactions to Croatian demands for greater economic and national autonomy within the Yugoslav federation. Western diplomats in Croatia were aware of both Croatian dissatisfaction with the existing Yugoslav economic system and of their inability to openly promote Croatian national identity. But in principle they supported the demands for greater national autonomy and economic decentralisation as the healthiest way to reconcile historical and cultural differences between the Yugoslav nations and regions.

The role of the Croatian leadership in the early phases of this process was approved of and supported by the West. The best examples are the reactions to the dismissal of Aleksandar Ranković in 1966, the Tenth Session of the Central Committee of the Croatian Communist Party in 1970, and the constitutional amendments of 1971. The reactions to the 'Declaration on the position and the name of the Croatian language' in 1967, and the Serbian response to it, revealed that the West was less forthcoming where Croatian and Serbian nationalism were concerned. Still, in this period the West tolerantly observed occasional nationalist outbursts and justified them as a relaxation of party discipline that would ultimately lead to a positive compromise on the future of the Yugoslav federation.

In early 1971, however, Western diplomats started to question whether such a course might further destabilise the country. The rise of the student movement and *Matica Hrvatska* in Croatia attracted special attention. While free student elections were interpreted as a step forward in the democratisation of Croatian society, its strong nationalist component was perceived with unease in Western diplomatic missions in both Zagreb and Belgrade. According to Western diplomats, *Matica Hrvatska* had the most negative role in the promotion of Croatian nationalism. Its insistence on promoting Croatian national and economic rights only exacerbated old animosities, which in turn had a negative impact on the process of liberalisation and democratisation.

But the greatest Western concerns were related to the activities of the Croatian party leadership. According to British and American diplomats, the Croatian party leaders found themselves caught between the need for popular support and pressure from the conservative wing of the Croatian and Yugoslav leadership to put an end to growing Croatian nationalism. Savka Dabčević-Kučar articulated this dilemma when she complained that modernisers were caught between 'unitarists' and 'chauvinists', leaving no room to shape the Yugoslavia they wanted to see.[3] Both London and Washington concluded that the Croatian leaders had lost control of events, which led to Tito's intervention in Karađorđevo in December 1971.

Despite some suspicions, there is no evidence that the 1971 crises in Croatia and Yugoslavia were orchestrated from abroad. Western diplomats were in most cases passive observers of the events in Yugoslavia and there was little Western states could have done to prevent or stop Tito's purge. Indeed, Tito and the communist regime would never allow foreign intervention of any kind to occur. The West, however, clearly supported Yugoslav integrity and independence by providing political and economic aid to the regime, and prioritised these over matters of liberty and democracy. Consequently, the breakdown of the Croatian Spring in December 1971 did not cause a negative reaction in the West comparable to similar purges in Hungary or Czechoslovakia.[4]

Tito's move to suppress the Croatian Spring was treated with a measure of relief in both London and Washington. The dilemma in Whitehall and Foggy Bottom was not whether Tito should intervene, but how and to what extent he should do it. The British government was more concerned with the bad press Tito was receiving in London than with the effects of the purge. A fear did exist in the West that Yugoslavia might turn the clock back and restore its centralist character, further deepening antagonistic relations between the Yugoslav nationalities. But there was never a shred of doubt that the West preferred a stable regime that would ensure the integrity and continuity of Yugoslav foreign policy over the democratic aspirations of Yugoslav nationalities.

The Soviets

The Soviet leadership had consistently objected to liberal policies in Croatia and Yugoslavia. Accordingly, Moscow exerted constant pressure on the Yugoslav authorities to slow down or put an end to the process of decentralisation and liberalisation. There is no evidence, however, that the Soviets were contemplating a military intervention and planning to overthrow the existing Yugoslav regime.

It is equally difficult to determine the exact nature and scope of Soviet actions with regard to Yugoslavia. The Kremlin publicly accepted Yugoslavia's right to build its unique path to socialism, but it is certain that the Soviets wished to have more influence over Yugoslavia, which they considered to be a part of its sphere of influence – for both its socialist orientation and geostrategic importance. Lack of access to Soviet archives still prevents us, however, from gaining detailed insight into Soviet intentions and the extent to which the Soviets were prepared to go to influence or subvert the situation in Yugoslavia.

The Soviet leadership recognised that open threats and direct pressures would be unacceptable to Tito and the Yugoslav communist regime. Other factors prevented the Soviets from intervening more decisively in Yugoslavia's internal situation: resentment among the wider population towards Soviet-style communism, and the Yugoslav regime's resolve to resist any Soviet interference in its internal affairs. The Soviets were equally aware that Tito would not allow any change of Yugoslavia's political orientation in his lifetime.

Another source of deterrence was Western support for Yugoslav unity and independence. A possible Soviet military intervention in Yugoslavia would provoke a harsh reaction from the West, especially where control over the strategically important Adriatic coast was concerned. In these circumstances, the Soviets focused their efforts on more subtle tactics of political and economic pressure, as well as undercover activity, in order to prepare the ground for a political incursion after Tito's death.

The most visible outcomes of Soviet activities relating to Yugoslavia in this period were the 'Spy Affair' that shook the Yugoslav political scene in the spring of 1971, and Brezhnev's call to Tito during the 17th session of the Presidency of the LCY in Brijuni in April 1971. Soviet contacts with Croatian émigrés were never proven, although it is likely that they did occur. Similarly, it cannot be accurately determined whether the Soviets had actual plans to support the formation of an independent Croatian state under the auspices of the Soviet Union, and what their incentive would be to pursue such a plan, because decentralisation had always accompanied a trend of democratisation that the Soviets opposed.

In the international situation of the time, the option of Soviet support for and control over a Croatian state would only be desirable for the Soviets if Yugoslavia was facing imminent collapse. The Soviets were certainly aware of the fears and negative views about 'the Russians' among the populations of all the Yugoslav republics. In such circumstances, a reasonable explanation would be that one of the few ways in which the Soviets could increase their influence in Yugoslavia was to discredit the Croatian reformist leadership in order to slow down the process of decentralisation and democratisation.

Brezhnev's call to Tito in April 1971 can be similarly interpreted as a form of pressure on the Yugoslav leadership in the midst of heightened inter-republican tensions over the Spy Affair and constitutional amendments. However, despite the fact that Tito and the Yugoslav political leadership feared Soviet interference in their internal affairs, just as in 1968, Tito overplayed the Soviet threat to justify his own political moves, both internally and towards the West.

With Tito still in firm control, neither the West nor the Soviet Union had an interest in destabilising Yugoslavia. Both Cold War parties shared an interest not to permit any major changes in Yugoslavia. The fear of a civil war was real, and at the time it could have meant that the West and the Soviet Union would be drawn in on opposite sides.

Lessons

It is still not entirely clear what was behind Tito's decision to put an end to the democratic processes that the Party initiated in the early 1960s and whether it was the Soviet threat or fear of losing personal influence that motivated him. He was certainly driven by fears that modernisation and liberalisation of society and the media would weaken the Party's authority. But it is fair to describe 1971 as a perfect storm of crises where legitimate grievances, overreaching ambitions, and misunderstandings accumulated to tip the scales in favour of Tito's decision to crack down on the liberal leadership of Croatia he had once supported.

He must have felt threatened by the rise of a younger, more liberal and modernising generation of politicians, in Croatia and across all the republics, who were beginning to challenge his position as undisputed national leader and arbiter. He did not initiate the removal of the Croatian leadership in December 1971 just for its tolerance towards nationalism, which was extended to nearly 2,000 individuals in public and cultural life who resigned or were dismissed. Because the Croatian purge was followed, on a smaller scale, by crackdowns on Serbian, Slovenian and Macedonian liberals throughout 1972 and 1973, there is some validity to the claim that it was an anti-modernist purge. In this respect, there had indeed been a form of 'Yugoslav Spring', although there was never a unified or pan-Yugoslav movement but rather a concurrent set of liberal-national political movements. These parallel trends within Yugoslavia mirrored similar movements across Eastern Europe.

Open calls and movements for democratisation and modernisation took shape in Hungary, Poland and Czechoslovakia in the 1950s and 1960s and, like Yugoslavia, all had been suppressed by the late 1960s and early 1970s. Some contemporary observers compared the 1971 dismissal of the Croatian leadership to the Soviet intervention in Czechoslovakia in August 1968. Chris Cviić noted:

> But just as the Czechoslovak reformers of 1968 became isolated within the communist block, the Croat leaders and their follow-ers became isolated in Jugoslavia. Their far-reaching demands annoyed many economic interests in the other Jugoslav repub-lics. [...] When the conservatives, led by President Tito in per-son, struck in December, no influential voices from the other republics spoke up for the Croat leaders.[5]

But Western diplomats, and most Western historians of Eastern Europe, do not see many similarities between the two events, because Czechoslovakia was an intervention by foreign powers in the internal affairs of another country while Yugoslavia is seen exclusively as an internal matter of the Yugoslav state.

The suppression of nationalism was nevertheless a suppression of liberalism. In Hungary in 1956 and Czechoslovakia in 1968 the national component played an important role in efforts to reduce the influence of the Soviet Union and strengthen the independence of the local socialist regimes. In both cases, Soviet military and political control was the main obstacle to these processes of liberalisation and reduction of the totalitar-ian nature of the communist regime. Similarly, in Croatia the national question played an important role in the fight to reduce the impact of the federal centre in Belgrade and the strengthening of republican autonomy.

One can therefore conclude that the common denominator of the events of 1956, 1968 and 1971 was an attempt to achieve liberalisation, democratisation, and greater political and economic autonomy, opposed to the forces that sought to maintain the centralised control of commu-nist ideology. The Prague Spring came to an end when the Soviet inter-vention in Czechoslovakia crushed the reformers, reinforced the status quo in Europe and strengthened Brezhnev and Soviet control. Similarly, the crackdown on the Croatian Spring strengthened Tito's position in the country, the international stability of socialist Yugoslavia, and would lead to stronger ties with the Soviet Union during the rest of the 1970s.

While Tito's role in preserving the communist regime in Yugoslavia can be compared with the role that Moscow had in the countries of Eastern Europe, it was ultimately supported both by the West and by the Soviet Union. It is ironic because the West viewed Tito's Yugoslavia as a strategic buffer that reduced Moscow's influence. Western diplomats and journalists sought to highlight the difference between Yugoslav socialism and the Soviet system in order to promote trade, but the irony is that the purge increased Moscow's influence. Despite *détente*, the question of liberty couldn't be brushed aside so easily.

It is interesting to consider the differences on this question between American and British diplomats who had served in Belgrade and in Zagreb. Although diplomats and policymakers were primarily based in Belgrade, the FCO and State Department were aware of the significant cultural, historical and economic differences between the individual republics and peoples. But with few exceptions the West failed to appreciate Croatian aspirations towards greater political and economic autonomy. Complaints about the inferior economic situation in Yugoslavia and the dominance of Serbian personnel in the police and the army were primarily interpreted as a reflection of Croatian nationalism rather than as legitimate political concerns.

Most Western diplomats were astute observers of developments in Yugoslavia, but the views from Belgrade were limited by weak communications and closeness to the federal administration and press. Unlike their colleagues in Zagreb, Western diplomats in Belgrade did not think that the Croatian economy was suffering because of their successful tourism and processing industries, because they received cheap agricultural products and raw materials from the south-eastern parts of the country. After Karađorđevo, different views on the causes of the crisis in Croatia led to disagreements among American and British diplomats in their respective Zagreb consulates and Belgrade embassies.

However, it cannot be said that British and American diplomats had an intentional bias toward Serbs or a Serbian vision for Yugoslavia, as is often implied. The fact is that Western governments and diplomats wished to see a strong united Yugoslavia, but not necessarily an administratively centralised state. The experience of pre-war Yugoslavia showed Serbian hegemony over the rest of Yugoslavia to be unsustainable, and a regulated federal Yugoslavia was welcomed as a long-term solution to inter-ethnic problems. Serbian nationalism was considered very dangerous by the West, but Western diplomats believed that the Serbian leadership, unlike the Croatians, successfully kept a lid on nationalist tendencies within Serbia. However, the Foreign Office and the State Department were fully aware that a non-democratic and totalitarian Yugoslav regime, even in a much milder form than the Soviet Union, could not truly solve the complex web of historical differences between the Yugoslav peoples and republics. Therefore the West hoped that decentralisation and economic progress could promote awareness of a common interest in the existence of a unified Yugoslav state, even without Tito's strong authority.

The events in Croatia in 1971 showed that the process of liberalisation and decentralisation, which began in the early 1960s and accelerated after the economic reforms of 1965 and the dismissal of Aleksandar Ranković in 1966, ultimately weakened the process of integration in Yugoslavia. But the West had no doubts about the choice between a liberal and decentralised but politically unstable Yugoslavia, and a stable country under the firm control of a communist regime.

It is difficult to predict what would have happened in Yugoslavia if Tito had not decided to put an end to the reforms. We can be certain, however, that the Karađorđevo meeting and subsequent purge stopped the last attempt to modernise and democratise the Yugoslav state. Equally tragic for Yugoslavia's future was that the key protagonists and supporters of these attempts were removed from the political scene, never to return. It is tempting, albeit controversial, to assume that they could have prevented the rise of Slobodan Milošević, and paved the way for the peaceful resolution of the Yugoslav crisis had they been given the opportunity.

Decentralisation was continued with the adoption of the new constitution in 1974, which served as a compromise that was supposed to cement existing relations in the Federation and to prepare for the time after Tito's death, but no effort was made to promote further democratisation. Instead, too much was still invested in Tito's mortal person.

The events that followed after 1980 confirmed the fears of Western analysts that the Party would lose authority and legitimacy after Tito's death.

In the 1980s, Yugoslavia found itself in a deep political and economic crisis, and the final blow came with the collapse of the Communist bloc and of Soviet control over Eastern Europe in 1989. The end of the Cold War eroded the Yugoslav regime's foreign policy and weakened its policy of non-alignment, while in the eyes of the West Yugoslavia lost its geopolitical importance as a defensive buffer against the Soviet threat. The democratisation of Eastern Europe affected Yugoslav political life, and brought to the surface all the suppressed contradictions within Yugoslav society.

Further Research

Despite increased efforts by historians to research different aspects of this controversial period, there is still much to be done. In addition to this study, which used extensive sources from archives in Croatia and Serbia, along with British and American diplomatic and press reports, further research may paint a fuller picture of the depth and connections of the Croatian Spring movement to other liberal leaderships in Slovenia, Macedonia and elsewhere. This is primarily related to economic grievances between the federation and the republics, as well as between the developed north-west and less developed south-east of the country. Special attention also needs to be given in future to link the events surrounding the purge in the early 1970s, with further developments in the 1970s and 1980s – and in particular with the circumstances that defined the adoption of the 1974 constitution, as well as the economic and political crisis of 1980s. Finally, greater access to Soviet archives would also contribute to explaining Yugoslavia's international position and answer the extent to which the Soviets were willing, or planning, to go to secure their influence over communist Yugoslavia.

Notes

1. The Cold War World

1. Tvrtko Jakovina, *Trenutak katarze, Predgovor u knjizi Đorđe Zelmanović, Mađarska Jesen 1956*, Fraktura: Zagreb, 2006a, 7.
2. Michael Schaller, *The United States and China in the Twentieth Century*, Oxford University Press, New York and Oxford 1990: 169; John W. Young, John Kent, *International History since 1945, A Global History*, Oxford University Press: Oxford, New York 2004: 408–9.
3. Vladislav Zubok, *A Failed Empire, The Soviet Union in the Cold War from Stalin to Gorbachev*, The University of North Carolina Press: Chapel Hill 2007: 192.
4. Antony Best et al.; *International History of the Twentieth Century and Beyond*, Second Edition, Routledge: London, New York 2008: 281.
5. Schaller, *The United States and China* 1990: 169; Young, Kent, *International History since 1945* 2004: 408–9.
6. Best et al., *International History of the Twentieth Century* 2008: 281–2; Jonathan Fenby, *Povijest suvremene Kine, Propast i uzdizanje velike sile 1850.-2008.*, Sandorf: Zagreb 2008: 469–524; Roy Medvedev, *China and the Superpowers*, Basil Blackwell: London, New York 1986: 45; Keith L. Nelson, *Making of Détente: Soviet American Relations in the Shadow of Vietnam*, John Hopkins University Press: Baltimore, London, 1995: 91; Rosemary Quested, *Sino-Russian Relations*, Routledge: London 2005: 106.
7. See Piers N. Ludlow, *European Integration and the Cold War, Ostpolitik-Westpolitik, 1965–1973*, Routledge: London, 2007.
8. Ibid., 68.
9. Julia Von Dannenberg, *Foundations of Ostpolitik: Making of the Moscow Treaty between West Germany and the USSR*, Oxford University Press: Oxford, 2008, 19; Dušan Nećak, *Hallsteinova doktrina i Jugoslavija, Tito između Savezne Republike Njemačke i Demokratske republike Njemačke*, Srednja Europa: Zagreb, 2004, 174–8. See: William Glenn Gray, *Germany's Cold War, Global Campaign to Isolate East Germany, 1949–1969*, University of North Carolina Press: Chapel Hill, 2003.
10. Best et al., *International History of the Twentieth Century* 2008: 282; Dannenberg, *Foundations of Ostpolitik* 2008: 33; Tomislav Mitrović, 'Berlinsko pitanje na dnevnom redu,' *Međunarodna politika* 494, XXI, Beograd, 1970, 5–8.

11. Dannenberg, *Foundations of Ostpolitik* 2008: 29; Nećak, *Hallsteinova doktrina i Jugoslavija* 2004: 174–8.
12. Maude Bracke, *Which Socialism, Whose Détente?: West European Communism and the Czechoslovak crisis, 1968*, Central European University Press: Budapest 2007, 209–23.
13. Zubok, *A Failed Empire* 2007: 209.
14. Dannenberg, *Foundations of Ostpolitik* 2008: 33.
15. Mary Elise Sarotte, *Dealing with the Devil*, University of North Carolina Press, Chapel Hill, 2001, 109.
16. The treaty of recognition of the border between Germany and Poland was signed in 1990.
17. Best et al., *International History of the Twentieth Century* 2008: 282; Dannenberg, *Foundations of Ostpolitik* 2008: 33; Mitrović, 'Berlinsko pitanje na dnevnom redu,' 1970: 5–8.
18. See Robert H. Donaldson and Joseph L. Nogee, *Foreign Policy of Russia: Changing Systems, Enduring Interests*, M.E. Sharpe: London, 1998.
19. Anthony R. De Luca, 'Soviet-American Politics and the Turkish Straits,' *Political Science Quarterly*, 92, 3, 1977: 505.
20. Ibid., 515.
21. A good example is Soviet policy towards Iran and Turkey, as well as China and Korea in the period 1945–53, cf. Odd Arne Westad, *The Global Cold War: Third World Interventions and the Making of our Times*, 2009: 85.
22. Ibid., 85.
23. Westad, *The Global Cold War* 2009: 110–12.
24. Michael MccGwire, Ken Booth and John McDonnell, *Soviet Naval Policy*, Praeger: New York, London, Washington, 1975: 248.
25. Nigel Ashton, ed., *Cold War in the Middle East, Regional Conflict and the Superpowers 1967–1973*, Routledge: London, 2007: 136–63.
26. Benjamin Miller, *States, Nations, and the Great Powers: Sources of Regional War and Peace*, Cambridge University Press: Cambridge, 2007: 236–8.
27. Tvrtko Jakovina, *Hrvatski izlaz u svijet. Hrvatska/Jugoslavija u svjetskoj politici 1945–1991, Hrvatska politika u XX. stoljeću*, Matica Hrvatska: Zagreb, 2006: 346; see Yaacov Ro'i et al., *e Soviet Union and the June 1967 Six Day War*, Stanford University Press: Washington, DC, Stanford, 1989: 35–59.
28. Stephen F. Larrabee, 'Changing Russian Perspectives in the Balkans,' *Survey* 18(3), 1972: 16.
29. Gavriel D. Ra'anan, *Yugoslavia after Tito – Scenarios and Implications, Westview Special Studies on the Soviet Union an Eastern Europe*, Westview Press: Boulder, 1977: 109; Nils H. Wessel, 'Yugoslavia: Ground Rules for Restraining Soviet and American Competition,' *Journal of International Affairs*, 34, 2, 1980: 316–17.
30. Jakovina, 'Jugoslavija, Hrvatsko proljeće i Sovjeti u Detantu,' 2005: 168–9; Ra'anan, *Yugoslavia after Tito* 1977: 50–2; Samuel L. Sharp, 'The Yugoslav

Experiment in Self-management: Soviet Criticism,' *Studies in Comparative Communism*, Vol. 4, 3–4, 1971: 169–78.

31. Stephen S. Anderson 'Yugoslavia: Diplomacy of Balance,' *Current History*, 56, 1969: 212.

32. NARA, Electronic FOIA Reading Room, CIA, Yugoslavia: An Intelligence Appraisal 00734, 27 July 1971, p. 55.

33. Zlatko Rendulić, *General avnojevske Jugoslavije*, Golden marketing-Tehnička knjiga: Zagreb, 2004: 284–8; FRUS, Nixon-Ford Administration, Volume XXIX, Eastern Europe; Eastern Mediterranean, 1969–72, Yugoslavia, Telegram from the Embassy in Yugoslavia to the Department of State, US–Yugoslav Military Relations, Belgrade, March 13, 1970, 1540Z, p. 532, http://www.state.gov/documents/organization/97933.pdf, Source: National Archives, Nixon Presidential Materials, NSC Files, Box 733, Country Files—Europe, Yugoslavia, Vol. I through Jul 70. Secret; Exdis.

34. Dušanka Špadijer, 'Jugoslavija u međunarodnim odnosima,' *Godišnjak Instituta za međunarodnu politiku i privredu 1967*, Beograd, 1967: 43–4.

35. John R. Lampe, *Balkans into Southeastern Europe*, Palgrave Macmillan: Basingstoke, NY, 2006: 223; Karen A. Mingst, 'From the Politics of Non-Alignment to the Economics of the Semi-Periphery: Case of Yugoslavia,' *East European Quarterly*, 18, 3, 1984: 318.

36. Nećak, *Hallsteinova doktrina i Jugoslavija*, 2004: 174–8.

37. Aleksander Clarkson, 'Home and Away: Immigration and Political Violence in the Federal Republic of Germany, 1945–90,' *Cold War History*, 8, 1, 2008: 8; William E. Griffith, *Ostpolitik of the Federal Republic of Germany*, MIT Press: Cambridge, MA, 1978: 156–8; Boris Šnuderl, 'SR Nemačka na prvom mestu u robnoj razmeni Jugoslavije,' *Međunarodna politika*, 506, Beograd, 1971: 26–7; Špadijer 'Jugoslavija u međunarodnim odnosima,' 1967: 40–1.

38. Karlovic, 'Internal Colonialism in a Marxist Society,' *Ethnic and Racial Studies*, 5, 3, 1982: 285; Lampe, *Balkans into Southeastern Europe* 2006: 222; William Zimmerman, *Open Borders, Nonalignment, and the Political Evolution of Yugoslavia*, Princeton University Press: Princeton, 1987: 74–6; Aleksandar Petković, 'Jugoslavenski radnici u inostranstvu,' *Međunarodna politika*, 506, XXII, Beograd, 1971: 23–5.

39. Zimmerman, *Open Borders, Nonalignment, and Political Evolution* 1987: 85.

40. Kent and Young, *International History since 1945* 2004: 324.

41. Zimmerman, *Open Borders, Nonalignment, and Political Evolution* 1987: 78–83.

42. Foreign Investment in Yugoslavia, Radio Free Europe Research, 13 July 1970, Open Society Archives, http://files.osa.ceu.hu/holdings/300/8/3/text/79-2-284.shtml; According to data of the Institute for Foreign Trade in Belgrade, by June 1970, 19 joint-venture contracts were negotiated with a total value of $170 million, cf. Vojislav Vlajić, 'Jugoslavenska i svetska privreda,' *Međunarodna politika* 490, XXI, Beograd, 1970: 36.

43. Foreign Investments in Yugoslavia Discussed, Radio Free Europe Research, 23 March 1973, Open Society Archives.
44. PRO, FCO 28/1628, Internal Political Situation in Yugoslavia, Past and Present, Terence Garvey to Michael Stewart, 2 April 1971. The best overview of Western influence on everyday life in Yugoslavia was provided by Igor Duda in his book *In Search of the Good Life* (in Croatian, *U potrazi za blagostanjem*, 2005), where he researched the history of leisure and spending in Croatia in the 1950s and 1960s.

2. Yugoslavia, 1945–65

1. Antifašističko vijeće narodnog oslobođenja Jugoslavije (Anti-fascist council of the people's liberation of Yugoslavia).
2. 'Stalin's tick on Churchill's note written at the Kremlin on 9 October 1944, dividing up the Balkans into spheres of influence', Britain's Public Record Office, PREM 3/66/7; and image library reference 3/66/7 (169) at https://images.nationalarchives.gov.uk.
3. Dušan Bilandžić, *Historija Socijalističke federativne republike Jugoslavije, Glavni procesi*, Školska knjiga: Zagreb, 1978: 76; Nikola Popović, *Jugoslovensko-sovjetski odnosi u drugom svetskom ratu (1941–1945)*, Institut za savremenu istoriju: Beograd, 1988: 150–6; Vladimir Volkov, 'Soviet Leadership and Southeastern Europe: Establishment of Communist regimes in Eastern Europe, 1944–1949,' ed. Norman Naimark and Leonid Gibianskii, Westview Press: Oxford, 1997: 58–60; Branko Petranović, *Istorija Jugoslavije 1918–1988, sv. I–III*, Nolit: Beograd, 1988, vol. II: 330–1.
4. Bilandžić, *Historija Socijalističke* 1978: 77–8.
5. Dušan Bilandžić, *Historija Socijalističke Federativne Republike Jugoslavije, Glavni procesi 1918–1985*, Školska knjiga, Zagreb, 1985: 102.
6. Vesselin Dimitrov, 'Communism in Bulgaria, Origins of the Cold War,' ed. Melvyn P. Lefler and David S. Painter, Routledge: New York, London, 2005: 190–205; Jerzy Holzer, *Komunizam u Europi, Povijest pokreta i sustava vlasti*, Srednja Europa: Zagreb, 2002: 64–7.
7. Ivo Banac, *Sa Staljinom protiv Tita, Globus – Plava biblioteka*, Zagreb, 1990: 33; Volkov, Soviet Leadership and Southeastern Europe 1997: 291.
8. Dušan Bilandžić, *Borba za samoupravni socijalizam u Jugoslaviji 1945–1969*, Institut za historiju radničkog pokreta Hrvatske: Zagreb, 1969: 24.
9. Ibid., 26.
10. Dennison Rusinow, *Yugoslav Experiment 1948–1974*, C. Hurst and Co. – Royal Institute of International Affairs: London, 1977: 20.
11. Tvrtko Jakovina, *Američki komunistički saveznik, Hrvati, Titova Jugoslavija i Sjedinjene Američke Države 1945–1955*, Profil International, Srednja Europa: Zagreb, 2003: 55.
12. Rusinow, *Yugoslav Experiment* 1977: 17.

13. Beatrice Heuser, *Western 'Containment' Policies in the Cold War – Yugoslav Case, 1948–53*, Routledge: London, 1989: 19; Jakovina, *Hrvatski izlaz u svijet.*, 2006: 339–42.

14. Zimmerman, *Open Borders, Nonalignment, and Political Evolution* 1987: 13.

15. Bilandžić, *Historija Socijalističke* 1985: 152, 154; Leonid Gibianskij, 'Soviet-Yugoslav Split and the Cominform, The Establishment of Communist regimes in Eastern Europe, 1944–1949,' ed. Norman Naimark i Leonid Gibianskii, Westview Press: Oxford 1997: 292–3.

16. Rusinow, *Yugoslav Experiment* 1977: 24; Leonid Gibianskij, '1948 Soviet-Yugoslav Conflict and the Formation of the 'Socialist Camp' Model, The Soviet Union in Eastern Europe, 1945–89,' ed. Odd Arne Westad, Sven Holtsmark, Iver B. Neuman, St. Martin's Press: New York, 1994: 26–56.

17. Trieste belonged to Italy under the terms of the 1954 London treaty; Ante Batović, '*Zadar na pariškoj mirovnoj konferenciji 1946. godine, Zadar i okolica od Drugog svjetskog rata do Domovinskog rata*,' Sveučilište u Zadru, Zadar, 2009: 40–55.

18. Branko Petranović, *Balkanska federacija 1943–1948*, IKP Zaslon: Beograd-Šabac, 1991.

19. Petranović, *Istorija Jugoslavije* 1988, 178; Thanasis D. Sfikas, 'Greek Civil War, Origins of the Cold War,' ed. Melvyn P. Lefler, David S. Painter, Routledge: New York, London, 2005: 139.

20. Banac, *Sa Staljinom protiv Tita* 1990: 42–55; Gibianskij, 'Soviet-Yugoslav Split and the Cominform,' 1997: 293–6.

21. Rusinow, *Yugoslav Experiment* 1977: 26.

22. Kent and Young, *International History since 1945* 2004: 74–7; Scott D. Parrish and Mikhail M. Narinsky, 'New Evidence on the Soviet Rejection of the Marshall Plan, 1947': Two Reports, *Cold War International History Project*, Working Paper No. 9, http://www.wilsoncenter.org/topics/pubs/ACFB73.pdf; Eduard Mark: 'Revolution By Degrees: Stalin's National-Front Strategy For Europe, 1941–1947,' *Cold War International History Project*, Working Paper No. 31, http://www.wilsoncenter.org/topics/pubs/ACFB11.pdf.

23. Vladislav Zubok, Constantine Pleshakov, *Inside the Kremlin's Cold War – From Stalin to Khrushchev*, Harvard University Press: Cambridge, 1996: 13; Gibianskij, '1948 Soviet-Yugoslav Conflict and the Formation of the 'Socialist Camp' Model, 1994: 39; Csaba Békés, 'Soviet Plans to Establish the COMINFORM in Early 1946: New Evidence from the Hungarian Archives', *Cold War International History Project*, Bulletin 10 (March 1998), http://www.wilsoncenter.org/topics/pubs/ACF183.pdf.

24. Leonid Gibianskij, 'The Soviet Bloc and the Initial Stage of the Cold War: Archival Documents on Stalin's Meetings with Communist Leaders of Yugoslavia and Bulgaria, 1946–1948', *Cold War International History Project*, Bulletin 10, March 1998, http://www.wilsoncenter.org/topics/pubs/ACF183.pdf.

25. Volkov, Soviet Leadership and Southeastern Europe 1997: 67–9.
26. Gibianskij, 'Soviet-Yugoslav Split and the Cominform,' 1997: 297–8.
27. Ibid., 298–301.
28. Banac, *Sa Staljinom protiv Tita* 1990: 121; Gibanskij, 'Soviet-Yugoslav Split and the Cominform,' 1997: 299–308.
29. Petranović, *Istorija Jugoslavije* 1988, sv. III: 234–5; Fejtö François, *A History of the People's Democracies: Eastern Europe since Stalin*, Penguin Books: London, 1971: 3–13.
30. Banac, *Sa Staljinom protiv Tita* 1990: 132; Jeronim Perović, 'The Tito-Stalin Split: A Reassessment in Light of New Evidence,' *Journal of Cold War Studies*, 9(2), 2007: 62; Holzer, *Komunizam u Europi* 2002: 79–83; Rusinow, *Yugoslav Experiment* 1977: 42; Joseps Rotschild, and Nancy M. Wingfield, *Return to Diversity, A Political History of East Central Europe Since World War II*, Oxford University Press: New York, Oxford, 2000: 125–46; David Childs, *Two Red Flags, European Social Democracy and Soviet Communism since 1945*, Routledge: London, New York, 2000: 41–5; Karel Bartošek, *Central and Sotheastern Europe: The Black Book of Communism, Crimes, Terror, Repression*, Harvard University Press: Cambridge, London, 1999: 424–36.
31. Rusinow, *Yugoslav Experiment* 1977: 34.
32. Banac, *Sa Staljinom protiv Tita* 1990: 127; Rusinow 1974: 34.
33. Bilandžić, *Borba za samoupravni socijalizam* 1969: 52.
34. Rusinow, *Yugoslav Experiment* 1977: 36.
35. Marijan Maticka, *Agrarna reforma i kolonizacija u Hrvatskoj od 1945 do 1948*, Školska knjiga: Zagreb, 1990.
36. Rusinow, *Yugoslav Experiment* 1977: 44.
37. Jakovina, *Američki komunistički saveznik* 2003: 56–72.
38. Best et al., *International History of the Twentieth Century* 2008: 226–9; Jakovina, *Američki komunistički saveznik* 2003: 106–9; Kent and Young, *International History since 1945* 2004: 74–7; Robert E. Wood, 'From the Marshall Plan to the Third World, Origins of the Cold War,' ed. Melvyn P. Lefler, David S. Painter, Routledge: New York, London, 2005: 249.
39. Best et al., *International History of the Twentieth Century* 2008: 226–31.
40. John C. Campbell, *Tito's Separate Road, America and Yugoslavia in World Politics, Harper and Row – Council on Foreign Relations*, New York, 1967: 18.
41. DNSA, 'The Attitude of This Government Toward Events in Yugoslavia,' *Secret, National Security Council Report*, NSC 18, 6 July 1948.
42. Campbell, *Tito's Separate Road* 1967: 20.
43. Heuser, *Western 'Containment' Policies in the Cold War* 1989: 109; Jakovina, *Američki komunistički saveznik* 2003: 286; 'Possibility of Direct Soviet Military Action During 1948–49', *Top Secret, Intelligence Estimate*, ORE 22–48, September 16, 1948.
44. Campbell, *Tito's Separate Road* 1967: 17.

45. Darko Bekić, *Jugoslavija u hladnom ratu*, Globus: Zagreb 1988: 104–6; Heuser, *Western 'Containment' Policies in the Cold War* 1989: 110.
46. Jakovina, *Američki komunistički saveznik* 2003: 291.
47. Heuser, *Western 'Containment' Policies in the Cold War* 1989: 82.
48. Rusinow, *Yugoslav Experiment* 1977: 45.
49. Campbell, *Tito's Separate Road* 1967: 28.
50. Heuser 1989: 144.
51. Ibid., 91.
52. Henry W. Brands, Redefining the Cold War: American Policy toward Yugoslavia, 1948–60, Diplomatic History, 11(1), 1987: 41–4; Bojan Dimitrijević, 'Jugoslavija i NATO 1951–1958 skica intenzivnih vojnih odnosa,' *Spoljna politika Jugoslavije 1950–1961*, Zbornik radova, Institut za noviju istoriju Srbije, Beograd, 2008: 255–74; Ivan Laković, 'Jugoslavija i projekti kolektivne bezbjednosti, Spoljna politika Jugoslavije 1950–1961,' *Zbornik radova*, Institut za noviju istoriju Srbije: Beograd, 2008: 275–91; Nemanja Milošević, 'Jugoslavija u američkoj vojnopolitičkoj strategiji odbrane Zapada od SSSR-a 1950–1954,' Spoljna politika Jugoslavije 1950–1961, Zbornik radova, Institut za noviju istoriju Srbije: Beograd, 2008: 307–21; Milan Terzić, 'Tito i balkanski pakt, Premošćivanja na putu ka neutralnosti,' Spoljna politika Jugoslavije 1950–1961, *Zbornik radova*, Institut za noviju istoriju Srbije: Beograd, 2008: 573–86; For more details on Yugoslav relations with the West in 1948–55, see Bekić, *Jugoslavija u hladnom ratu* 1988; Nick Ceh, *US Diplomatic Records On Relations With Yugoslavia During the Early Cold War, 1948–1957*, Columbia University Press: New York 2002; Jakovina, *Američki komunistički saveznik* 2003; Loraine M. Lees, *Keeping Tito afloat: the United States, Yugoslavia and the Cold War*, Pennsylvania State University Press, 1997.
53. Campbell, *Tito's Separate Road* 1967: 26; Rusinow, *Yugoslav Experiment* 1977: 46; Jakovina, *Američki komunistički saveznik* 2003: 296; v. Jadranka Jovanović, *Jugoslavija u Organizaciji Ujedinjenih Nacija (1945–1953)*, Institut za savremenu istoriju: Beograd, 1985.
54. Jakovina, *Američki komunistički saveznik* 2003: 296.
55. Pleshakov and Zubok, *Inside the Kremlin's Cold War* 1996: 158
56. Anatolij Semenovič Anikejev 'Načalni period normalizacii sovetsko-jugoslavskih otnošenij (1953–1954), Spoljna politika Jugoslavije 1950–1961,' Zbornik radova, Institut za noviju istoriju Srbije: Beograd, 2008: 66–92; Fejtö, *A History of the People's Democracies* 1974: 32; Andrej Edemskij, 'The Turn in Soviet-Yugoslav Relations, 1953–55,' Cold War International History Project, Bulletin 10, March 1998; Rajak, 'The Tito-Khruschev Correspondence,' Cold War International History Project, Bulletin 12/13, Fall/Winter 2001.
57. Clissold, Stephen, *Yugoslavia and the Soviet Union 1939–1973 – A Documentary Survey*, Oxford University Press: Oxford, 1975: 63.
58. Pleshakov and Zubok, *Inside the Kremlin's Cold War* 1996: 171.

59. Belgrade Declaration, Part I (26 May 1955) cf. *Borba*, 3 June 1955.
60. Robert F. Byrnes, *U.S. Policy Toward Eastern Europe and the Soviet Union, Selected Essays, 1956–1988*, Westview Press, 1989: 33; Jakovina, *Američki komunistički saveznik* 2003: 495–505; 2009: 459–64; Jan Pelikan, 'The Yugoslav State Visit to the Soviet Union, June 1956, Spoljna politika Jugoslavije 1950–1961' *Zbornik radova*, Institut za noviju istoriju Srbije, Beograd, 2008: 93–117.
61. On the Yugoslav role in the Hungarian events of 1956, see: Jakovina, Tvrtko *Trenutak katarze, Predgovor u knjizi Đorđe Zelmanović, Mađarska Jesen 1956*, Fraktura: Zagreb, 2006: 5–21; ibid. 2009: 472–5; Leonid Gibianskij; 'On Soviet-Yugoslav Relations and the Hungarian Revolution of 1956', *Cold War International History Project*, Bulletin 10 (March 1998); Alexander S. Stykalin, 'Soviet–Yugoslav Relations and the Case of Imre Nagy', *Cold War History*, Vol. 5, No. 1, February 2005: 3–22; Leonid Gibianskij, 'Nikita Sergeevich Khrushchev, Josip Broz Tito, and the Hungarian Crisis of 1956', Russian Studies in History 44 (3), 2005–6: 7–34; Johanna Granville, 'Tito and the Nagy Affair in 1956,' *East European Quarterly* 32 (1), 1998: 23–55; Johanna Granville, 'Hungary, 1956: The Yugoslav Connection', *Europe-Asia Studies* 50 (3), 1998: 493–517; Granville, Johanna, 'The Soviet-Yugoslav Détente, Belgrade-Budapest Relations and the Hungarian Revolution', *Hungarian Studies Review* 24 (1), 1997: 15–63; Đorđe Zelmanović, *Mađarska jesen 1956*, Fraktura: Zagreb, 2006.
62. Nećak, *Hallsteinova doktrina i Jugoslavija* 2004: 117–26.
63. Jakovina, *Hrvatski izlaz u svijet.*, 2006: 345.
64. Clissold, *Yugoslavia and the Soviet Union* 1975: 75; Dragan Bogetić, 'Drugi jugoslovensko-sovjetski sukob, Sudar Titove i Hruščovljeve percepcije politike miroljubive koegzistencije, Spoljna politika Jugoslavije 1950–1961', Zbornik radova, Institut za noviju istoriju Srbije, Beograd, 2008: 49–65; Tvrtko Jakovina, 'Je li predsjednik SAD-a Nixon doista podupirao 'hrvatsko proljeće'?', Zbornik uz 70. godišnjicu života Dragutina Pavličevića, Pro historia Croatica 1, Zagreb, 2002: 121–8; Svetozar Rajak, Yugoslavia and the Soviet Union in the Early Cold War: Reconciliation, Comradeship, Confrontation, 1953–1957, Routledge, Abingdon, 2010: 205.
65. Ross A. Johnson, 'Yugoslavia and the Sino-Soviet Conflict: The Shifting Triangle, 1948–1974', *Studies in Comparative Communism*, Vol. 7, 1–2, 1974: 31.
66. Larson 1979: 261, Jakovina, *Američki komunistički saveznik*, 2002: 84–7.
67. Jakovina, *Američki komunistički saveznik*, 2002: 87–91; Jakovina, *Američki komunistički saveznik* 2003: 508–13.
68. John R. Lampe, Russel O. Prickett, and Ljubiša S. Adamovic, *Yugoslav-American Economic Relations Since World War II*, Duke University Press: Durham, London, 1990: 48–57.
69. Gray, *Germany's Cold War* 2003: 58–86; Lampe 1990: 57–64.
70. Lampe et al., *Yugoslav-American Economic Relations* 1990: 283; see Nećak, *Hallsteinova doktrina i Jugoslavija*, 2004.

71. Larson 1979: 306; Jakovina, *Američki komunistički saveznik*, 2002: 166–74.
72. Lampe et al., *Yugoslav-American Economic Relations* 1990: 64–72; Lampe, *Yugoslavia as History* 1999: 271; Rusinow, *Yugoslav Experiment* 1977: 178.
73. Jakovina *Američki komunistički saveznik* 2003: 514–22; Jovan Čavoški, 'Jugoslavija i Azija (1947–1953); *Spoljna politika Jugoslavije 1950–1961*, Zbornik radova, Institut za noviju istoriju Srbije, Beograd, 2008: 526–43; Bogetić, Dragan, *Nova strategija spoljne politike Jugoslavije 1956–1961* 2006; Leo Mates, *Međunarodni odnosi socijalističke Jugoslavije*, Nolit: Beograd, 1976.
74. Bekić, *Jugoslavija u hladnom ratu* 1988: 160–200.
75. Alvin Z. Rubinstein, *Yugoslavia and the Nonaligned World*, Princeton University Press, 1970: 35; Jovanović, Jugoslavija u Organizaciji Ujedinjenih Nacija 1985.
76. Bekić, *Jugoslavija u hladnom ratu* 1988: 318–21.
77. Vladimir Petrović, 'Pošteni posrednik'. Jugoslavija između starih i novih spoljnopolitičkih partnerstava sredinom pedesetih godina, Spoljna politika Jugoslavije 1950–1961; *Zbornik radova*, Institut za noviju istoriju Srbije: Beograd, 2008: 459–72; Aleksandar Životić, 'Jugoslavija i Bliski istok (1945–1956); *Spoljna politika Jugoslavije 1950–1961, Zbornik radova*, Institut za noviju istoriju Srbije: Beograd, 2008: 483–96; Dmitar Tasić, 'Otkrivanje Afrike, Jugoslovensko-etiopski odnosi i počeci jugo-slovenske afričke politike 1954–1955; *Spoljna politika Jugoslavije 1950–1961, Zbornik radova*, Institut za noviju istoriju Srbije: Beograd, 2008. Ante Batović, *Britansko-jugoslavenski odnosi od Bagdadskog pakta do Sueske krize*, Spoljna politika Jugoslavije 1950–1961, Institut za noviju istoriju Srbije, Beograd, 2008: 363–80.
78. Rubinstein, *Yugoslavia and the Nonaligned World* 1970: 78.
79. Jakovina, *Američki komunistički saveznik*, 2002: 162–6; Peter Willetts, *The Non-Aligned Movement: Origins of a Third World Alliance*, Pinter: London, 1978.
80. Bilandžić, Historija Socijalističke Federativne Republike Jugoslavije 1985: 171; Lampe et al., *Yugoslav-American Economic Relations* 1990: 80.
81. Rusinow, *Yugoslav Experiment* 1977: 62, 78; Ivo Goldstein, *Hrvatska 1918–2008*, Europapress holding – Novi liber: Zagreb, 2008: 464–7; Sabrina P. Ramet *Tri Jugoslavije, Izgradnja države i izazov legitimacije 1918–2005*, Golden marketing-Tehnička knjiga: Zagreb, 2009: 255–7.
82. Bilandžić, *Borba za samoupravni socijalizam u Jugoslaviji* 1969: 68.
83. See the constitutional law of 1953: 'Ustavni zakon o osnovama društvenog i političkog uređenja FNR Jugoslavije i saveznim organima vlasti 1953', which fully translates as the 'Law on the Basics of Social and Political Management of the FNRJ and the federal institutions.'
84. Russinow, *Yugoslav Experiment* 1977: 78.
85. Dušan Bilandžić, *Hrvatska moderna povijest*, Golden marketing: Zagreb, 1999: 355.
86. Russinow, *Yugoslav Experiment* 1977: 86–7.

87. Bilandžić, Historija Socijalističke Federativne Republike Jugoslavije 1985: 234; Dijana Pleština, *Regional Development in Communist Yugoslavia*, Westview Press: Oxford, 1992: 47.
88. Bilandžić, Historija Socijalističke Federativne Republike Jugoslavije 1985: 72.
89. Bilandžić, *Hrvatska moderna povijest* 1999: 410.
90. Ibid.: 427; Fejtö, *A History of the People's Democracies* 1974: 200.
91. Bilandžić, *Borba za samoupravni socijalizam u Jugoslaviji* 1969: 113; Milorad Simić, 'Bankarski sistem Jugoslavije,' *Međunarodna politika* 410, Beograd, 1967: 26–7.
92. Vinod Dubey, *Yugoslavia: Development with Decentralization, Report of a Mission sent to Yugoslavia by the World Bank*, Johns Hopkins University Press, 1975: 37.
93. Paul Shoup, *Communism and the Yugoslav National Question*, Columbia University Press, 1968: 212.
94. Russinow, *Yugoslav Experiment* 1977: 155
95. Shoup, *Communism and the Yugoslav National Question* 1968: 186.
96. Ibid.: 193.
97. Joseph T. Bombelles, *Economic development of Communist Yugoslavia 1947–1964*, Hoover Institution Publications: Stanford, 1968: 154.
98. Shoup, Communism and the Yugoslav National Question 1968: 241.
99. More on this topic in Harold Lydall, *Yugoslav Socialism – Theory and Practice*, Clarendon Press: Oxford, 1986.
100. Bilandžić, *Hrvatska moderna povijest* 1999: 400.
101. Josip Šentija, *Razgovori s Mikom Tripalom o hrvatskom proljeću*, Profil: Zagreb, 2005: 42–3.

3. Economic Reforms and the Fall of Aleksandar Ranković

1. NARA, RG 59, *General Records of the Department of State*, Central Foreign Policy Files 1964–66, Political and Defense, From: Pol 12–5 Laws. Statues Yugo to Pol 15-1 Yugo, 'Happenings Associated with Rankovic's Dismissal', July 12, 1966.
2. Lampe et al., *Yugoslav-American Economic Relations* 1990: 81–2; Pleština, *Regional Development* 1992: 58; Susan L. Woodward, Socialist *Unemployment: The Political Economy of Yugoslavia, 1945–1990*, Princeton University Press: Princeton, 1995: 225
3. Richard P. Farkas, *Yugoslav Economic Development and Political Change: The Relationship between Economic Managers and Policy-Making Elites*, Praeger Publishers: New York, London, 1975: 13.

4. Dubey, *Yugoslavia: Development with Decentralization* 1975: 18.
5. Lampe, *Balkans into Southeastern Europe* 2006: 222; Lampe et al., *Yugoslav-American Economic Relations*, 1990: 83–5.
6. Biljana Stojanović, 'Exchange Rate Regimes of the Dinar 1945–1990: An Assessment of Appropriateness and Efficiency', in Proceedings of OeNB Workshops, 13, 2008: 202.
7. Ibid.: 202.
8. Boris Krajger, *New Economic Measures, The Economic Reform in Yugoslavia, Socialist Tought and Practice*, Belgrade 1965: 77; Duncan Wilson, *Tito's Yugoslavia*, Cambridge University Press: Cambridge, 1979: 156.
9. Lydall, *Yugoslav Socialism* 1986: 257.
10. Lampe, *Balkans into Southeastern Europe* 2006: 230; Ljuba Veljković, 'The Meaning of the Economic Reform in Yugoslavia: The Economic Reform in Yugoslavia, Socialist Tought and Practice,' Belgrade, 1965: 12.
11. Rudolf Bičanić, *Economic Policy in Socialist Yugoslavia*, Cambridge University Press: Cambridge, 1968: 211–20; Pleština, *Regional Development* 1992: 69.
12. Ante Cuvalo, *The Croatian National Movement 1966–1972, East European Monographs*, 1990: 90–1; Lampe et al., *Yugoslav-American Economic Relations* 1990: 89–92; Rusinow, *Yugoslav Experiment*, 1977: 174.
13. Sabrina P. Ramet, *Nationalism and Federalism in Yugoslavia, 1962–1991*, Indiana University Press: Bloomington, 1992: 150; Sabrina P. Ramet, *The Three Yugoslavias: State-Building and Legitimation, 1918–2005*, Woodrow Wilson Center Press, Indiana University Press: Washington DC, Bloomington, 2006: 275–8.
14. John R. Lampe, *Yugoslavia as History: Twice there was a Country*, Cambridge University Press: Cambridge, 1999: 276–9; Lydall 1986: 84; Woodward, *Socialist Unemployment* 1995: 191–221.
15. Bičanić, *Economic Policy in Socialist Yugoslavia* 1973: 200; Ramet, *The Three Yugoslavias* 2006: 214–15.
16. Pedro Ramet, *Nationalism and Federalism in Yugoslavia, 1963–1983*, Indiana University Press: Bloomington, 1984: 91–4.
17. Wilson, *Tito's Yugoslavia* 1979: 158.
18. NARA, RG 59, *General Records of the Department of State*, Central Foreign Policy Files, 1964–1966, Political and Defense, From: Pol Yemen-USSR to Pol 2-1 Joint Weekas Yugo, Zagreb Political Cabaret Pokes Fun at Yugoslav System, December 21, 1964.
19. Ibid., From: Pol Yugo to Pol 6-3 Yugo, Croatian and Slovenian Nationalism, March 15, 1966.
20. See Miroslav Akmadža, 'Uzroci prekida diplomatskih odnosa između Vatikana i Jugoslavije 1952. godine,' *Croatica Christiana, Periodica*, XXVII, 2003: Miroslav Akmadža, 'Razvoj odnosa Katoličke crkve i komunističkog režima u Jugoslaviji od 1945. do 1966. godine, Spomenica Filipa Potrebice,'

FF press, Zagreb, 171–202; Miroslav Akmadža, *Razvoj odnosa Katoličke crkve i komunističkoga režima u Jugoslaviji od 1945 do 1966 godine*, Otokar Keršovani: Rijeka, 2004: Miroslav Akmadža, 'Pregovori Svete Stolice i Jugoslavije i potpisivanje protokola iz 1966. godine,' *Časopis za suvremenu povijest*, 36 (2) 377–408; 'Pregovori Svete Stolice i Jugoslavije i potpisivanje protokola iz 1966. godine,' *Časopis za suvremenu povijest*, 36 (2), 2004: 473–503; Katarina Spehnjak, *Tumačenja Protokola o odnosima Jugoslavije i Vatikana iz 1966. u političkoj javnosti Hrvatske, Dijalog povjesničara/istoričara*, Friedrich Naumann Stiftung: Zagreb, 2001: 473–85.

21. NARA, RG 59, *General Records of the Department of State*, Central Foreign Policy Files, 1964–66, Political and Defense, From: Pol Yugo to Pol 6-3 Yugo, Croatian and Slovenian Nationalism, March 15, 1966.

22. April Carter, *Democratic Reform in Yugoslavia: The Changing Role of the Party*, Pinter: London, 1982: 16.

23. Šentija, *Razgovori s Mikom Tripalom* 2005: 42; Miko Tripalo, *Hrvatsko proljeće*, Nakladni zavod Matice hrvatske: Zagreb, 2001: 81–97; Dabčević Kučar, Savka, *'71: Hrvatski snovi i stvarnost*, Interpublic: Zagreb, 1997: 82–5.

24. The Yugoslav state security service changed names several times since its official founding in 1944. It was first known as *Odjeljenje za zaštitu naroda* (OZN-A) ('Department for the Protection of the People') until 1946, when it was renamed *Upravu državne bezbjednosti* (UDB-a) ('Department for State Security'); finally, in 1964, it was renamed in Croatia *Službu državne sigurnosti* (SDS) and in Serbia *Služba državne bezbednosti* (SDB), (both 'State Security Service'). As most diplomatic documents use the abbreviation 'Udba' we will only use this one in this book, instead of SDS or SDB. In Yugoslav parlance 'Udba' has become a term to refer to the organisation, as well as to a particular type of man, the notorious 'Udbaš'; Katarina Spehnjak, 'Brionski plenum' – odjeci IV. Sjednice CK SKJ iz srpnja 1966. godine u hrvatskoj političkoj javnosti,' *Časopis za suvremenu povijest*, 31, 3, 1999: 463.

25. Šentija, *Razgovori s Mikom Tripalom* 2005: 42–8.

26. Vojin Lukić, *Brionski plenum, Obračun sa Aleksandrom Rankovićem – sećanja i saznanja*, Stručna knjiga: Beograd, 1990: 13. Lukić does not mention the country of the ambassador. From the US and the UK documents that I have researched, I could not find any trace of this information. But it is hard to believe that Bakarić would reveal such sensitive information to a foreign ambassador.

27. The Croatian party official Miko Tripalo did not consider Ranković to be close to the Soviets, despite his centralist attitudes. Šentija, *Razgovori s Mikom Tripalom*, 2005: 45.

28. Petranović, *Istorija Jugoslavije* 1988: 382–8.

29. *Vjesnik*, 2 July 1966, no. 6957, 2.

30. Lukić, *Brionski plenum* 1990: 37; Rusinow, *Yugoslav Experiment* 1977: 190

31. PRO, FO 371/189011, A letter from Duncan Wilson to Howard F.T. Smith, 13 July 1966.

32. Ibid., Personal and Secret.

33. PRO, FO 371/189011, Report of the fourth plenum of the Central Committee of the League of Communists, 2 July 1966.

34. PRO, FO 371/189011, 'The Fall of Vice-President Rankovic, and the following reorganisation of the Yugoslav Secret Police', 6 July 1966.

35. Ibid., 'Developments in Yugoslavia, Concerning the recent upheaval in the Yugoslav Security Service', 6 July 1966.

36. Udba controlled the foreign ministry, or DSVP, via its Coordination Department, established in 1952. Through this formal channel Ranković had control over the foreign ministry since 1952, not 1964, as the US document indicates; cf. Ranko Petković, *Subjektivna istorija jugoslovenske diplomacije*, Službeni list SCG: Beograd, 1995: 116; Šuvar 2001: 377–8.

37. Aleksandar Nenadović, *Mirko Tepavac – Sećanja i komentari*, Radio B92: Beograd, 1989: 143–7.

38. CIA FOIA Electronic Reading Room, Current Intelligence Weekly Special Report, *Yugoslavia-The Fall of Rankovic*, 5 August 1966, p. 8, http://www.foia.cia.gov/sites/default/files/document_conversions/89801/DOC_0000720786.pdf.

39. Ibid., pp. 8–9.

40. NARA, RG 59, *General Records of the Department of State*, Central Foreign Policy Files 1964–66, Political and Defense, From: Pol 12-5 Laws. Statues Yugo to Pol 15-1 Yugo, 'Dismissal of RANKOVIC and Related Matters', 12 July 1966.

41. NARA, RG 59, *General Records of the Department of State*, Central Foreign Policy Files 1964–66, Political and Defense, From: Pol 12-5 Laws. Statues Yugo to Pol 15-1 Yugo, 'Arrest of Zagreb Radio and Television Station Personnel', 10 July 1966.

42. Ibid., 'Happenings Associated with Rankovic's Dismissal', 12 July, 1966.

43. Ibid., Telegram 65 from US Embassy Belgrade to Secretary of State, 'Rankovic's Fall – Part VI', 8 July 1966.

44. Ibid., 'Reaction to Foreign Press Coverage of the "Brioni Plenum"', 16 August 1966; Zvonimir Kristl, 'Politika i demokracija: IV Plenum CK SKJ u ogledalu svjetske štampe', *Vjesnik* 7 August 1966; Spehnjak '"Brionski plenum"' 1999: 481.

45. NARA, RG 59, *General Records of the Department of State*, Central Foreign Policy Files, 1964–66, Political and Defense, From: Pol Yugo to Pol 12-3 Yugo, 'Telegram 1051 from US embassy Belgrade to Secretary of State', 4 October 1966.

46. Ibid., 'US Reaction to Ranković Ouster, Memorandum of Conversation between Cvijeto Job and Dudley W. Miller', 18 July 1966; David Binder, 'Ranković's Fall From Power', *New York Times*, 8 July 1966; Jakovina, 'Titovi ciljevi sukladni su našima', 2003: 1037–9.

4. The Language Question

1. 'After all, it's not exactly Babel', *The Economist*, 1 April 1967.
2. The Association for Diplomatic Studies and Training Foreign Affairs Oral History Project, Donald C. Tice Interviewed by Charles Stuart Kennedy 10 February 10, 1997, p. 35.
3. Rusinow, *Yugoslav Experiment*, 1977: 224.
4. Branko Franolić, *An Historical Survey of Literary Croatian*, Nouveles Editions Latines: Paris, 1984: 34; Robert D. Greenberg, *Jezik i identitet na Balkanu – Raspad srpsko-hrvatskoga*, Srednja Europa: Zagreb, 2005: 13, 55.
5. Franolić, *An Historical Survey of Literary Croatian* 1984: 114–15; Mile Mamić, *Hrvatsko jezično zakonodavstvo i jezična politika u 20. stoljeću*, Hrvatski jezik u XX. stoljeću, Matica hrvatska: Zagreb, 2006: 65; Milan Moguš, 'Značenje Deklaracije u povijesti hrvatskog jezika', *Kolo* 1–2, 2009: 90; Samardžija, Marko, *Hrvatski jezik od početka XX. stoljeća do godine 1945.*, Hrvatski jezik u XX. stoljeću, Matica hrvatska: Zagreb, 2006: 12–16.
6. The Anti-Fascist Council of the People's Liberation of Yugoslavia.
7. Stjepan Babić, 'Za ravnopravnost, ali čega?', *Jezik*, 16, 5, 1968–9: 140; Pranjković, *Hrvatski jezik od godine 1945. do 2000., Hrvatski jezik u XX. stoljeću*, Matica hrvatska: Zagreb, 2006: 30.
8. Ustav FNRJ (Constitution of the Federal Republic of Yugoslavia), 1946; Babić 1969: 140–2; During the proclamation of the new constitution in 31 January 1946, Moša Pijade read Articles 1–43 in the Serbian language, Zvonko Brkić read Articles 44–76 in Croatian, Marijan Brecelj read Articles 77–114 in Solvenian, and Vlado Malevski read Articles 115–39 in Macedonian.
9. Tripalo, Miko, 'Deklaracija o hrvatskom jeziku', *Republika* 7–8, 1992, Zagreb 1992: 27; Only the 31st Amendment to the 1971 constitution partially corrected this situation, with the decision to leave the question of official languages to the republics and their constitutions. The amendments to the 1971 and 1974 Croatian constitutions, the official language of the People's Republic of Croatia is defined as the 'Croatian literary language – the standard form of the national language of Croats and the Serbs in Croatia, which is called Croatian or Serbian'; Constitution of the Federal Republic of Yugoslavia 1971: 74, 188; Stjepan Babić, 'O Deklaraciji – činjenice i pretpostavke', *Kolo* 1–2, 2009: 110; Pranjković, *Hrvatski jezik*, 2006: 43.
10. Bilandžić, *Historija Socialističke*, 1978: 212.
11. Predrag J Marković, *Titova shvatanja nacionalnog i jugoslovenskog identiteta, Dijalog povjesničara – istoričara 2*, Friedrich Naumann Sti ung: Zagreb, 2000: 255.
12. Miroslav Brandt, 'Povjesno mjesto Deklaracije o imenu i položaju hrvatskoga književnoga jezika iz 1967 godine', Radovi *Zavoda za hrvatsku povijest*, 27, 1994: 348–9; Robert D. Greenberg, *Language and Identity in the Balkans: Serbo-Croatian*

and its Disintegration, Oxford University Press: Oxford, 2004: 26–32; Ljudevit Jonke 'Razvoj hrvatskoga književnog jezika u 20. stoljeću,' *Jezik*, 16, 1, 1968: 17–18; Moguš 2009: 91; Pranjković, *Hrvatski jezik*, 2006: 31; Babić 1969: 143; Zdenko Radelić, *Hrvatska u Jugoslaviji 1945–1991 – od zajedništva do razlaza*, Školska knjiga: Zagreb, 2006: 403.

13. Jonke, 'Razvoj hrvatskoga književnog jezika,' 1968: 18; Pranjković, *Hrvatski jezik*, 2006: 32–5.

14. Jonke, Ljudevit, 'Aktualna jezična pitanja danas,' *Jezik*, 16, 3, 1968–9: 73.

15. Pavle Ivić, 'Za ravnopravnost, a protiv cepanja jezika,' *Jezik*, 16, 4, 1968–9: 118.

16. Robert D. Greenberg, 'The Politics of Dialects among Serbs, Croats, and Muslims in the Former Yugoslavia,' *East European Politics & Societies* 10, 1996: 393–415; Jonke, 'Aktualna jezična pitanja danas,' 1969: 73; Pranjković, *Hrvatski jezik*, 2006: 38–40; *Upravni odbor Matice o jeziku*, 1969: 114–17.

17. Greenberg, *Jezik i identitet na Balkanu* 2005: 44–5; Ramet, *Nationalism and Federalism in Yugoslavia*, 1992: 102.

18. Radelic, *Hrvatska u Jugoslaviji 1945–1991*, 2006: 404.

19. Brandt 1994: 350.

20. *Telegram*, 17 March 1967, br. 359.

21. Babić 2009: 103; Hekman, '*Deklaracija o nazivu i položaju hrvatskog književnog jezika: građa za povijest Deklaracije,*' 1997: 101; Jandrić 1994: 393.

22. Ramet, *Nationalism and Federalism in Yugoslavia*, 1992: 102; *Telegram*, no. 359, 17 March 1967.

23. Rusinow, *Yugoslav Experiment* 1977: 225.

24. Jelena Hekman, '*Deklaracija o nazivu i položaju hrvatskog književnog jezika: građa za povijest Deklaracije,*' Matica hrvatska: Zagreb, 1997: 85–94; Ivičević-Bakulić, 'Deklaracija o nazivu i položaju hrvatskoga književnog jezika u sklopu suvremene hrvatske povijesti,' *Kolo* 1–2, 2009: 146.

25. Jovan Kesar, Đuro Bilbija and Nenad Stefanović, *Geneza Maspoka u Hrvatskoj*, Književne novine: Beograd, 1990: 4

26. Ibid.: 33; NARA, RG 59, Central Foreign Policy Files 1967–69, Political and Defense, From pol 7 Yugo to pol 12 Yugo, Language Declaration Universally Condemned: Individual Signers Threatened, March 30, 1967.

27. NARA, RG 59, Central Foreign Policy Files 1967–69, Political and Defense, From POL 7 Yugo to POL 12 Yugo, Language Declaration Universally Condemned: Individual Signers Threatened, March 30, 1967.

28. Ibid., POL 15-2 Yugo to POL 29 Yugo, Surprise Croatian Language Declaration Causes Official Concern, March 22, 1967; Katarina Spehnjak, Većeslav Holjevac u političkim događajima u Hrvatskoj 1967. godine, *Časopis za suvremenu povijest*, 32, 2, 2000: 577.

29. Radelic, *Hrvatska u Jugoslaviji 1945–1991*, 2006: 404; Jure Bilić, '*71 koja je to godina*, Centar za informacije i publicitet: Zagreb, 1990: 64; Tripalo, 'Deklaracija o hrvatskom jeziku,' 1992: 26–7; Tripalo, *Hrvatsko proljeće*, 2001: 109.

30. Brandt, 'Povjesno mjesto Deklaracije o imenu i položaju hrvatskoga književnoga jezika iz 1967 godine,' 1994: 351; Hekman, '*Deklaracija o nazivu i položaju hrvatskog književnog jezika: građa za povijest Deklaracije*,' 1997: 116.

31. NARA, RG 59, Central Foreign Policy Files 1967–69, Political and Defense, POL 15-2 Yugo to POL 29 Yugo, Surprise Croatian Language Declaration Causes Official Concern, April 10, 1967.

32. NARA, RG 59, Central Foreign Policy Files 1967–69, Political and Defense, POL 15-2 Yugo to POL 29 Yugo, Serbs Bite Back in Language Feud, March 31, 1967; Kesar et al., *Geneza Maspoka u Hrvatskoj*, 1990: 44–5; Radelic, *Hrvatska u Jugoslaviji 1945–1991*, 2006: 406; Rusinow 2008: 140.

33. NARA, RG 59, Central Foreign Policy Files 1967–1969, Political and Defense, POL 15-2 Yugo to POL 29 Yugo, 'Foreign Services' implicated in Language Controversy, April 10, 1967. (The American diplomatic reports do not mention intelligence agencies playing any role, nor would it be in the American interest to destabilise Yugoslavia in this way.); Denison Rusinow, 'Reopening of the 'National Question' in the 1960s, State Collapse in South-Eastern Europe,' ed. Lenard J. Cohen and Jasna Dragovic Soso, Purdue University Press: West Lafayette, 2008, 140.

34. NARA, RG-59, Central Policy Files 1967–69, Political and Defense, From POL 7 Yugo to POL 12 Yugo, Bakaric Speech on Declaration and Croatian Nationalism at Seventh Plenum of Croatian Party, 25 April 1967.

35. NARA, RG 59, Central Foreign Policy Files 1967–69, Political and Defense, POL 15-2 Yugo to POL 29 Yugo; Significance of Furor Over Croatian 'Declaration' on Language, 12 April 1967; Babić 2009: 105; Jandrić 1994: 397. Božidar Novak, an editor at the daily *Vjesnik*, argued that Vladimir Bakarić knew of and deliberately allowed the publication of the declaration in order to discredit its signatories (cf. Interview with Božidar Novak 17 August 2009).

36. NARA, RG 59, Central Foreign Policy Files 1967–69, Political and Defense, POL 15-2 Yugo to POL 29 Yugo, Language Controversy, 15 April 1967.

37. Tripalo, 'Deklaracija o hrvatskom jeziku,' 1992: 28; Tripalo, *Hrvatsko proljeće*, 2001: 110–11; Šentija, *Razgovori s Mikom Tripalom*, 2005: 51.

38. NARA, RG 59, Central Foreign Policy Files 1967–69, Political and Defense, POL 7 Yugo to POL 12 Yugo, Croatian Writer Krleza Forced to Resign Croatian Central Committee Membership, 25 April 1967.

39. NARA, RG 59, Central Foreign Policy Files 1967–69, Political and Defense, POL 15-2 Yugo to POL 29 Yugo, Language Controversy, 15 April 1967.

40. Ibid.

41. Ibid.

42. NARA, RG 59, Central Foreign Policy Files 1967–69, Political and Defense, POL 15-2 Yugo to POL 29 Yugo, Leaflets Denouncing Croatian Party Leadership Scattered in Zagreb, 19 April 1967.

43. Ibid., Additional Resignations and Expulsions in Croatia as Aftermath of Language Declaration, 19 April 1967.
44. NARA, RG 59, Central Foreign Policy Files 1967–69, Political and Defense, POL 7 Yugo to POL 12 Yugo, Further Resignations and Expulsions in Croatia as Aftermath of Language Declaration, 3 May 1967.
45. Ibid., POL 15-2 Yugo to POL 29 Yugo, Lull in Croatia Concerning Language Controversy, 17 May 1967.
46. Ibid., POL 7 Yugo to POL 12 Yugo, Croatia's Elder Writer KRLEZA Continues Limited Activity; May Visit West Germany, 26 June 1967.
47. Ibid., Status of Party Literary Intellectual Miroslav Krleza, 8 November 1967; Ibid, Miroslav Krleza's Public Appearances, 11 October 1967.
48. Dušan Bilandžić, *Povijest izbliza, Memoarski zapisi 1945–2005*, Prometej: Zagreb, 2006: 62; Radelic, *Hrvatska u Jugoslaviji 1945–1991*, 2006: 434; Spehnjak, Već eslav Holjevac u politič kim događajima u Hrvatskoj 1967 2000: 594.
49. Branko Petranović, and Momčilo Zečević, *Jugoslovenski federalizam II*, Prosveta: Beograd, 1987: 743.
50. NARA, RG 59, Central Foreign Policy Files 1967–69, Political and Defense, POL 7 Yugo to POL 12 Yugo, Croatian Party Executive Committee Meeting on Language Controversy, 27 December 1967.
51. Ibid., Language Controversy Incident at Anniversary Celebration of Birth of Croatian Poet Petar Preradovic, 26 March 1967.
52. Krunoslav Pranjić, Krunoslav, 'Zakonski prijedlog: četiri jezika,' *Jezik* 16, 1, 1968–9: 5.
53. R. Eder, 'Serbo-Croatian Dispute Becomes Political Issues in Yugoslavia,' *New York Times*, 23 March 1967.
54. 'Anxiety in Belgrade – Linguistic Quarrel Stirring Fears Of a Widened Serbo-Croat Rivalry,' *New York Times*, 25 March 1967.
55. Vjesnik u srijedu, Na marginama događaja oko Deklaracije i Predloga i jednog članka, *New York Times*, Snaga plebiscita, čvrstina ili slabost?, 5 April 1967.
56. 'Croats claim full language rights,' *The Times*, 25 March 1967.
57. 'Serbs and Croats climb down,' *The Times*, 5 April 1967.
58. 'After all, it's not exactly Babel,' *The Economist*, 1 April 1967.
59. 'Belgrade Pushes On,' *The Economist*, 22 April 1967.

5. Liberal Reforms

1. Dušan Bilandžić, *Društveni razvoj socijalističke Jugoslavije*, Naklada Cdd: Zagreb, 1975: 262–4; Morača et al., *Istorija Saveza komunista Jugoslavije* 1976: 278; Radelic, *Hrvatska u Jugoslaviji 1945–1991*, 2006: 366–7.
2. Pero Morača, et al., *Istorija Saveza komunista Jugoslavije*, Rad: Beograd, 1976: 281.

3. Already in 1964, the Eighth Congress of the LCY tackled the relations between nationalities. The practice of pursuing the policy of integral 'Yugoslavism' ceased, and was replaced with affirmative attitudes to 'national belonging'. At this congress, Tito declared himself to be a Croat; cf. Bilandžic, *Historija Socijalističke*, 1978: 300–4; *Practice and Theory of Socialist Development in Yugoslavia 1965*: 36–45.

4. Bilandžic, *Historija Socijalističke*, 1978: 331; Rusinow 1977: 195–6.

5. Bilandžić, *Hrvatska moderna povijest*, 1999: 510.

6. Rusinow, *Yugoslav Experiment* 1977: 197–202.

7. Bilandžic, *Društveni razvoj socijalističke Jugoslavije*, 1975: 304–5.

8. Stevan L. Burg, 'Ethnic Conflict and the Federalization of Socialist Yugoslavia: The Serbo-Croat Conflict', *Publius*, Vol. 7, 4, *Federalism and Ethnicity*, Oxford University Press, 1977: 125–6; Petranović, *Istorija Jugoslavije 1918–1988* 1988: 396; *Vjesnik u srijedu*, 'Vijeće naroda' ('Chamber of nationalities'), 4 January 1967.

9. Constitution of the FSRY 1971: 89–90.

10. Burg, 'Ethnic Conflict and the Federalization of Socialist Yugoslavia' 1977: 126.

11. Rusinow, *Yugoslav Experiment*, 1977: 225, Tripalo, *Hrvatsko proljeće*, 2001: 97–8.

12. Bilandžic, *Hrvatska moderna povijest* 1999: 529.

13. Bilandžic, *Historija Socijalističke*, 1978: 330; Rusinow, *Yugoslav Experiment*, 1977: 225–6; Constitution of the SFRY 1971: 133–6.

14. Latinka Perović, *Zatvaranje kruga*, Svjetlost, 1991: 92.

15. Constitution of the SFRY 1971: 139–53

16. Bilandžić, *Hrvatska moderna povijest* 2006: 91; Burg, 'Ethnic Conflict and the Federalization of Socialist Yugoslavia' 1977: 131; Radelic, *Hrvatska u Jugoslaviji 1945–1991*, 2006: 383; Spehnjak, 'Izbori u Hrvatskoj 1967 i 1969' 1998: 321.

17. NARA, RG 59, General Records of the Department of State, Central Foreign Policy Files 1967–69, Political and Defense, From: Pol 7 Yugo to Pol 12 Yugo; 'Interview with Miko Tripalo', *New York Times*, 24 July 1967.

18. Rusinow, *Yugoslav Experiment*, 1977: 261; Spehnjak, 'Izbori u Hrvatskoj 1967 i 1969', *Časopis za suvremenu povijes*, 30, 2, 1998: 332.

19. At the Eighth Congress of the LCY in 1964 it was decided that republic and regional congresses should precede the federal congress of the LCY; Lampe 1999: 281; Radelic, *Hrvatska u Jugoslaviji 1945–1991*, 2006: 346.

20. Bilandžic, *Historija Socijalističke*, 1978: 345–6, Bilandžic, *Hrvatska moderna povijest* 2006: 78; Tripalo, *Hrvatsko proljeće*, 2001: 129–31.

21. Tripalo, *Hrvatsko proljeće*, 2001: 98.

22. See the film *Underground*.

23. Bilandžic, *Hrvatska moderna povijest* 1999: 535; 2006: 76.

24. *Novi list*, 'Interview Dušanom Bilandžićem: Spašavajući Jugoslaviju Tito inicirao hrvatsko proljeće', 4 October 1999, vol. (16) 594; Bilandžić, *Hrvatska moderna povijest* 1999: 506, 515, 535–7.

25. Stevan L. Burg, 'Republican and Provincial Constitution Making in Yugoslav Politics, State Constitutional Design in Federal Systems,' *Publius*, Vol. 12, 1, Oxford University Press 1983: 80, Morača et al.: 291.

26. Perovic, *Zatvaranje kruga*, 1991: 90.

27. Bilandžić, *Hrvatska moderna povijest* 2006: 77–8; Burg, Republican and Provincial Constitution Making in Yugoslav Politics 1982: 133.

28. Bilandžić, *Društveni razvoj socijalistič ke Jugoslavije* 1975: 305–6, 1978: 348; Morača et al., *Istorija Saveza komunista Jugoslavije* 1976: 279–80, 290–1.

29. NARA, RG 59, General Records of the Department of State, Central Foreign Policy Files 1967–69, Political and Defense, From: Pol 7 Yugo to Pol 12 Yugo, Yugoslavia: Ninth Party Congress Reaffirms Liberal and Independent Note, March 20, 1969.

30. AJ, 507, Izvršni komitet – biro PSKJ 1966–1971, Sednice Izvršnog komiteta u 1971. godini, 1971. VI 9CK SKJ, IV/145, Magnetofonske beleške sa 83. sednice Izvršnog biroa SKJ od 9. VI. 1971.

31. NARA, RG 59, General Records of the Department of State, Central Foreign Policy Files 1967–69, Political and Defense, From: Pol 7 Yugo to Pol 12 Yugo, Yugoslavia's Political System: The Drift from the Center; 25 February 1967.

32. NARA, RG 59, General Records of the Department of State, Central Foreign Policy Files 1967–69, Political and Defense, From: Pol 13 Yugo to Pol 15-1 Yugo, Yugoslavia's Political System: The Drift from the Center, 25 February 1967; Nenadović 1989: 143–7.

33. Ibid., From: Pol 7 Yugo to Pol 12 Yugo, Repercussions from TRIPALO's Speech Reflected in Bakaric's and Spiljak's Comments, 9 January 1967; Tripalo – Spomenica 1996: 321.

34. NARA, RG 59, General Records of the Department of State, Central Foreign Policy Files 1967–1969, Political and Defense, From: Pol 13 Yugo to Pol 15-1 Yugo, Who Rules? – Changes in the Yugoslav Power Structure Since the Brioni Plenum; 4 September 1967.

35. Denitch 1976: 114; Radelic, *Hrvatska u Jugoslaviji 1945–1991*, 2006: 395–6; *Vjesnik u srijedu*, 'Ključ za republički ključ', 1 October 1969; Savka Dabčević-Kučar wrote that 80 per cent of workers in the Croatian interior ministry were Serbs, Dabčević-Kučar, '71: Hrvatski snovi i stvarnost, 1997: 324, 413.

36. Bogdan Denis Denitch, *The Legitimation of a Revolution, The Yugoslav Case*, Yale University Press: New Haven and London, 1976: 107–13.

37. Mitja Ribičič, 'Ne želim činovničku vladu', *Vjesnik u srijedu*, 9 April 1969.

38. 'Ključ za republički ključ', *Vjesnik u srijedu*, 1 October 1969.

39. Tripalo, *Hrvatsko proljeće*, 2001: 101.

40. Bilandžic, *Hrvatska moderna povijest* 1999: 515; Dragutin Haramija, 'Ustavne promjene, pravni sustav, aktivnosti Izvršnog vijeća Sabora SRH, 25. obljetnica boljševičkog udara i sjećanje na hrvatsko proljeće, zbornik radova,' ed. Slobodan Kaštela et al., Hrvatska akademija znanosti i umjetnosti: Zagreb, 1997: 64–5.

41. Bilandžić, *Povijest izbliza, Memoarski zapisi 1945–2005*, Prometej: Zagreb 2006: 68.
42. Dabčević-Kučar, *'71: Hrvatski snovi i stvarnost*, 1997: 103.
43. NARA, RG 59, General Records of the Department of State, Central Foreign Policy Files 1967–1969, Political and Defense, From: Pol 13 Yugo to Pol 15-1 Yugo, New Croatian Assembly Constituted and Top Officials of New and leading members of the Croatian Executive Council, 25 May 1967.
44. Ibid., From Pol 15-2 Yugo to Pol 29 Yugo, Courtesy Call on New Croatian Premier Dabcevic-Kucar, 22 May 1967.
45. Dabčević-Kučar, *'71: Hrvatski snovi i stvarnost*, 1997: 113; Božidar Novak, *Hrvatsko novinstvo u 20. stoljeću*, Golden marketing-Tehnička knjiga: Zagreb, 2005: 613.
46. NARA, RG 59, General Records of the Department of State, Central Foreign Policy Files 1967–69, Political and Defense, From: Pol 7 Yugo to Pol 12 Yugo, Changes in Croatian Top Party Leadership, 2 April 1969.
47. Zdravko Vuković, *Od deformacija SDB-a do Maspoka i liberalizma*, Narodna knjiga: Beograd, 1989: 305–6.
48. Bilandžić, *Historija Socijalističke*, 1978: 360–1; Radelic, *Hrvatska u Jugoslaviji 1945–1991*, 2006: 382.
49. Vlado Gotovac, 'Skica o hrvatskom proljeću, 25. obljetnica boljševičkog udara i sjećanje na hrvatsko proljeće, zbornik radova,' ed. Slobodan Kaštela et al., Hrvatska akademija znanosti i umjetnosti: Zagreb, 1997: 89.
50. Bilandžić, *Hrvatska moderna povijest* 1999: 556.
51. Božidar Novak, 'Uloga i doprinos medija i hrvatskog novinstva u Hrvatskom proljeću,' *Medijska istraživanja*, 7, 1–2, Zagreb, 2001: 118.
52. Ibid.
53. Novak, *Hrvatsko novinstvo*, 2005: 573.
54. *Vjesnik u srijedu*, 'Vusovi razgovori, Ostavka vlade – Kada i zašto', 19 October 1966.
55. Josip Šentija, 'Jezik i jezična politika u medijima uoči Deklaracije,' *Kolo* 1–2, 2009: 170–1.
56. HDA, 1220, D-3565, Komisija za meñunarodnu politiku i odnose u meñunarodnom radničkom pokretu, Bilten Predsedništva Saveza komunista Jugoslavije, 3, 1969, Poruka CK KPSS i Vlade SSSR, Odgovor Vlade SFRJ i Predsedništva SKJ, 19 July 1969.
57. Novak, *Hrvatsko novinstvo*, 2005: 606.

6. Democratising Foreign Policy

1. The US consul-general Helen Batjer reported in March 1967 on the meeting of the Split branch of the Croatian UN Society. Although the society

had existed for over 10 years, it had been reactivated over the previous six months with the help of Mika Tripalo, Savka Dabčević-Kučar and Pero Pirker. According to the American source, the society was intended as a source of pressure on the federal government. cf. NARA, RG 59, Central Foreign Policy Files, 1967–1969, Political and Defense, Pol 15-2 Yugo to Pol 29 Yugo, UN Organization Revived as Croatian Affairs Voice, 22 March 1967.

2. HDA, 1220, D-4033, *Komisija za meñunarodnu politiku i odnose u meñunarodnom radničkom pokretu*, 'Zapisnik sjednice Komisije održane' 10 February 1970.; *Vjesnik u srijedu*, 'Tribina VUS-a: Tko da kreira jugoslavensku vanjsku politiku'(3) Prilog republike', 18 January 1967; From 1967 the first president of the first Council for International Relations was the diplomat and politician Vjekoslav Prpić, cf. Josip Šentija, *Jedna hrvatska sudbina, Priča o Vjekoslavu Prpiću ispričana s njim samim na kraju puta*, Školska knjiga: Zagreb, 2007: 188–95.

3. *Vjesnik u srijedu*, 'Vjerovali su doušnicima, a ne meni', 9 November 1966.

4. Ibid., Tribina VUS-a: 'Tko da kreira Jugoslavensku vanjsku politiku (1), 28 December 1966; The American consulate in Zagreb believed that the publication of the articles was a sign that the Croats wanted to increase their influence over Yugoslav foreign policy, cf. NARA, RG 59, Central Foreign Policy Files, 1967–69, Political and Defense, Pol 15-2 Yugo to Pol 29 Yugo, U.N. Organization Revived as Croatian Affairs Voice, 22 March 1967.

5. Ibid., Tribina VUS-a: Tko da kreira jugoslavensku vanjsku politiku (3), Prilog republike, br. 18 January 1967.

6. Ibid., Tribina VUS-a: Tko da kreira jugoslavensku vanjsku politiku (4), *Novi impulsi*, 25 January 1967.

7. *Vjesnik u srijedu*, Tribina VUS-a: Tko da kreira jugoslavensku vanjsku politiku (6), Domena svih naroda i nacionalnosti, 8 February 1967.

8. Ibid., Tribina VUS-a: Tko da kreira jugoslavensku vanjsku politiku (7), Općinski ambasadori, 15 February 1967.

9. HDA, 1220, D-4725, Komisija za meñunarodnu politiku i odnose u meñunarodnom radničkom pokretu, Informacija o polemici VUS – *Politika – Vjesnik* na temu jugoslavenske nesvrstane politike, 9 November 1967.

10. *Vjesnik u srijedu*, Ni lobiranje ni stečaj, 11 October 1967.

11. HDA, 1220, D-4823, Komisija za meñunarodnu politiku i odnose u meñunarodnom radničkom pokretu, Javno mnijenje stanovništva SR Hrvatske u lipnju 1970.

12. The study entitled *International Relations and Foreign Policy in Self-Managed Socialist Society* was presented by Dr Davorin Rudolf in November 1969. At the time he was an assistant professor in the law faculty at the University of Split. The study was subsequently heavily criticised by the state leadership and Tito himself, primarily for expressing negative views on the role of the Federal Assembly and Tito's exclusive role in shaping foreign policy, cf. Rudolf, 1969; Vuković, *Od deformacija SDB-a do Maspoka i liberalizma*, 1989: 352.

13. HDA, 1220, D-4033, Komisija za meñunarodnu politiku i odnose u meñunarodnom radničkom pokretu, Zapisnik sjednice Komisije održane, 10 February 1970.

14. Budimir Lončar was a long-standing Yugoslav diplomat, and at the time also a member of the Croatian party commission on international policy. He would later be the last foreign minister of socialist Yugoslavia.

15. HDA, 1220, D-4033, Komisija za meñunarodnu politiku i odnose u meñunarodnom radničkom pokretu, Zapisnik sjednice Komisije održane 10. veljače 1970. O tome vidi i u: Dabčević-Kučar, '71: Hrvatski snovi i stvarnost, 1997: 490–3; Šentija, Jedna hrvatska sudbina, 2007: 195.

16. The Yugoslav diplomats Mirko Tepavac, Cvijeto Job and Vladimir Velebit believed that the Croats who worked in the foreign secretariat were uneasy with the pressures coming from Zagreb, cf. AJ, 507, Izvršni komitet – biro PSKJ 1966–71, 1971. III 23 – CK SKJ, IV/139, Sednice Izvršnog biroa u 1971. godini, Sedamdeset sedma sednica IB Predsedništva SKJ, od 23. marta 1971; Jakovina, 'Titovi ciljevi sukladni su našima', 2003: 1038–9, 1042–3; Cvijeto Job, *Yugoslavia's Ruin – Bloody Lessons of Nationalism, A Patriot's Warning*, Rowman and Little eld Publishers: Oxford, 2002, 77–8; Aleksandar Nenadović, *Mirko Tepavac – Sećanja i komentari*, Radio B92: Beograd, 2002: 77–8; Nenadović 1998: 149; Šuvar Mira, *Vladimir Velebit – Svjedok historije*, Razlog: Zagreb, 2001: 378–9.

17. HDA, 1220, D-4033, Komisija za meñunarodnu politiku i odnose u meñunarodnom radničkom pokretu, Zapisnik sjednice Komisije održane 10. veljače 1970.

18. AJ, 507, Izvršni komitet – biro PSKJ 1966–71, 1969. VII 1. – CK SKJ, IV/75, Sednice Izvršnog komiteta u 1969. godini, Stenografske beleške sa Trinaesta sednica Izvršnog biroa Predsedništva održane 1. jula 1969., Kadrovska pitanja u Državnom sekretarijatu za inostrane poslove; Job 2002: 77–8; Šuvar 2001: 378–9; Jakovina, 'Titovi ciljevi sukladni su našima', 2003: 1038–9, 1042–3.

19. *Vjesnik u srijedu*, 'Neprivlačni frak', 22 January 1969.

20. AJ, 507, Izvrsni komitet – biro PSKJ 1966–71, 1969. VII 1. – CK SKJ, IV/75, Sednice Izvršnog komiteta u 1969. godini, Stenografske beleške sa Trinaesta sednica Izvršnog biroa Predsedništva održane 1 jula 1969, Kadrovska pitanja u Državnom sekretarijatu za inostrane poslove.

21. PRO, FCO 28/1176, Proposed Reorganisation of State Administration of Yugoslavia, Yugoslav Foreign Relations, 17 August 1971.

22. NARA, RG 59, General Foreign Policy Files, 1967–69, Political and Defense, Pol 13 Yugo to Pol 15-1 Yugo, New Foreign Affairs Legislation, 15 November 1969.

23. The US report does not clearly define the nationality of the personnel from Dalmatia, although it is quite clear that this is a quota for the Croatian republic.

24. This category of 'problematic' diplomats includes Maks Baće, Veljko Mićunović, Jovo Kapičić and Vladimir Rolović, cf. Petković 1995: 127–31.

25. Mišo Pavičević would eventually become ambassador to Italy in 1971.

26. PRO, FCO 28/1176, Proposed Reorganisation of State Administration of Yugoslavia, Yugoslav Foreign Relations, 23 August 1971.

27. NARA, RG 59, General Records of the Department of State, Subject Numeric Files 1970–1973, Political and Defense, From: Pol 7 Yugo to Pol 7, Croatian and Slovenian Contacts with East Block, 31 March 1971.

28. These initiatives were the beginnings of today's Alps-Adriatic Alliance, an economic and cultural association; cf. Haramija: 1997, 76.

29. NARA, RG 59, General Records of the Department of State, Subject Numeric Files 1970–1973, Political and Defense, From: Pol 7 Yugo to Pol 7 Yugo, Croatian and Slovenian Contacts with East Block, March 31, 1971.

30. Ibid., Recent Croatian 'Foreign Policy' Initiatives Culminate in 27–30 June Visit by Premier Haramija to Neighbouring Italian Autonomous Region Friuli-Venezia Giulia, 14 July 1971; Tvrtko Jakovina, 'Titovi ciljevi sukladni su našima', Američki izvori o hrvatskom proljeću', *Historijski zbornik*, LVI–LVII, 2003–4: 77, Ibid, 'Sjećanja koja čine povijest – razgovori s Cvijetom Jobom, dugogodišnjim diplomatom i veleposlanikom FNRJ/SFRJ', *Časopis za suvremenu povijest*, 35, 3, Zagreb, 2003: 303–5.

31. *Vjesnik*, Strategija agresije; U skladu s globalnom politikom svjetske dominacije; Pion za druge; Novi odnos s Arapima, 11 June 1967.

32. Jakovina, *Hrvatski izlaz u svijet.*, 2006: 346; AJ, KPR I-2/33, Put J. B. Tita u SSSR, 9–10.06.1967, Konferencija KP socijalističkih zemalja.

33. FCO 28/518, Minutes, Richard Kindersley, 19 July 1967.

34. Ibid.

35. Dragan Bogetić, 'Arapsko-izraelski rat 1967 godine i jugoslavensko-američki odnosi, Istorija 20 veka', 1, Beograd, 2008: 99–101; Ursine 1978: 210–11.

36. *Vjesnik*, 'Spriječiti novi München', 13 June 1967.

37. Dušan Bilandžić observed in 1968 in his diaries that there were two opposing policies in the foreign ministry: Tito's pro-Eastern, pro-Arab position, and the pro-Western position supported by Nikezić; cf. Bilandžić 2006: 68.

38. Bogetić 2008: 107–8.

39. Jakovina, *Hrvatski izlaz u svijet.*, 2006: 364; Tripalo, *Hrvatsko proljeće*, 2001: 125–6.

40. NARA, RG 59, General Records of the Department of State, Central Foreign Policy Files 1967–9, Political and Defence, Pol 7 Yugo to Pol 12 Yugo, *New York Times* Interview with Miko Tripalo, Burk Elbrict to Department of State, 24 July 1967; the *New York Times* did not publish Tripalo's remark on the Yugoslav Middle Eastern policy. Instead, the American diplomats received the transcript of the full interview from Richard Eder, the *New York Times* correspondent in Belgrade. cf. Jakovina 'Titovi ciljevi sukladni su našima', 2003: 1045.

41. DA, Fond 1220, 2437, CK SKH, Komisija za meñunarodnu politiku i odnose u meñunarodnom radničkom pokretu, Informacija o reagiranju grañana u vezi situacije na Bliskom istoku, 9 June 1967.

42. NARA, RG 59, General Records of the Department of State, Central Foreign Policy Files 1967–1969, Political and Defence, Pol 7 Yugo to Pol 12 Yugo, The Intelligentsia and the Party-Is There a Rift? Burk Elbrick to Department of State, 12 January 1968.

43. NARA, RG 59, General Records of the Department of State, Central Foreign Policy Files 1967–1969, Political and Defence, Pol 13 Yugo to Pol 15-1 Yugo, Who Rules? – Changes in the Yugoslav Power Structure Since the Brioni Plenum, Tobin to Department of State, 4 September 1967.

44. PRO, FCO 28/518, Yugoslav Foreign Policy, Duncan Wilson to George Brown, 25 September 1967.

45. FCO 28/518, Minutes, 19 July 1967.

46. Hutchings 1983: 46; Retegan 2000: 158.

47. Andrzej Paczkowski, *Pola stoljeća povijesti Poljske: 1939–1989. godine*, Pro l, Srednja Europa: Zagreb, 2001: 283–4.

48. Mihail Retegan, *In the Shadow of the Prague Spring*, The Centre for Romanian Studies, 2000: 91.

49. Tvrtko Jakovina, 'Tito, the Bloc-Free Movement and the Prague Spring, e Prague Spring and the Warsaw Pact Invasion of Czechoslovakia in 1968,' e *Harvard Cold War Studies Book Series*, ed. Gübter Bischof et al., Lexington Books, 2009a: 406–7; Hrvoje Klasić, *Unutrašnjopolitičke i vanjskopolitičke aktivnosti Jugoslavije nakon intervencije Varšavskog pakta u Čehoslovačkoj 1968. godine, 1968 – Četrdeset godina posle*, Institut za noviju istoriju Srbije: Beograd, 2008: 519–47.

50. Retegan 2000: 197.

51. Thomas Franck, *Nation Against Nation: What Happened to the U.N. Dream and What the U.S. Can Do About It.* (1985), p. 71.

52. PRO, FCO 28/559, Yugoslavia: Defence: Security against external agression, A Soviet Threat to Yugoslavia, 3. September 1968; Jakovina, 'Where has War for Hearts and Souls Gone?' 2008: 151–3; Jakovina, *Vrhunac jugoslavenske vanjske politike* 2009: 408–10.

53. PRO, FCO 28/560, Yugoslavia: Defence: Security against external aggression, Yugoslavia, P. Dean to Denis Greenhill, 4 October 1968.

54. The full title was 'Federal Secretary of People's Defence of Yugoslavia'.

55. Dabčević-Kučar, '*71: Hrvatski snovi i stvarnost*, 1997: 99–100; Tripalo 1989: 97–103; Pero Simić published the transcript of the meeting of the Presidency of the Executive Committee of the Central Committee of the LCY from 2 September 1968, where this discussion between Gošnjak and Koče Popović occured; cf. Tvrtko Jakovina, *1956. godina naše ere: Vrhunac jugoslavenske vanjske politike, Spomenica Josipa Adamčeka*, FF-Press: Zagreb, 2009: 406; Rendulić 2004: 279–84; Pero Simić, *Svetac i magle*, Službeni list SCG: Beograd, 2005: 211–12, 214–22.

56. Burg, Republican and Provincial Constitution Making in Yugoslav Politics, 1983, str. 85.

57. Peter Prifti, 'Albania and the Sino-Soviet Con ict,' *Studies in Comparative Communism*, Vol. 6, 3, 1973: 241–66

58. Robert R. King, 'Rumania and the Sino-Soviet Conflict,' *Studies in Comparative Communism*, Vol. 5, 4, 1972: 373–93.

59. Larrabee, Changing Russian Perspectives 1972: 19.

60. Stjepan Brezarić, Jugoslavija i NR Kina, *Međunarodna politika* 508, XXII, Beograd, 1971: 1–3; Larrabee, Changing Russian Perspectives 1972: 22; Ranko Petković, *Jugoslavija u međunarodnim odnosima, Godišnjak Instituta za međunarodnu politiku i privredu 1971*, Institut za međunarodnu politiku i privredu: Beograd, 1972: 38.

61. Johnson Yugoslavia and the Sino-Soviet Conflict 1974: 184–203.

7. Nixon in Yugoslavia

1. The Croatian writer Zlatko Tomičić was the editor of *Hrvatski književni list*, and it was published by the *Zajednica samostalnih pisaca* ('Union of independent writers'). HKL was founded in April 1968 and banned in October 1969.

2. *Borba*, 'O listu koji nije ni hrvatski ni književni: Povampirene sablasti malograñanskog hrvatstva I-VII,' 14–20 February 1969. Instead of Žanko's articles, *Vjesnik* published an article by Dražen Vukov Colić entitled 'Meek Croatian bleating,' in which he also mildly criticised the HKL; Kesar et al., *Geneza Maspoka u Hrvatskoj*, 1990: 136.

3. Kesar et al., *Geneza Maspoka u Hrvatskoj*, 1990: 173–89; Mihailo Blečić, Ivica Dolenčić, *Slučaj Žanko*, Kosmos: Beograd, 1986: 123–4.

4. Kesar et al., *Geneza Maspoka u Hrvatskoj*, 1990: 191–2, 239; AJ, KPR, II-4b, 169 (170), 1968–80.

5. *Borba*, 'U toj (nacionalističkoj) ludosti – ima sistema,' 'O nacionalističkoj platformi i djelovanju Matice hrvatske i njenih časopisa "Kolo", "Kritika", "Dubrovnik (I-V)', 17–21 November 1969.

6. Novak, *Hrvatsko novinstvo*, 2005: 619.

7. Dabčević-Kučar, *'71: Hrvatski snovi i stvarnost*, 1997: 128–9; Kesar et al., *Geneza Maspoka u Hrvatskoj*, 1990: 296–321; Šentija, *Razgovori s Mikom Tripalom*, 2005: 54.

8. Bilandžić, *Hrvatska moderna povijest* 1999: 559–63; Dabčević-Kučar, *'71: Hrvatski snovi i stvarnost*, 1997: 125; Hrvoje Klasić, *Hrvatsko proljeće u Sisku*, Srednja Europa: Zagreb, 2006: 64–6, 72–3; Šentija, *Razgovori s Mikom Tripalom*, 2005: 56; Zdravko Vuković, the long-standing director of TV Belgrade, noted in his memoirs that Savka Dabčević-Kučar said in a meeting of the federal party executive bureau, in March 1970, that Todorović and Popović were not working with Žanko; Vuković, *Od deformacija SDB-a do Maspoka i liberalizma*, 1989: 354.

9. Novak, *Hrvatsko novinstvo*, 2005: 617.
10. Dabčević-Kučar, *'71: Hrvatski snovi i stvarnost*, 1997: 129.
11. Novak, *Hrvatsko novinstvo*, 2005: 621.
12. Vuković, *Od deformacija SDB-a do Maspoka i liberalizma*, 1989: 342, 352.
13. Novi list, Interview s Dušanom Bilandžićem: Spašavajući Jugoslaviju Tito inicirao hrvatsko proljeće, 4. 10. 1999; Bilandžić 1999: 515; Tripalo, *Hrvatsko proljeće*, 2001: 98–9.
14. Burg, Republican and Provincial Constitution Making in Yugoslav Politics 1983: 107; see Deseta sjednica CK SKH 1970, ur. Milovan Baletić, Zdravko Židovec.
15. Vuković, *Od deformacija SDB-a do Maspoka i liberalizma*, 1989: 343, 352–3; Šentija, *Razgovori s Mikom Tripalom*, 2005: 56–7.
16. Dabčević-Kučar, *'71: Hrvatski snovi i stvarnost*, 1997: 156–75; Vuković, *Od deformacija SDB-a do Maspoka i liberalizma*, 1989: 353–4, 373; Šentija, *Razgovori s Mikom Tripalom*, 2005: 58.
17. Vuković, *Od deformacija SDB-a do Maspoka i liberalizma*, 1989: 347.
18. Dabčević-Kučar, *'71: Hrvatski snovi i stvarnost*, 1997: 93–4, 135.
19. Ibid., 557.
20. *The Economist*, 'The Conservatives turn on the Croats', 7 February 1970; 'First round to the liberals', 18 April 1970.
21. NARA, RG 59, General Records of the Department of State, Central Foreign Policy Files 1967–1969, Political and Defense, From: Pol 13 Yugo to Pol 15-1 Yugo, Who Rules? – Changes in the Yugoslav Power Structure Since the Brioni Plenum, September 4, 1967.
22. For American diplomatic reports on the Croatian Spring, see Jakovina, 'Titovi ciljevi sukladni su našima', 2003–4.
23. PRO, FCO 28/1171, League of Communist of Yugoslavia, The Zhanko Affair, 22 January 1970.
24. Ibid.
25. NARA, RG 59, General Records of the Department of State, Subject Numerical Files, 1970–73, Political and Defense, From: Pol 12 Yugo to POL 13-2 Yugo, LCC Deals With Nationalism, Chastizes Milos Zanko For 'Unitarism' In Widely Publicized Tenth Plenum, 21 January 1970; Jakovina, 'Titovi ciljevi sukladni su našima', 2003–4: 74.
26. PRO, FO 28/1171, League of Communist of Yugoslavia, 10th Plenum of the CC of LC of Croatia: the Žanko Case, 27 January 1970.
27. Ibid., Unitarism and Nationalism, 17 February 1970.
28. Ibid., Cominformism, 17 February 1970; Vjesnik u srijedu, Cvjetanje inform-biroovskih tikava, 11 February 1970.
29. NARA, RG 59, General Records of the Department of State, Subject Numerical Files, 1970–3, Political and Defense, From: Pol 12 Yugo to Pol 13-2 Yugo,

Croatian Party Secretary Pero Pirker Attacks 'Unitarists' As Enemies of Reform, Implies Soviet Connections With Them, March 11, 1970.

30. PRO, FCO 28/1171, League of Communist of Yugoslavia, The Žanko Case, 3 March 1970.

31. Ibid., The Žanko Case, 14 April 1970; NARA, RG 59, General Records of the Department of State, Subject Numerical Files, 1970-3, Political and Defense, From: Pol 12 Yugo to Pol 13-2 Yugo, Federal Assembly Vice President Zanko Refuses To Resign, Formal Proceedings For Recall to Be Instituted, 3 March 1970.

32. PRO, FCO 28/1171, League of Communist of Yugoslavia, The Žanko Case, 30 June 1970.

33. Ibid., The Žanko Case, 28 April 1970.

34. NARA, RG 59, General Records of the Department of State, Subject Numerical Files, 1970-73, Political and Defense, From: Pol 12 Yugo to Pol 13-2 Yugo, Businesslike Croatian Party Plenum and Recall of Milos Zanko Signal End to Zanko Affair in Croatia, 14 April 1970; Jakovina, 'Titovi ciljevi sukladni su našima', 2003-4: 75.

35. NARA, RG 59, General Records of the Department of State, Subject Numerical Files, 1970-3, Political and Defense, From: Pol 12 Yugo to Pol 13-2 Yugo, Discreet Rehabilitation Of Some Prominent Croatians Who Were Censored During 1967 Language Controversy For Excessive Nationalism, 5 August 1970; Jakovina, 'Titovi ciljevi sukladni su našima', 2003-4: 74.

36. Richard Nixon's visit to Croatia and Yugoslavia was covered extensively in the following articles by Tvrtko Jakovina, 'Što je značio Nixonov usklik 'Živjela Hrvatska'?', Društvena istraživanja, 8, 2–3 (40–1), 1999; 'Je li predsjednik SAD-a Nixon doista podupirao 'hrvatsko proljeće'?', Zbornik uz 70. godišnjicu života Dragutina Pavličevića, Pro historia Croatica 1, Zagreb, 2002; 'Nixon i Tito: Kako je pripreman i što je značio Titov posjet Washingtonu 1971?', Historijski zbornik LV, 2002, 167–97; 'Sjećanje na Nixona i Tita', Spomenica Filipa Potrebice, Zagreb, 2004.

37. Jakovina, 'Što je značio Nixonov usklik 'Živjela Hrvatska'?', 1999: 366; 2003a: 1037–9.

38. Jakovina, 'Sjećanja koja čine povijest' 2003: 1037–9.

39. Miriam Joyce, Anglo-American Support for Jordan: e Career of King Hussein, Palgrave Macmillan: New York, 2008: 49–66.

40. Digital National Security Archive (DNSA), Kissinger Telephone Conversations KA03734, President Nixon's Remarks to Chicago Press, Kissinger/Laird, 17 September 1970, The location of the original: National Archives. Richard Nixon Presidential Library and Museum. Henry A. Kissinger Telephone Conversation Transcripts (Telcons). Chronological File. Box 6. 12–17 September 1970; National Archives. Richard Nixon Presidential Library and Museum. Henry A. Kissinger Telephone Conversation Transcripts (Telcons). Jordan File. Box 30. 5–19 September 1970.

41. KA03733, President Nixon's Remarks on US Intervention in the Middle East, Kissinger/Rogers, 17 September 1970, Lokacija originala: National Archives. Richard Nixon Presidential Library and Museum. Henry A. Kissinger Telephone Conversation Transcripts (Telcons). Chronological File. Box 6. 12–17 September 1970; National Archives. Richard Nixon Presidential Library and Museum. Henry A. Kissinger Telephone Conversation Transcripts (Telcons). Jordan File. Box 30. 5–19 September 1970.

42. AJ, KPR, I-5-C, 303, Bliski istok 1968–80, Beleška, Nacrt izjave Predsednika SIV-a povodom najnovijih dogañaja u Jordanu, 19 September 1970.

43. Digital National Security Archive (DNSA), Kissinger Telephone Conversations KA03680, Receiving Heads of State During UN Meeting, 12 September 1970, Location of the original: National Archives. Richard Nixon Presidential Library and Museum. Henry A. Kissinger Telephone Conversation Transcripts (Telcons). Chronological File. Box 6. 12–17 September 1970.

44. Ibid., KA03682, President Nixon's Visit to Europe, 12 September 1970, Lokacija originala: National Archives. Richard Nixon Presidential Library and Museum. Henry A. Kissinger Telephone Conversation Transcripts (Telcons). Chronological File. Box 6. 12–17 September 1970.

45. Ibid., KA03692, President Nixon's Visit to Yugoslavia, 14 September 1970, Lokacija originala: National Archives. Richard Nixon Presidential Library and Museum. Henry A. Kissinger Telephone Conversation Transcripts (Telcons). Chronological File. Box 6. 12–17 September 1970.

46. Ibid., KA03702, President Nixon's Visit to Yugoslavia, 15 September 1970; KA03704, President Nixon's Visit to Europe, Rogers/Kissinger, 15 September 1970, Lokacija originala: National Archives. Richard Nixon Presidential Library and Museum. Henry A. Kissinger Telephone Conversation Transcripts (Telcons). Chronological File. Box 6. 12–17 September, 1970.

47. Ibid., KA03755, Richard Nixon to Visit Yugoslavia, 19 September 1970; KA03756, Richard Nixon to Visit Yugoslavia, 19 September 1970, Lokacija originala: National Archives. Richard Nixon Presidential Library and Museum. Henry A. Kissinger Telephone Conversation Transcripts (Telcons). Chronological File. Box 6. 18–21 September 1970.

48. NARA, Nixon Presidential Materials Staff, National Security Council (NSC) Files, President's Trip Files, Presidential European Trip, 27 September – 3 October 1970, Vol. I to Presidential European Trip 27 September – 3 October 1970, Vol. III (Part 2), Memorandum for the President, From Henry A. Kissinger, Your Visit to Yugoslavia, 30 September – 2 October 1970; Jakovina, 'Sjećanje na Nixona i Tita,' 2004: 438.

49. In his report to the Presidency of the LCY on Nixon's visit, Tito claimed that the Lusaka conference brought Nixon to Belgrade, and that the Americans took the outcome of the conference very seriously. Vuković, *Od deformacija SDB-a do Maspoka i liberalizma*, 1989: 404.

50. Jakovina 'Je li predsjednik SAD-a Nixon doista podupirao 'hrvatsko proljeće'?,' 2002: 384–6.

51. DNSA, Kissinger Telephone Conversations, KA03885, President Nixon's Trip to Yugoslavia; United Nations Development Program Leadership, Kissinger/ McNamara, 6 October 1970, Lokacija originala: National Archives. Richard Nixon Presidential Library and Museum. Henry A. Kissinger Telephone Conversation Transcripts (Telcons). Chronological File. Box 7. 5–10 October 1970.

52. '221. Memorandum of Conversation', *Foreign Relations 1969–1976*, Vol. XXIX, pp. 542–52.

53. NARA, Nixon Presidential Materials Staff, National Security Council (NSC) Files, Country Files-Europe, Yugoslavia – through July 70 – Vol. I to Yugoslavia – Aug 70 – Aug 71 Vol. II, The President's Visit to Yugoslavia: Impact and Initial Sequels, Telegrame no. 8686, October 1970.

54. Jakovina 'Je li predsjednik SAD-a Nixon doista podupirao 'hrvatsko proljeće'?,' 2002: 388–90.

55. Zabeleška o razgovoru s Henri Kisingerom, voñenim u četvrtak, 1 oktobra 1970, u avionu na povratku iz Zagreba, Source: Josip Broz Tito Archives, KPR I-3-a USA. Visit of Richard Nixon 30 September–2 October 1970. Translated for CWIHP by Lana Obradovic, Cold War International History Project.

56. DNSA, Kissinger Telephone Conversations, KT00190, Vietnam; Soviet Foreign Policy; US Reaction to Brezhnev Doctrine and Any Attack on Yugoslavia, Kissinger/ Tepavac, Aboard the President's aircraft returning from Zagreb to Belgrade, 1 October 1970, Lokacija originala: National Archives. Nixon Presidential Materials Project. National Security Council Files. Box 467. President's European Trip 27 September – 5 October 1970 Memoranda of Conversation.

57. Dabčević-Kučar, '71: Hrvatski snovi i stvarnost, 1997: 604–8; Novak, *Hrvatsko novinstvo*, 2005: 624; Tripalo, *Hrvatsko proljeće*, 2001: 216.

58. NARA, RG 59, General Records of the Department of State, Subject Numerical Files, 1970–1973, Political and Defense, From Pol Yemen-A to Pol 7 Yugo, Situation in Yugoslavia, Conversation between Adolph Dubs and Radovan Vukadinovic, 27 April 1971.

59. AJ, KPR I-5-b/164-18, SAD, 21 January 1970–31 August 1971, Jugoslavensko-američki odnosi (naglasak na odnose u posljednjih deset mjeseci), 23 June 1971.

60. *New York Times*, 'Belgrade Asked to Clarify Aide's Charge That Nixon Backed Croatian Dissent', 14 December 1976; Močnik 2008: 118.

8. 1971: Yugoslavia in Crisis

1. PRO, FCO 28/1176, Proposed Reorganisation of State Administration of Yugoslavia, Tito's Reorganization, 5 October 1970.

2. *Borba*, 'Tito: Više nego ikada potrebno nam je jedinstvo naše zemlje' ['Tito: more than ever we need unity in our country'], 23 September 1970;

Bilandžić, *Historija Socijalističke*, 1978: 373; Savka Dabčević-Kučar wrote in her memoirs that Tito informed the Croatian leadership about his decision at the opening of the Zagreb trade fair, a day before it was publicly announced; Dabčević-Kučar, '71: *Hrvatski snovi i stvarnost*, 1997: 361–3.

3. Marko Vrhunec in his memoirs revealed that Tito announced the creation of the state presidency as early as July 1969, at the meeting of the representatives of the republican and regional socialist alliances. Marko Vrhunec, *Šest godina s Titom (1967–1973), Pogled s vrha i izbliza*, Nakladni zavod Globus: Adamić, Zagreb, 2001: 184–5.

4. Dabčević-Kučar, '71: *Hrvatski snovi i stvarnost*, 1997: 357–80; Perović, *Zatvaranje kruga*, 1991: 143; Tripalo, *Hrvatsko proljeće*, 2001: 155–67; Vuković, *Od deformacija SDB-a do Maspoka i liberalizma*, 1989: 394–5.

5. PRO, FCO 28/1176, Proposed Reorganisation of State Administration of Yugoslavia, The Presidency of the SFRY, 29 September 1970.

6. Ibid., Proposed Reorganisation of State Administration of Yugoslavia, Tito's Reorganization, 5 October 1970.

7. Bilandžić 1978: 375–7; Rusinow 1978: 222–9; Tripalo, *Hrvatsko proljeće*, 2001: 143–55.

8. PRO, FCO 28/1176, Proposed Reorganisation of State Administration of Yugoslavia, Tito's Reorganization, 5 October 1970.

9. Ibid., Proposed Reorganisation of State Administration of Yugoslavia, Tito's Reorganization, 5 October 1970.

10. Dabčević-Kučar, '71: *Hrvatski snovi i stvarnost*, 1997: 357–77; Šentija 2007: 188–96; Rusinow 1978: 279–87; Bilandžić , Historija Socijalističke federativne republike Jugoslavije, 1978: 378–81; PRO, FCO 28/1176, Proposed Reorganisation of State Administration of Yugoslavia, The Constitutional Amendments, 17 February 1971; Ustav SFRJ 1971: 237–9; Tripalo, *Hrvatsko proljeće*, 2001: 147–67; PRO, FCO 28/1176, Proposed Reorganisation of State Administration of Yugoslavia, Constitutional Amendments XX through XLII, Translated from: Official Gazette of the SFRJ, No. 29, July 8, 1971, pp 525–38; Proposed Reorganisation of State Administration of Yugoslavia, Yugoslav Governmental Changes, 30 June 1970; NATO Political Committee, The Situation in Yugoslavia, 29 October, 1971; PRO, FCO 28/1176, Proposed Reorganisation of State Administration of Yugoslavia, Constitutional Amendments Round 4: Coordination Commision, 6 August 1971. Ustav SFRJ 1971: 157–209.

11. PRO, FCO 28/1176, Proposed Reorganisation of State Administration of Yugoslavia, Constitution Changing in Yugoslavia, 18 August 1971.

12. PRO, FCO 28/1630, Internal Situation in Croatia, Region of Yugoslavia, Croatian Nationalism, 15 February 1971.

13. Jakovina, 'Titovi ciljevi sukladni su našima', 2003–4: 78–80.

14. PRO, FCO 28/1630, Internal Situation in Croatia, Region of Yugoslavia, Croatian Nationalism, 15 February 1971.

15. Ibid., Internal Situation in Croatia, Region of Yugoslavia, 1/9 S, Croatian Nationalism, 3 March 1971.

16. Ibid., Internal Situation in Croatia, Region of Yugoslavia, 15 March 1971.

17. NARA, RG 59, General Records of the Department of State, Subject Numerical Files, 1970–3, Political and Defense, From: Pol 12 Yugo to Pol 13-2 Yugo, The Symbols and Myths of Croatian Nationalism, 12 May 1971.

18. Jakovina, 'Titovi ciljevi sukladni su našima', 2003–4: 78.

19. NARA, RG 59, General Records of the Department of State, Subject Numerical Files, 1970–3, Political and Defense, From: Pol 12 Yugo to Pol 13-2 Yugo, The Symbols and Myths of Croatian Nationalism, 12 May 1971; Jakovina, 'Titovi ciljevi sukladni su našima', 2003–4: 86.

20. NARA, RG 59, General Records of the Department of State, Subject Numerical Files, 1970–3, Political and Defense, From: Pol Yemen to Pol 7 Yugo, Croatian Nationalism Manifest at Zagreb Opera Opening, 8 October 1971.

21. PRO, FCO 28/1630, Internal Situation in Croatia, Region of Yugoslavia, The North of Yugoslavia, 4 June 1971.

22. *Vecernje novosti*, 25 May 1971.

23. NARA, RG 59, General Records of the Department of State, Subject Numerical Files, 1970–73, Political and Defense, From: Pol 12 Yugo to Pol 13-2 Yugo, Anti-Croatian Cartoon causes ban of Belgrade newspaper in Zagreb, 2 June 1971.

24. PRO, FCO 28/1630, Internal Situation in Croatia, Region of Yugoslavia, The North of Yugoslavia, 4 June 1971.

25. Dabčević-Kučar, '71: Hrvatski snovi i stvarnost, 1997: 751–63; Čičak, Ivan Zvonimir, 'Bio sam dogmatik i manipulator, Ljudi iz 1971 – Prekinuta šutnja', Vjesnik, Zagreb, 1990: 92–9; Tihomir Ponoš, *Na rubu revolucije-studenti '71*, Pro l: Zagreb, 2007: 71–9; Rusinow Dennison, 'Reopening of the 'National Question' in the 1960s, State Collapse in South-Eastern Europe', ed. Lenard J. Cohen and Jasna Dragovic Soso, Purdue University Press: West Lafayette, 2008: 167–75; Supek 1990: 158–9.

26. PRO, FCO 28/1628, Internal Situation of Yugoslavia, The Čičak Affair, 4 January 1971.

27. *The Economist*, 'Zagreb's Cicero', 16 January 1971.

28. For the American sources on the Croatian Spring, see Jakovina 'Sjećanje na Nixona i Tita', 2004.

29. NARA, RG 59, General Records of the Department of State, Subject Numerical Files, 1970–3, Political and Defense, From: Pol 12 Yugo to Pol 13-2 Yugo, To Its Chagrin and Outrage, Croatian Student Association Loses Election for Prestigious New Post of Zagreb University Student Prorector, January 20, 1971; Jakovina, 'Titovi ciljevi sukladni su našima', 2003–4: 78–9; Ponoš, *Na rubu revolucije*, 2007: 92–3, 97.

30. NARA, RG 59, General Records of the Department of State, Subject Numerical Files, 1970–3, Political and Defense, From: Pol 12 Yugo to Pol 13-2. Yugo, The

Čičak Affair: Zagreb University Rector Supek and Church Against University Party Organisation, January 27 1971.

31. Ponoš, *Na rubu revolucije*, 2007: 88.

32. Dabčević-Kučar, *'71: Hrvatski snovi i stvarnost*, 1997: 751–63; Ponoš, *Na rubu revolucije*, 2007: 130.

33. NARA, RG 59, General Records of the Department of State, Subject Numerical Files, 1970–73, Political and Defense, From: Pol 12 Yugo to Pol 13-2 Yugo, An Impression of Ivan Zvonimir Cicak – Student Prorector at Zagreb University, 26 April 1971; Jakovina, 'Titovi ciljevi sukladni su našima', 2003–4: 79–80.

34. Izjava Matice hrvatske u povodu saopćenja Matice srpske, *Jezik*, 3, 1970–1, 72–5; *Kritika* 16, 1971, 167–9.

35. NARA, RG 59, General Records of the Department of State, Subject Numerical Files, 1970–73, Political and Defense, From: Pol 15-5 Yugo to Pol 29 Yugo, Renewed Language Dispute Between Croatia and Serbia, 26 January 1971.

36. NARA, RG 59, General Records of the Department of State, Subject Numerical Files, 1970–73, Political and Defense, From: Pol Yemen-A to Pol 7 Yugo, Yugoslav Notes – January 1971, 23 February 1971.

37. NARA, RG 59, General Records of the Department of State, Subject Numerical Files, 1970–73, Political and Defense RG 59, From: Pol 12 Yugo to Pol 13-2 Yugo, Matica Hrvatska Formally Renounces 1954 Novi Sad Language Agreement, April 28, 1971; Novosadski dogovor odbačen, *Jezik* 5, 1970–1: 136–7; Pranjković, *Hrvatski jezik*, 2006: 40–1; *Kritika* 17, 1971: 381.

38. NARA, RG 59, General Records of the Department of State, Subject Numerical Files, 1970–3, Political and Defense, From: Pol 15-5 Yugo to Pol 29 Yugo, Another Croatian Nationalist Complaint: Alleged Anti-Croatian Bias in Federal Census, February 10, 1971; 'Izjava Upravnog odbora Matice hrvatske o pripremama za popis stanovništva SFRJ', *Kritika*, 16, 1971: 174–6.

39. Savka Dabčević-Kučar noted in her memoirs that in June 1970, the Socialist Alliance had complained about these contentious issues related to the upcoming census, *Kritika*, 16, 1971: 173–4.

40. PRO, FCO 28/1630, Internal Situation in Croatia, Region of Yugoslavia, 18/6, The 1971 Census, 4 March 1971; *Borba*, 'Kratkoročni krediti za obrtna sredstva', 26 February 1971.

41. PRO, FCO 28/1630, Internal Situation in Croatia, Region of Yugoslavia, The 1971 Census, 25 February 1971.

42. NARA, RG 59, General Records of the Department of State, Subject Numerical Files, 1970–73, Political and Defence, From: Pol 15-5 Yugo to Pol 29 Yugo, Another Croatian Nationalist Complaint: Alleged Anti-Croatian Bias in Federal Census, 10 February 1971; In her memoirs, Savka Dabčević-Kučar qualifies the census affair as an 'organised conspiracy aimed at reducing the number of Croats'. Dabčević-Kučar, *'71: Hrvatski snovi i stvarnost*, 1997: 303–5.

43. NARA, RG 59, General Records of the Department of State, Subject Numerical Files, 1970–3, Political and Defense, From: Pol Yemen-A to Pol 7 Yugo, Yugoslav Notes – April 1971, 15 May 1971.

44. NARA, Electronic FOIA Reading Room, CIA Propaganda Perspectives, Yugoslavia: Can Moscow Tolerate an Independent Marxist State, July 1971.

45. For a more extensive discussion of the spy affair, see Dabčević-Kučar, '71: Hrvatski snovi i stvarnost, 1997: 483–543.

46. NARA, RG 59, General Records of the Department of State, Subject Numerical Files, 1970–73, Political and Defense, From: Pol 7 Yugo to Pol 7 Yugo, Telegram 169 from US Consulate Zagreb to Secretary of State, April, 1971; Keser et al., Geneza Maspoka u Hrvatskoj, 1990: 699–702.

47. Velimir Tomulić was a close associate of Branko Jelić.

48. AJ, Fond 507, CK SKJ, Izvršni komitet – biro PSKJ 1966–71, 1971. III 23 – CK SKJ, IV/139, Sednice Izvršnog biroa u 1971. godini, Sedamdeset sedma sednica IB Predsedništva SKJ, od 23 marta 1971, Neka pitanja neprijateljske delatnosti protiv SFRJ i rad obaveštajne službe; Dabčević-Kučar, '71: Hrvatski snovi i stvarnost, 483–96; Tripalo, 'Deklaracija o hrvatskom jeziku,' 1992: 29–30.

49. AJ, Fond 507, CK SKJ, Izvršni komitet – biro PSKJ 1966–71, 1971. III 23 – CK SKJ, IV/139, Sednice Izvršnog biroa u 1971. godini, Sedamdeset sedma sednica IB Predsedništva SKJ, od 23. marta 1971, Neka pitanja neprijateljske delatnosti protiv SFRJ i rad obaveštajne službe; Dabčević-Kučar, '71: Hrvatski snovi i stvarnost, 483–96; Tripalo 1992: 29–30.

50. Ibid.

51. The foreign minister at the time, Mirko Tepavac, noted in his memoirs that there was no conspiracy, but he explained the accusations by the reluctance of the Croatian leadership to confront Tito's authority directly. Instead, they attacked the federal bodies as a symbol of centralism, Nenadović 1998: 150.

52. PRO, FCO 28/1175, Internal Situation of Croatia Region of Yugoslavia, Croatian Emigrés, 6 October 1970.

53. NARA, RG 59, General Records of the Department of State, Subject Numerical Files, 1970–3, Political and Defense, From: Pol 12 Yugo to Pol 13-2 Yugo, Soviet Interest in Croat Party Communique, 14 April 1971; Jakovina 'Je li predsjednik SAD-a Nixon doista podupirao 'hrvatsko proljeće'?,' 2002: 392.

54. 64 NARA, Electronic FOIA Reading Room, CIA Central Intelligence Bulletin, Yugoslavia-USSR: Belgrade speaks of the Soviet hand in Croatian separatism, 26 April 1971; Tvrtko Jakovina, 'Jugoslavija, Hrvatsko proljeće i Sovjeti u Detantu,' Kolo, 4, 2005: 168–73.

55. AJ, KPR I-3-a/101–127, SSSR, Prijem otpravnika poslova Dimitrija Sevjana, 24.06.1971.

56. NARA, Electronic FOIA Reading Room, CIA Propaganda Perspectives, Yugoslavia: Can Moscow Tolerate an Independent Marxist State, July 1971.

57. Dabčević-Kučar, '71: Hrvatski snovi i stvarnost, 1997: 515–17.
58. NARA, RG 59, General Records of the Department of State, Subject Numerical Files, 1970–73, Political and Defense, From: Pol 12 Yugo to Pol 13-2 Yugo, Developments Related to the April 7, 1971 Croat Party Communique, April 21 1971.
59. NARA, RG 59, General Records of the Department of State, Subject Numerical Files, 1970–3, Political and Defense, From: Pol 12 Yugo to Pol 13-2 Yugo, Investigation of Croatian Charges: Re Security Police, May 1971.
60. All historians of socialist Yugoslavia, as well as memoirs, wrote extensively about the 17th meeting. See more details in Bilandžić, Hrvatska moderna povijest, 1999; Tripalo, Hrvatsko proljeće, 2001; Dabčević-Kučar, '71: Hrvatski snovi i stvarnost, 1997; Perović, Zatvaranje kruga, 1991; Vuković, Od deformacija SDB-a do Maspoka i liberalizma, 1989.
61. Jakovina, 'Jugoslavija, Hrvatsko proljeće i Sovjeti u Detantu,' 2005: 169–73; Tripalo, Hrvatsko proljeće, 2001: 181; Vuković, Od deformacija SDB-a do Maspoka i liberalizma, 1989: 516.
62. The American report from 3 August mentions the information – or disinformation – obtained from Yugoslav military intelligence that the Soviets sent six divisions into Central Asia, to train them for a possible attack on Yugoslavia. FRUS, Nixon-Ford Administration, Volume XXIX, Eastern Europe; Eastern Mediterranean, 1969–72, Intelligence Information Cable, TDCS DB–315/04377–71, August 2, 1971, Appeal by President Tito for Croatian Party Unity in Face of Danger From the USSR, Source: National Archives, Nixon Presidential Materials, NSC Files, Box 733, Country Files—Europe, Yugoslavia, Vol. II Aug 70–Aug 71. Similarly, in July 1971 Yugoslav intelligence provided the Soviet report to Yugoslav leadership which names the key anti-Soviet people in Yugoslavia. These included the editor-in-chief of Vjesnik, Milovan Baletić Jakovina, 'Jugoslavija, Hrvatsko proljeće i Sovjeti u Detantu,' 2005: 174.
63. AJ, KPR, I-5-b/99-23, SSSR, 06.1-30.11. 1970, Osvrt na stanje odnosa SFRJ-SSSR, početkom 1970, 16.01.1970.
64. Jakovina, 'Jugoslavija, Hrvatsko proljeće i Sovjeti u Detantu,' 2005: 158–9; Veljko Mićunović, Moskovske godine 1969-1971, Jugoslovenska Revija: Beograd, 1984: 83.
65. Jakovina, 'Jugoslavija, Hrvatsko proljeće i Sovjeti u Detantu,' 2005: 165–7.
66. NARA, Electronic FOIA Reading Room, no. 00733, CIA, Yugoslavia: An Intelligence Appraisal (In Response to NSSM 129), 27 July 1971.
67. The National Security Archive, Memorandum of Conversation between Richard Nixon, Henry Kissinger and Zhou Enlai, 23 February 1972, p. 31, http://www.gwu.edu/~nsarchiv/NSAEBB/NSAEBB106/NZ-2.pdf, Location of original: National Archives, Nixon Presidential Materials Project, White House Special Files, President's Office Files, box 87, Memoranda for the President Beginning February 20 1972.

68. Bilić, '71 koja je to godina, 1990: 85–7; Dabčević-Kučar, '71: Hrvatski snovi i stvarnost, 1997: 659–68; In his memoirs, the Croatian politician Dušan Dragosavac noted that minutes from the meeting with the central committee were reproduced with the help of notes made by Milke Planinc, Eme Derossi- Bjelajac, Jelice Radojčić and Ante Josipovića, cf. Dušan Dragosavac, Zbivanja i svjedočenja, Globus: Zagreb, 1985: 49–52; Tripalo, Hrvatsko proljeće, 2001: 184–6, AJ, KPR II-1/06, K 27, Poseta Zagrebu 4.-5. VII 1971. Riječ druga Tita na sastanku sa Izvršnim komitetom 4. VII. 1971. u Vili Zagorje u Zagrebu.

69. Mićunović 1984: 127–31; KPR, I-5-b/99-24, SSSR, 04.01.1971–25.10.1971.

70. AJ, 507, Izvršni komitet – biro PSKJ 1966–1971, 1971. III 23 – CK SKJ, IV/145, Magnetoskopske beleške 83. sednice Izvršnog biroa Predsedništva SKJ, od 9. VI. 1971.

71. Mate Krpan was at the time the Croatian interior minister.

72. AJ, 507, Izvršni komitet – biro PSKJ 1966–71, 1971. III 23 – CK SKJ, IV/145, Magnetoskopske beleške 83. sednice Izvršnog biroa Predsedništva SKJ, od 9. VI. 1971.

73. NARA, RG 59, General Records of the Department of State, Subject Numerical Files, 1970–3, Political and Defense, From: Pol 12 Yugo to Pol 13-2 Yugo, Aftermath to Brioni LCY Presidium: The CC LCC XX Plenum, May 26, 1971.

74. NARA, RG 59, General Records of the Department of State, Subject Numerical Files, 1970–3, Political and Defense, From: Pol Yugo 12 to Pol 13-2 Yugo, Zagreb Garrison Commander Publicly Backs Constitutional Reforms, Attacks 'Statists'; Zagreb Military District Party Conference More Conservative Stance, April 30 1971.

75. NARA, RG 59, General Records of the Department of State, Subject Numerical Files, 1970–3, Political and Defense, From: Pol 12 Yugo to Pol 13-2 Yugo, Aftermath to Brioni LCY Presidium: The CC LCC XX Plenum, May 26, 1971.

76. NARA, RG 59, General Records of the Department of State, Subject Numerical Files, 1970–3, Political and Defense, From: Pol Yemen-A to Pol 7 Yugo, Zagreb Citizens Cheer LCC President Dabčević-Kučar as She Reassures Them Reform Will be Carried Through, 12 May 1971; Dabčević-Kučar, '71: Hrvatski snovi i stvarnost, 1997: 616–20.

77. NARA, RG 59, General Records of the Department of State, Subject Numerical Files, 1970–3, Political and Defense, From: Pol 12 Yugo to Pol 13-2 Yugo, The Controversial Mika Tripalo: Still Very Much in the Croatian Limelight, 9 June 1971; Bilić, '71 koja je to godina, 1990: 78–9; Jakovina, 'Titovi ciljevi sukladni su našima', 2003–4: 75–6; Stijepo Obad, 'Hrvatsko proljeće u Zadru, Zadarska smotra', 54, 1–2, Zadar, 2005: 140; Stijepo Obad Zadar i okolica u Hrvatskom proljeću 1971. godine, Zadar i okolica od Drugog svjetskog rata do Domovinskog rata, HAZU, Sveučilište u Zadru, Zadar, 2009: 173.

78. 'Will he make it?', The Economist, 1 May 1971.

79. 'Drama in the Balkans', *Christian Science Monitor*, 11 May 1971.
80. 'Tito Says Party Will Keep Unity', *Washington Post*, 2 May 1971; 'All Tito Wants is a Little Bit of Unity', *New York Times*, 2 May 1971.
81. NARA, RG 59, General Records of the Department of State, Subject Numerical Files, 1970–3, Political and Defense, From: Pol 7 Yugo to Pol 7 Yugo, Tensions within Croatian Party as Fourth Congress Approaches: Stipe Prolic Expelled, other Unitarists under Attack-but Counterattack from Elements within Veterans' Organization, 14 July 1971.
82. Dabčević-Kučar, *'71: Hrvatski snovi i stvarnost*, 1997: 672–3.
83. NARA, RG 59, General Records of the Department of State, Subject Numerical Files, 1970–3, Political and Defense, From: Pol 7 Yugo to Pol 7 Yugo, Two Prominent Croatian Nationalists, Veselica and Đodan, Expelled from the Party, 28 July 1971; Dabčević-Kučar, *'71: Hrvatski snovi i stvarnost*, 1997: 672–4; Tripalo, *Hrvatsko proljeće*, 2001: 189.
84. Ponoš, *Na rubu revolucije*, 2007: 145.
85. Ibid., 146–7; NARA, RG 59, General Records of the Department of State, Subject Numerical Files, 1970–3, Political and Defense, From: Pol 7 Yugo to Pol 7 Yugo, Reaction Since July 23 Expusion of Veselica and Đodan from the LCC, August 4, 1971; Dabčević-Kučar 1997: 673.
86. NARA, RG 59, General Records of the Department of State, Subject Numerical Files, 1970–3, Political and Defense, From: Pol Yemen A to Pol 7 Yugo, Croatian Student Leaders Congratulate President Nixon on Independence Day, Discuss Various Political Subjects, 14 July 1971.
87. Hrvatski tjednik, Dramatični trenutak Hrvatske, 30 srpnja 1971.
88. NARA, RG 59, General Records of the Department of State, Subject Numerical Files, 1970–3, Political and Defense, From: Pol 7 Yugo to Pol 7 Yugo, Banned Front Page of Hrvatski Tjednik Smuggled Onto Zagreb Streets, 9 September 1971.
89. NARA, RG 59, General Records of the Department of State, Subject Numerical Files, 1970–3, Political and Defense, From: Pol 7 Yugo to Pol 7 Yugo, Attempt to Drum up Consensus for Expulsion of Veselica and Đodan from Croatian Party Fails to Quiet Students or Matica Hrvatska, 25 August 1971.

9. Two Visits

1. Mićunović 1984: 144.
2. Tito's views on the Soviet engagement in the Middle East were confirmed by the US Assistant Secretary of Defense for International Security, Warren Nutter, after he visited Yugoslavia. On this visit, which took place immediately before Nixon's 1970 visit, Nutter spoke to Yugoslav military and political leaders; Jakovina Je li predsjednik SAD-a Nixon doista podupirao 'hrvatsko proljeće'?,' Zbornik uz 70. godišnjicu života Dragutina Pavličevića, Pro historia Croatica 1, Zagreb, 2002: 382–3.

3. AJ, 507, Izvršni komitet – biro PSKJ 1966–71, 1971. III 23 – CK SKJ, IV/151, Magnetofonske beleške sa 89. (proširene) sednice Izvršnog biroa PSKJ, od 14. IX. 1971.
4. Tito did convey Brezhnev's message to Nixon, Jakovina, *Socijalizam na američkoj pšenici* 2002: 186.
5. 'MEMO number Title', *Foreign Relations 1969–1976*, Vol. XXIX, p. 587.
6. '231. Memorandum for the Record,' 13 September 1971, Ibid.: pp. 574–7.
7. https://www.youtube.com/watch?v=TAZbEC_VWRk.
8. '221. Memorandum of Conversation', Belgrade 1 October 1970, *Foreign Relations, 1969–1976, Volume XXIX*, pp. 542–52.
9. '232. Memorandum for the President's File', ibid.: pp. 578–86.
10. '233. Editorial Note', transcript of phone call between Rogers and Nixon at 10:36 am on 29 October 1971, ibid.: pp. 586–9.
11. '234. Memorandum for the President's Files', Washington 30 October 1971, 10–11 am, ibid.: pp. 590–7.

10. Purge

1. PRO, FCO 28/2114, Internal Situation in Yugoslavia, Croatian Nationalism, 12 January 1972.
2. Changes in the Constitution of the Socialist Republic of Croatia, draft Amendment 19.
3. NARA, RG 59, General Records of the Department of State, Subject Numerical Files, 1970–3, Political and Defense, From: Pol 7 Yugo to Pol 7 Yugo, Debate on Croatian Constitutional Amendments: CC LCC Member Rade Bulat Proposes 'Chamber of Nationalities' in Sabor to Protect Serb Rights, Croatian Nationalists Rally in Opposition, September 24, 1971; Kesar et al., *Geneza Maspoka u Hrvatskoj*, 1990: 797; Baletić, Milovan, *Hrvatska simultanka, prosinac sedamdeset prve*, Naklada Pavičić, Zagreb, 2003: 211–12; Cuvalo, *The Croatian National Movement*, 1990: 174–6.
4. This was *Hrvatski Pravopis*, also known as the 'London grammar', because a certain number of copies made it to London, where it was republished in 1972. The grammar was meant to replace the project of a joint-grammar for Serbian and Croatian that was abandoned (see Chapter 4). The new grammar was supposed be taught in schools from the autumn of 1971 onwards. But due to the political situation the distribution was postponed and after the collapse of the spring movement most copies were destroyed. The unchanged version of the 1971 grammar was reissued in London in 1971 and 1984 by the magazine *Nova Hrvatska*. Lada Badurina, 'Hrvatska pravopisna norma u 20. stoljeću, Hrvatski jezik u XX. stoljeću,' Matica hrvatska, Zagreb, 2006: 148–9; Novak, *Hrvatsko novinstvo*, 2005: 689–90; Pranjković, *Hrvatski jezik*, 2006: 42; Stjepan Babić et al., 'Finka Božidar, Moguš Milan,

Hrvatski pravopis, Školska knjiga: Zagreb, 1971, banned and destroyed; reprint: London 1972 (2nd edition); Zagreb, 1990 (3rd edition).

5. Stjepan Babić et al., *Hrvatski Pravopis* 1972: Preface in English.

6. PRO, FCO 28/1630, Internal Situation in Croatia, Region of Yugoslavia, Croatian Nationalism and Draft Amendment no I(2) to the Croatian Constitution, 11 October 1971; Babić et al., 1971.

7. In practice, the separation of two languages would not diminish the status of the Croatian Serbs, because the Croatian-Serbian language version was using the Croatian literal standard. *Promjene u Ustavu Socijalističke republike Hrvatske* 1971: 19–20.

8. PRO, FCO 28/1630, Internal Situation in Croatia, Region of Yugoslavia, Croatian Constitutional Amendments, 2 November 1971.

9. Ibid., 1 December 1971.

10. Ibid.

11. PRO, FCO 28/1630, Internal Situation in Croatia, Region of Yugoslavia, The Struggle for Power in Croatia, 18 November 1971.

12. NARA, RG 59, General Records of the Department of State, Subject Numerical Files, 1970–3, Political and Defense, From: Pol 13-2 Yugo to Pol Yugo 15-1, Tito Concludes Unusually Lengthy Visit to Croatia with Warm Exchange of Toasts with LCC President Dabčević-Kučar; Terms 'Absurd' Allegation that Croatian Chauvinism Flourishes, September 24, 1971; Dabčević-Kučar *71: Hrvatski snovi i stvarnost*, 1997: 679–84; Dragutin Haramija, *Nisam želio biti statist, Ljudi iz 1971 – Prekinuta šutnja*, Vjesnik: Zagreb, 1990: 328–9; Tripalo, *Hrvatsko proljeće*, 2001: 190–3.

13. Tripalo noted in his memoirs that Tito only learnt about the motto 'Croatia in the United Nations' during his visit to Canada. He was particularly angered by the provocative conclusion drawn by Canadian journalists that Yugoslavia is falling apart while he is promoting Yugoslavia abroad. Šentija, *Razgovori s Mikom Tripalom*, 2005: 83; Jakovina, 'Idealističkoj, hrabroj (i ludoj) mladosti, Predgovor knjizi Tihomira Ponoša: Na rubu revolucije, studenti '71,' *Pro l*, Zagreb, 2007: 5; Ponoš, *Na rubu revolucije*, 2007: 167–9.

14. NARA, RG 59, General Records of the Department of State, Subject Numerical Files, 1970–3, Political and Defense From POL 7 Yugo to POL 7 Yugo, University Student Pro-Rector Cicak hopes for Exchange of Student Visits with US Universities, September 16, 1971; Jakovina, 'Titovi ciljevi sukladni su našima', 2003–4: 80–1.

15. Ibid.

16. PRO, FCO 28/1654, Protests and Demonstrations of Students of Yugoslavia, Students, 16 September 1971.

17. NARA, RG 59, General Records of the Department of State, Subject Numerical Files, 1970–3, Political and Defense, From: Pol 12 Yugo to Pol 13 Yugo, 22nd CC LCC Plenum: Croatian Party President Dabcevic- Kucar Demands

Acceptance of Croatian Position on Foreign Exchange as a 'Test' of Good Faith Re Constitutional Reform and Respect for Croatia's Vital Interests, November 12, 1971; Dabčević-Kučar '71: *Hrvatski snovi i stvarnost*, 1997: 689–94.

18. Bilić, '*71 koja je to godina*, 1990: 89–90; According to Dušan Dragosavac and Božidar Novak, Tito decided to remove the Croatian leadership during his visit to the US and Canada, Dušan Dragosavac, *Zbivanja i svjedočenja*, Globus: Zagreb, 1985: 70–7; Jakovina 'Sjećanja koja čine povijest – razgovori s Mirjanom Krstinić, visokom dužnosnicom u vladama SRH i SFRJ,' *Časopis za suvremenu povijest*, 35, 1, Zagreb, 2003: 304–5; Novak, *Hrvatsko novinstvo*, 2005: 688; Tripalo, *Hrvatsko proljeće*, 2001: 201–3.

19. AJ, KPR, II-4-a, 'O situaciji na zagrebačkom sveučilištu,' Informacija IK CK SKH, 'O situaciji na zagrebačkom sveučilištu,' 24 November 1971.

20. Tait based his assessment on information only from the Belgrade newspapers *Borba* and *Večernje Novosti*.

21. The workers of the Zagreb factories Rade Končar and Nikola Tesla initially supported the student demands; Ponoš, *Na rubu revolucije*, 2007: 182.

22. PRO, FCO 28/1654, Protests and Demonstrations of Students of Yugoslavia, The Zagreb Student Strike, 26 November 1971; Tripalo, *Hrvatsko proljeće*, 2001: 221–2.

23. FCO 28/1630, Concluding speech by Comrade Tito at the session of the Presidium of the LCY, 4 December 1971, (Extract Translated from *Borba*).

24. DAZD, Spisi OK SKH Zadar, 1971, 'Video footage from the meeting Tito with members of the Executive Committee and the heads of socio-political organization of the Parliament and the Executive Council of the Croatian republic'. ('Magnetoskopska snimka sa sastanka druga Tita s članovima Izvršnog komiteta i rukovodiocima društveno-političkih organizacija Sabora i Izvršnog vijeća SR Hrvatske'), held on 30 November and 1 December 1971 in Karađorđevo, 1466: 307–49.

25. 'Tito: Ne smije oslabiti budnost prema najopasnijem klasnom neprijatelju, a to su šovinizam i nacionalizam,' *Vjesnik* 3 December 1971.

26. Dušan Bilandžić noted the thoughts of Mika Špiljak, that Tito was reluctant to remove the Croatian leadership until he read the letter signed by 67 prominent Yugoslav party members on 6 December, where they demanded the removal of the Croatian leadership. Bilandžić 2006: 265; Baletić 2003: 98–100; Dabčević-Kučar, '71: *Hrvatski snovi i stvarnost*, 1997: 963–5, Klasić 2006: 176.

27. Baletić 2003: 112–13; Dr. Vladimir Bakarić, 'Čitav je ovaj period bio takav da radnička klasa nije obavljala svoj utjecaj na SKH,' *Vjesnik*, 9 December 1971.

28. Ibid.

29. NARA, RG 59, General Records of the Department of State, Subject Numerical Files, 1970–3, Political and Defense, From: Pol 12 Yugo to Pol 13-2 Yugo, Tito and Croatian Communist Party, Telegram 5277 fromm US Embassy Belgrade to Secretary of State, December 1971.

30. Croatian Communist Party Affairs, Telegram 833 from US Consulate Zagreb to Secretary of State, December 1971.

31. General Janko Bobetko would be Chief of Staff of the Croatian armed forces during the 1990s conflicts.

32. New Croatian Party Leadership, Telegram 5392 from US Embassy Belgrade to Secretary of State, December 1971; Dabčević-Kučar, '71: Hrvatski snovi i stvarnost, 1997: 981–5; Janko Bobetko, Sve moje bitke, Zagreb, 1996: 74.

33. New Croatian Executive Bureau Member Police Official, Telegram 5405 from Us Embassy to Secretary of State, December 1971.

34. Student Arrests in Zagreb, Telegram 5382 from US Embassy Belgrade to Secretary of State, December 1971.

35. Resignation of Croatian Party Leaders; Zagreb Student Leaders Arrested, Telegram 5357 from US Embassy Belgrade to Secretary of State, December 1971.

36. Developments in Croatia, Telegram 5447 from US Embassy Belgrade to Secretary of State, December 1971.

37. PRO, FCO 28/1630, Internal Situation of Croatia, Region of Yugoslavia, Change of Croatian Party Leadership, 17 December 1971.

38. Editor of Komunist on Recent Events in Croatia, Telegram 5470 from US Embassy Belgrade to Secretary of State, December 1971.

39. Ibid., Telegram 5481 from US Embassy Belgrade to Secretary of State, December 1971; Altman's views on Blažević are puzzling, because Blažević had stood by the reformist wing of the Croatian party until the very end. Other contemporaries also confirmed this, cf. Jakovina, Mozaik hrvatskog reformskog pokreta 1971, Hrvatsko proljeće, 40 godina poslije, Zbornik radova: Zagreb, 2012: 408.

40. 'Tito Rebukes Croatian Leaders on "Chauvinist" Student Strike', New York Times, December 3, 1971; 'Warning to Croats by President Tito', The Times, 3 December 1971.

41. Email from David Binder, 24 July 2008.

42. David Binder, 'Croatian Capital Is Quiet After 4 Nights of Riots Stirred by Nationalist Resentment Against Belgrade', New York Times, 17 December 1971.

43. Ivo Škrabalo, Samoodređenje i odcjepljenje, Pouke iz nastanka države Bangladeš, Školske novine: Zagreb, 1997.

44. DASMIP, Jugoslavija, 1971, Telegram from the Yugoslav mission to the UN. 1364, 18 December 1971.

45. David Binder, 'Clash With Croatians Reported Gravely Damaging Yugoslavia', New York Times, 20 December 1971.

46. NARA, RG 59, General Records of the Department of State, Subject Numerical Files, 1970–3, Political and Defense, From: Pol 12 Yugo to Pol 13-2 Yugo, Resignation of President Croatian Executive Council Haramija and Other Top Officials, Telegram 5578 from US Embassy Belgrade to Secretary of State, December 1971; Dragutin, Haramija, Nisam želio biti statist, Ljudiiz 1971 – Prekinuta šutnja, Vjesnik: Zagreb 1990: 329–30; Haramija, Ustavne promjene,

pravni sustav, aktivnosti Izvršnog vijeća Sabora SRH, 25. obljetnica boljševičkog udara i sjećanje na hrvatsko proljeće, zbornik radova,' eds Slobodan Kaštela et al., Hrvatska akademija znanosti i umjetnosti : Zagreb 1997: 80–1.

47. Zagreb's Situation December 20, Telegram 849 from US Consulate Zagreb to Secretary of State, December 1971.

48. NARA, RG 59, General Records of the Department of State, Subject Numerical Files, 1970–3, Political and Defense, From: Pol 15-5 Yugo to Pol 29 Yugo, Zagreb Archbishop's Christmas Message, 30 December 1971; Ibid, The Roman Catholic Church in Croatia After Karadjordjevo, 17 March 1972.

49. Executive Bureau Member Dolanc's Comments on Croatian Events, Telegram 5616 from US Embassy Belgrade to Secretary of State, December 1971.

50. Stane Dolanc on Croatian Events, Telegram 20 from US Embassy Belgrade to Secretary of State, January 1972.

51. Mood Music in Belgrade, Telegram 120 from US Embassy Belgrade to Secretary of State, January 1972.

52. Croatian News Media and the Housecleaning, Airgram A-10, US Consulate Zagreb to Department of State, 25 January 1972; Novak, *Hrvatsko novinstvo*, 2005: 707, 709.

53. Vrhovec says Croatian 'Counter-Revolutionaries' Sought to Split Up Yugoslav Federation, Telegram 242 from US Embassy Belgrade to Secretary of State, January 1972.

54. Crisis in Croatian Party – Summary and View from Belgrade, Telegram 503 from US Embassy Belgrade to Secretary of State, February 1972.

55. On 2 August 1971, the police attacked and arrested pilgrims during procession that celebrated the Catholic holiday of 'Our Lady of the Angels' in the Dalmatian village of Karin. One pilgrim was killed. Both Western diplomats and Croatian leaders interpreted this as a manifestation of ethnic animosities between a predominantly Serb police and Croat pilgrims.

56. PRO, FCO 28/1630, Internal Situation of Croatia, Region of Yugoslavia, Croatian Nationalism, 14 December 1971; Change of Croatian Party Leadership, 17 December 1971.

57. Ibid.

58. Ibid., Internal Situation of Croatia, Region of Yugoslavia, Croatian Nationalism, 31 December 1971; Tito hosted a hunting event for diplomatic corps in Karađorđevo on 10 December 1971, 'Tito priredio lov za diplomatski kor', *Vjesnik*, 11 December 1971; *The Economist* article 'An old man in panic' was written by their Eastern European correspondent Chris Cviić; Jakovina, 'Idealističkoj, hrabroj (i ludoj) mladosti' 2007: 7.

59. PRO, FCO 28/2114, Internal Situation in Yugoslavia, Croatia, 4 January 1972.

60. Slobodan Lang (1945–2016) was a physician and remained politically active, and served as a human rights activist, and organised humanitarian convoys during the 1990s wars.

61. Ponoš, *Na rubu revolucije*, 2007: 105.
62. PRO, FCO 28/2114, Internal Situation in Yugoslavia, Record of Conversation on 19 December 1971 With Mr Slobodan Lang, One-Time President of the Zagreb Student Union, 29 December 1971.
63. Ibid., Internal Situation in Yugoslavia, Record of Conversation on 20 December 1971 With Mr Novak Pribičević, Member of the Executive Council of SR Croatia, 29 December 1971.
64. Ibid., Internal Situation in Yugoslavia, Croatia, 21 January 1972.
65. Ibid., Internal Situation in Yugoslavia, Yugoslavia, 4 January 1972.
66. Ibid., Internal Situation in Yugoslavia, Croatia, 5 January 1972.
67. Ibid., Internal Situation in Yugoslavia, Yugoslav Internal, Croatia, 13 January 1972; Supek, Ivan, *Krivovjernik na ljevici*, Globus: Zagreb, 1992: 201–14.
68. PRO, FCO 28/2114, Internal Situation in Yugoslavia, Croatia, 14 January 1972.
69. Ibid.
70. Ibid, Internal Situation in Yugoslavia, Post-Karadjordjevo Events in Serbia, 7 January 1971.
71. Ibid., Internal Situation in Yugoslavia, Call on Mr. Nikezic, President of LC Serbia, 7 January 1972.
72. Ibid., Internal Situation in Yugoslavia, Croatia, 10 January 1972.
73. NARA, RG 59, General Records of the Department of State, Subject Numerical Files, 1970–3, Political and Defense, From: Pol 12 Yugo to Pol 13-2 Yugo, Telegram 1922 from US Embassy Belgrade to Secretary of State, December 1971.
74. PRO, FCO 28/2114, Internal Situation in Yugoslavia, Croatia, 14 January 1972.

11. 1972: Aftermath

1. PRO, FCO 28/1630, Internal Situation of Croatia, Region of Yugoslavia, Croatian Nationalism, 31 December 1971.
2. The Association for Diplomatic Studies and Training Foreign Affairs Oral History Project, Thomas P. H. Dunlop interviewed by Charles Stuart Kennedy, (July 12, 1996), 96.
3. Jozo Ivičević, 'Kako su montirani politički procesi,' *Hrvatska revija*, 2, 2002: 23–33.
4. PRO, FCO 28/2115, Internal political situation in Yugoslavia, Yugoslavia after the upheaval in Croatia, 18 February 1972.
5. PRO, FCO 28/2115, Internal political situation in Yugoslavia, Record of Conversation Between HMA and Mr Novak Pribičević, President of the Council of Foreign Affairs of the Croatian Government, at the Hotel Metropol on Sunday, 12 March, 14 March 1972.
6. Visit of President Tito to Zagreb: 19 to 24 April, G. H. Baker to D. L. Stewart, 25 April 1972; Dabčević-Kučar, *'71: Hrvatski snovi i stvarnost*, 1997: 681.

7. Croatia, 1 June 1792; Dabčević Kučar, Savka, *Htjeli smo Hrvatsku dovesti u Evropu, Ljudi iz 1971 – Prekinuta šutnja*, Vjesnik: Zagreb, 1990: 287–8; Hrvatsko proljeće – Presuda Partije 2003; Baletić 2003: 198–202; Džeba, Krešimir and Božidar Novak, *Zašto se dogodila '71, Ljudi iz 1971 – Prekinuta šutnja*, Vjesnik: Zagreb, 1990: 267–8, 272–3.

8. *The Economist*, 'Softly, softly catchee Croat', 11 May 1972.

9. *The Economist*, 'The trouble with terrorism', 8 July 1972.

10. PRO, FCO 28/2115, Internal political situation in Yugoslavia, Yugoslav Internal Affairs, Serbia, 10 August 1972; PRO FCO 28/2116, The present situation in Yugoslavia, 21 November 1972; Slavoljub Đukić, *Slom srpskih liberala: Tehnologija političkih obračuna Josipa Broza*, Filip Višnjić: Beograd, 1990: 170–4.

11. PRO, FCO 28/2116, A letter from D. L. Stewart to Julian Bullard, 15 December 1972.

12. Jakovina, 'Jugoslavija, Hrvatsko proljeće i Sovjeti u Detantu,' 2005: 182.

13. *The Economist*, 'An Old Man in a Panic', 18 December 1971.

14. FCO 28/1630, Letter from Dugald Stewart to Julian Bullard, 31 December 1971.

15. Lajos Lederer was the *Observer's* correspondent for Eastern Europe and he had reported on Yugoslavia since the 1948 split with Stalin. Chris (Krsto) Cviić was born in Croatia, and was *The Economist's* long-standing correspondent for Central and Eastern Europe; *The Economist*, 'An Old Man in a Panic', 18 December 1971; Lajos Lederer, 'Tito losing grip on his country', 12 December 1971.

16. PRO, FCO 28/2114, Internal Situation in Yugoslavia, Croatia, 20 January 1972

17. Lajos Lederer, 'Tito losing grip on his country', 12 December 1971.

18. Tito met with Ceauşescu on 23 November 1971. On the same day, the student protests started in Zagreb. *Vjesnik*, 'Danas sastanak Tito-Ceausescu', 'Danas (hitan) plenum Saveza studenata Hrvatske', 23 November 1971.

19. *The Economist*, 'An Old Man in a Panic', 18 December 1971; Jakovina, 'Idealističkoj, hrabroj (i ludoj) mladosti' 2007: 7.

20. Paul Lendvai, 'New Croatian leaders pledge support for Tito', 14 December 1971.

21. Cyrus Leo Sulzberger II (1912–93), the nephew of lthe publisher of the *New York Times* Arthur Hays Sulzberger, was their leading foreign correspondent in the from 1944 to 1954, when he became a columnist, which he kept up until 1978.

22. C.L. Sulzberger, 'Old Clouds in Eastern Europe', *International Herald Tribune*, 3 December 1971.

23. C.L. Sulzberger, 'Reading Soviet Tea Leaves', *International Herald Tribune*, 17 January 1972.

24. Internal Situation in Yugoslavia, Western Press on Croatia, 26 January 1972.

25. Paul Lendvai, 'Croatia wants a fair deal, *FT* 10 December 1971; 'Croatia tense after purge', 12 December 1971; 'New Croatian leaders pledge support for

Tito', 14 December 1971; 'A blow to the 'new Yugoslavia', 17 December 1971; 'Croatian Premier resigns as purges continue', 22 December 1971; 'Croatian concessions by Tito', 29 December 1971; 'Arrests and searches in Zagreb', 13 January 1972.

26. Aleksander Lebl, 'Tito attacks "sluggish" Croatian party leaders', 3 December 1971.

27. Paul Lendvai (b. 1929), of Hungarian origin, was one of the most highly regarded *FT* correspondents for Eastern Europe, based in Vienna. Aleksandar Lebl (b. 1922), a Serbian Jew and Holocaust survivor, was also a highly regarded *FT* correspondent, based in Belgrade. Michael Simmons (1935–2015) joined the foreign news desk of the *FT* in 1967 as correspondent for Eastern Europe and joined The *Guardian* in 1977. Howard Wilson was the Labour leader, and at the time Leader of Her Majesty's Opposition.

28. 'Pro-Tito party leaders take over in Croatia', 14 December 1971; 'The Southern Slavs face old enmities', 15 December 1971; 'Yugoslav unity proved, President says', 17 December 1971; 'Premier of Croatia resigns after criticism', 23 December 1971; 'Yugoslav student editors may be put on trial', 1 January 1972; 'Croat leader resigns from Yugoslav parliament', 7 January 1972; '11 Croatian intellectuals on plot charges', 13 January 1971.

29. *The Times*, 'The Way Forward For Yugoslavia', 24 January 1972.

30. *The Times*, 'Shadows over Croatia', 28 January 1972.

31. PRO, FCO 28/2114, Internal Situation in Yugoslavia, Croatia, 20 January 1972.

32. A.M. Rendel, 'President Tito's gamble on good sense', *The Times*, 10 November 1972.

33. Michael Simmons, 'A climate of uncertainty'; Paul Lendvai, 'Industry unbalanced'; Aleksander Lebl, 'Rule by consensus', *Financial Times*, 29 March 1972.

34. Ben Wright, 'Yugoslavia's potential', *Financial Times*, 6 May 1972.

35. Michael Simmons, 'The man who keeps Moscow guessing', 23 May 1972.

36. PRO, FCO 28/2115, Internal political situation in Yugoslavia, British Press Coverage of Croatia, 9 February 1972.

37. 'The only ally', *The Economist*, 22 January 1972.

38. PRO, FCO 28/2114, Internal Situation in Yugoslavia, Croatia, 28 January 1972.

39. 'Tito tries to unscramble things', *The Economist*, 19 February 1972.

40. 'Softly, softly catchee Croat', 13 May 1972; 'The trouble with terrorism', 8 July 1972; 'Mopping up operations', 29 July 1972; 'No defence', 12 August 1972; 'Backward twists', 16 September 1972; 'From Russia with intent', 16 September 1972; 'King Tito at home to the Queen', 14 October 1972; 'Now Serbia too', 28 October 1972.

41. Lajos Lederer, 'Tito uses army to break revolt', *Observer*, 19 December 1971; 'Tito's firm line pays off', *Observer*, 2 January 1972; 'Tougher tactics in Croatia', *Observer*, 16 January 1972; 'Tito sacks Marxist professors', the *Observer*, 15 April 1972; 'Tito clamps down on millionaires', *Observer*, 13 August 1972; 'Tito sacks top party opponents', *Observer*, 12 November 1972.

42. Lajos Lederer, Tito lets the KGB return, *Observer*, 25 November 1973
43. PRO FCO 28/2145, Yugoslav Government complaints about BBC programmes on Yugoslavia, BBC 2 Europa Programme on Yugoslavia, 28 January 1972.
44. 'Pregled svjetskog tiska: Pala je maska!', *Hrvatska revija* 1, 1972, 74–140; Maticka, Marijan, 'Hrvatski prosinački događaji 1971. i svjetska javnost: primjer pariškog "Le Mondea"', *Časopis za suvremenu povijest*, 3, 2006: 1121–30.
45. PRO, FCO 2115, Internal political situation in Yugoslavia, British Press Coverage and Croatia, 9 February 1972.
46. Interview by the author with Stewart Kennedy, August 2008.
47. *The Association for Diplomatic Studies and Training Foreign Affairs Oral History Project*, Thomas P. H. Dunlop, interviewed by Charles Stuart Kennedy, 12 July 1996; Donald C. Tice, interviewed by Charles Stuart Kennedy, 10 February 1997. Kennedy was interviewed three times in his own programme: by Victor Wolf Jr. 24 July 1986; by Jewell Fenzi, 17 November 1986; and by Brandon Grove, 4 September 1996. All interviews can be found at: http://adst.org/oral-history/oral-history-interviews/.
48. Dunlop interview, p. 22.
49. Ibid., p. 34.
50. Ibid., p. 85.
51. Ibid., p. 86.
52. Ibid., p. 88.
53. Tice interview, p. 55.
54. Dunlop interview, p. 89.
55. http://archives.nato.int/polads.
56. PRO, FCO 28/1647, Political Relations Between Yugoslavia and NATO, Yugoslavia, 28 January 1971.
57. Ibid. Proposed Discussion of Yugoslavia in the Political Committee, 22 January 1971.
58. Ibid. Political Relations Between Yugoslavia and NATO, Davidson's Letter to Sparrow of 22 January, 29 January 1971.
59. Ibid. Political Relations Between Yugoslavia and NATO, Yugoslav Request for NATO Status, 12 August 1971.
60. NARA, RG 59, General Records of the Department of State, Subject Numerical Files, 1970–3, Political and Defense, From: Pol Yemen-A to Pol 7 Yugo, Austrian Concern over Yugoslavia.
61. Ibid., From: Pol Yemen-A to Pol 7 Yugo, From Embassy Rome to Secretary of State, July 1971.
62. FRUS, Nixon-Ford Administration, Volume XXIX, Eastern Europe; Eastern Mediterranean, 1969–72, Yugoslavia, 'Statement of US Interest in Yugoslavia,' 13 September 1971, http://www.state.gov/documents/organization/97933.pdf, Source: National Archives, Nixon Presidential Materials, NSC Files, NSC

Institutional Files (H-Files), Box H-185, National Security Study Memoranda, NSSM 129.

63. NARA, RG 59, General Records of the Department of State, Subject Numerical Files, 1970–3, Political and Defense, From: Pol Yemen-A to Pol 7 Yugo, NATO and Yugoslavia, 20 January 1971.

64. Ibid., Political and Defense, From Embassy Belgrade to US Mission NATO, February 1971.

65. Nato archives, IMSM-567-71, North Atlantic Military Committee, Memorandum for the members of the Military Committee, Briefing on the Yugoslav All Peoples Defense Exercise 'FREEDOM 71', 6 December 1971; Manevri, Vojna enciklopedija, 5, 269–70.

66. Dabčević-Kučar, '71: Hrvatski snovi i stvarnost, 1997: 684–9; Novak, Hrvatsko novinstvo, 2005: 687; Tripalo, Hrvatsko proljeće, 2001: 193–5.

67. NARA, RG 59, General Records of the Department of State, Subject Numerical Files, 1970–3, Political and Defense, From: Pol Yemen-A to Pol 7 Yugo, POLADS Considerations of Yugoslav Developments, From US Mission NATO to Secretary of State, December 1971.

68. DASMIP, PA, Jugoslavija, 1971, Telegram jugoslavenskog veleposlanstva u Bruxellesu, br. 651, 31 December 1971.

69. PRO, FCO 28/2114, Yugoslavia, R. H. Smith (UK Delegation to NATO) to B. Sparrow, 28 January 1972; Access to NATO's original report is still restricted. The aforementioned limited information was obtained from British diplomatic documents.

70. NARA, RG 59, General Records of the Department of State, Subject Numerical Files, 1970–3, Political and Defense, From: Pol 7 Yugo to Pol 7 Yugo, Soviet–Yugoslav Visits, Telegram no. 8535, March 1972; Bilic Visit to USSR, Telegram no. 2610, March 1972, Jakovina, 'Jugoslavija, Hrvatsko proljeće i Sovjeti u Detantu,' 2005: 174.

71. DASMIP, PA, Jugoslavija, 1971, Telegram jugoslavenskog veleposlanstva u Moskvi br. 1189, 8 December 1971.

72. Ibid., Moskvi br. 1172, 6 December 1971; 1221, 20 December 1971.

73. Jakovina, 'Jugoslavija, Hrvatsko proljeće i Sovjeti u Detantu,' 2005: 176–7; Dubey, Yugoslavia: Development with Decentralization, 1975: 268; Singleton, Fred et al., The Economy of Yugoslavia, Croom Helm: London, 1982.

74. Dunlop interview, p. 96.

Conclusion

1. The Association for Diplomatic Studies and Training Foreign Affairs Oral History Project, Charles Kenney interviews Thomas Dunlop, 12 July 1996, pp. 101–2.

2. 'The only ally', The Economist, 22 January 1972.

3. 'Tito tries to unscramble things', *The Economist*, 19 February 1972.
4. In Poland in 1968, the violent suppression of student protests following the dismissal of intellectuals, and the subsequent anti-Jewish campaign and expulsion of the last Polish Jews similarly received little attention in the West. Poland is the exception here, because nationalism was mobilised for clearly anti-liberal ends by the communist authorities against both intellectuals and Jews. In the 1980s, however, the *Solidarność* movement was both nationalist and anti-communist.
5. 'The only ally', *The Economist*, 22 January 1972.

Bibliography

Archives

National Archives, London:

The National Archives (TNA), Public Record Office (PRO)

> *FO 371, Foreign Office: Political Departments: General Correspondence from 1906–66.*
>
> *FCO 28, Foreign Office and Foreign and Commonwealth Office: Northern Department and East European and Soviet Department: Registered Files (N and EN Series).*

National Archives and Record Administration, Washington, DC:

National Archives and Record Administration, (National Archives II at College Park, Maryland, NARA)

> *Record Group 59, General Records of the Department of State.*
>
> *Nixon Presidential Materials Project, National Security Council (NSC) Files.*
>
> *Electronic FOIA Room.*

Republic of Croatia, Zagreb:

Hrvatski državni arhiv (HDA)

> *Komisija za međunarodnu politiku i odnose u međunarodnom radničkom pokretu CK SKH.*

Državni arhiv u Zadru (DAZD)

> *Spisi OK SKH Zadar.*

Republic of Serbia, Belgrade:

Arhiv Jugoslavije (AJ)
> Izvršni komitet – biro PSKJ 1966–71.
> Kabinet predsednika Republike (KPR).

Diplomatski arhiv Ministarstva inostranih poslova Republike Srbije (DASMIP)

Kingdom of Belgium, Brussels:

NATO Archives
> North Atlantic Military Committee.

Digital Archives

Cold War International History Project (CWIHP), Woodrow Wilson Center for Scholars, Washington, DC, http://www.wilsoncenter.org/
> CWIHP Virtual Archive, Yugoslavia in the Cold War.
> CWIHP Working Paper 9.
> CWIHP Working Paper 31.
> CWIHP Bulletin, Issue 10, March 1998.
> CWIHP Bulletin, Issue 12/13, Fall/Winter 2001.

Digital National Security Archive (DNSA), George Washington University, Washington, DC, http://nsarchive.chadwyck.com/

Foreign Relations of the United States (FRUS), http://history.state.gov/
> Nixon-Ford Administration, Volume XXIX, Eastern Europe; Eastern Mediterranean, 1969–1972, Yugoslavia.

The Library of Congress, The Foreign Affairs Oral History Collection of the Association for Diplomatic Studies and Training,
> http://memory.loc.gov/ammem/collections/diplomacy/ and http://adst.org/oral-history/.

The National Security Archive, http://www.gwu.edu/~nsarchiv/

Open Society Archives, http://files.osa.ceu.hu/
> HU OSA 300-8-3, Records of Radio Free Europe/Radio Liberty Research Institute (RFE/RL RI).

Published Documents

Blečić, Mihailo, *Dolenčić, Ivica, Slučaj Žanko*, Kosmos: Beograd, 1986.

Ceh, Nick, *US Diplomatic Records On Relations With Yugoslavia During the Early Cold War, 1948–1957*, Columbia University Press: New York, 2002.

Hrvatsko proljeće – Presuda Partije, Dom i svijet, Zagreb, 2003.

Kesar, Jovan, Bilbija Đuro, and Nenad Stefanović, *Geneza maspoka u Hrvatskoj*, Književne novine: Beograd, 1990.

Petranović, Branko and Momčilo Zečević, *Jugoslovenski federalizam II*, Prosveta: Beograd, 1987.

Promjene u Ustavu Socijalističke Republike Hrvatske, Zagreb, 1971.

Ustav Federativne Narodne Republike Jugoslavije, Izdanje 'Službenog lista FNRJ', Beograd, 1949.

Ustav Socijalističke Federativne Republike Jugoslavije sa ustavnim amandmanima i ustavnim zakonima, Službeni list Socijalističke Federativne Republike Jugoslavije, Beograd, 1971.

Ustavni zakon o osnovama društvenog i političkog uređenja Federativne Narodne Republike Jugoslavije i saveznim organima vlasti, NIP: Zagreb, 1953.

Books

Akmadža, Miroslav, *Razvoj odnosa Katoličke crkve i komunističkoga režima u Jugoslaviji od 1945 do 1966 godine*, Otokar Keršovani: Rijeka, 2004.

Baletić, Milovan, *Hrvatska simultanka, prosinac sedamdeset prve*, Naklada Pavičić, Zagreb, 2003.

Babic Stjepan, Finka Božidar and Moguš Milan, *Hrvatski pravopis, Školska knjiga*, Zagreb, 1971, banned and destroyed; re-print: London 1972 (2nd edition); Zagreb, 1990 (3rd edition).

Banac, Ivo, *Sa Staljinom protiv Tita, Globus – Plava biblioteka*, Zagreb, 1990.

Bekić, Darko, *Jugoslavija u hladnom ratu*, Globus: Zagreb, 1988.

Bellamy, Alex J., *The Formation of Croatian National Identity*, Manchester University Press: Manchester, 2003.

Best, Antony et al., *International History of the Twentieth Century and Beyond*, 2nd edn, Routledge: London, New York 2008.

Bičanić, Rudolf, *Economic Policy in Socialist Yugoslavia*, Cambridge University Press: Cambridge, 1973.

Bilandžić, Dušan, *Borba za samoupravni socijalizam u Jugoslaviji 1945–1969*, Institut za historiju radničkog pokreta Hrvatske: Zagreb, 1969.

———, *Društveni razvoj socijalističke Jugoslavije*, Naklada Cdd: Zagreb, 1975.

———, *Historija Socijalističke federativne republike Jugoslavije, Glavni procesi*, Školska knjiga: Zagreb, 1978.

———, *Historija Socijalističke Federativne Republike Jugoslavije, Glavni procesi 1918–1985*, Školska knjiga, Zagreb, 1985.

———, *Jugoslavija poslije Tita (1980–1985)*, Globus: Zagreb, 1986.

———, *Hrvatska moderna povijest*, Golden marketing: Zagreb, 1999.

———, *Povijest izbliza, Memoarski zapisi 1945–2005*, Prometej: Zagreb, 2006.

Bilić, Jure, *'71 koja je to godina*, Centar za informacije i publicitet: Zagreb, 1990.

Bobetko, Janko, *Sve moje bitke*, Zagreb, 1996.

Bogetić, Dragan, *Nova strategija spoljne politike Jugoslavije 1956–1961*, Institut za savremenu istoriju: Beograd, 2006.

Bombelles, Joseph, T., *Economic development of Communist Yugoslavia 1947–1964*, Hoover Institution Publications: Stanford, 1968.

Borisov, Oleg Borisovich, *Soviet-Chinese Relations 1945–1970*, Indiana University Press: Bloomington and London, 1975.

Bracke, Maude, *Which Socialism, Whose Détente?: West European Communism and the Czechoslovak crisis, 1968*, Central European University Press: Budapest 2007.

Byrnes, Robert F., *U.S. Policy Toward Eastern Europe and the Soviet Union, Selected Essays, 1956–1988*, Westview Press, 1989.

Campbell, John C., *Tito's Separate Road, America and Yugoslavia in World Politics*, Harper and Row – Council on Foreign Relations, New York, 1967.

Carter, April, *Democratic Reform in Yugoslavia: The Changing Role of the Party*, Pinter: London, 1982.

Childs, David, *The Two Red Flags, European Social Democracy and Soviet Communism since 1945*, Routledge: London, New York, 2000.

Clissold, Stephen, *Yugoslavia and the Soviet Union 1939–1973 – A Documentary Survey*, Oxford University Press: Oxford, 1975.

Cuvalo, Ante, *The Croatian National Movement 1966–1972, East European Monographs*, New York, 1990.

Dabčević Kučar, Savka, *'71: Hrvatski snovi i stvarnost*, Interpublic: Zagreb, 1997.

Dannenberg, Julia Von, *The Foundations of Ostpolitik: The Making of the Moscow Treaty between West Germany and the USSR*, Oxford University Press: Oxford, 2008.

Denitch, Bogdan Denis, *The Legitimation of a Revolution, The Yugoslav Case*, Yale University Press: New Haven and London, 1976.

Deseta sjednica Centralnog komiteta Saveza komunista Hrvatske, ur. Baletić, Milovan, Židovec, Zdravko, Vjesnik: Zagreb, 1970.

Donaldson, Robert H. and Joseph L. Nogee, *The Foreign Policy of Russia: Changing Systems, Enduring Interests*, M.E. Sharpe: London, 1998.

Dragosavac, Dušan, *Zbivanja i svjedočenja*, Globus: Zagreb, 1985.

Dubey, Vinod, *Yugoslavia: Development with Decentralization, Report of a Mission sent to Yugoslavia by the World Bank*, Johns Hopkins University Press, 1975

Duda, Igor, *U potrazi za blagostanjem*, Srednja Europa: Zagreb, 2005.

Đukić, Slavoljub, *Slom srpskih liberala: Tehnologija političkih obračuna Josipa Broza*, Filip Višnjić: Beograd, 1990.

Farkas, Richard P., *Yugoslav Economic Development and Political Change: The Relationship between Economic Managers and Policy-Making Elites*, Praeger Publishers: New York, London, 1975.

Fejtö François, *A History of the People's Democracies: Eastern Europe since Stalin*, Penguin Books: London, 1974.

Fenby, Jonathan, *Povijest suvremene Kine, Propast i uzdizanje velike sile 1850–2008*, Sandorf: Zagreb, 2008.

Franolić, Branko, *An Historical Survey of Literary Croatian*, Nouveles Editions Latines: Paris, 1984.

Goldstein, Ivo, *Hrvatska 1918–2008*, Europa press holding – Novi liber: Zagreb, 2008.

Gray, William Glenn, *Germany's Cold War, The Global Campaign to Isolate East Germany, 1949–1969*, University of North Carolina Press: Chapel Hill, 2003.

Greenberg, Robert D., *Language and Identity in the Balkans: Serbo-Croatian and its Disintegration*, Oxford University Press: Oxford, 2004.

——, *Jezik i identitet na Balkanu – Raspad srpsko-hrvatskoga*, Srednja Europa: Zagreb, 2005.

Griffith, William E., *Albania and the Sino-Soviet Rift*, The MIT Press: Cambridge, MA, 1963.

——, *The Ostpolitik of the Federal Republik of Germany*, The MIT Press: Cambridge, MA, 1978.

Haug, Hilde Katrine, *Creating a Socialist Yugoslavia*, I.B.Tauris: London, 2015.

Heuser, Beatrice, *Western 'Containment' Policies in the Cold War – The Yugoslav Case, 1948–53*, Routledge: London, 1989.

Holzer, Jerzy, *Komunizam u Europi, Povijest pokreta i sustava vlasti*, Srednja Europa: Zagreb, 2002.

Hutchings, Robert L., *Soviet-East European Relations*, University of Wisconsin Press: Madison and London, 1983.

Jakovina, Tvrtko, *Socijalizam na američkoj pšenici*, Matica hrvatska: Zagreb, 2002.

——, *Američki komunistički saveznik, Hrvati, Titova Jugoslavija i Sjedinjene Američke Države 1945–1955, Profil International*, Srednja Europa: Zagreb 2003.

Job, Cvijeto, *Yugoslavia's Ruin – The Bloody Lessons of Nationalism, A Patriot's Warning*, Rowman and Littlefield Publishers: Oxford, 2002.

Jovanović, Jadranka, *Jugoslavija u Organizaciji Ujedinjenih Nacija (1945–1953)*, Institut za savremenu istoriju: Beograd, 1985.

Joyce, Miriam, *Anglo-American Support for Jordan: The Career of King Hussein*, Palgrave Macmillan: New York, 2008.

Klasić, Hrvoje, *Hrvatsko proljeće u Sisku*, Srednja Europa: Zagreb, 2006.

Lampe, John R., *Yugoslavia as History: Twice there was a Country*, Cambridge University Press: Cambridge, 1999.

——, *Balkans into Southeastern Europe*, Palgrave Macmillan: Basingstoke, NY, 2006.

BIBLIOGRAPHY

Lampe, John R., Russel O. Prickett, and Ljubiša S. Adamovi, *Yugoslav-American Economic Relations Since World War II*, Duke University Press: Durham, London, 1990.

Larson, David L., *United States Foreign Policy Toward Yugoslavia 1943–1963*, University Press of America, 1979.

Lees, Loraine M., *Keeping Tito afloat: the United States, Yugoslavia and the Cold War*, Pennsylvania State University Press, 1997.

Loth, Wilfried, *Overcoming the Cold War: A History of Detente, 1950–1991*, Palgrave, 2002.

Low, Alfred D., *The Sino-Soviet Dispute*, Fairleigh Dickinson University Press, 1976.

Ludlow, Piers N., *European Integration and the Cold War, Ostpolitik-Westpolitik, 1965–1973*, Routledge: London, 2007.

Lukić, Vojin, *Brionski plenum, Obračun sa Aleksandrom Rankovićem – sećanja i saznanja*, Stručna knjiga: Beograd, 1990.

Lydall, Harold, *Yugoslav Socialism – Theory and Practice*, Clarendon Press: Oxford, 1986.

Marković, Dragoslav, *Život i politika*, Rad: Beograd, 1987.

Mates, Leo, *Međunarodni odnosi socijalističke Jugoslavije*, Nolit: Beograd, 1976.

Maticka, Marijan, *Agrarna reforma i kolonizacija u Hrvatskoj od 1945 do 1948*, Školska knjiga: Zagreb, 1990.

Matković, Hrvoje, *Povijest Jugoslavije: 1918–1991–2003*, Naklada Pavičić: Zagreb, 2003.

MccGwire, Michael, *Soviet Naval Policy*, Praeger Publishers: New York, London, Washington, 1975.

MccGwire, Michael and John McDonnell, *Soviet Naval Influence*, Praeger Publishers: New York, London, 1977.

Medvedev, Roy, *China and the Superpowers*, Basil Blackwell: London, New York, 1986.

Mićunović, Veljko, *Moskovske godine 1969–1971*, Jugoslovenska Revija: Beograd, 1984.

Miller, Benjamin, *States, Nations, and the Great Powers: The Sources of Regional War and Peace*, Cambridge University Press: Cambridge, 2007.

Močnik, Josip, 'United States-Yugoslav Relations, 1961–80: The Twilight of Tito's Era and the Role of Ambassadorial Diplomacy in the Making of America's Yugoslav Policy, Graduate College of Bowling Green State University,' Doctoral Dissertation: Bowling Green, 2008.

Morača, Pero i dr., *Istorija Saveza komunista Jugoslavije*, Rad: Beograd, 1976.

Nećak, Dušan, *Hallsteinova doktrina i Jugoslavija, Tito između Savezne Republike Njemačke i Demokratske republike Njemačke*, Srednja Europa: Zagreb, 2004.

Nelson, Keith L., *The Making of Détente: Soviet American Relations in the Shadow of Vietnam*, John Hopkins University Press: Baltimore, London, 1995.

Nenadović, Aleksandar, *Mirko Tepavac – Sećanja i komentari*, Radio B92: Beograd, 1998.

————, *Razgovori s Kočom*, Globus: Zagreb, 1989.

Novak, Božidar, *Hrvatsko novinstvo u 20. stoljeću*, Golden marketing-Tehnička knjiga: Zagreb, 2005.

Ouimet, Matthew J., *The Rise and Fall of the Brezhnev Doctrine in Soviet Foreign Policy*, University of North Carolina Press, 2003.

Paczkowski, Andrzej, *Pola stoljeća povijesti Poljske: 1939–1989. godine*, Profil, Srednja Europa: Zagreb, 2001.

Perović, Latinka, *Zatvaranje kruga*, Svjetlost, 1991.

Petković, Ranko, *Subjektivna istorija jugoslovenske diplomacije*, Službeni list SCG: Beograd, 1995.

Petranović, Branko, *Istorija Jugoslavije 1918–1988, sv. I–III*, Nolit: Beograd, 1988.

————, *Balkanska federacija 1943–1948*, IKP Zaslon: Beograd-Šabac, 1991.

Pleština, Dijana, *Regional Development in Communist Yugoslavia*, Westview Press: Oxford, 1992.

Ponoš, Tihomir, *Na rubu revolucije-studenti '71*, Profil: Zagreb, 2007.

Popović, Nikola, *Jugoslovensko-sovjetski odnosi u drugom svetskom ratu (1941–1945)*, Institut za savremenu istoriju: Beograd, 1988.

Quested, Rosemary, *Sino-Russian Relations*, Routledge: London, 2005.

Ra'anan, Gavriel D., *Yugoslavia after Tito – Scenarios and Implications, Westview Special Studies on the Soviet Union an Eastern Europe*, Westview Press: Boulder, 1977.

Radelić, Zdenko, *Hrvatska u Jugoslaviji 1945–1991 – od zajedništva do razlaza*, Školska knjiga: Zagreb, 2006.

Ramet, Pedro, *Nationalism and Federalism in Yugoslavia, 1963–1983*, Indiana University Press: Bloomington, 1984.

Ramet, Sabrina, P., *Nationalism and Federalism in Yugoslavia, 1962–1991*, Indiana University Press: Bloomington, 1992.

————, *The Three Yugoslavias: State-Building and Legitimation, 1918–2005*, Woodrow Wilson Center Press, Indiana University Press: Washington DC, Bloomington, 2006.

————, *Tri Jugoslavije, Izgradnja države i izazov legitimacije 1918–2005*, Golden marketing-Tehnička knjiga: Zagreb, 2009.

Rendulić, Zlatko, *General avnojevske Jugoslavije*, Golden marketing-Tehnička knjiga: Zagreb, 2004.

Retegan, Mihail, *In the Shadow of the Prague Spring*, The Centre for Romanian Studies, 2000.

Ro'i Yaacov et al., *The Soviet Union and the June 1967 Six Day War*, Stanford University Press: Washington, DC, Stanford, 2008.

Rotschild, Joseps and Nancy M. Wingfield, *Return to Diversity, A Political History of East Central Europe Since World War II*, Oxford University Press: New York, Oxford, 2000.

Rubinstein, Alvin Z., *Yugoslavia and the Nonaligned World*, Princeton University Press, 1970.

Rusinow, Dennison, *The Yugoslav Experiment 1948–1974*, C. Hurst and Co. – Royal Institute of International Affairs: London, 1977.

——, *Yugoslavia: Oblique Insights and Observations*, University of Pittsburgh Press: Pittsburgh, 2008.

Sarotte, M.E., *Dealing with the Devil*, The University of North Carolina Press: Chapel Hill, 2001.

Scaller, Michael, *The United States and China in the Twentieth Century*, Oxford University Press: New York, Oxford, 1990.

Šentija, Josip, *Razgovori s Mikom Tripalom o hrvatskom proljeću*, Profil: Zagreb, 2005.

——, *Jedna hrvatska sudbina, Priča o Vjekoslavu Prpiću ispričana s njim samim na kraju puta*, Školska knjiga: Zagreb, 2007.

Shoup, Paul, *Communism and the Yugoslav National Question*, Columbia University Press, 1968.

Simić, Pero, *Svetac i magle*, Službeni list SCG: Beograd, 2005.

Singleton, Fred et al., *The Economy of Yugoslavia*, Croom Helm: London, 1982.

Sirotković, Jakov, *Hrvatsko gospodarstvo, Privredna kretanja i ekonomska politika, HAZU*, Golden marketing: Zagreb, 1996.

Škrabalo, Ivo, *Samoodređenje i odcjepljenje, Pouke iz nastanka države Bangladeš*, Školske novine: Zagreb, 1997.

Stojanović, Biljana, 'Exchange Rate Regimes of the Dinar 1945–1990: An Assessment of Appropriateness and Efficiency', in Proceedings of OeNB Workshops, 13: 2007, 202.

Supek, Ivan, *Krivovjernik na ljevici*, Globus: Zagreb, 1992.

Šuvar, Mira, *Vladimir Velebit – Svjedok historije*, Razlog: Zagreb, 2001.

Tripalo, Miko, *Hrvatsko proljeće*, Nakladni zavod Matice hrvatske: Zagreb, 2001.

——, *spomenica, Institut otvoreno društvo*, Zagreb, 1996.

Vrhunec, Marko, *Šest godina s Titom (1967–1973), Pogled s vrha i izbliza*, Nakladni zavod Globus: Adamić, Zagreb, 2001.

Vuković, Zdravko, *Od deformacija SDB-a do Maspoka i liberalizma*, Narodna knjiga: Beograd, 1989.

Westad, Odd Arne, *Globalni hladni rat – Velike sile i Treći svijet*, Golden marketing-Tehnička knjiga: Zagreb, 2009.

Willetts, Peter, *The Non-Aligned Movement: The Origins of a Third World Alliance*, Pinter: London, 1978.

Wilson, Duncan, *Tito's Yugoslavia*, Cambridge University Press: Cambridge, 1979.

Woodward, Susan L., *Socialist Unemployment: The Political Economy of Yugoslavia, 1945–1990*, Princeton University Press: Princeton, 1995.

Young, John W. and John Kent, *International History since 1945: A Global History*, Oxford University Press: Oxford, New York, 2004.

Zelmanović, Đorđe, *Mađarska jesen 1956*, Fraktura: Zagreb, 2006.

Zimmerman, William, *Open Borders, Nonalignment, and the Political Evolution of Yugoslavia*, Princeton University Press: Princeton, 1987.

Zubok, Vladislav and Constantine Pleshakov, *Inside the Kremlin's Cold War - From Stalin to Khrushchev*, Harvard University Press: Cambridge, 1996.

Zubok, Vladislav M., *A Failed Empire: The Soviet Union in the Cold War from Stalin to Gorbachev*, University of North Carolina Press: Chapel Hill, 2007.

Articles

Akmadža, Miroslav, 'Uzroci prekida diplomatskih odnosa između Vatikana i Jugoslavije 1952. Godine,' *Croatica Christiana, Periodica*, XXVII, 2003.

———, 'Razvoj odnosa Katoličke crkve i komunističkog režima u Jugoslaviji od 1945. do 1966. godine, Spomenica Filipa Potrebice,' *FF press*, Zagreb, 2004.

———, 'Pregovori Svete Stolice i Jugoslavije i potpisivanje protokola iz 1966. godine,' *Časopis za suvremenu povijest*, 36 (2), 2004.

Anderson, Stephen S., 'Yugoslavia: The Diplomacy of Balance,' *Current History*, 56, 1969.

Anikejev, Anatolij Semenovič, '*Načalni period normalizacii sovetsko-jugoslavskih otnošenij (1953-1954), Spoljna politika Jugoslavije 1950-1961*,' Zbornik radova, Institut za noviju istoriju Srbije: Beograd, 2008.

Artisien, Patrick F.R. and Peter J. Buckley, 'Joint Ventures in Yugoslavia: Opportunities and Constraints,' *Journal of International Business Studies*, 16, 1, Palgrave Macmillan Journals, 1985.

Ashton, Nigel, ed., *The Cold War in the Middle East, Regional Conflict and the Superpowers 1967-1973*, Routledge: London, 2007.

Babić, Stjepan, 'Za ravnopravnost, ali čega?,' *Jezik*, 16, 5, 1968-9.

———, 'O Deklaraciji – činjenice i pretpostavke,' *Kolo* 1-2, 2009.

Badurina, Lada, '*Hrvatska pravopisna norma u 20. stoljeću, Hrvatski jezik u XX. stoljeću*,' Matica hrvatska, Zagreb, 2006.

Bartošek, Karel, *Central and Southeastern Europe: The Black Book of Communism, Crimes, Terror, Repression*, Harvard University Press: Cambridge, London, 1999.

Batović, Ante, '*Zadar na pariškoj mirovnoj konferenciji 1946. godine, Zadar i okolica od Drugog svjetskog rata do Domovinskog rata*,' Sveučilište Hazu, u Zadru, Zadar, 2009.

Békés, Csaba, 'Soviet Plans to Establish the COMINFORM in Early 1946: New Evidence from the Hungarian Archives,' *Cold War International History Project Bulletin* 10, March 1998.

Bešlin, Milivoj, '*Liberalna koalicija' između saradnje i nerazumevanja: odnos političkih elita Srbije i Hrvatske 1969-1971*,' Hrvatsko proljeće, 40 godina poslije, Zbornik radova, Zagreb, 2012.

Bogetić, Dragan, 'Arapsko-izraelski rat 1967 godine i jugoslavensko-američki odnosi, Istorija 20 veka,' 1, *Beograd*, 2008.

———, 'Drugi jugoslovensko-sovjetski sukob, Sudar Titove i Hruščovljeve percepcije politike miroljubive koegzistencije, Spoljna politika Jugoslavije 1950–1961,'
Zbornik radova, Institut za noviju istoriju Srbije, Beograd, 2008.

———, 'Približavanje Jugoslavije socijalističkom lageru tokom arapsko-izraelskog
rata 1967 godine,' *Tokovi istorije* 3–4, Beograd, 2008.

Brands, ry W., 'Redefining the Cold War: American Policy toward Yugoslavia,
1948–60,' *Diplomatic History*, 11 (1), 1987.

Brandt, Miroslav, 'Povjesno mjesto Deklaracije o imenu i položaju hrvatskoga
književnoga jezika iz 1967 godine,' Radovi *Zavoda za hrvatsku povijest*, 27,
1994.

Brezarić, Jugoslavija i NR Kina, *Međunarodna politika* 508, XXII, Beograd, 1971.

Burg, Stevan L., 'Ethnic Conflict and the Federalization of Socialist Yugoslavia: The
Serbo-Croat Conflict,' *Publius*, Vol. 7, 4, *Federalism and Ethnicity*, Oxford
University Press, 1977.

———, 'Republican and Provincial Constitution Making in Yugoslav Politics,
State Constitutional Design in Federal Systems,' *Publius*, Vol. 12, 1, Oxford
University Press 1982.

Čavoški, Jovan, 'Jugoslavija i Azija (1947–1953),' *Spoljna politika Jugoslavije 1950–
1961*, Zbornik radova, Institut za noviju istoriju Srbije, Beograd, 2008.

Čičak, Ivan Zvonimir, 'Bio sam dogmatik i manipulator, Ljudi iz 1971 – Prekinuta
šutnja,' Vjesnik, Zagreb, 1990.

Clarkson, Aleksander, 'Home and Away: Immigration and Political Violence in the
Federal Republic of Germany, 1945–90,' *Cold War History*, 8, 1, 2008.

Cviić, Krsto, 'Hrvatska 1971 – Jedan pogled izvana,' *Erasmvs*, 15, 1996.

Dabčević Kučar, Savka, *Htjeli smo Hrvatsku dovesti u Evropu, Ljudi iz 1971 –
Prekinuta šutnja*, Vjesnik: Zagreb, 1990.

De Luca, Anthony R., 'Soviet-American Politics and the Turkish Straits,' *Political
Science Quarterly*, 92, 3, 1977.

Đilas, Milivoj, *1971 Ljetopis srpskog kulturnog društva Prosvjeta*, 7, 2002.

Dimitrijević, Bojan, 'Jugoslavija i NATO 1951–1958 skica intenzivnih vojnih
odnosa,' *Spoljna politika Jugoslavije 1950–1961*, Zbornik radova, Institut za
noviju istoriju Srbije, Beograd, 2008.

Dimitrov, Vesselin, 'Communism in Bulgaria, Origins of the Cold War,' ed. Melvyn
P. Leffler and David S. Painter, Routledge: New York, London, 2005.

Džeba, Krešimir and Božidar Novak, *Zašto se dogodila '71, Ljudi iz 1971 – Prekinuta
šutnja*, Vjesnik: Zagreb, 1990.

Edemskij, Andrej, 'The Turn in Soviet-Yugoslav Relations, 1953–55,' *Cold War
International History Project Bulletin* 10, March 1998.

Gibianskij, Leonid, 'The 1948 Soviet-Yugoslav Conflict and the Formation of
the 'Socialist Camp' Model, The Soviet Union in Eastern Europe, 1945–89,'
eds Odd Arne Westad, Sven Holtsmark and Iver B. Neuman, St. Martin's
Press: New York, 1994.

———, 'The Soviet-Yugoslav Split and the Com-inform, The Establishment of Communist regimes in Eastern Europe, 1944–1949,' eds Norman Naimark and Leonid Gibianskii, Westview Press: Oxford, 1997.

———, 'Soviet-Yugoslav Relations and the Hungarian Revolution of 1956,' *Cold War International History Project Bulletin* 10, March 1998.

———, 'The Soviet Bloc and the Initial Stage of the Cold War: Archival Documents on Stalin's Meetings with Communist Leaders of Yugoslavia and Bulgaria, 1946–1948,' *Cold War International History Project Bulletin* 10, March 1998.

Gibianskij, Leonid and Nikita Sergeevich Khrushchev, 'Josip Broz Tito, and the Hungarian Crisis of 1956,' *Russian Studies in History* 44 (3), 2005–6.

Gotovac, Vlado, *Moj slučaj, Ljudi iz 1971 – Prekinuta šutnja*, Vjesnik: Zagreb, 1990.

———, 'Skica o hrvatskom proljeću, 25. obljetnica boljševičkog udara i sjećanje na hrvatsko proljeće, zbornik radova,' eds Slobodan Kaštela et al., Hrvatska akademija znanosti i umjetnosti: Zagreb, 1997.

Granville, Johanna, 'The Soviet-Yugoslav Détente, Belgrade-Budapest Relations and the Hungarian Revolution,' *Hungarian Studies Review* 24 (1), 1997.

———, 'Tito and the Nagy Affair in 1956,' *East European Quarterly* 32 (1), 1998.

———, 'Hungary, 1956: The Yugoslav Connection,' *Europe-Asia Studies* 50 (3), 1998.

Grbić, Srđan, *Čedo Grbić o Hrvatskom proljeću: Prilog o ideologiji jednog vremena, Hrvatsko proljeće, 40 godina poslije*, Zbornik radova, Zagreb, 2012.

Greenberg, Robert D., 'The Politics of Dialects among Serbs, Croats, and Muslims in the Former Yugoslavia,' *East European Politics & Societies* 10, 1996.

Haramija, Dragutin, *Nisam želio biti statist, Ljudi iz 1971 – Prekinuta šutnja*, Vjesnik: Zagreb 1990.

———, 'Ustavne promjene, pravni sustav, aktivnosti Izvršnog vijeća Sabora SRH, 25. obljetnica boljševičkog udara i sjećanje na hrvatsko proljeće, zbornik radova,' ed. Slobodan Kaštela et al., Hrvatska akademija znanosti i umjetnosti: Zagreb, 1997.

Ivić, Pavle, 'Za ravnopravnost, a protiv cepanja jezika,' *Jezik*, 16, 4, 1968–9.

Ivičević, Jozo, 'Kako su montirani politički procesi,' *Hrvatska revija*, 2, 2002.

Ivičević-Bakulić, 'Deklaracija o nazivu i položaju hrvatskoga književnog jezika u sklopu suvremene hrvatske povijesti,' *Kolo* 1–2, 2009.

'Izjava Matice hrvatske u povodu saopćenja Matice srpske,' *Jezik* 3, 1970–1.

'Izjava Upravnog odbora Matice hrvatske o pripremama za popis stanovništva SFRJ,' *Kritika*, 16, 1971.

Jakovina, Tvrtko, 'Što je značio Nixonov usklik 'Živjela Hrvatska'?,' *Društvena istraživanja*, 8, 2–3 (40–1), 1999.

———, 'Život u limenci sa crvima, (Kako su živjeli i doživljavali Titovu Jugoslaviju? – razgovori američkih diplomata skupljenih u Foreign Affairs Oral History Program Udruge za diplomatske studije i Sveučilišta Georgetown u Washington),' *Historijski zbornik*, LIV: Zagreb, 2001.

————, 'Je li predsjednik SAD-a Nixon doista podupirao 'hrvatsko proljeće'?,' Zbornik uz 70. godišnjicu života Dragutina Pavličevića, Pro historia Croatica 1, Zagreb, 2002.

————, 'Nixon i Tito: Kako je pripreman i što je značio Titov posjet Washingtonu 1971?,' Historijski zbornik LV, 2002, 167–97.

————, 'Sjećanja koja čine povijest – razgovori s Cvijetom Jobom, dugogodišnjim diplomatom i veleposlanikom FNRJ/SFRJ,' Časopis za suvremenu povijest, 35, 3, Zagreb, 2003.

————, 'Sjećanja koja čine povijest – razgovori s Mirjanom Krstinić, visokom dužnosnicom u vladama SRH i SFRJ,' Časopis za suvremenu povijest, 35, 1, Zagreb, 2003.

————, 'Titovi ciljevi sukladni su našima', Američki izvori o hrvatskom proljeću,' Historijski zbornik, LVI–LVII, 2003–4.

————, 'Sjećanje na Nixona i Tita,' Spomenica Filipa Potrebice, Zagreb, 2004, 435–54.

————, 'Jugoslavija, Hrvatsko proljeće i Sovjeti u Detantu,' Kolo, 4, 2005.

————, Hrvatski izlaz u svijet. Hrvatska/Jugoslavija u svjetskoj politici 1945–1991, Hrvatska politika u XX. stoljeću, Matica Hvatska: Zagreb, 2006.

————, Trenutak katarze, Predgovor u knjizi Đorđe Zelmanović, Mađarska Jesen 1956, Fraktura: Zagreb, 2006.

————, 'Idealističkoj, hrabroj (i ludoj) mladosti, Predgovor knjizi Tihomira Ponoša: Na rubu revolucije, studenti '71,' Profil, Zagreb, 2007.

————, 'Where has War for Hearts and Souls Gone? The United States of America and Liberals in Yugoslavia in 1960 and Early 1970, 125 Years of Diplomatic Relations between the USA and Serbia,' ed. Ljubinka Trgovičević, Faculty of Political Sciences, University of Belgrade: Belgrade, 2008.

————, 1956. godina naše ere: Vrhunac jugoslavenske vanjske politike, Spomenica Josipa Adamčeka, FF-Press: Zagreb, 2009.

————, 'Tito, the Bloc-Free Movement and the Prague Spring, The Prague Spring and the Warsaw Pact Invasion of Czechoslovakia in 1968,' The Harvard Cold War Studies Book Series, eds Gübter Bischof et al., Lexington Books, 2009.

————, Mozaik hrvatskog reformskog pokreta 1971, Hrvatsko proljeće, 40 godina poslije, Zbornik radova: Zagreb, 2012.

Jandrić, Berislav, 'Sveučilišni nastavnici Filozofskog fakulteta u Zagrebu u obrani sastavljača i potpisnika Deklaracije o nazivu i položaju hrvatskog književnog jezika,' Radovi zavoda za hrvatsku povijest, 27, 1994.

Johnson, Ross A., 'Yugoslavia and the Sino-Soviet Conflict: The Shifting Triangle, 1948–1974,' Studies in Comparative Communism, Vol. 7, 1–2, 1974.

————, 'Yugoslavia: In the Twilight of Tito,' The Washington Papers, Vol. 2, SAGE Publications, 1974.

Jonke, Ljudevit, 'Aktualna jezična pitanja danas,' Jezik, 16, 3, 1968–9.

————, 'Razvoj hrvatskoga književnog jezika u 20. stoljeću,' Jezik, 16, 1, 1968–9.

BIBLIOGRAPHY

Karlovic, N.L., 'Internal Colonialism in a Marxist Society,' *Ethnic and Racial Studies*, 5, 3, 1982.

King, Robert R., 'Rumania and the Sino-Soviet Conflict,' *Studies in Comparative Communism*, Vol. 5, 4, 1972.

Klasić, Hrvoje, *Unutrašnjopolitičke i vanjskopolitičke aktivnosti Jugoslavije nakon intervencije Varšavskog pakta u Čehoslovačkoj 1968. godine, 1968 – Četrdeset godina posle*, Institut za noviju istoriju Srbije: Beograd, 2008.

Krajger, Boris, *New Economic Measures, The Economic Reform in Yugoslavia, Socialist Thought and Practice*, Belgrade, 1965.

Laković, Ivan, 'Jugoslavija i projekti kolektivne bezbjednosti, Spoljna politika Jugoslavije 1950–1961,' *Zbornik radova*, Institut za noviju istoriju Srbije: Beograd, 2008.

Larrabee, Stephen F., 'Changing Russian Perspectives in the Balkans,' *Survey* 18(3), 1972.

Lukšić, Mislav Elvis, *Hrvatska jezična deklaracija iz 1967. i njeni odjeci na zadarskom području*, Zadar i okolica od Drugog svjetskog rata do Domovinskog rata, HAZU, Sveučilište u Zadru, Zadar, 2009.

Magner, Thomas F. 'Yugoslavia and Tito: The Long Farewell,' *Current History* 74, 1978.

Mamić, Mile, *Hrvatsko jezično zakonodavstvo i jezična politika u 20. stoljeću, Hrvatski jezik u XX. stoljeću*, Matica hrvatska: Zagreb, 2006.

Mark, Eduard, 'Revolution By Degrees: Stalin's National-Front Strategy For Europe, 1941–1947,' *Cold War International History Project*, Working Paper No. 31.

Marković, Predrag J., *Titova shvatanja nacionalnog i jugoslovenskog identiteta, Dijalog povjesničara – istoričara 2*, Friedrich Naumann Stiftung: Zagreb, 2000.

Maticka, Marijan, 'Hrvatski prosinački događaji 1971. i svjetska javnost: primjer pariškog "Le Mondea"', *Časopis za suvremenu povijest*, 3, 2006.

Milošević, Nemanja, 'Jugoslavija u američkoj vojnopolitičkoj strategiji odbrane Zapada od SSSR-a 1950–1954,' Spoljna politika Jugoslavije 1950–1961, Zbornik radova, Institut za noviju istoriju Srbije: Beograd, 2008.

Mingst, Karen A., 'From the Politics of Non-Alignment to the Economics of the Semi-Periphery: The Case of Yugoslavia,' *East European Quarterly*, 18, 3, Fall 1984.

Mitrović, Tomislav, 'Berlinsko pitanje na dnevnom redu,' *Međunarodna politika* 494, XXI, Beograd, 1970.

Moguš, Milan, 'Značenje Deklaracije u povijesti hrvatskog jezika,' *Kolo* 1–2, 2009.

Novak, Božidar, 'Uloga i doprinos medija i hrvatskog novinstva u Hrvatskom proljeću,' *Medijska istraživanja*, 7, 1–2, Zagreb, 2001.

'Novosadski dogovor odbačen,' *Jezik*, 5, 1970–1.

Obad, Stijepo, 'Hrvatsko proljeće u Zadru, Zadarska smotra,' 54, 1–2, Zadar, 2005.

———, *Zadar i okolica u Hrvatskom proljeću 1971. godine*, Zadar i okolica od Drugog svjetskog rata do Domovinskog rata, HAZU, Sveučilište u Zadru, Zadar, 2009.

Parrish, Scott D. and Mikhail M. Narinsky, 'New Evidence on the Soviet Rejection of the Marshall Plan, 1947: Two Reports,' *Cold War International History Project Working Paper No. 9.*

Pelikan, Jan, 'The Yugoslav State Visit to the Soviet Union, June 1956, Spoljna politika Jugoslavije 1950–1961,' *Zbornik radova*, Institut za noviju istoriju Srbije, Beograd, 2008.

Perović, Jeronim, 'The Tito-Stalin Split: A Reassessment in Light of New Evidence,' *Journal of Cold War Studies*, 9 (2), 2007.

Perović, Latinka, *Prilog proučavanju Hrvatskog proljeća, Hrvatsko proljeće, 40 godina poslije*, Zbornik radova: Zagreb, 2012.

Petković, Aleksandar, 'Jugoslavenski radnici u inostranstvu,' *Međunarodna politika*, 506, XXII, Beograd, 1971.

Petković, Ranko, *Jugoslavija u međunarodnim odnosima, Godišnjak Instituta za međunarodnu politiku i privredu 1971*, Institut za međunarodnu politiku i privredu: Beograd, 1972.

Petrović, Vladimir, '"Pošteni posrednik". Jugoslavija između starih i novih spoljnopolitičkih partnerstava sredinom pedesetih godina, Spoljna politika Jugoslavije 1950–1961,' *Zbornik radova*, Institut za noviju istoriju Srbije: Beograd, 2008.

'Practice and Theory of Socialist Development in Yugoslavia, VIIIth Congress of the League of Communist of Yugoslavia,' *Međunarodna politika*, Beograd, 1965.

Pranjić, Krunoslav, 'Zakonski prijedlog: četiri jezika,' *Jezik* 16, 1, 1968–9.

Pranjković, Ivo, *Hrvatski jezik od godine 1945. do 2000., Hrvatski jezik u XX. stoljeću*, Matica hrvatska: Zagreb, 2006.

'Pregled svjetskog tiska: Pala je maska!,' *Hrvatska revija*, 1, 1972.

Prifti, Peter, 'Albania and the Sino-Soviet Conflict,' *Studies in Comparative Communism*, Vol. 6, 3, 1973.

'Prosvjed Upravnog odbora DKH protiv načina predstojećeg popisivanja stanovništva,' *Kritika*, 16, 1971.

Rajak, Svetozar, 'The Tito-Khruschev Correspondence,' *Cold War International History Project Bulletin* 12/13, Fall/Winter 2001.

Rusinow, Dennison, 'Reopening of the 'National Question' in the 1960s, State Collapse in South-Eastern Europe,' eds Lenard J. Cohen and Jasna Dragovic Soso, Purdue University Press: West Lafayette, 2008.

Samardžija, Marko, *Hrvatski jezik od početka XX. stoljeća do godine 1945., Hrvatski jezik u XX. stoljeću*, Matica hrvatska: Zagreb, 2006.

Šentija, Josip, 'Jezik i jezična politika u medijima uoči Deklaracije,' *Kolo* 1–2, 2009.

Sfikas, Thanasis D., 'The Greek Civil War, Origins of the Cold War,' eds Melvyn P. Leffler and David S. Painter, Routledge: New York, London 2005.

Sharp, Samuel L., 'The Yugoslav Experiment in Self-management: Soviet Criticism,' *Studies in Comparative Communism*, Vol. 4, 3–4, 1971.

Shoup, Paul, *The League of Communist of Yugoslavia: The Communist Parties of Eastern Europe*, Columbia University Press: New York, 1979.

Simić, Milorad, 'Bankarski sistem Jugoslavije,' *Međunarodna politika* 410, Beograd, 1967.

Šnuderl, Boris, 'SR Nemačka na prvom mestu u robnoj razmeni Jugoslavije,' *Međunarodna politika*, 506, Beograd, 1971.

Špadijer, Dušanka, 'Jugoslavija u međunarodnim odnosima,' *Godišnjak Instituta za međunarodnu politiku i privredu 1967*, Beograd, 1968.

Spehnjak, Katarina, 'Izbori u Hrvatskoj 1967 i 1969,' *Časopis za suvremenu povijest*, 30, 2, 1998.

———, '"Brionski plenum" – odjeci IV. Sjednice CK SKJ iz srpnja 1966. godine u hrvatskoj političkoj javnosti,' *Časopis za suvremenu povijest*, 31, 3, 1999.

———, Većeslav Holjevac u političkim događajima u Hrvatskoj 1967. godine, *Časopis za suvremenu povijest*, 32, 2, 2000.

———, *Tumačenja Protokola o odnosima Jugoslavije i Vatikana iz 1966. u političkoj javnosti Hrvatske, Dijalog povjesničara/istoričara*, Friedrich Naumann Stiftung: Zagreb, 2001.

Stewart, Phillip D. et al., 'Modeling the 1973 Soviet Decision to Support Egypt,' *The American Political Science Review*, 83, 1, 1969.

Stykalin, A.S., 'Soviet–Yugoslav Relations and the Case of Imre Nagy,' *Cold War History*, Vol. 5, No. 1, February 2005.

Supek, Ivan, *Pobjeda grupe crvenih radikala, Ljudi iz 1971. – Prekinuta šutnja*, Vjesnik: Zagreb 1990.

Tasić, Dmitar, 'Otkrivanje Afrike, Jugoslovensko-etiopski odnosi i počeci jugoslovenske afričke politike 1954–1955,' *Spoljna politika Jugoslavije 1950–1961, Zbornik radova*, Institut za noviju istoriju Srbije: Beograd, 2008.

Terzić, Milan, 'Tito i balkanski pakt, Premošćivanja na putu ka neutralnosti,' *Spoljna politika Jugoslavije 1950–1961, Zbornik radova*, Institut za noviju istoriju Srbije: Beograd, 2008.

Tripalo, Miko, 'Deklaracija o hrvatskom jeziku,' *Republika* 7–8, 1992, Zagreb 1992.

———, 'Hrvatska 1971. – u povodu dvadesete obljetnice (II),' *Republika* 1–2, Zagreb 1992.

'Upravni odbor Matice hrvatske o jeziku,' *Jezik*, 16, 4, 1968–9.

Veselica, Vladimir, '25. obljetnica boljševičkog udara i sjećanje na hrvatsko proljeće, zbornik radova,' eds Slobodan Kaštela et al., Hrvatska akademija znanosti i umjetnosti: Zagreb, 1997.

Vlajić, Vojislav, 'Jugoslavenska i svetska privreda,' *Međunarodna politika* 490, XXI, Beograd, 1970.

Vojna enciklopedija, *Redakcija vojne enciklopedije*, Beograd, 1973.

Volkov, Vladimir, 'The Soviet Leadership and Southeastern Europe: The Establishment of Communist regimes in Eastern Europe, 1944–1949,' eds Norman Naimark and Leonid Gibianskii, Westview Press: Oxford, 1997.

Veljković, Ljuba, 'The Meaning of the Economic Reform in Yugoslavia: The Economic Reform in Yugoslavia, Socialist Thought and Practice,' Belgrade, 1965.

Vujić, Antun, 'Političke osnove nekih interpretacija Hrvatskog proljeća,' *Hrvatsko proljeće, 40 godina poslije*, Zbornik radova, Zagreb, 2012.

Wessel, Nils H., 'Yugoslavia: Ground Rules for Restraining Soviet and American Competition,' *Journal of International Affairs*, 34, 2, 1980.

Whitehorn, Alan J., 'Yugoslav Constitutional Developments: An expression of Growing Nationality Rights and Powers (1945–1972),' *East European Quarterly*, Vol. 9, 3.

Wood, Robert E., 'From the Marshall Plan to the Third World, Origins of the Cold War,' eds Melvyn P. Leffler and David S. Painter, Routledge: New York, London, 2005.

Životić, Aleksandar, 'Jugoslavija i Bliski istok (1945–1956),' *Spoljna politika Jugoslavije 1950–1961, Zbornik radova*, Institut za noviju istoriju Srbije: Beograd, 2008.

Index

INDEX